Archetypes of Mythology

Cover image: Saint George Slaying the Dragon. Painting, tempura and gold on wood, by Carlo Rivelli, 1470.
Title page image: Saint George Killing the Dragon. Woodcut by Albrecht Dürer, c. 1504.

Archetypes
of
Mythology

Jungian Theories on Myth and Religion Examined

Stefan Stenudd

Stefan Stenudd is a Swedish author, artist, and historian of ideas. He has published a number of books in Swedish as well as English, both fiction and non-fiction. Among the latter are books about mythology, Taoism, the cosmology of the Greek philosophers, the Japanese martial arts, Tarot, astrology, and life force concepts.

His novels explore existential subjects from Stone-Age drama to science fiction, but lately he focuses increasingly on the present.

In the history of ideas, he researches the thought patterns in creation myths, as well as theories about those myths through history.

He is also a 7 dan instructor in the peaceful martial art aikido, which he has practiced for 50 years.

He has his own extensive website: stenudd.com

Books by Stefan Stenudd:
Psychoanalysis of Mythology: Freudian Theories on Myth and Religion Examined, 2022.
Fake Lao Tzu Quotes: Erroneous Tao Te Ching Citations Examined, 2020.
Ever Young, 2017, 2018, 2020.
Sunday Brunch with the World Maker, 2016, 2018, 2020.
All's End, 2007, 2015.
Occasionally I Contemplate Murder, 2006, 2011, 2015.
Cosmos of the Ancients: The Greek Philosophers on Myth and Cosmology, 2007, 2011, 2015.
Tao Te Ching: The Taoism of Lao Tzu Explained, 2011, 2015.
Tao Quotes, 2013, 2015.
Tarot Unfolded: Imaginative Reading of the Divination Cards, 2012, 2015.
Life Energy Encyclopedia, 2009, 2015.
Qi: Increase Your Life Energy, 2008, 2009, 2015.
Aikido Principles, 2008, 2016.
Attacks in Aikido, 2008, 2009, 2015.
Aikibatto: Sword Exercises for Aikido Students, 2007, 2009.
Your Health in Your Horoscope: Introduction to Medical Astrology, 2009, 2015.

Archetypes of Mythology:
Jungian Theories on Myth and Religion Examined.
© Stefan Stenudd, 2022. All rights reserved.
Book design by the author.
Publisher: Arriba, Malmö, Sweden, arriba.se
ISBN: 978-91-7894-002-8

Contents

Introduction 7
    A Critical Examination 11

Carl G. Jung 21
    Three Basic Jungian Concepts 25
    A Theory takes Form 36
    Psychology of the Unconscious 36
    Two Essays, Multiple Versions 52
    Men, Women, and Races 60
    Individuation, Alchemy, and Tao 64
    Archetypes in Transformation 67
    The Blessing and Curse of Religion 74
    Mythological Dreams 77
    The Psyche of a God 84
    The Inwards Eastern Path 92
    The Elusive Unconscious 104
    The Collective Unconscious 117
    Seeing by Symbols 128
    Archetypes Beyond Jung 142
    Acted Archetypes 144
    List of Jungian Archetypes 153
    Dramaturgical Archetypes 157
    Archetypal Literary Criticism 175
    Myth as Self-Realization 186
    Personal Myth 191
    Myths Are Stories 195

Jungians 210
    Erich Neumann 212
    New Ethics in the Shadow 212
    Consciousness through Mythology 214
    Woman as an Archetype 221
    Károly Kerényi 224
    Primordial image 226

Joseph L. Henderson 229
Reading Dreams 229
Repeated Initiation 234
Fear of Death 236
Joseph Campbell 238
Monomyth Hero 239
Primeval Mythology 254
East Versus West 266
Four Ages of Western Mythology 273
Individual Mythology 279
Mircea Eliade 287
Other Archetypes 287
The Sacred 293
Marie-Louise von Franz 300
Pure Fairy Tales 301
Preconscious Creation Myths 307
Charles H. Long 318
Symbolic Creation Myths 319
James Hillman 330
Inward Search 331
Archetypal Psychology 341
Anthony Stevens 357
In Defense of the Archetypes 358
Mythological Symbols 371
David Adams Leeming 395
Voyage of the Hero 395
Creation Myths 399
Religious Myth 404
Jordan B. Peterson 414
Meaning and Belief 415
Rules for Life 449

Literature 469
Web Sources 481

Introduction

This is my second book on so-called depth psychology perspectives on mythology and religion. The first one was about how Sigmund Freud and his followers tackled the subjects,[1] and this one is about the thoughts of Carl G. Jung and those who have applied his theories. Initially, it was to be one book, but it swelled beyond reasonable size, so I decided to divide it into two.

Also, it made sense regarding the content. The Freudian and the Jungian views differ considerably and profoundly. Therefore, each tradition is better to treat separately, for the sake of clarity and consistency.

Still, an examination of those theories is not complete without comparing them, which is what is done in this introduction. That is why some of its content is the same in both books. Here, though, a certain emphasis is on the characteristics of Jungian thought, as that of Freudian thought was in the previous book.

Background

The psychoanalytical perspective on mythology was unavoidable. When the study of myths and religions from all over the world intensified during the 19th century, patterns in them were extracted and compared, and theories on what they revealed about common human conditions were proposed. Myths were increasingly seen as expressions of needs of the human psyche.

The beliefs expressed in myths, as well as in rites, gradu-

[1] Stefan Stenudd, *Psychoanalysis of Mythology: Freudian Theories on Myth and Religion Examined*, Malmö 2022.

ally ceased to be dismissed as merely heathen misconceptions as opposed to the sacred truth of the Christian doctrine. Instead, they became respected fields of study of the human nature, inspired by the quickly growing mass of documented myths and increasing knowledge about religious traditions among distant and obscure cultures.

By the end of the 19th century, the literature on the subject was immense, and mostly pointing to psychological explanations to the structure and content of myths, as well as for the birth of religions and their spiritual meaning.

To name a few:

English anthropologist Edward Burnett Tylor's *Primitive Culture: Researches into the Development of Mythology, Philosophy, Religion, Language, Art, and Custom* was published in 1871 and made a lasting impression. A few years earlier, in 1865, he had written *Researches into the Early History of Mankind* on the same theme.

The German philologist and orientalist Max Müller, who is regarded as the initiator of comparative religion, became Oxford's first professor of comparative theology in 1868. He edited *Sacred Books of the East*, published in 50 volumes from the years 1879 to 1910.

Scottish anthropologist James George Frazer's *The Golden Bough*, presenting a vast material on myth, lore, and ritual around the world, was originally published in 1890, as a two-volumes work. In the following decades it expanded considerably, reaching twelve volumes in its third edition, published between 1906 and 1915.

The Scottish author Andrew Lang's *Myth, Ritual, and Religion* in two volumes preceded Frazer by just a few years, getting published in 1887. There were also journals of anthropology published since the mid-1800s, frequently containing documentations of myths and rituals in nonliterate societies.

This rapid growth of interest in the traditions of other cultures was taking place simultaneously with the establishment of the science of psychology, and they influenced one another continuously. Anthropologists used psychological concepts to analyze and explain beliefs and religious practices of societies they studied, and psychologists searched anthropological material for support of their theories about the mentality of man. This is still the case.

Freudians and Jungians
The two persons most influential in the emergence of psychological treatments of myth were Sigmund Freud and Carl Gustav Jung, the latter to a much wider extent than the former. Since both were connected to the psychoanalytical movement — Freud as its founder and Jung as his most prominent disciple until they parted ways — and their perspectives on man and myth involved unconscious parts of the psyche supposed to play much more of a role than mere emotions and instinctive stimuli, it is possible to label their theories on myth psychoanalytical.

It can certainly be said about Freud's followers, who stuck with the term and what it contained. Jung was to change his name for the discipline to *analytical psychology*, which is not that different.

The term *depth psychology* is often used in this framework, but that would imply the existence of a shallow counterpart, which can be questioned, and it also suggests a vertical grading of the components of the psyche that is not necessarily shared by other psychologists.

By psychoanalytical perspectives on myths, I here refer to the theories of Freud, Jung, and their followers. For the 20th century, these two groups of theorists are so clearly defined that they can be treated as such without doing their individual thoughts any significant injustice. Freudians have treated myth and religion from the paradigm established by Freud, and Jungians have done the same from that of Jung.

For the future, though, both groups are sure to lose some of their homogeneity, since both Freudian and Jungian ideas about myth and religion are increasingly questioned and altered in differing directions, where they are not altogether abandoned. The latter seems to be more the case for Freud's ideas than for those of Jung. Freud has not stood the test of time to the extent that his former disciple has — especially in regard to theories about mythology, its psychological roots, and how it should be interpreted.

While Freud's psychology as a whole had a considerably wider reputation and respect than Jung's — and to some extent still does, although questioned on many central points — his take on myths in particular did not fare so well. There, Jung's influence grew to overshadow Freud all but completely, not that it has managed to find any consensus among either psychologists or mythologists.

The Freudian perspective can be described as one of mythology stemming from personal urges that may be shared by all, but are strictly internal and based on each individual's instinctual emotions. Jungian theories, on the other hand, involve social causes and a symbolism formed and upheld by the human species, more or less independently of individual minds. Where Freudians see a pattern of instincts, Jungians point to imagination nurtured by cultural heritage. One focuses on strictly internal factors, and the other emphasizes external influence.

Although these two perspectives sometimes lead to similar conclusions regarding the causes and effects of myth and religion, they display fundamentally different views on the human psyche. So, they may just as well be treated separately, in order to explore each approach adequately.

In examining the Freudian and Jungian theories about myth and religion, I have turned to their own writing on the subject, just about exclusively. Neither contemporary nor later commentators on their views are treated more than occasionally in passing, since their own words speak well for themselves and are enough material for an examination of them.

This book is about their theories on mythology, and not aiming at presenting other aspects of their psychology. It is also the reason for some significant Freudians and Jungians being excluded for not treating the subject at hand in any substantial way, if at all. Only those who in their writing showed an interest in myth and religion are included. I may not have caught all of them, nor all of their writing on the subject, but I am confident that most of them are treated, as well as their most notable texts.

A Critical Examination

As is certainly evident in both books, my examination of the Freudians and Jungians who theorized about the psychological causes behind mythology and religion is quite critical. I trust that it is also evident why. Anything else would be a betrayal of the book's objective. A serious investigation of this subject unavoidably leads to criticism, since there is such a discrepancy between Freudian and Jungian claims and their arguments for them. So much is stated and so little is proven.

It is blatantly obvious already with what Sigmund Freud had to say about the emergence of religion and its constant fuel — the Oedipus complex, which he regarded as the root to just about all expressions of the male psyche. He would not admit to the existence of something similar in the female mind.

The theory is, especially but not only when applied to religion, as preposterous as Freud's insistence on it is obstinate. He stuck with it until his death, refusing even to consider a nuanced view or alternative hypotheses. What he claimed to be a verified scientific theory was really a doctrine not to be questioned. A decree.

His followers were anxious to comply and did so with a reverence akin to that given high priests in religious congregations. This fidelity was clearly demonstrated by the formation and activities of the so-called Secret Committee, working to protect Freud's dogma from any modification, described in my previous book. That kind of loyalty is not unheard of in many kinds of subcultures, but it is gravely detrimental to scientific research.

The Freudians were more obsessed with defending the dogma of Freud than trying to expand the understanding of the human psyche. This explains the high degree of conformity in their theories about mythology and religion. Those who followed other lines of thought were condemned and expelled.

What made this situation possible and consolidated it was the fragile nature of the science in which they worked. Psychology was still very much limited to speculation and little was proven by hard empirical facts, during the first few decades of psychoanalysis. Freud was the father of this emerging science, and therefore his paradigm was the foundation on which his followers built their understanding.

That changed when Carl G. Jung broke free and developed his own paradigm, which was quite different and deviated increasingly as he continued to develop it. He was quite peripheral at first. Freud dominated the scene. But by time, Jung's alternative attracted more and more attention, though not primarily from psychologists and psychiatrists. Instead, he was increasingly read and respected by anthropologists, mythologists, authors, artists, and the general public.

In accordance with the variety of his audience, those who picked up on his ideas in their own writing were quite a diverse group. Many were not even primarily interested in psychological aspects, but focused on the myths and Jung's ideas as tools to explore them.

That had the distinct benefit of the Jungian line being much less constrained and controlled than that of the Freudians. It is strikingly obvious in the Jungian texts. They dare to deviate considerably from Jung, even when praising him as their source and guiding light. There is something about Jung's thoughts that invites creativity instead of conformity. He is used as a trampoline by which to reach new heights and perspectives, and not at all a standard to obediently repeat.

This is definitely a winning recipe, indicating that Jung will remain much longer and with more appreciation than Freud — at least regarding speculations about mythology and religion. As for therapeutical benefits, both are probably going to be of diminishing value, until they fade away completely. They just don't have the track record to be sustainable.

The Jungian perspective on myths has proven to inspire innovation and creativity in the pursuit of their meaning, which Freud's constraining doctrine just does not allow. Also, the scope of the Jungian view is so much wider and so are its applications. Right or wrong, it is a tool of greater use.

That liberty is what a science needs the most, especially in its primal stage, and I would argue that this is still the stage of a nonprejudiced study of mythology and religion. It is only a hundred years or so since these subjects were treated from a perspective where Christianity was the norm and everything else an oddity. Already the concept of religion was based on its Christian form, and the same was the case with the narrow idea of what constituted a god. Many mythological traditions are so far from how these concepts were defined that they can hardly be called religions.

Jung and his followers were not completely free from Christian prejudice, but they explored the myths of other cultures with both respect and curiosity, since they searched for a common essence in all myths, including those of Christianity. Whether they found it may certainly be debatable, but that aim made them regard all traditions as equal in significance. No mythology was superior or inferior, since they were all believed to contain universal meanings on which none of them had any patent.

The Jungian attitude in general was also distinctly more welcoming towards critique and questioning of its claims, than what the Freudians had shown to be. Of course, criticism is still very much needed also in regard to Jungian claims, as will be evident in the following pages of this book. The significant thing is that they practically invited it. They usually confessed to being speculative, which is vastly different from falsely stating something as an established fact. There were exceptions, but that is to be expected.

Jung in his writing was certainly insisting on the accuracy of his claims, but he did so with sort of a fictional style, a speculative twist, which opened for doubt and rebuttal. He did not lock the door to contradictory views, although he was not exactly asking for them. Frequently, he even seemed to intentionally provoke them. He was serving a palette, and not a finished painting.

Well, that palette was kind of rigged, with a set number of particular colors. Still, a palette. Jung invited creativity, where Freud demanded conformity.

Clinical and Textual

Systematic testing of a psychological hypothesis is an intricate matter already because it is very difficult to repeat the test with a similar setting, which is necessary in an empirical process. Even if the hypothesis is defined with precision and clear delimitation, which is particularly problematic in psychology, repeated testing is not sure to isolate the item to be studied from other known or unknown variables. If the hypothesis is vague, the task is practically impossible.

The human mind is just too much of a maze to be trapped in repeated clinical experiments, without lots of circumstances bound to deviate from one test to the next. And people are far too different, in ways impossible to predict, for their results to be confidently compared even if the tests are deemed identical — in itself something very hard to assess.

In addition, the psyche is not enough understood and its processes not sufficiently mapped, for test results to be adequately observable and measurable in an empirically trustworthy manner. There are too many unknowns in the equation.

The simple cause and effect of, say, what the lack of one vitamin does to the body or how a broken bone is healed, is objectively observable. But that is rare to find in psychology. In the mind, everything is subjective. That gives room for speculations, but few affirmed conclusions.

What modern psychology often relies on to make conclusions are statistical correlations: more people than pure chance would have it react in a certain way to something. It is a precarious path of inquiry, and its application is limited to strictly simplified assumptions. At best, it can show correlation, but rarely causation. Still, it is used a lot by psychologists, mainly because they have few other tools by which to experiment and get tangible results.

The Freudian psychoanalysts used a method to reach their conclusions, which was similar to the statistical one, but with even more alarming shortcomings. They referred to their own experiences with patients treated by psychoanalysis, and used that as evidence of their theories. But those numbers were far too few to make any statistical evaluation, and they did not bother to present any figures. Instead, they regarded their thesis as true because they had patients whose behavior confirmed it. They often settled for just one case to prove their point, no matter how far-fetched or intricate it was.

As a method in empirical science, it has little value. It lacks any more weight than saying, "I once knew someone who was like that."

The Jungians who were active therapists, which was far from all of them, used much the same flawed method of proving by examples from their patients. Jung certainly did so repeatedly. Apart from that, though, they also based their theories on the content of mythology and the symbolism they extracted from it.

That second route made it possible for people without therapeutic training to join the discussion, coming up with their own applications of Jungian principles based solely on what they found the myths to reveal. Their analysis can be described as textual instead of clinical.

The main problem with this approach was that the analysis tended to be biased, favoring an interpretation of the myths that would confirm the Jungian theories. It was bound to lead to a flawed understanding of the content of the myths, sometimes absurdly so. There are many examples of it in this book.

Furthermore, the Jungian theory of the archetypes and the collective unconscious is so vaguely and insufficiently defined that just about anything can be molded to fit it.

As for the archetypes, there is neither an authoritative and complete list of them, nor a precise definition of what does and what does not constitute an archetype. As for the collective unconscious, there is no evidence of its existence and no precise account of what it does and does not contain.

There is not even a plausible explanation to how it could exist at all, the way it is described in Jungian theory. A container in the brain with a multitude of symbols, innate from previous generations and identical in all of us, is not genetically possible. It is so much more plausible that the archetypes, said to be the content of the collective unconscious, are learned from generation to generation, and not genetically inherited. That also accounts for the variation of such symbols and how they are regarded in different cultures.

What it boils down to, for Freudians and Jungians alike, is that their theories are pure speculation. That is fine, if not pretending to be proven fact. The Freudians made rigid claims of scientific certainty, which have not aged well.

The Jungians, due to the complexity of their theories and their focus on the meaning of myths instead of just their therapeutical function, were less categorical with their scientific claims — mostly. They tended to allow the speculative nature of the myths they studied to influence their reasoning and descriptions, so that the results became mythical, too. They created myths of what myths were all about. Stories about stories.

That may be unavoidable. Analysis of fiction is also fiction.

Unconscious as a Noun

Both Freudian and Jungian psychology are based on the erroneous assumption of an unconscious, inaccessible to the conscious mind and still controlling very much of our psyche, our emotions, and our perception of ourselves as well as the world around us. This claim is so central that their psychological models would collapse all but completely if it were removed from the equation. So, it has not been questioned by them, but held as a paradigm to which they adapted the whole structure of their psychology. They were building their castles in the sand.

There is no evidence of an unconscious as an entity in the mind, even less so of such an entity being a hidden ruler of it. Also, there is nothing of a thinking nature going on in the brain that is inaccessible to the conscious mind. It may be ignored, in the constant flow of impressions, reflections, and considerations going on in our heads, but it is accessible, or it simply could not affect us.

There is just one exception — what we dream in our sleep. We only get a glimpse of the dream going on as we wake up, but our dreaming before that has faded away completely, and it is not stored in our memory. It happened, but then it's gone. This phenomenon has intrigued people for as long as our species has been around, and still does.

Freudians and Jungians have put a lot of emphasis on dreams, using them as arguments for their theories about the unconscious. But of course, the only dreams they have had access to in their research are the ones remembered by the dreamer, i.e., the ones at the moment of waking up — at which point they are accessed by the conscious mind of the dreamer. Previous dreams are not, and since they are not memorized at all, they have no lasting effect on the mind.

Something so fleeting is a fragile base for a theory of psychology. Dream interpretation is a risky business, for several reasons. It cannot be used as empirical evidence, but that has not stopped Freudians and Jungians from making such claims. Both my previous book and this one have many examples of it, where their reliability — or rather lack thereof — is discussed.

Returning to the unconscious, the problem with the concept is when it is used as a noun instead of an adjective, the difference between having an unconscious and being unconscious. The latter is no mystery. We may be unconscious of thoughts spinning around in our minds that we do not give any attention, of habitual behavior, of instinctual reactions, and so on. We can also become unconscious in the drastic meaning of fainting, losing consciousness for a while.

But the noun has no bearing. Our thoughts neither flee to nor emerge from some hidden part of the brain, with its own agenda.

Verdict

This project started with a paper I presented for a seminar in 2006 at the Department of the History of Ideas at Lund University, thinking that would be the end of it. But in 2014, I decided to return to it for a substantial editing and expansion of the text, mainly by not only treating Freud and Jung more at depth, but also their followers. The text turned out to have swelled almost twentyfold.

After having spent several years, to and fro, on this examination of Freudian and Jungian theories about myths and religion, I ask myself what to conclude. Within the history of ideas, my work has been concentrated on the thought patterns of creation myths, where this was one of many aspects explored.

Somewhat like many Jungians, and less so with the Freudians, I was and still am more interested in what the myths meant to those who created and upheld them, than what they may mean to us today. It is my conviction that this is also how we can find them relevant to us — not as a basis for religious belief or therapeutic technique, but to find ancient patterns of thought that are compatible to ours. There is an abundance of them.

Upon scrutiny, it is not at all difficult to see how our distant ancestors came up with those myths, even when they superficially seem absurd. We just have to consider what the world looked like to our predecessors, and what they were able to conclude about it. Also, and this is the most important thing, what they were able to imagine about it.

Where knowledge ends, fantasy begins. Human creativity is not boundless, since it depends on what is fathomable, but that gets us very far indeed.

Myths are stories, first and foremost. They may have started with speculations about the beginning of the world and the invisible powers that act on it, but the rules they follow are those of stories and storytelling, or they would not have stayed with us for so tremendously long. Way before the development of writing, they were transmitted orally between generations. That means they had to make some kind of sense to those who told them as well as to those who listened. And they had to engage, fascinate, scare, or enchant — preferably all of it combined. Just like good fiction or drama.

This is what Freudians and Jungians got wrong. They insisted that myths were not consciously invented, but sprang from unconscious sources, dealing with other issues completely than those told by the stories.

To Freudians, they were expressions of suppressed emotions, usually of guilt and more often than not related to the Oedipus complex. To Jungians, they stemmed from the collective unconscious and symbolized the quest towards individuation, which is in essence becoming aware of that part of the unconscious. They were, so to speak, calls from that hidden depth. Both theories were based on the claim that myths were not products of conscious efforts and conscious ideas.

With such a premise, it is impossible to even try looking objectively at the myths and what they might actually have meant to their creators and their original audiences. It is brutally ethnocentric and arrogant to assume that they meant what they may mean to us. The interpretation made by our present culture doesn't have precedence over how our predecessors saw it.

The only reasonable starting point is to accept that it meant something to them, and trying to find out what that was.

The myths preserved to our time are expressions of the times and cultures in which they appeared. Anything else is preposterous to claim. It would be sort of a colonialism of cultural heritage.

That attitude was certainly present at the time Freud and Jung developed their theories, when missionaries travelled the world to make everyone Christian, and European rule and law were established by military force in numerous distant regions. The cultural appropriation was used as an excuse for the exploitation. Populations of the conquered territories were not even acknowledged to understand their own traditions correctly.

Whether knowingly or not, Freud and Jung took part in this process with their theories on how to understand the myths of faraway cultures, without considering what the myths meant to those cultures. They did so in a time when few would object to it, or even understand the problem. Still, it is alarming with what confidence they made firm statements about things way beyond their own experiences, without even giving alternative explanations a thought.

It is at least equally sad to see those shortcomings of Freud and Jung repeated later, when their followers continued on the same track, assuming that they understood the old myths better than did the people of the cultures where they were formed. None of those Western theorists would have accepted that done to the biblical myths by people from other traditions.

On the other hand, some of the elaborate interpretations of mythology, especially those from Jungian writers, are rather ingenious in their treatments of the material, widening the perspectives considerably. They recognize the complexity and refinement of those ancient stories, by finding in them the possibilities of such far-fetched assumptions about their meaning.

That is what constitutes excellent fiction — it allows for all kinds of disparate impressions. Therein lies a proper homage to the clever imagination of our ancestors. They made stories that still intrigue us and nourish our speculations.

Carl G. Jung

Carl Gustav Jung (1875-1961) was born in Switzerland, the son of a Protestant priest who died when Carl was 21. He studied medicine in Basel until 1900, where his interest in psychiatry was awakened by the end of his studies, and led him to work at a psychiatric hospital in Zürich. In 1902 he got his MD with the dissertation *On the Psychology and Pathology of So-Called Occult Phenomena*, about a somnambulistic girl of 15 years, who was a medium.

Between 1905 and 1913 he was a lecturer of psychiatry at the University of Zürich. In 1909 he opened a private practice, which he would run until his death.

He sent his 1906 book *The Psychology of Dementia Praecox* (the ailment later by Eugen Bleuler renamed schizophrenia) to Sigmund Freud, which was the start of a collegial friendship between them. This was turned into dispute and separation, especially with Jung's 1912 book *Wandlungen und Symbole der Libido*, (published in English 1916 as *Psychology of the Unconscious*), which questioned Freud's focus on sexual trauma and the Oedipus complex, arguing for his own alternative theories about the psyche.

Jung's writing on mythology is not to be found concentrated to a few books on this subject, as is the case with Freud, but sprayed all over his works. There is rarely a text of his that does not touch on the subject, and just as rarely one devoted exclusively to it.

So, Jung's theories on myth come to us in bits and pieces, spread over all his writing. The job of systematizing has mainly been left in the hands of his pupils and followers. Among them, though, it is equally difficult to find one with the intention to bring together and present Jung's theories on myth in any authoritative and organized fashion. His gospel remains an elusive one, presenting few straightforward answers. That is quite befitting his psychological doctrine, which is in itself rather mythological.

Considerable Influence

Jung's ideas on myth and religion have made far more of an impact than those of Freud, among scholars as well as to an even larger extent on the general public. Where Freud remains little more than a joke in the field of history of religion and the study of mythology, Jung has made a lasting impression through most of the 20th century, to partly fade only in the last decade or so of it. And he is far from forgotten yet.

Apart from his own widely read writing, which deals considerably with myths, mythology, and many elements of religion, he has greatly influenced a number of significant scholars and other writers on these themes. The most important of them are Mircea Eliade (1907-86) and Joseph Campbell (1904-87).

Eliade wrote many books on myths and how they should be interpreted. He also formed the minds of numerous students as the head of the University of Chicago History of Religion department for almost 30 years. Campbell's books have become bestsellers and made deep impressions on the general public as to how myth should be understood. He was the central participant in a 1987 TV series about mythology, which received a huge audience in many countries.

In addition, there is the continued work of Jungian theorists and psychologists more often than not involving their perspective on myth in their writing on the mind of man and the inner workings of society. Notable Jungian theorists dealing extensively with myth are Erich Neumann (1905-1960), Marie-Louise von Franz (1915-1998), and James Hillman (1926-2011).[2]

By the sheer mass of it, Jungian literature on myth has set a standard and its theories have become a paradigm of sorts as

---

[2] Robert A. Segal, *Jung on Mythology*, Princeton 1998, p. 43.

to how myths should be understood. The Jungian perspective has widely influenced how mythological material is presented and interpreted.

For most of the 20th century, a substantial part of the literature on myth and lore used a Jungian viewpoint, whether or not that was adequate to the material. Myths were often even translated into the Jungian vocabulary, to the extent that their original content got distorted.

It can be compared to how the missionaries, who collected myths around the world in the 19th century, interpreted these myths through a Christian filter. Especially when they recorded exclusively oral traditions in this manner, they left us with flawed material of primary sources difficult to reconstruct. Our world has since become increasingly integrated, whereby orally transmitted mythology free from outside influence is nowadays almost impossible to find.

Washing off the Jungian influence from much of the literature on mythology of the 20th century is a challenge comparable to doing the same with the Christian influence on the literature of the preceding century.

Opposing Freud

Where Freud was mainly interested in the origin of religion and explaining the functions of rituals, Jung focused on myth and legend, the stories told within religions. To him, these stories were the essence of any religion, and therefore he was keener to explore the origin of myths than of religion as a whole.

Also contrary to Freud, Jung found myth and its meaning within the individual psyche. In spite of myths and their components being shared by all members of a society — and essentially by all mankind — he saw their workings as strictly personal. According to Jung, man is on a quest towards self-realization, and myths serve as clues to this process. Although every person is on this quest, fulfilling it to various degrees, it is a solo venture, each man for himself.

This difference between Freud and Jung can be loosely compared to the generalizations of *Mahayana* and *Hinayana* in Buddhism. The former is characterized as a joint effort together with people of the same conviction to find spiritual perfection, while the latter is doing it in solitude. Freud saw the individual as deeply dependent on society and anxious to conform to it, while Jung saw society as little more than a number of individuals of similar nature.

Therefore, to Jung the myths contain messages to the individuals, not the group, no matter how many people are involved in retelling and listening to them. Myths speak to each of us in the same way, but have to be dealt with individually as opposed to collectively.

Jung himself pointed out other differences to Freud, mainly regarding how to interpret dreams and fantasies:

I did not reduce them to personal factors, as Freud does, but — and this seemed indicated by their very nature — I compared them with the symbols from mythology and the history of religion, in order to discover the meaning they were trying to express.[3]

That may seem like a collective perspective and not an individual one, but the general symbols he found were messages for the individual to deal with according to personal needs, in a process he fittingly called *individuation*.

Jung also objected to the sexual themes Freud mostly found in dream interpretation:

Whereas he will always look for sexual causes, I trace the origin of dreams back to age-old mythological influences. Deriving from our remotest ancestors, there slumber in all

<hr>

[3] Carl G. Jung, "Introduction to Kranefeldt's Secret Ways of the Mind," transl. R. F. C. Hull from the German book *Die Psychoanalyse* published in 1930. *The Collected Works of C. G. Jung*, volume 4, Princeton 1985, p. 330.

of us subconscious memories which awaken at night and seek to compensate the false attitude modern man has towards nature.[4]

The above quotes demonstrate what utter importance Jung put on myths. To him they were little less than manifestations of a worldwide premise from the dawn of man, comparable to the divine *"Fiat!"* ("Let there be!") by which the god of the Bible created the world.[5] Myths, in his view, were clues to the inner workings of the human mind and its mission, no less.

He expressed it as if certain that he had revealed the very key to how the human mind works. His students were just as convinced of the same. Time has gnawed on this conviction, but still far from discarded it completely. Jung's vision is far too attractive and exciting to be ignored. In that way, it shares the quality of the myths it explores. Whether accurate of false, it is a wonderful story.

Three Basic Jungian Concepts

In the following, I have as much as possible used the original English translations of Jung's texts, since they have been more or less altered in later editions — either by Jung or by new translators. Sticking to the earliest versions was necessary when searching for the timeline of the emergence of his ideas and his terminology for them.

There are three basic concepts in Jung's psychology and analysis of myth: the *collective unconscious*, the *archetypes*, and

[4] Reports from a press conference in Vienna 1928, *Jung Speaking: Interviews and Encounters*, edited by William McGuire and R. F. C. Hull, Princeton 1977, p. 44.

[5] Jung had his own relation to *Fiat*. He regarded God's utterance "Let there be light!" as "the projection of that immemorial experience of the separation of the conscious from the unconscious." Carl G. Jung & Károly Kerényi, *On a Science of Mythology: The Myth of the Divine Child and the Mysteries of Eleusis*, transl. R. F. C. Hull, New York 1949 (originally published in German 1942), p. 119.

individuation. They are closely connected, describing the human mind as on a quest for self-realization. The collective unconscious is where the archetypes are stored. They emerge to the conscious mind, urging it to realize the existence and function of the collective unconscious. That is the process of individuation.

Already in his first written work, the dissertation from 1902, Jung's interest in the unconscious and the imagery emanating from it was evident. He describes the case of a 15 years old girl who acted out a wild imagination, thinking of herself as a medium, who in her frequent trances expressed the personalities of deceased persons. This girl, Hélène Preiswerk, was Jung's cousin, which he neglected to mention in his dissertation.[6]

Unconvinced of her medial abilities, Jung was still amazed by her fantasy in creating them and making them believable. He regarded it as a form of cryptomnesia,[7] the error of believing that images and ideas are new, when they are actually deeply hidden memories of the past. The visions of the patient were examples of cryptomnesic images from the unconscious. He says about their nature:

> *It is characteristic of cryptomnesia that the picture which emerges does not bear the obvious mark of the memory-picture, is not, that is to say, bound up with the idiosyncratic super-conscious ego-complex.*[8]

[6] Eugene Taylor, *The Mystery of Personality: A History of Psychodynamic Theories*, New York 2009, p. 41.

[7] The term cryptomnesia was first used by the Swiss psychologist Théodore Flournoy in a study of the medium Hélène Smith from 1900 (*Des Indes à la planète Mars: Étude sur un cas de somnambulisme avec glossolalie*), published in English the same year. Théodore Flournoy, *From India to the Planet Mars: A Study of a Case of Somnambulism with Glossolalia*, transl. Daniel B. Vermilye, New York 1900, p. 59 and other pages.

[8] Carl G. Jung, "On the Psychology and Pathology of So-Called Occult

It makes him think of Freud's investigations of dreams in *The Interpretation of Dreams*, "which disclose the independent growth of repressed thoughts."[9] But Jung expresses a sense of more to be found in the phenomenon. In the conclusion, Jung writes:

> *I naturally examined occultistic literature pertinent to the subject, and discovered a store of parallels from different centuries with our gnostic system, but scattered through all kinds of work mostly quite inaccessible to the patient.*[10]

That is very close to his later ideas of the archetypes and their seat in the collective unconscious. But it would take him quite some time to get there.

The Collective Unconscious

Neither Jung nor Freud were the first to use the term unconscious (*Unbewusste*) as a noun, representing a certain entity within the psyche. It was the German philosopher Friedrich Schelling in his book *System des transcendentalen Idealismus* from 1800.

He discussed the dynamics between the conscious and the unconscious, calling the former the absolutely subjective and the latter the absolutely objective.[11] To Schiller, the unconscious should have priority over the conscious, and he explained:

Phenomena" (originally published in German 1902), *Collected Papers on Analytical Psychology*, transl. M. D. Eder, ed. Constance E. Long, London 1916, p. 86.

[9] Ibid., p. 82.

[10] Ibid., p. 93.

[11] Friedrich von Schelling, *System of Transcendental Idealism*, transl. Peter Heath, Charlottesville 1978 (originally published in German 1800), p. 208.

> *The objective world is simply the original, as yet uncon-*
> *scious, poetry of the spirit; the universal organon of philos-*
> *ophy — and the keystone of its entire arch — is the philos-*
> *ophy of art.*[12]

But a book which left much more of a mark on the ideas of an unconscious was Eduard von Hartmann's *Philosophie des Unbewussten* from 1869 (translated into English 1884 as *Philosophy of the Unconscious*).

The massive text had a significant impact at the time, making the concept of the unconscious widely established long before the works of Freud and Jung.

Jung mentions in his memoirs that he read Eduard von Hartmann "assiduously" already in his university years.[13] But the text is most definitely the philosophy of the unconscious, and not the psychology of it. The unconscious of von Hartmann's interpretation is metaphysical, if not to say cosmological, discussed alongside the thoughts of Schelling as well as Kant, Leibnitz, and other philosophers. He still spoke of an unconscious in the psyche of man, but it led him to speculate way beyond the mind:

> *One of the most important and familiar manifestations of*
> *the Unconscious is Instinct, and the conception of Instinct*
> *rests on that of Purpose.*[14]

This purpose, without which instinct would be pointless, led him on to seeing an aim in nature and a design to it. It took

---

[12] Ibid., p. 12.

[13] Carl G. Jung, *Memories, Dreams, Reflections*, edited by Aniela Jaffé, transl. Richard and Clara Winston, New York 1965 (originally published in German 1962), p. 101.

[14] Eduard von Hartmann, *Philosophy of the Unconscious*, transl. William Chatterton Coupland, London 1884 (originally published in German 1869), vol 1, p. 43.

him quite far from the psychological application made by Freud and Jung.

The collective unconscious is a concept of Jung's own invention. His first description of it was in a 1916 lecture, which was the same year translated into French. It was published in English the following year.[15]

In this text, he describes the conflict inside every individual mind between personal aspirations and the collective demands. When one dominates the other, the person suffers. This tension exists in the conscious as well as the unconscious. Jung considers the risk of the collective material taking over, because of its quantity. Individuation is the process by which a personality can develop in spite of the overwhelming collective material in both the conscious and the unconscious.[16]

He does not yet use the expression collective unconscious, but implies it. The English translation has other terms, such as *collective psyche* and *impersonal unconscious*, whereof the latter may be what Jung later called collective unconscious.

In a summary at the end of the text Jung expresses the need for dividing both the conscious and the unconscious contents into individualistic and collectivistic, defining the latter: "A content is collectivistic whose developing tendency aims at universal validity."[17] The individualistic content, on the other hand, tends towards differentiation from the collective. He also states:

[15] Carl G. Jung, "La Structure de l'inconscient", transl. M. Marsen, *Archives de Psychologie XVI*, Geneva 1916. An English translation, "The Conception of the Unconscious", was published in Carl G. Jung, *Collected Papers on Analytical Psychology*, 2nd ed., London 1917. The original German lecture manuscript, *Über das Unbewusste und seine Inhalte*, was lost until after Jung's death in 1961, when it was found in his personal archives.

[16] Carl G. Jung, "The Conception of the Unconscious", *Collected Papers on Analytical Psychology*, transl. M. D. Eder, ed. Constance E. Long, 2nd ed., London 1917, pp. 455f.

[17] Ibid., p. 473.

There are insufficient criteria by which to designate a given content as simply individual or collective, for uniqueness is very difficult to prove, although it is a perpetually and universally recurrent phenomenon.

He was soon to tackle that insufficiency.

The Archetypes

Jung's first treatment of the term archetype was in the 1919 symposium text *Instinct and the Unconscious*.[18] Before that he had used the expression 'primordial image' (*Urbild* in German), derived from the Swiss art historian Jacob Burckhardt.[19] In this text, he also talks about the collective unconscious, smoothly bringing them together in one simple formula.

After defining what belongs to the personal unconscious, he talks about another stratum of the unconscious, containing "supra-individual" qualities which were not acquired but inherited, like instincts and impulses. He continues:

Moreover, in this stratum we discover the pre-existent forms of apprehension, or the congenital conditions of intuition, viz. the 'archetypes' of apperception, which are the a priori *determining constituents of all experience. Just as instincts compel man to a conduct of life that is specifically human, so the archetypes or categories* a priori *compel intuition and apprehension to forms specifically human. I propose to designate the sum of such inherited psychic qualities as instincts and archetypes of apprehension by the term 'collective unconscious'.*[20]

[18] Carl G. Jung, "Instinct and the Unconscious", transl. C. F. and H. G. Baynes, first published in the *British Journal of Psychology* X, London 1919.

[19] Carl G. Jung, *The Portable Jung*, ed. Joseph Campbell, New York 1971, p. 52.

[20] Carl G. Jung, "Instinct and the Unconscious," *Contributions to Analytical Psychology*, transl. H G. and Cary F. Baynes, London 1928, pp. 275f.

Jung states that he takes the term archetype from St. Augustine, although briefly discussing its use also by Plato, Descartes, Malebranche, Spinoza, Kant, and Schopenhauer.[21] In a later text he clarifies:

The term "archetype" is not found in St. Augustine, but the idea of it is. Thus in De diversis quaestionibus LXXXIII he speaks of "ideae principales, 'which are themselves not formed . . . but are contained in the divine understanding.'"[22]

Augustine in turn connected the concept to Plato's world of ideas, and thought of these principal ideas to "exist nowhere but in the very mind of the Creator."[23] Like Plato's ideas or forms, they are the very molds of anything to be materialized:

The ideas are certain original and principal forms of things, i.e., reasons, fixed and unchangeable, which are not themselves formed and, being thus eternal and existing always in the same state, are contained in the Divine intelligence. And though they themselves neither come into being nor pass away, nevertheless, everything which can come into being and pass away and everything which does come into being and pass away is said to be formed in accord with these ideas.[24]

[21] Ibid., pp. 278f.

[22] Carl G. Jung, "Archetypes and the Collective Unconscious," *The Collected Works of C. G. Jung*, volume 9.1, transl. R. F. C. Hull, Princeton 1969, p. 4. The essay is an edited version of a text from 1934, which just states that the term archetype "derives" from Augustine. Carl G. Jung, *The Integration of the Personality*, transl. Stanley Dell, London 1940, p. 53.

[23] Augustine, *Eighty-three Different Questions*, qu. 46, transl. David L. Mosher, Washington D.C. 1982, p. 80.

[24] Ibid., p. 80.

The similarities to Jung's archetype concept are not hard to spot, but to Augustine these original and principal forms were tools by which God created from his mind, and not existing outside of it.

Individuation

The term individuation I have not found Jung use before 1912, when he did so briefly in *Wandlungen und Symbole der Libido*, translated to English in 1916 as *Psychology of the Unconscious*. Discussing sacrifice, he calls the individual mask the veil of individuation, and later in a footnote he describes the separation from the mother as an individuation. In both cases he puts the word within quotes.[25]

As mentioned earlier, Jung also used the term in his 1916 lecture "The Conception of the Unconscious," where he describes individuation as a necessary process to avoid drowning in one's unconscious:

> *Upon close consideration it is astonishing to note how much of our so-called individual psychology is really collective; so much that the individual element quite disappears. Individuation, however, is an indispensable psychological requirement. The crushing predominance of what is collective should make us realize what peculiar care and attention must be given to the delicate plant "individuality," if it is to develop.*[26]

Clearly, the concept of individuation had by then rooted in Jung's theories on the psyche and its needs. Five years later, in 1921, he published the book substantially devoted to the process of individuation: *Psychologische Typen*.

[25] Carl G. Jung, *Psychology of the Unconscious*, transl. Beatrice M. Hinkle, New York 1916 (originally published in German 1912), pp. 433 and 554.

[26] Jung, "The Conception of the Unconscious," pp. 455f.

The English translation from 1923 had the subtitle *The Psychology of Individuation*. In the definitions of terms at the end of the book, he writes about individuation:

In general, it is the process of forming and specializing the individual nature; in particular, it is the development of the psychological individual as a differentiated being from the general, collective psychology.[27]

There is no separate definition of the collective unconscious, but the one about the unconscious explains what he means about the personal unconscious and the collective unconscious. He describes the contents of the latter as originating in "the inherited possibility of psychic functioning in general, viz. in the inherited brain-structure." He adds:

These are the mythological associations — those motives and images which can spring anew in every age and clime, without historical tradition or migration.[28]

Archetype, too, lacks its own entry among the definitions, but is described in that about image:

The primordial image (elsewhere also termed the 'archetype') is always collective, i.e. it is at least common to entire nations or epochs. In all probability the most important mythological motives are common to all times and races.[29]

He prefers the expression primordial image as opposed to personal image, explaining it as having an archaic character

---

[27] Carl G. Jung, *Psychological Types or The Psychology of Individuation*, transl. H. Godwin Baynes, London 1923 (originally published in German 1921), p. 561.

[28] Ibid., p. 616.

[29] Ibid., pp. 555f.

"in striking unison with familiar mythological motives" based on material from the collective unconscious.

In the definition of intuition, he also describes the archetypes, and here with that term:

> These archetypes, whose innermost nature is inaccessible to experience, represent the precipitate of psychic functioning of the whole ancestral line, i.e. the heaped-up, or pooled, experiences of organic existence in general, a million times repeated, and condensed into types. Hence, in these archetypes all experiences are represented which since primeval time have happened on this planet.[30]

The last sentence makes a claim close to the absurd. All experiences since primeval time — that is a lot. But what he implies is that the archetypes are condensations of significant experiences, numerously repeated by generations of humankind. Not just any trivial thing or events that have been so rare that they are long forgotten before repeated.

Apart from in the definitions, Jung uses the word archetype in only two of the chapters. Individuation is used three times, but collective unconscious twenty times, most of them in a chapter discussing the type-problem in poetry.

The poets, at least the major ones and in their principal and most inspired work, "create from the very depths of the collective unconscious, voicing aloud what others only dream." But they lack conscious understanding of the true meaning of what emerges.[31]

So, by this time, in 1921, Jung was comfortable with the three concepts archetypes, collective unconscious, and individuation, and how to utilize them in his psychology. But he had not yet started making a habit of it. He settled with arguing for their utility when used to understand the psyche.

[30] Ibid., pp. 507f.

[31] Ibid., pp. 237f.

It would take additional years before he did so himself consistently, without hesitation.

A Theory takes Form

Although it would take quite some time before Jung settled for an exact and consistent terminology, his path towards a psychology all of his own was evident quite early, probably already by his dissertation in 1902, *On the Psychology and Pathology of So-Called Occult Phenomena*. He might have reached his own take on psychology sooner, had he not become a disciple of Sigmund Freud for a number of years.

Psychology of the Unconscious

The definite break between them came with Jung's 1912 book *Wandlungen und Symbole der Libido*, published in English in 1916 with the title *Psychology of the Unconscious*. In this book, Jung contradicted some of Freud's theories about the psyche, especially by giving less importance to sexuality as the root to just about all problems of the psyche.

From then on, Jung was definitely on his own course, and there was no stopping his own theory of psychology from taking its form. As he says in the author's note of the book:

> *My task in this work has been to investigate an individual phantasy system, and in the doing of it problems of such magnitude have been uncovered, that my endeavor to grasp them in their entirety has necessarily meant only a superficial orientation toward those paths, the opening and exploration of which may possibly crown the work of future investigators with success.*[32]

Of course, that future investigator was none other than Jung himself.

---

[32] Carl G. Jung, *Psychology of the Unconscious: A Study of the Transformations and Symbolisms of the Libido, A Contribution to the History of the Evolution of Thought*, transl. Beatrice M. Hinkle, New York 1916, p. xlvii.

The Longing for Rebirth

In the book, Jung spends 560 pages discussing the dynamics between the conscious and the unconscious, and what they imply about the dilemmas of the human psyche. It is an extensive text. The end notes alone cover 76 pages.

Jung bases his treatment of the subject on the "poetical unconsciously formed phantasies" of Miss Frank Miller, published in 1906 in *Archives de Psychologie*, with the title "Quelque faits d'imagination créatrice subconsciente."[33] In the following year it was translated into English by Miss Miller and published with the title "Some Instances of Subconscious Creative Imagination" in an American journal on parapsychology.

The theme of Miss Miller's text is what can be called a strong sense of empathy, "at certain moments, and for a few instants only, the impressions and feelings of another suggest themselves so vividly to me that they appear to be mine."[34] She goes on to describe dreams and fantasies that made lasting impressions on her, sometimes inspiring her to write poems in her sketchbook, and speculates about where she got the ideas to them.

She finds quite natural explanations — they are all fragments in her memory of past experiences, be that her own or from what she has read. She can even list those specific memories, and it comes as no surprise to her:

> *It is alleged that whatever enters into the mind is never completely lost, that the association of ideas, or a certain combination of circumstances suffices to bring back the faintest impression.*[35]

[33] Ibid., p. 41.

[34] Miss Frank Miller, "Some Instances of Subconscious Creative Imagination", *Journal of the American Society for Psychical Research*, vol. 1 no. 6, New York 1907, pp. 293-308.

[35] Ibid., p. 307.

That would make her experiences examples of cryptomnesia, forgotten memories reappearing and believed to be new thoughts. This was a phenomenon Jung had treated already in his first book *On the Psychology and Pathology of So-Called Occult Phenomena*, the dissertation from 1902, where he used it to explain odd instances with the young medium examined.

Regarding Miss Miller, though, Jung had a completely different take — in spite of her own conclusions.

It is puzzling that Jung would venture to analyze the thoughts and emotions of a woman he had never met, based only on a text of hers. Otherwise, he had numerous experiences of patients from his practice, and frequently referred to these in his writing. Although Miss Miller was a complete stranger, it did not stop him from making firm assumptions about her state of mind.

Not only that, but while his own patients remained anonymous when he wrote about them, this was not a discretion he granted Miss Miller, although his text explores her psyche intimately, to say the least. Jung simply assumed — wrongly — that she used a pseudonym.[36] The oddity of her male first name Frank might have convinced him of it.[37]

Analyzing Miss Miller's text with its dream-like fantasies, visions, and poetry, Jung traces a psychological process he regards as a basic human conflict — the unconscious libido urges versus the inhibitions of the conscious. In particular, he points out the human longing to return to childhood, thereby escaping decay and death:

[36] In the foreword to the second German edition, 1924, Jung writes: "an unknown young American woman, pseudonymously known as Frank Miller." *Collected Works of C. G. Jung*, volume 5, 2nd edition, transl. R. F. C. Hull, Princeton 1976, p. xxviii.

[37] The facts in the case of Miss Miller have been examined in Sonu Shamdasani, "A woman called Frank," *Spring: Journal of Archetype and Culture*, volume 50 (1990), New York 1991, pp. 25-56.

> *But man wishes to remain a child too long; he would fain*
> *stop the turning of the wheel, which, rolling, bears along*
> *with it the years; man wishes to keep his childhood and*
> *eternal youth, rather than to die and suffer corruption in*
> *the grave.*[38]

In the unconscious, this longing becomes an incestuous one directed at the mother, since she is the one who gave birth and therefore, she is also the one holding the key to rebirth. The incestuous urge is not sexual at its core, but symbolic. It represents the wish to return to the maternal uterus, of "coming into the mother once more in order to be born again."[39]

Still, it creates a reaction of denial — because incest, also in a symbolic form, is condemned by society since primeval times, "the original sin of incest weighs heavily for all time upon the human race."[40] The forbidden incest has had a tremendous impact on the evolution of the human mind:

> *It was only the power of the incest prohibition which cre-*
> *ated the self-conscious individual, who formerly had been*
> *thoughtlessly one with the tribe, and in this way alone did*
> *the idea of individual and final death become possible.*[41]

Jung sees this dilemma as the root to just about every neurosis. The solution lies not in denying it, but in recognizing it and thereby growing out of it. The conscious needs to be aware of this longing in the unconscious and how it expresses itself. That is the process of the psyche growing up, which is necessary for its health.

This is all quite straightforward, and not that very far from

[38] Jung, *Psychology of the Unconscious*, p. 434.

[39] Ibid., p. 251.

[40] Ibid., p. 63.

[41] Ibid., pp. 303f.

Freud's idea of the Oedipus complex. But there are significant differences, and Jung points them out. He states clearly that he no longer can support Freud's view that every neurotic symptom is caused by oppressed sexuality. Jung even uses biology to oppose Freud's idea of the overall dominance of the sexual influence on the psyche:

> *Biology, as a science of objective experience, would have to reject unconditionally Freud's proposition, for, as we have made clear above, the function of reality can only be partly sexual; in another equally important part it is self-preservation.*[42]

Not even when the unconscious expresses itself in sexual imagery is its content necessarily sexual: "The sexuality of the unconscious is not what it seems to be; *it is merely a symbol.*"[43]

Instead, Jung sees the seemingly sexual expressions from the unconscious as symbols of the true urge — that of rebirth through the mother, which in turn is a confused expression of the longing to return to childhood and thereby avoiding or at least postponing death.

The unconscious uses images that are remnants from man's primitive past. They must be interpreted as representations of basic urges and not assumed to be only what they appear to be on the surface.

This is also how Jung's definition of libido deviates from that of Freud. About Freud's book from 1905 on sexual theory,[44] Jung says: "There the term libido is conceived by him in the original narrow sense of sexual impulse, sexual need." But since then, "a change has taken place in the libido conception; its field of application has been widened. An extremely clear

[42] Ibid., p. 459.

[43] Ibid., p. 433.

[44] Sigmund Freud, *Drei Abhandlungen zur Sexualtheorie*, 1905, translated into English 1910 by A. A. Brill as *Three Contributions to the Sexual Theory*.

example of this amplification is this present work."[45]

To Jung, libido is not a sexual urge, but urge and longing as such, the energy that drives us onward, much like many ancient ideas of a life force or a primus motor of the human mind. It is what makes us wish, whatever we wish for. Without it, we would complacently sit down and do nothing with our lives. We would be dormant.

Denying this urge can be very detrimental, but it is not a force without its own hazards:

> *The passionate longing, that is to say, the libido, has its two sides; it is power which beautifies everything, and which under other circumstances destroys everything.*[46]

Humongous Excavation

Now, what takes Jung as much as 560 pages is that he sets out to prove his thesis by finding its pattern in numerous myths and legends, as well as in works of poetry and fiction.

Among the latter he repeatedly turns to Goethe's *Faust* and the writings of Friedrich Nietzsche. As for the former, he uses many examples from Mithraism and Christianity, but also explores countless other mythologies from all over the world.

Jung spends several pages analyzing *Hiawatha*, which he calls "a poetical compilation of Indian myths."[47]

But *The Song of Hiawatha* by Henry Wadsworth Longfellow from 1855 is a very free compilation of Indian myths turned into a fictional story, ending with Hiawatha adopting Christianity. Speaking about visiting missionaries, he tells his tribe:

> *Listen to their words of wisdom,*
> *Listen to the truth they tell you,*

[45] Jung, *Psychology of the Unconscious*, pp. 139f.

[46] Ibid., p. 116.

[47] Ibid., pp. 347ff.

For the Master of Life has sent them
From the land of light and morning![48]

Then he leaves in his canoe for the land of the Hereafter. There was an historical figure named Hiawatha, but Longfellow's poem does in no way relate to him.

Jung sees mythology and the like as an age-old "phantastic form of thought — of the infantile in general," and explains:

From this type of thinking proceed all those numerous contacts with mythological products, and that which we consider as original and wholly individual creations are very often creations which are comparable with nothing but those of antiquity.[49]

Also, he is fond of utilizing etymology, comparing words and their meanings from different languages and eras. For example, this is what he has to say about the etymological context of the word *libido*:

libido *or* lubido *(with* libet, *more ancient* lubet*), it pleases me, and* libens *or* lubens = *gladly, willingly. Sanskrit,* lúbhyati = *to experience violent longing,* lôbhayati = *excites longing,* lubdha-h = *eager,* lôbha-h = *longing, eagerness. Gothic =* liufs, *and Old High German* liob = *love. Moreover, in Gothic,* lubains *was represented as hope; and Old High German,* lobôn = *to praise,* lob = *commendation, praise, glory; Old Bulgarian,* ljubiti = *to love,* ljuby = *love; Lithuanian,* liáupsinti = *to praise.*[50]

It is hard to see how this would clarify the concept.

---

[48] Henry Wadsworth Longfellow, *The Song of Hiawatha*, London 1855, p. 294.

[49] Jung, *Psychology of the Unconscious*, p. 159.

[50] Ibid., pp. 137f.

Jung's excavation is humongous, if not to say manic. The book is almost impenetrable with its repeated detours around numerous examples from myth and poetry. And he allows himself great freedom in interpreting all kinds of elements as examples of the unconscious symbols of the human urge for rebirth. Often his explanations are far-fetched, indeed. Often, too, they seem contradictory.

Here is one example of his reasoning, when presenting a creation story from the *Brihadaranyaka Upanishad*, which he sees as representing the "transition of the sexual libido through the onanistic phase in the preparation of fire." He begins by quoting the text, and then follows his explanation of its meaning:

"In truth, he (Atman) was as large as a woman and a man, when they embrace each other. This, his own self, he divided into two parts, out of which husband and wife were formed. With her, he copulated; from this humanity sprang. She, however, pondered: 'How may he unite with me after he has created me from himself? Now I shall hide!' Then she became a cow; he, however, became a bull and mated with her. From that sprang the horned cattle. Then she became a mare; he, however, became a stallion; she became a she-ass; he, an ass, and mated with her. From these sprang the whole-hoofed animals. She became a goat; he became a buck; she became an ewe; he became a ram, and mated with her. Thus were created goats and sheep. Thus it happened that all that mates, even down to the ants, he created — then he perceived: 'Truly I myself am Creation, for I have created the whole world!' Thereupon he rubbed his hands (held before the mouth) so that he brought forth fire from his mouth, as from the mother womb, and from his hands." [51]

[51] Ibid., pp. 174f. In the original German text, Jung quoted from Paul Deussen, *Die Geheimlehre des Veda*, probably the 2nd ed., Leipzig 1907.

And here is Jung's interpretation of it:

We meet here a peculiar myth of creation which requires a psychologic interpretation. In the beginning the libido was undifferentiated and bisexual; this was followed by differentiation into a male and a female component. From then on man knows what he is. Now follows a gap in the coherence of the thought where belongs that very resistance which we have postulated above for the explanation of the urge for sublimation. Next follows the onanistic act of rubbing or boring (here finger-sucking) transferred from the sexual zone, from which proceeds the production of fire. The libido here leaves its characteristic manifestation as sexual function and regresses to the presexual stage, where, in conformity with the above explanation, it occupies one of the preliminary stages of sexuality, thereby producing, in the view expressed in the Upanishad, the first human art, and from there, as suggested by Kuhn's idea of the root "manth," perhaps the higher intellectual activity in general. This course of development is not strange to the psychiatrist, for it is a well-known psychopathological fact that onanism and excessive activity of phantasy are very closely related. (The sexualizing-autonomizing of the mind through autoerotism is so familiar a fact that examples of that are superfluous.)

Jung has found a myth that contains both an onanistic act of sorts and incest of sorts in the same initial sexual act. Atman copulates with himself in the form of a woman born out of himself. But this is easily explained in other words than those of Jung.

Several creation myths deal with the problem of how one sole initial being can give birth to others. Here he does so by splitting himself into two, who mate. Their first children are human beings, indicating their importance in this cosmogony.[52] Mankind is closest to this supreme deity by being the first ones created. Then the deity has to transform in order to give birth to the lesser creatures in the world, one species after the other. Without these transformations, the children would all be human. The story makes good sense without the psychological symbolism Jung suggests.

There is an Egyptian creation myth that Jung would surely have liked to include on this topic. Here speaks the creator Khepera (usually transliterated Khepri), who was all alone in the beginning. This is what he did to change that:

> *I, even I, had union with my clenched hand, I joined myself in an embrace with my shadow, I poured seed into my mouth, my own, I sent forth issue in the form of Shu, I sent forth moisture in the form of Tefnut.*[53]

Like Atman, he had to find a way to multiply from an original state of solitude. Being the very creator god, Khepera could out of his own seed only create other gods. Human beings came later, created by his tears, a lesser fluid. Plants and animals appeared after that.

The Khepera and Atman myths present similar solutions to the primary problem of creation myths — how was the start, the very start? A sole primordial being is left no other choice than to impregnate itself, in one or other fashion.

One may wonder why it is usually a he instead of a she. If I am allowed to speculate, it is probably due to ancient misunderstanding of reproduction as an act of impregnation of the woman, where she was believed to be nothing more than a vessel for the fetus. Nothing was known of the egg needed. The man's seed alone was thought to be the carrier of new life.

In this very ambitious inventory of mythology and leg-

---

[52] *Cosmogony*, theory about the origin of the cosmos.

[53] E. A. Wallis Budge, *The Gods of the Egyptians: Studies in Egyptian Mythology*, volume 1, London 1904, pp. 310f.

ends, Jung has most definitely been inspired by James George Frazer's *The Golden Bough*. He does not refer to it that many times in his book, but enough to make it clear that he is familiar with and impressed by it.

This multitude of examples was common in texts about mythology of that period, as the writers searched for universal patterns and explanations to the emergence of myths. So did Edward Burnett Tylor, Andrew Lang, and many others. They had to, because of their subject-matter being mythology. In Jung's text, dealing mainly with aspects of the human psyche, this vast quantity is less convincing. It is like he tries to drown any opposition to his theories by this flood of indicia, none of which is much proof on its own.

The pattern that this quantity forms is one of circular arguments: The myths are supposed to confirm Jung's theory about symbols from the unconscious, since they can be interpreted as such. But there are, of course, alternative interpretations of them.

That goes already for the text of Miss Miller, which is the recurring theme of Jung's book. She explains her visions as stemming from nothing fancier than old memories and past experiences, which would make them examples of cryptomnesia. But Jung discards those explanations, meaning instead that they emerged from the imagery of her unconscious — because they fit his interpretation of them.

That does not mean he must be wrong. But he is still to prove being right. The mere quantity of arguments does not suffice. And his constant unwillingness to try other modes of explanation hardly increases his credibility.

Dream, Chicken, and Egg

Jung starts his book by referring to Freud's *The Interpretation of Dreams* from 1899, and expanding on what dreams represent and contain. He states that "the dream images are to be understood symbolically," and "the dream arises from a part of the mind unknown to us, but none the less important, and is concerned with the desires for the approaching day." Although the dreams may seem contradictory and nonsensical, they rise from "psychologic material which yields a clear meaning."[54]

He goes on to claim that dreams are symbolic for the purpose of not being understood by the dreamer, or specifically "in order that the wish, which is the source of the dream, may remain unknown."[55] It is to protect the conscious mind from what lurks in the unconscious, which would be very hard to face.

Not that these wishes are necessarily abominable in essence, but they may seem so because of the form they take — as is the case with the hidden incestuous urge discussed above. It is a mere representation of the longing for rebirth, which may be naïve, but not as deplorable as its representation.

It is interesting that Jung uses dreaming as an entry to the symbolic workings of the unconscious, and then traces similar symbolism in mythology. Such similarities are not hard to find, as has been pondered both before and after his book by writers on the topics of mythology and religion.

It would not be preposterous to claim that the fact that we dream and how we do it may be what caused us to come up with ideas of an invisible world and parallel realities of some obscure but utter significance. We dream about those who passed away, as if they are alive somewhere and come to visit our dreams. And dreams have their own absurd logic in how one thing leads to another, as if the laws of nature ceased to apply.

So, there may be another reality to find than the one our eyes see when we are awake. Dreams suggest, even insist, that there is more to life than what we perceive with our senses.

But Jung goes further, when he claims that the dreams as well as any material in the unconscious represent something fixed and definable. He gives one explanation to them, refus-

[54] Jung, *Psychology of the Unconscious*, pp. 8f.
[55] Ibid., p. 12.

ing alternatives. Maybe he takes it too far already by claiming that they can at all be explained in a rational way.

Furthermore, there is the problem of the chicken and the egg. Is the symbolic nature of the unconscious the source to such patterns in our dreams and in mythology, or can the mythology we have adapted influence how we think and how we perceive our dreams?

We have no trace of the human psyche and its expressions before the emergence of mythology, so we do not know for sure how that happened. But in every culture we can study, we see its mythology and other forms of belief influence the children increasingly by each year they live. Santa Claus is not an invention of each child's own imagination, and the same goes for just about every conceivable mythical narrative and symbol.

I doubt that there is any way to extract from a human mind what has to be a mythical symbol of its own unconscious origin. But it is not too complicated to suggest how any such symbol can have been ingested from the outside world — either from fellow humans or from conclusions through personal observations. Our ideas of the surreal and the unreal are shaped by what is real.

Miss Miller points this out with her matter-of-factly statements of what brought her visions. Maybe Jung would have been inclined to trust her explanations more if the two had actually met.

Our dreams say the same. They consist of material from our experiences when awake, though often twisted and strangely altered, and really nothing else. No hidden clues to our psychological needs, no synthesis of insights reached, no maze by which we can find our true selves. They are just dreams, a haphazard collage of what we have stored in our memories. Their meaning is something we invent in our conscious minds when we are awake.

The many similarities Jung finds between mythologies from all over the world, he wants to explain by their origin in identical unconscious urges we all share, as well as the symbols for them. To him, that is the simple truth about mythology:

> We take mythologic symbols much too concretely and wonder at every step about the endless contradictions. These contradictions arise only because we constantly forget that in the realm of phantasy "feeling is all." Whenever we read, therefore, "his mother was a wicked sorcerer," the translation is as follows: The son is in love with her, namely, he is unable to detach his libido from the mother-imago; he therefore suffers from incestuous resistance.[56]

But there are so many other experiences common to people all over the world than incestuous urges, and human observations were even more homogenous in the distant past when mythologies emerged. The sun goes up and down, changing day to night. We are born, we grow and struggle to survive, until we inevitably die. We hunt and we are hunted, we use what we know and fear what we do not know, and so on. We have so much in common with people of other cultures and with our distant ancestors, it would be strange if our mythologies lacked similarities.

But there are also differences in the world we perceive around us, depending on where or when we live, just as there are distinct differences between mythologies. The differences of the latter are often readily explained by the differences of the former. Would the differences be just as easily explained by Jung's model? Hardly. He would need the added component of the outer influence of environment or events.

So, why would he not pursue that line of reasoning, to see how far it might take him? At least once, he should have tried to see if there is anything not explainable by outer influence and the conscious mind's response to it. Granted, that would

[56] Ibid., p. 249.

have taken him quite some time and surely increased the number of pages of his book considerably.

Still, the search for patterns in mythologies and their symbolic imagery is a fruitful one. It has been done by all who researched mythology at any depth. It is also evident that mythologies can give clues to the nature of the human psyche and what needs they might aim to fulfill. The difficult question is what those clues are, and how they are to be interpreted.

The Theory before the Terminology

In his text, Jung does not use the terms later to be central in his theory: the collective unconscious, archetypes, and individuation. But what he describes definitely fits those concepts.

He speaks of the unconscious containing material common to us all, expressing itself in symbolic tales of equally symbolic characters, which are "primitive figures of phantasies and religious myths streaming up from the unconscious."[57] But he speaks of the unconscious as a whole, not dividing it into a personal and a collective part. One time he mentions an "individual unconscious" as a retrogressive tendency overcoming the forward strife of the conscious, but does not explore the concept further.[58]

He describes a process of becoming aware of the conflict between unconscious urges and the conscious as a method of healing. And he presents symbolic types of utter significance, staying the same through history, but without using the word archetype. He does speak of a father-imago and a mother-imago, explaining in a note that he chooses "imago" instead of the expression "complex."[59] He makes no use of it for any other type than the parents.

The two types that stand out in the book are the mother and the hero. About the latter he states, "No man is or, indeed,

---

[57] Ibid., p. 456.

[58] Ibid., pp. 335f.

[59] Ibid., p. 492.

ever was, a hero, for the hero is a god, and, therefore, impersonal and generally applicable to all."[60]

He speaks of "the abundance of ancient symbolic possibilities, latent in the human mind" stimulating it to create mythological figures, adding:

> *But the products always contain the same old problems of humanity, which rise again and again in new symbolic disguise from the shadowy world of the unconscious.*[61]

He touches on individuation, but it seems not to be in the meaning he later gave the term. Here "the veil of 'individuation'" is the individual mask with which each person is equipped.[62] And in a footnote he has another definition:

> *The separation and differentiation from the mother, the "individuation" creates that transition of the subjective into the objective, that foundation of consciousness. Before this, man was one with the mother. That is to say, with the world as a whole.*[63]

In this voluminous text from 1912, Jung clearly moves away from the psychology of Freud and explores in detail his own version of what forms and triggers the human mind. He is to stay on that course, though it takes him a number of years before deciding on a fixed terminology.

In 1952, forty years after *Psychology of the Unconscious* was published, Jung had edited the work thoroughly and released the new version as *Symbole der Wandlung*, which was published in English as *Symbols of Transformation*, in 1956.

---

[60] Ibid., p. 379.

[61] Ibid., p. 391.

[62] Ibid., p. 433.

[63] Ibid., p. 554.

Two Essays, Multiple Versions

At this point in searching Jung's development of his theories, it is necessary to have a look at the texts of his known as *Two Essays on Analytical Psychology*. They have their origin in the 1910s, at least partly, but it gets complicated because of the revisions they have gone through. That goes for most of Jung's texts — changes either by his own hand, by editors and translators, or both.

The latest English version of the two essays is found in *The Collected Works by C. G. Jung*, volume 7, 2nd edition from 1966. It is an edited and expanded version of the 1st edition from 1953. They are based on two German essays, "Über die Psychologie des Unbewussten" originally published in 1917, and "Die Beziehungen zwischen dem Ich und dem Unbewussten" from 1928.

The English titles to the essays in the 1966 version are "On the Psychology of the Unconscious" and "The Relations between the Ego and the Unconscious." Before the publishing in *The Collected Works*, the essays were translated by H. G. and C. F. Baynes and published as *Two Essays on Analytical Psychology* in 1928, with slightly different titles.[64] The translator's preface mentions that there was an earlier publication of the essays (in 1917), and there have been substantial changes since then:

> *Of the first essay only the framework of its earlier form can be recognized, and so much new material has been added to the second essay that both works start afresh, so to speak, full of the amazing vitality of Jung's mind.*[65]

As for the second essay, it was originally printed in the *Archives de Psychologie*, under the title "La structure de l'incons-

---

[64] "The Unconscious in the Normal and Pathological Mind" and "The Relation of the Ego to the Unconscious."

[65] Carl G. Jung, *Two Essays on Analytical Psychology*, transl. H. G. and C. F. Baynes, London 1928, p. v.

cient" in 1916. It is just 28 pages, whereas the 1928 version is 145 pages. By that time, it was yet to appear in German.[66]

An earlier book, the second edition from 1917 of *Collected Papers on Analytical Psychology* contains several texts, not just the two above-mentioned essays. The first one is translated by Dora Hecht, with the title "The Psychology of the Unconscious Processes." Jung explains in his foreword to this edition of the book that this part of it "has been fundamentally altered, and I have used the opportunity to incorporate an article that should describe the results of more recent researches."[67]

The first edition of *Collected Papers on Analytical Psychology* was published the year before, in 1916. The essay is just called "New Paths in Psychology" and contains merely 27 pages, whereas the 1917 edited version has swelled to 93 pages. That is a lot happening in but one year.

In his 1917 foreword to the essay Jung makes it clear why he was so anxious to edit the text substantially: "This essay was originally written in 1913, when I limited myself entirely to presenting an essential part of the psychological point of view inaugurated by Freud."[68] He stepped away from Freudian psychology and was well on the way to replace it with a Jungian one, although still somewhat modestly:

> *In this new edition some expositions about Freud's theories are shortened, whilst Adler's psychological views are more fully considered, and — so far as the scope of this paper permits — a general outline of my own views are given.*

The second essay does not appear in the 1916 edition, but in 1917, with the title "The Conception of the Unconscious." Here it is 31 pages, since it is a translation of the original text

[66] Ibid., p. 125.

[67] Carl G. Jung, *Collected Papers on Analytical Psychology*, 2nd edition, London 1917, p. ix.

[68] Ibid., p. 352.

in French. I have discussed the essay earlier, using this version of it. The 1966 translation in *The Collected Works*, based on a 1935 German version, is well over a hundred pages.

The differences between these versions are so substantial that they could, or even should, be regarded as completely separate texts.

Jung had a habit of so to speak recycling old texts. He edited and expanded them to be published again, often with a new title. That may be efficient, but it makes following his track through time utterly complicated and uncertain. He allowed himself to revise his earlier writing so that it would conform to his later views, making the appearance that he always thought the same. That is understandable, but misleading.

Strangely, the problem is the same with *The Collected Works of C. G. Jung*. This 20 volumes series is not chronological, but divided into themes. Also, the texts have been revised, often quite substantially. Before his death in 1961, Jung himself supervised that process. After his death, new revisions were made, based on manuscripts found on his estate.

For example, the editors have readily admitted to changing the terminology in older texts to make it conform to later practice. As for volume 7, containing the essays discussed here, the editors write: "The texts of the two main essays have also been revised, for consistency."[69] It is a strange practice.

There is no problem defending the established order of collecting the works of an author chronologically. As shown previously in this book, it certainly makes sense also with Jung's writing. To base the order on themes, on the other hand, is particularly questionable with the work of Jung.

Readers of his texts can easily see that he usually dealt with a lot of subjects, whatever the theme of the essay at hand might have been. He would touch on all components of his psychology, apply them to personal therapy as well as cultural

[69] "Editorial Note to the Second Edition", *The Collected Works of C. G. Jung*, volume 7, Princeton 1972.

phenomena, current events, and what-not. He was not the kind of author to stick to a specific subject-matter slavishly. On the contrary, his texts often give the impression of being random thoughts, with the subject at hand as little more than an excuse.

Of course, that largely has to do with his theories being of the kind that sees correlations just about everywhere. To him, everything was connected by archetypes, and the collective unconscious was never passive in the lives of men. So, how could he stick to a subject containing anything less than all?

Still, it makes the collection of his works based on themes an odd choice. It is hard to see as something else than the effort to create an illusion of order in the lifework of someone happily scouting through chaos.

Already finding Jung's work in books is a bit confusing, since his major writing was in the form or articles, essays, forewords, and the like. His texts rarely exceed, say, a hundred pages. Most of them were originally published in magazines, yearbooks, and anthologies with texts also by other writers.

That is yet another argument for collecting them chronologically instead of by theme. The combination of those essays from different times of his life into books, as if written consecutively with that purpose, is misleading.

Absolutes and Dominants

The first of the two essays, "The Psychology of the Unconscious Processes," represents a turning point in Jung's work and his boldness in proclaiming it. He had decisively left the path of Freud to walk his own way, never to look back.

I use the 1917 version of the text. It is an edit and significant expansion (from 27 to 93 pages) of the 1916 version, which is a clear sign of Jung's commitment to his own theories, uncompromisingly, at this point. He had still found neither the final terminology nor the exact workings of the processes he described, but he had definitely decided that this was the path of his research. Although the structures of his psychology were somewhat incomplete, all the elements were there.

The book was published in a setting darkly clouded by World War I. Jung could not leave that uncommented, and his words are bitter. He writes in the foreword to this essay, dated March 1917, "This war has inexorably shown to the man of culture that he is still a barbarian."[70]

Later in the essay he calls the war "an epidemic of madness" and continues, "The several parties project their unconscious upon each other, hence the mad confusion of ideas in every head." He compares it to the legend of the Tower of Babel.[71]

The essay begins by going through the claims of existing psychological theories at the time, especially but not only those of Sigmund Freud. But let us focus on Jung's own theory of the collective unconscious, the archetypes, and how they are applied to mythology.

He does not yet use the terms consistently. The word archetype is never used in the essay. The collective unconscious is mentioned as such, but only in two of the chapters. In the chapter about the two sides of the unconscious he calls them the personal and the impersonal unconscious.[72] But about the latter Jung explains, "that is to say that it is collective."[73] It is quite something:

The collective unconscious is the sediment of all the experience of the universe of all time, and is also an image of the universe that has been in process of formation for untold ages.[74]

[70] Carl G. Jung, "The Psychology of the Unconscious Processes", transl. Dora Hecht, *Collected Papers on Analytical Psychology*, 2nd edition, London 1917, p. 353.

[71] Ibid., p. 416.

[72] Ibid., p. 408.

[73] Ibid., p. 457.

[74] Ibid., p. 432.

He also suggests the expression "absolute unconscious" for it, because it is absolutely universal.[75] This is actually the expression he uses most often for this concept. Another expression used for the same thing is "super-personal unconscious."[76]

Instead of archetypes, he uses "primordial images," giving praise to Jacob Burckhardt for coming up with the expression, and states that these "inherited potentialities of human imagination" have always been "potentially latent in the structure of the brain." Jung continues:

The fact of this inheritance also explains the otherwise incredible phenomenon, that the matter and themes of certain legends are met with all the world over in identical forms.[77]

Because these ancient and universal images are feelings as much as thoughts, Jung suggests they might also be called original thought-feelings.

Jung gives one example of a primordial image from primitive, so-called dynamistic religions — the idea of "some universal magical power upon which everything depends," which is what Tylor and Frazer termed animism. To Jung, this has nothing to do with souls or spirits, but rather "primitive energetics." The image has many manifestations:

This notion comprises the idea of soul, spirit, God, health, physical strength, fertility, magic power, influence, might, prestige, curative remedies, as well as certain states of mind which are characterised by the setting loose of affects.[78]

[75] Ibid., p. 410.

[76] Ibid., p. 426.

[77] Ibid., p. 410.

[78] Ibid., p. 413.

It is also the first rendering of the concept of god among primitive people, and there are many variations of it through history:

> *In the Old Testament this magic power is seen in the burning bush, and shines in the face of Moses. It is manifest in the Gospels as the outpouring of the Holy Spirit, as cloven tongues of fire from heaven. In Heraclitus it appears as universal energy, as "eternally living fire"; for the Persians it is the fiery brightness, haôma, divine mercy; for the Stoics it is heimarmene, the power of destiny. In mediæval legend it is seen as the aura, or the halo of the saint.*

Jung also sees it in Buddhistic and other conceptions of metempsychosis (transmigration of souls). This wide-spread thought, then, has been "imprinted on the human brain for untold ages," ready to appear under certain conditions.

But the primordial images are far from only pleasant. They contain all sides of what we can be and what we have been through history, "also every deed of shame and devilry of which human beings have ever been capable."[79] Such images can be very detrimental to a person's psyche. They can lead to ideas of demons as well as gods. About the latter, Jung states:

> *The concept of God is simply a necessary psychological function of an irrational nature that has altogether no connection with the question of God's existence.*

While we are on the subject: Jung also presents the concept of dominants of the super-personal unconscious, to which gods would definitely belong.[80] The dominants are particularly powerful figures emerging from the collective uncon-

---

[79] Ibid., p. 414.

[80] Ibid., p. 426.

scious, such as the magician or the demon. Jung accredits them with "not human but mythological qualities." By mythological he means that they stem from the collective and not from the individual psyche.[81]

By these figures from the collective unconscious Jung obviously refers to what he later was to call archetypes. Their traits are the same. Their forms are easily, if not to say intuitively, associated with certain specific qualities, they emerge from the same place, and Jung treats them the same way in his therapy sessions with patients.

In this essay, he claims that the dominants usually make their appearance as projections on persons in the patient's immediate surrounding, by abnormal under- or over-valuations of them. Furthermore, "They also give rise to the formation of modern myths, that is, fantastic rumours, suspicions and prejudices."[82]

The dominant almost always encountered in psychoanalysis of projections is the magical demon, of which Jung says, "The picture of this demon is the lowest and most elementary concept of God."[83] But there are also images from an even more distant past:

The animal symbol specially refers to what is extra human, that is super-personal; for the contents of the absolute unconscious are not merely the residue of archaic human functions, but also the residue of functions of the animal ancestry of mankind.[84]

The personal struggle to overcome the projections of those dominants from the collective unconscious, Jung finds strikingly similar to the hero-myth. He goes on to describe the typ-

[81] Ibid., p. 430.

[82] Ibid., pp. 432f.

[83] Ibid., pp. 433f.

[84] Ibid., p. 435.

ical hero-myth in those terms: "The typical combat of the hero with the monster (the unconscious content) frequently takes place on the banks of some water; sometimes at a ford." In this battle, the hero is swallowed by the monster, but kills it by cutting off a valuable piece of the viscera, such as the heart, "that is, the valuable energy by which the unconscious was activated." The monster drifts ashore and the hero steps forth, "born anew through the transcendental function."

> *This enables the normal state to be restored, as the unconscious having been robbed of its energy no longer occupies a preponderating position.* [85]

In a footnote, Jung points out that he has treated the parallels of hero-myths in great detail in *The Psychology of the Unconscious* from 1912, discussed here earlier.

In the conclusion at the end of the essay, Jung admits that his findings are likely to be questioned. He knows that their merit is still to be proven. But things that are not yet true may be true tomorrow. He regards himself as a pioneer and can handle scorn, because he is pleased with what he has done:

> *Our age is seeking a new spring of life. I found one and drank of it and the water tasted good. That is all that I can or want to say.*[86]

Men, Women, and Races

In 1927, contributing to the symposium *Mensch und Erde* (Man and Earth), Jung wrote the essay "Die Erdbedingtheit der Psyche" ("The Earth Conditioning of the Psyche") on the subject of mind and earth, which was used for the title it got in the English translation published the following year.

It is a strange text, where Jung intends to shed light on

[85] Ibid., p. 436.

[86] Ibid., p. 444.

"the question of the conditioning of mind by the earth."[87]

In the text, he expresses his basic psychological principles with clarity and bold certainty. He states, "The whole of mythology could be taken as a kind of projection of the collective unconscious."[88] And he explains that "the unconscious, as the totality of all archetypes, is the deposit of all human experience back to its most remote beginnings."[89]

He sees archetypes as forms that the instincts have assumed, at the same time images and emotions, working as systems of preparedness, stemming from prehistoric irrational psychology.[90] And he presents a simple recipe for what constitutes an archetype:

> *I would like to suggest that every psychic reaction that is out of proportion to its exciting cause should be investigated as to whether it is not in part conditioned by an unconscious archetype.[91]*

The problem for man's psyche is to adapt to these demands from deep within, especially since they are invisible to his conscious.

> *If consciousness had never split off from the unconscious — an event eternally repeated, and symbolized as the fall of the angels and the disobedience of the first parents — this problem would never have arisen, nor would there be a question of environmental adaption.[92]*

[87] Carl G. Jung, "Mind and the Earth", *Contributions to Analytical Psychology*, transl. H. G and C. F. Baynes, London 1928, p. 100.

[88] Ibid., p. 111.

[89] Ibid., p. 116.

[90] Ibid., pp. 117f.

[91] Ibid., p. 120.

[92] Ibid., p. 117.

He claims that there is a feminine archetype in man, and a masculine archetype in woman, which he has given the names anima and animus.[93] Then follow several pages of generalizations about the masculine, and even more so the feminine, also their respective archetypes. These descriptions are dated, to put it mildly.

For example, he calls self-mastery a typically masculine ideal, achieved by repressed feelings, while feeling is instead a feminine virtue. The anima in man balances this by bringing out feelings according to need: "As is well known it is just the most masculine men who inwardly are most subject to feminine feeling." The animus in women, though, does not make her feelings disappear, but she begins to discuss and rationalize. Yet, "these feminine arguments are illogical and unreasonable."[94]

Jung also claims that biological differences of the sexes include these behavioral patterns:

On the biological level woman's chief interest is to hold a man, whereas the interest of the man is to conquer a woman, and nature does not encourage him to stick to a conquest.[95]

That would make infidelity a male activity, which can indeed be discussed. To Jung, it also makes man "emphasize the legal and social aspects of marriage, whereas the woman sees it as an exclusively personal relation." That, too, is balanced by the anima and animus. But consciously, men and women are far apart:

Man, in his conscious activity, plans ahead and seeks to

[93] Ibid., p. 127.

[94] Ibid., p. 130.

[95] Ibid., p. 131.

*create the future, whereas it is specifically feminine to be-
labour the mind with such questions as, who was some-
body's great great aunt.*[96]

One must wonder what his conversations with women
were like.

Even more disturbing is what follows about race, as he
speaks about how European immigrants to America were unconsciously influenced by both the natives they conquered and
the Africans they brought to be slaves. Describing that influence, he reveals an alarming prejudice, which he sadly shared
with many in that time. He even refers to the absurd nonsense
of measurements of the skull.[97]

Racial biology was still regarded as proper science at the
universities and as legitimate cause for political decisions. So
were ideas along the line of social Darwinism. In Jung's use, it
is a warning example of how "the earth" influences people:

*Certain Australian primitives assert that one cannot con-
quer foreign land, for in foreign soil live strange ancestor
spirits, and therefore the strange spirits will inhabit the
new-born. There is a great psychological truth in this. The
strange land assimilates the conqueror.*[98]

Strictly speaking, that would not be the land but its people. Furthermore, Jung neglects that he has also pointed out
the influence of the African Americans, although they were
moved to foreign soil, too. Not to mention the striking fact that
in the 1920s, the influence of the European immigrants on both
the other groups was even more obvious.

I mention this text of Jung because it shows how he, at the
time of writing it, had become accustomed to the use of arche-

types and the collective unconscious in the way he was to keep and propagate. It is obvious also in what playful delight he applied them.

As for his views on gender and race, one would hope he soon abandoned them.

Individuation, Alchemy, and Tao

In the 1930s Jung produces several texts devoted to his ideas of individuation, the archetypes, and the collective unconscious, no longer the least hesitant about the terms and their use. He seems to have reached his conviction in three steps. Establishing the idea of the collective unconscious, he found the archetypes to be its building blocks, and individuation its ultimate function.

In 1934, his essay "A Study in the Process of Individuation" was published in German. The English translation appeared five years later.[99] He describes the case of a woman whom he guides through a step-by-step realization of what emerges from her collective unconscious and how to understand it. They do so by drawings of hers, which upon Jung's examination are found filled with mythical, archetypal ingredients of considerable age and spread across otherwise very different human cultures.

He elaborately compares the woman's imagery to alchemy, finding them to use identical symbols and describe an identical process — that of making gold as an allegory for personal development. The alchemist philosophers "understood by it a spiritual transmutation, or what we would today call a psychological transformation or readjustment."[100] This revela-

---

[99] The German title of his text was "Zur Empirie des Individuationsprozesses" and it was published in *Eranos-Jahrbuch 1933*, Zürich 1934. The English translation was published in New York 1939 and London 1940, in the book *The Integration of the Personality*, transl. Stanley Dell.

[100] Carl G. Jung, "A Study in the Process of Individuation", *The Integration of the Personality*, transl. Stanley Dell, London 1940, p. 49.

tion was not just new to the woman, but also to Jung: "As a matter of fact, it was this very case that led me to the study of alchemy."[101]

He doesn't only compare the individuation process and its symbols to alchemy. He starts his text by quoting the 20th chapter of the *Tao Te Ching*, where its legendary author Lao Tzu ponders his isolation in being the only one to see clearly how the world really works. Lao Tzu ends the chapter by finding comfort in being nourished by the great mother, which is Tao, the Way.[102]

It is easy to see how Jung finds this illustrative of the individuation process, and how lost people are who have not commenced it. He goes on to quote the next chapter of the *Tao Te Ching*, which is about Tao as the origin of all, and its evasive nature. Jung regards this chapter as the answer to the questions contained in the previous one. It appears that Jung sees Tao as identical to the collective unconscious.

This is significant to Jung's reasoning, and an unsurprising consequence of his theories about the psyche's components. His definitions are so vague and wide that they can smoothly be applied to just about anything equally vague and wide. The devil, though, is in the detail.

Regarding the *Tao Te Ching*, the book as a whole does not at all point to an inner psychological entity, other than human misconception of the nature of the world, as described in chapter 20.

Lao Tzu presents a cosmology, the basic principle by which all of nature works and out of which it came to be. It describes what can be called a natural law.

If anything, the Tao concept relates to Einstein's dream of a unified field theory. Lao Tzu writes in chapter 25: "Man is ruled by Earth. Earth is ruled by Heaven. Heaven is ruled by

[101] Ibid., p. 51.
[102] Ibid., p. 30.

the Way. The Way is ruled by itself."[103]

Lao Tzu would most likely have discarded the idea of a tumultuous and myth-laden unconscious undercurrent. His text is famously straightforward, not even bothering about things like gods and the afterlife. If people are confused, it is because their minds are misled by nonsense. The chapter right before the one with which Jung starts his essay states, "Behave simply and hold on to purity. Lessen selfishness and restrain desires. Abandon knowledge and your worries are over."[104]

Alchemy, on the other hand, does fit Jung's application more readily. That is of no surprise, since it is a European tradition consisting of philosophical and mythological materials that are deeply entwined in the history of Western culture.

But when he claims it to be closely comparable to Taoist alchemy in China, he is jumping to conclusions.[105] The Chinese version is by no means some self-realization process. It is simply a search for longevity, which was inspired by a misconception of another *Tao Te Ching* chapter.

The last line of chapter 33 was thought to say, "Those who die without perishing get longevity." Therefore, some Taoists started to experiment with potions supposed to have that effect. Heavy metals were used, so the potions had the opposite effect. Findings in the 1970s of *Tao Te Ching* manuscripts older than the ones known before, showed that the line actually reads, "Those who die without being forgotten get longevity."[106] Taoism is definitely no alchemy.

Jung's theories need to be applicable through time and across any borders, since they make statements about the nature of the human mind in general. But that remains to be proven. He did no such thing in his 1934 study of individua-

---

[103] Stefan Stenudd, *Tao Te Ching: The Taoism of Lao Tzu Explained*, Malmö 2015, p. 123.

[104] Ibid., p. 100.

[105] Jung, "A Study in the Process of Individuation", p. 50.

[106] Stenudd 2015, p. 150.

tion. Claiming the words of Lao Tzu to support his case is twisting them beyond reason.

Archetypes in Transformation

The year after the above-mentioned essay, in 1935, Jung had another text in the same publication, *Eranos*, this time on archetypes of the collective unconscious, which was its title in the English translation, published in the same book as the previously discussed essay.

In this text, he explores the archetypes in some depth, with several examples. He credits them with a lot. Every important idea and view have their historical antecedent:

> *They are all founded upon archetypal, primordial forms, whose sensuous nature dates from a time when consciousness did not yet think, but merely perceived.*[107]

The archetypes are such primordial types. They surface from the collective unconscious to the conscious in myth, esoteric teaching, and fairy tale. But they also have their immediate manifestations by dreams and visions, which are "much more natural, less understandable or naiver than in the myth, for example. In this respect the fairy tale is, no doubt, much truer to nature."[108]

To Jung, myths are first and foremost psychic manifestations that represent the nature of the psyche. They have nothing to do with explanations of natural and other phenomena, for which the primitive mind of man in the past had little concern. Instead, "its unconscious psyche has an irresistible urge to assimilate all experience through the outer senses into inner, psychic happening."

It is not the mind trying to understand what is outside of

---

[107] Carl G. Jung, "Archetypes of the Collective Unconscious", *The Integration of the Personality*, transl. Stanley Dell, London 1940, p. 83.
[108] Ibid., p. 54.

it, but making the outside connect to man's inner life, or even
copy it:

> *All the mythologized occurrences of nature, such as sum-
> mer and winter, the phases of the moon, the rainy seasons,
> and so forth, are anything but allegories of these same ob-
> jective experiences, nor are they to be understood as "ex-
> planations" of sunrise, sunset, and the rest of the natural
> phenomena. They are, rather, symbolic expressions for the
> inner and unconscious psychic drama that becomes acces-
> sible to human consciousness by way of projection — that
> is, mirrored in the events of nature.*[109]

Esoteric teachings have the same inward focus. They "try
to grasp the unseen happening of the psyche." That is true for
primitive lore, and even more so for the world religions: "They
contain what was originally the hidden knowledge of revelation and have set forth the secrets of the psyche in glorious images."[110]

Doing so, the religions drain the unconscious of its powerful imagery to substitute it by dogma: "Dogma advises us
not to have an unconscious."[111] Jung regards Catholicism as
most successful in this, baring the collective unconscious completely of its functions:

> *The whole life of the collective unconscious has been ab-
> sorbed without remainder, so to speak, in the dogmatic ar-
> chetypes, and flows like a well-controlled stream in the
> symbolism of ritual and of the church calendar.*

He goes on to describe how Protestantism has failed to do
the same, by gradually removing that powerful imagery. Sure

[109] Ibid., pp. 54f.

[110] Ibid., p. 56.

[111] Ibid., p. 60.

enough, "the power of the church has gone with that loss of symbolism, too."[112]

Jung gives an example from his own childhood of this weakening of Protestantism, as it has been stripped of its esoteric components. His father, who was a priest, was giving him a confirmation lesson that he found utterly boring, except for the idea of the Trinity. But when they reached that particular subject, his father just said, "We will skip this section; I cannot make anything out of it myself."[113]

The bulk of his text is about a few patients struggling with this alienation from the collective unconscious, and the transformation processes they go through, by means of archetypes, to reestablish a connection to it — at least some understanding of its workings. That process is through dreams and fantasies, not myths, but they are filled with mythical figures and objects.

Jung uses these cases to present some of those archetypes in detail and explore their complexity. First and foremost in this exploration is *anima*, the female archetype in males. That automatically excludes woman from the analysis, and Jung's explanation for this is simply absurd: "But traditional symbolism is chiefly a product of the masculine psyche and is, therefore, not a suitable object of imitation for woman." He even has the audacity to add in Latin: "Exempla sunt otiosa!" (Examples are odious!)[114]

We are left with having to take his words for it. Well, we don't.

In addition to the anima, Jung also describes the workings of the archetypes *the shadow* and *the old wise man*. But the archetypes are not separate in the unconscious. Normally, the shadow is largely identical with the anima. Still, "the shadow, according to its definition, is the historically older human be-

[112] Ibid., p. 61.

[113] Ibid., p. 64.

[114] Ibid., p. 95.

ing."[115] It is the meeting with the shadow by which a transformation begins. Already at this stage, a person can get completely lost into the distant past and its ideals, i.e., the domain of the shadow:

> For the shadow is a formidable thing. The harder and more disappointing are the conditions of life, and the more despondent consciousness becomes, so much the more grows the shadow, till the darkness at last is overpowering.[116]

As an example of this, Jung mentions France in the 11th century, tormented by famines and plagues, where disillusioned people invented the cult of Satan and the Black Mass. Jung states that "the attempt to escape to the metaphysical and spiritual was right, but the regression to the past and to the dark, opposite principle was wrong." This archetype is a dangerous one, but also a tremendous resource in a transformation:

> Taking it in its deepest sense, the shadow is the invisible saurian tail that man still drags behind him. Carefully amputated, it becomes the serpent of healing of the mystery.[117]

So, the shadow seems to be the remainder in the collective unconscious of primeval man, perhaps even before he had become man.

The old wise man is a different kind of old. Here age is an indication of acquired wisdom. This archetype appears as the magician or the medicine man of primitive society. It is an enlightener and teaching master, who "penetrates the chaotic darkness of mere life with the light of meaning."[118]

---

[115] Ibid., p. 91.

[116] Ibid., p. 92.

[117] Ibid., p. 93.

[118] Ibid., p. 87.

By far the most complex of these archetypes is the anima. It plays shifting roles in Jung's process of transformation, being involved in just about all of it. Actually, it is always the a priori element in "moods, reactions, impulses and whatever else is spontaneous in psychic life." The anima is the major archetype in the male psyche, which "satisfactorily subsumes every pronouncement of the unconscious and of the primitive mind that gave form to language and religion."[119]

Jung finds the anima in the mythical nixie, a half-woman fish dragging men into the deep, also in the siren, the wood nymph, and succubus — all of them seductive but lethal to young men. The anima is "the serpent in the paradise of the harmless man with good resolutions and still better intentions." For the child, it lurks in the supremacy of the mother.[120]

In addition to archetypes with personalities, like the three mentioned above, there is another class that Jung calls the archetypes of transformation, because they appear in that process. They are "typical situations, places, ways, animals, plants, and so forth that symbolize the kind of change, whatever it is,"[121] and they can be as ambiguous as the personal ones. Their meaning is just as manifold.

By the end of his text, Jung lists a number of such archetypes of transformation, readily admitting that his rapid survey is far too brief. He sorts them according to what phase of the transformation process they tend to appear in.[122]

In the beginning they are mostly in animal form, such as a bird, horse, wolf, bull, lion, or serpent, which has a kinship in myth with the dragon. Also symbols like the cellar and cave, watery depths and the sea, fire, weapons, and instruments belong to this phase. They represent different aspects of this phase and of the person going through it.

[119] Ibid., p. 76.

[120] Ibid., pp. 73, 77, and 79.

[121] Ibid., 89.

[122] Ibid., pp. 93f.

To the phase Jung calls intermediate belong the frog, the hermaphrodite, the crossing, the dangerous passage, the transitus, corpse, tree, cross, hanging, soaring, and swimming.

To the last phase belong all the symbols of the self in its various aspects. Among them he mentions the cross with equal arms, the circle, the square, the fourfold opposed to the three-fold in all possible forms, the flower, the wheel, star, egg, sun, and the child. He also mentions negative forms, presumably when the transformation is about to fail: the spider, the net, and the prison.

What Is Not an Archetype?

This listing is unusually generous. In most of his texts, Jung discussed archetypes one at a time, here and there, frequently stating that there are many more of them, but without making any effort to list them. No doubt, it would be a very long list, maybe even impossible to complete. And that is the main problem with Jung's theory.

Neither in the text discussed here or other ones, as far as I have seen, does Jung define what an archetype is in such a way that it would be possible to state what is not an archetype. His description of the concept is so vague, and his examples so haphazard, his claim cannot be falsified. Anything could be an archetype — or not.

The only way to decide is to track if it plays a role in the psychological process of personal development. But that is cir-cular reasoning. An archetype is an archetype if it can be de-scribed as one. Then, what cannot be described as one? Are there characters or objects that can never have an archetypal role? For example, how about a middle-aged woman or man, a zebra or hippopotamus, a kitchen, a spoon, a blade of grass, a promenade, parallel lines, and so on?

Furthermore, when is an old man an archetype and when is he simply an old man? The same question can be asked about every archetype Jung mentions. He gives no definition by which to decide.

Another weakness in his theory of the archetypes is his claim that they reside in the unconscious, and therefore they are uninfluenced by the conscious. But that, too, remains to be proven. Why can't they be symbols created and fostered by the conscious mind?

Looking at Jung's list, most — if not all — of the archetypes need no hidden unconscious design to get their significance. Our perception of snakes, spiders, dark cellars, lions, deep seas, weapons, the sun, and children, is full of significance already to the conscious mind, without any need for hidden amplifications. The hermaphrodite is an obvious symbol of an in-between stage, a child of both fragility and potential, a burning fire is an image of destruction and renewal, a serpent of danger, a crossing of options, a prison of confinement, of course, and so forth.

There is no need for an unconscious process to explain the symbolic meanings of such things. It is easily explained by our conscious perception and impressions we consciously share with each other. The burden of proof is on Jung. He must show how such symbolic meanings could not have appeared in the conscious mind alone. He does not.

Jung's perspective all through the essay is that of the psyche and experience of the individual, although he regards these things as common human conditions. He does not explore myths as such, but mentions their connection to the archetypes and their dynamics.

This continued to be his recurring focus in later works, but he turned increasing attention to how these processes of the psyche have created and formed myths and whole mythologies — if not all our perception of life and the world we live in. Even more so did his followers.

The Blessing and Curse of Religion

Jung's writing tended by time towards religion and its importance to the human psyche. His reflections on religion can be traced back to his earliest writings, but by the 1930s he had developed a keener interest and a clearly spoken support for the importance of religion in mental health.

This turn from the individual patient to society as a whole, with the psychological tools he had at hand, sprung out of the deep disappointment that was World War I. It is quite clear in his essay "The Spiritual Problem of Modern Man" from 1933, which is an edited and expanded version of the 1928 German original "Das Seelenproblem des modernen Menschen." He laments:

> *Think of nearly two thousand years of Christian ideals followed, instead of by the return of the Messiah and the heavenly millennium, by the World War among Christian nations and its barbed-wire and poison-gas. What a catastrophe in heaven and on earth!*[123]

The text describes modern man in search of a new spiritual framework to replace the old religion in which he has lost trust. Jung speaks appreciatively of the Eastern spiritual traditions receiving rising interest in the West, hoping that this might contribute to calm down the beastly behavior Europeans have recently expressed.

There is a need of the soul that repeatedly manifests itself in monstrosities of the Western world, to itself as well as to the other cultures it comes across.

Jung quotes a Native American friend of his: "We don't understand the whites, they are always wanting something —

---

[123] Carl G. Jung, "The Spiritual Problem of Modern Man," *Modern Man in Search of a Soul*, transl. W. S. Dell and Cary F. Baines, London 1933, p. 230.

always restless — always looking for something. What is it?"[124]

A good question, indeed. To Jung, the answer is coming to peace with the unconscious.

A 1932 lecture, "Die Beziehungen der Psychotherapie zur Seelsorge," was the following year published in English with the title "Psychotherapists or the Clergy" in the same book as the previously mentioned text about the spiritual problems of modern man. Their subjects are similar.

Jung states that modern medicine disregards the psychological perspective and is therefore unable to treat illnesses of the mind. He claims without hesitation that "organic medicine fails completely in the treatment of neuroses, while psychic methods cure them."[125] The same problem he sees with Sigmund Freud's and Alfred Adler's therapies, because they refuse to leave the perspective of natural science and therefore "they give too little value to fictional and imaginative processes,"[126] which are to the human psyche as real as anything physical is to its body.

What needs to be considered is something as profound as the patient's lack of meaning of life. Faced with the patient's unrest not being physical but existential, the doctor without recognition of the psyche is helpless:

> *What will he do when he sees only too clearly why his patient is ill; when he sees that it arises from his having no love, but only sexuality; no faith, because he is afraid to grope in the dark, no hope, because he is disillusioned by the world and by life; and no understanding, because he has failed to read the meaning of his own existence?*[127]

---

[124] Ibid., p. 246.

[125] Carl G. Jung, "Psychotherapists or the Clergy," *Modern Man in Search of a Soul*, transl. W. S. Dell and Cary F. Baines, London 1933, p. 258.

[126] Ibid., p. 259.

[127] Ibid., p. 260.

That would be the domain of the clergy, but modern man has no faith in the church and is therefore quite unwilling to consult a priest, even if the ailment is spiritual. Also, modern churches are reluctant towards the complexity of the psyche and what it hides in its depth.

That is particularly true for Protestantism. As an example of this, Jung mentions that his own texts "were seriously studied in Rome long before any Protestant pastor thought them worthy of a glance."[128] He finds Catholicism much more relevant to human spiritual needs:

I am firmly convinced that a vast number of people belong to the fold of the Catholic Church and nowhere else, because they are most suitably housed there.[129]

That is exactly why Protestants are in far greater need of therapy. They are, indeed, the vast majority of his patients, whereas only five or six have been Catholics.[130]

Jung calls on the clergy, Protestants in particular, to stand up to this challenge by assimilating the discoveries about the psyche and its needs: "It is indeed high time for the clergyman and the psychotherapist to join forces to meet this great spiritual task."[131] But that means the clergy must recognize and accept modern man's search for a meaning of life relevant to him, instead of sermons about guilt and sin.[132]

Although Jung studied ancient Eastern traditions with enthusiasm, his main perspective remained Christian, with the Bible as a major source. His writing reveals that it was also a personal process, not without frustration. When discussing the

[128] Ibid., p. 263.

[129] Ibid., p. 282.

[130] Ibid., p. 264.

[131] Ibid., p. 265.

[132] Ibid., p. 274.

dilemmas of patients of his, as well as tendencies in society around him, his own processing of religious issues — even wrestling with them — is visible.

Two of his works stand out: *Psychology and Religion* from 1938 and *Answer to Job* from 1952. The former lands in a praise of religion as a blessing for well-being of the human psyche, whereas the latter is a bitter confrontation with the ruthlessness of God. Surely, another world war taking place between the two books had its influence on Jung's mood.

Mythological Dreams

In 1937, Jung gave three lectures on psychology and religion at Yale University. It was part of the annual Terry Lectureship on the theme of religion in the light of modern science. His lectures were published in a book the following year.[133]

For his speculations on the sources and workings of religion, Jung analyzed the dreams of one of his patients, who was an intellectual with little conscious interest in religious questions. Nor had he ever studied psychology. Out of a series of more than 400 dreams, Jung selected and published 74 of "a peculiar religious interest." That does not mean their content was evidently religious — only two of the 400 dreams "obviously deal with religion."[134]

The patient was given the task of recording his dreams, without any guidance by Jung during this process:

The dreams were not analyzed or explained to him and it was only very much later that we began with their analysis. Thus the dreams I am going to demonstrate have not been tampered with at all. They represent an entirely uninfluenced natural sequence of events.[135]

---

[133] Carl G. Jung, *Psychology and Religion*, New Haven 1938 (1977 reprint).

[134] Ibid., pp. 26f. The dreams were published in Carl G. Jung, "Traumsymbole des Individuationsprozesses," *Eranos-Jahrbuch 1935*, Zürich 1936.

[135] Jung, *Psychology and Religion*, pp. 26f.

Jung's measurements to ensure a clinical experiment free of his own influence are questionable. The patient would surely not have been unaware of the reputation and specialties of his therapist to begin with, and the more dreams he delivered, the clearer to him it must have been what was searched for. Also, Jung's selection of 74 out of the more than 400 dreams is cause for alarm.

Already the detailed recollections of the dreams raise questions about how they were assembled. Dreams are fleeting by nature and particularly difficult to reconstruct backwards from the moment of waking up. This patient's dreams are notably detailed, even containing long dialogues word by word. One of the two dreams with evident religious content written down by the patient, covers two and a half pages of the book.[136]

In these dreams of a significantly mythical nature, Jung finds several archetypes and archetypal ingredients on which he bases his interpretation. Among them is the unknown woman, who represents *anima*, the female entity in man's unconscious, "since time immemorial man in his myths always manifested the idea of a coexistence of male and female in the same body."[137]

There is also a voice of unknown origin, which speaks in an archaic way about the essence of religion:

Religion is no substitute, but it is the ultimate accomplishment added to every other activity of the soul. Out of the fullness of life thou shalt give birth to thy religion, only then shalt thou be blessed.[138]

After this utterance of the voice, there is music from an organ, reminding the dreamer of Wagner's *Feuerzauber*.

[136] Ibid., pp. 28-30.

[137] Ibid., p. 34.

[138] Ibid., p. 42.

Jung also finds in the dreams several examples of what he calls the *quaternarium* or *quaternity*, the symbol of four. He also finds it in Christian iconology, Gnostic philosophy, and medieval alchemy.[139] To Jung, it symbolizes a fourth entity to complement the Trinity, which is the evil principle of the devil.[140]

He can't be speaking only of Christianity, since he claims the "suffering God-Man" to be at least five thousand years old and "the Trinity is probably even older."[141] He mentions no support for that probability, nor a definition of the Trinity by which to spot it in ancient cultures. So, it is difficult indeed to falsify. A suffering God-Man, on the other hand, is easier to find in mythologies of the distant past — well, depending on how he is defined. But surely, in the old myths there have been many gods and men of grandeur suffering, possibly as far back as five thousand years.

To Jung, the quaternity is "a more or less direct representation of the God manifested in his creation." Therefore, in dreams it signifies the God within, by which he means the very important archetypal image of the Deity.[142] The quaternity symbols occur 71 times in the 400 dreams of Jung's patient, as well as frequently in dreams of other patients. They are always of an unconscious origin, since the four, contrary to the Trinity, "conveys no more than any other number."[143]

That statement must be questioned, though, since four is the number of seasons, of basic directions on a map, of the Greek elements, of the Gospels, of corners in the square and any rectangle, of dimensions in the physical world, and so on. It would be hard to find a society where four is not as significant to all of its members as one, two, and three.

[139] Ibid., p. 44 (and notes).

[140] Ibid., pp. 73f.

[141] Ibid., p. 57.

[142] Ibid., p. 73.

[143] Ibid., p. 65.

He also speaks of an evolution of the deities through time, from polytheism to monotheism. It is a view he shared with several scholars at the time, starting with Edward Burnett Tylor's *Primitive Culture* from 1871. The theory was that when societies became more advanced, the primitive polytheism was replaced by monotheism. To Jung, the last step of this progression is god's descent into the psyche of man:

> *The gods first lived in superhuman power and beauty on the top of snow-clad mountains or in the darkness of caves, woods and seas. Later on they drew together into one god, and then that god became man.*[144]

That doesn't stop the gods from being as powerful as ever, "in spite of their new disguise." Jung warns against the growing atheism following the progress of natural science: "Since the throne of god could not be discovered among the galactic systems, the inference was that god had never existed."[145] He even calls atheism a stupid error,[146] of which "people believe, hope and expect just as much as they formerly did of God."[147]

Jung uses dreams to explore what is going on in the patient's unconscious, which is the main source to them: "The dream occurs when consciousness and will are to a great extent extinguished." In Jung's view of the psyche, it means that only the unconscious remains. Dreams are neither created nor controlled by the conscious mind. He even quotes the Talmud: "The dream is its own interpretation."[148]

Emerging from the unconscious, dreams are far from unique to the individual:

[144] Ibid., p. 102.

[145] Ibid., p. 103.

[146] Ibid., p. 100.

[147] Ibid., p. 104.

[148] Ibid., p. 31.

*Even dreams are made of collective material to a very high
degree, just as, in the mythology and folklore of different
peoples, certain motives repeat themselves in almost identical form.*[149]

He goes on to explain that these motives are the archetypes, forms or images of a collective nature occurring in
myths, and also as autochthonous (aboriginal) individual
products of unconscious origin. Presumably, they start from
the archetypal patterns of the human mind, transmitted by tradition and migration, but also by heredity. Their heredity he
finds indispensable since they "can be spontaneously reproduced without any possible direct tradition."

He finds support for the concept of preconscious, primordial ideas within psychology in Adolf Bastian, Friedrich Nietzsche, Henri Hubert and Marcel Mauss, and also in Lucien
Lévy-Bruhl. Hubert and Mauss spoke of categories and gave
mana, the Polynesian concept of personal power, as an example. As for Nietzsche, who used the expression *atavistic relic*,
Jung quotes from *Human, All-Too-Human*:

*In our sleep and in our dreams we pass through the whole
thought of earlier humanity. I mean, in the same way that
man reasons in his dreams, he reasoned when in the waking state many thousands of years.*[150]

Jung finds the dreams of this particular patient to reveal a
struggle with his religious needs, in spite of his intellectual dismissal of them. It is not that religious beliefs as such are
needed, but they protect against the chaotic content hidden in
the unconscious. Jung sees religion and its rituals as a safe-
guard against that vast space of the self which is the uncon-

[149] Ibid., p. 63.

[150] Ibid., p. 122.

scious, completely incomprehensible to the conscious mind. The self (or psyche) is the sum of the two, but they are far from equal:

> *The psyche reaches so far beyond the boundary line of consciousness that the latter could be easily compared to an island in the ocean.*[151]

Religion acts as sort of an orderly representation of the unconscious, making the glimpses of it bearable and much less threatening. Religion can be said to pretend to explain them. And since time immemorial, ritual has been "a safe way of dealing with the unaccountable forces of the unconscious mind."[152]

This major function of religion is best served by religious rites and symbols accepting a mysterious reality beyond the palpable and visible one. Reason is not enough, by far. There has to be magnificence, magic, and a strong sense of metaphysical meaning.

Jung sees Catholicism as a good example of this, whereas Protestantism has become far too bland and de-mythologized to do the trick, "because dogma and ritual have become so pale and faint that they have lost their efficacy to a high degree."[153] He warns against the continued decay of Protestantism:

> *If it keeps on disintegrating as a church, it succeeds in depriving man of all his spiritual safeguards and means of defense against the immediate experience of the forces waiting for liberation in the unconscious mind.*[154]

He is convinced that this is a costly shortcoming, leading

[151] Ibid., p. 102.
[152] Ibid., p. 58.
[153] Ibid., p. 53.
[154] Ibid., pp. 59f.

to mental suffering, and argues for the healing capacity of the religious experience. Whether it is an illusion or not is irrelevant. For the psyche, it is still beneficial, if not absolutely necessary. Jung expresses a very high regard for religion and its effects:

> *No matter what the world thinks about religious experience, the one who has it possesses the great treasure of a thing that has provided him with a source of life, meaning and beauty and that has given a new splendor to the world and to mankind. He has pistis and peace.*[155]

Jung ends his book repeating his conviction of the overwhelmingly positive values of the religious experience:

> *And if such experience helps to make your life healthier, more beautiful, more complete and more satisfactory to yourself and to those you love, you may safely say:*
> *"This was the grace of God."*[156]

Jung's praise of religion is difficult not to perceive as naïve. Surely, it was influenced by the experience of World War I as well as the growth of fascism and Nazism in Europe. In the 1930s, the longing for a force accomplishing piety and compassion among men, be it real or imagined, was understandable.

But Jung cannot have been blind to the many drawbacks of religious belief and practice — also in relation to mental health. His own experience as a therapist for decades must have shown to him that religion can cause at least as much anguish as it can cure. And upon inspection, worshipers don't prove to be more at peace, healthier or more satisfied than those who discard religion from their minds. His text certainly shows no evidence of it.

[155] Ibid., p. 113. In the New Testament, *pistis* is translated as faith or belief.
[156] Ibid., p. 114.

Whatever perils from the unconscious religion can hinder or soften, it remains to be proven that the absence of this mental filter leads to increased suffering. Religious practice and rites may even increase the burdens. The life of the pious is not an easy one.

This is constantly pointed out in Christianity, the religion with which Jung was the most familiar ever since his childhood. Man should prepare to suffer for his faith, as did Christ, and humbly accept it. As Joe Hill wrote in his song from 1911, the reward is not to come in this life, but, "You'll get pie in the sky when you die."

The Psyche of a God

In 1939, Sigmund Freud's book on Moses was published. That was also the year when World War II began. A few years after the end of it, in 1952, Jung published a book about another biblical figure: *Antwort auf Hiob*. Its English translation by R. F. C. Hull, *Answer to Job*, came two years later.

The severe testing of Job's faith made Jung wonder about the nature of the biblical god Yahweh and what drove him to put Job through such torment: "Yahweh's behaviour is so revolting that one has to ask oneself whether there is not a deeper motive hidden behind it."[157]

Jung saw evidence of an imperfection in Yahweh: "Job stands morally higher than Yahweh. In this respect the creature has surpassed the creator."[158]

But the book soon moves from the Old Testament and Job to Christ of the New Testament, where Jung finds the explanations to Yahweh's behavior — it is the god's wish to become a man, all but completely. Thereby, he would be able to perfect himself. This is done through Christ:

[157] Carl G. Jung, "Answer to Job," transl. R. F. C. Hull, *The Collected Works of C. G. Jung*, volume 11, New York 1958, p. 375.

[158] Ibid., p. 405.

The life of Christ is just what it had to be if it is the life of a god and a man at the same time. It is a symbolum, a bringing together of heterogeneous natures, rather as if Job and Yahweh were combined in a single personality. Yahweh's intention to become man, which resulted from his collision with Job, is fulfilled in Christ's life and suffering.[159]

Jung compares it to a process of individuation, "the father wants to become the son, God wants to become man, the amoral wants to become exclusively good, the unconscious wants to become consciously responsible."[160] He sees traces of this divine urge all the way from the creation of Adam to the Apocalypse and beyond. But it is an urge with mixed feelings, complicating the process considerably:

The unconscious wants to flow into consciousness in order to reach the light, but at the same time it continually thwarts itself, because it would rather remain unconscious. That is to say, God wants to become man, but not quite.[161]

So, Jung's perspective is completely Christian, although his starting point is a tale from hundreds of years before the days of Jesus. Furthermore, his arguments weigh heavily on the principle of the Trinity — the Father, the Son, and the Holy Spirit being one and the same god — which is not even biblical, but took its form in the 4th century, following the First Council of Nicaea.

It is strange that Jung chooses to explain the meaning of one biblical story with others at that time yet to be written. Thereby he ignores considering explanations based on the *Book of Job* and its contextual setting. His choice is theological. He

---

[159] Ibid., p. 409.

[160] Ibid., p. 424.

[161] Ibid., p. 456.

analyzes the fate of Job and what it says about Yahweh with arguments from within the mythology of the Bible, also some of its Apocrypha, as if the texts speak the truth, the whole truth and nothing but the truth.

That does not necessarily mean he confesses to the Christian faith. He complains about how many times he has been asked if he believes in the existence of God, finding the question irrelevant. What he states firmly is that God is real in the psyche, but can never be proven to exist anywhere else:

God is an obvious psychic and non-physical fact, i.e., a fact that can be established psychically but not physically.[162]

God is an archetype within us, a splendid one of wholeness.[163] As such it is just as real as anything else of the psyche, influencing our thoughts and actions.

So, Jung's choice of making his analysis theological has a psychological reason. The theology of mythology is real, whether objectively true or not, because it speaks accurately of the way the mind works, especially the unconscious and its relation to the conscious.

This psychological theology is a maze. Jung's steps of reasoning are hard to follow and often lack convincing arguments, whether psychological or theological. We are mainly left with accepting his statements because he knows them to be true.

His bold idea of applying analytical psychology to a god is intriguing, but the picture he paints is obscured by numerous symbols and mythological detours. God remains hard to figure out and his psyche continues to evade our understanding.

If Jung's book were a novel, we would have to say that the character of Yahweh remains vague and contradictive to the

<hr>

162 Ibid., p. 464.

163 Ibid., p. 469.

last page. His actions remain irrational and frequently out of character, to the extent that the character can at all be envisioned.

For example, Jung claims that though Yahweh is omniscient he often forgets this. Jung has no better explanation to this forgetfulness than that "Yahweh was so fascinated by his successive acts of creation, so taken up with them, that he forgot about his omniscience altogether."[164] If he had not, he would have no question remaining to be answered and no insecurity to upset his temper. If he had used his omniscience all through, his creation would have been perfect in every way.

It is hard to see that this oblivious omniscience fits Yahweh as well as it fits Jung's need of it in his reasoning. If Jung had not decided to argue completely within the theology of Christianity, he would have concluded that omniscience is much easier to say than to imagine. Just like omnipotence. They are absurdities that ruin any story when pursued.

In other words, an omniscient god may forget, but he must know that he does and what it is he forgets. So, he can't really forget. It is as paradoxical as the old trap of omnipotence: creating a stone too heavy to lift, i.e., a problem too big to be solved. Both omniscience and omnipotence are impossible.

Most mythologies don't have these contradictions, because their deities are neither all-knowing nor all-powerful. But they do have characters that stand out for all to see. Jung's method may have proven much more fruitful if applied to any other deity than one of monotheism.

Contrary to the gods Jung calls pagan, Yahweh had "no origin and no past, except his creation of the world." On the other hand, the colorful biographies of the pagan gods were the reasons for their undoing:

It was precisely the details of their mythological biography that had become their nemesis, for with his growing capac-

[164] Ibid., p. 402.

Regarding the Greek gods, their questionable behavior
was discussed already in the time of the Greek philosophers,
and several of the philosophers did not hesitate to dismiss
them because of it. Others blamed Homer and Hesiod for de-
picting the gods as immoral monsters. Aristotle dismissed
their texts as nonsense: "About those who have invented clever
mythologies it is not worthwhile to take a serious look."[166]

Still, the Greek gods would all be much more exciting objects of psychoanalysis than the sole invisible observer of his
own creation who is Yahweh.

Actually, the problem of monotheism is another angle on
Christianity that might prove both intriguing and complicated.
The Trinity is a questionable way of trying to secure monotheism, as is Jung's alternative of a quaternity, where the fourth
apparition of God would be the woman — either Sophia, the
wisdom Yahweh frequently seems lacking, or Maria the virgin
mother of Christ, whose ascension decreed by the pope in 1950
Jung applauds.[167] Or is the fourth alias in his view Satan, whom
he calls the dark son of Yahweh?[168] Jung's claims are neither
clear nor consistent on this point.

The lacking monotheism of the monotheisms makes for a
number of anomalies in their theology that needs a wider
scope to reflect upon — a scope comparing with other mythologies and how they interfered and competed with the monotheisms. Faithfully following the theological doctrine doesn't
solve the riddle.

[165] Ibid., p. 373.

[166] Aristotle, *Metaphysics*, 1000a, transl. Hugh Lawson-Tancred, London
1998, pp.68f.

[167] Jung, "Answer to Job," p. 458.

[168] Ibid., p. 410.

Power Corrupts

Returning to Job, his story is not hard to figure out on its own. It addresses the question of how bad things can happen to a good man. This is the problem named *theodicy* by Gottfried Leibnitz in 1710, but it had been discussed long before: How can there be evil in a world created by a good god?

Not that the god testing Job seems the least bit good. He is far too swiftly persuaded by Satan to strike Job with terrible misfortune, although saying about him that "there is none like him in the earth, a perfect and an upright man, one that feareth God, and escheweth evil."[169] And when Job's torments are over, Yahweh has given no reason for it, nor any kind of excuse, but just insisted that his deeds cannot be questioned because none other than he has the power to perform them. Might makes right.

Still, Yahweh does give credit to Job's complaints, albeit indirectly, when dismissing the arguments of his friends who criticized him, "ye have not spoken of me the thing that is right, as my servant Job hath."[170]

But the literary value of the Book of Job lies between the appearances of Yahweh in the beginning and the end. That is where Job argues with his three old friends, who repeatedly condemn him for daring to question their god's wisdom. They insist that Job must have sinned or he would not have been struck so severely by Yahweh's wrath. Job persists with his surprisingly outspoken critique of Yahweh's judgment, until his friends give up against his stubbornness and fall silent.

At that point, another person opens his mouth to continue the dispute. It is the young man Elihu, who repeats the complaints of Job's friends, but also introduces new arguments as to the meaning of Yahweh's action and the nature of Job's sin. As for the former, Yahweh strikes people with suffering to warn them and give them incentive to repent.

[169] Job 1:8, *King James Bible*.
[170] Job 42:7.

There, their fate is decided, and not before:

If they obey and serve him, they shall spend their days in prosperity, and their years in pleasures. But if they obey not, they shall perish by the sword, and they shall die without knowledge.[171]

As for Job's sin, it lies in what Job says about his suffering, and not before it. He has failed Yahweh's test by not accepting it.

Neither Elihu nor anyone else mentions it, but one circumstance is cause for questioning Job's character: When he lost all his children and his riches, he remained faithful and praised his god — but when his own body was struck with disease, his patience ran out. He loved himself more than both Yahweh and his own children.

The end of the story proves to be rightly divined by Elihu, when Job repents and is given back even more than was taken away from him.

But the speech of Elihu is by many Bible scholars regarded as a later addition to the text. Others claim that it has always belonged there. Without Elihu's additional arguments, the dispute between Job and his friends would have been little more than a quarrel between Job claiming not to have sinned and his old friends claiming that he had.

Yahweh, when he speaks at the end, adds surprisingly little to the big question of what is fair and what is not. He simply demands to be obeyed because he is so tremendously mighty.

Just as god is not necessarily good and just, life is simply not always fair. Nor are the repeated cruel tests of Job's faith that he has to endure necessarily fair (even less so to his children). The story would have the same meaning with or without a god. In his misfortune, Job must wonder — why bother to be good? And there is just one answer to be found: Even

[171] Job 36:11-12.

when struck by bad things, it is good to be good. The ideal withholds, whether tested by a god or by fate.

Of course, since the story contains a god, an almighty one at that, there is someone to blame. Then the question is how this god can allow such injustice. But in his might he doesn't allow to be questioned and sees no obligation to explain. Jung writes, "Yahweh is no friend of critical thoughts which in any way diminish the tribute of recognition he demands."[172] He is what he is, and man just has to accept — even worship him — without question.

Such a god is an interesting object of analytical psychology, without the introduction of the Trinity or a quaternity and other symbols of another incarnation of the deity. The god Job meets has a psyche mainly formed by his omnipotence.

In the words of Lord Acton: "Power tends to corrupt, and absolute power corrupts absolutely." In his 1887 letter to Archbishop Mandell Creighton, Lord Acton continues with words also relevant here: "Great men are almost always bad men, even when they exercise influence and not authority: still more when you superadd the tendency or the certainty of corruption by authority. There is no worse heresy than that the office sanctifies the holder of it."[173]

As Jung also points out, Yahweh acts without any consideration or remorse: "God does not want to be just; he merely flaunts might over right."[174] He does so because he can. In his absolute state he can do nothing else, because his almightiness is the dominant thing about him, overshadowing anything else. Since he has all power, he is nothing but power.

That's a psyche worth analyzing, probably not so different from some men who have made blood-drenched footprints in history.

[172] Jung, "Answer to Job," p. 373.

[173] Lord Acton, *Acton-Creighton Correspondence (1887)*, libertyfund.org.

[174] Jung, "Answer to Job," p. 378.

The Inwards Eastern Path

There is one more aspect of Jung's writing relevant to this exploration — his interest in Eastern thought. For that I go to a text of his originally from 1939, "The Difference between Eastern and Western Thinking," which was published in 1954 as a psychological commentary in *The Tibetan Book of the Great Liberation*. It is not the only text of his on the subject, but an adequate representation of his views.

Jung wrote his text in English. It was edited for the 1954 publication, which is evident from — for example — its mention of man's ability to produce the atom bomb.[175] Below, I use the 1958 additionally edited version of the text in the 11th volume of *The Collected Works of C. G. Jung*, since this late edit a few years before his death in 1961 is likely to show his definitive thoughts on the subject.

Comparing East and West, Jung sees the mentality of the former as essentially introverted, and the latter extroverted:

Introversion is, if one may so express it, the "style" of the East, a habitual and collective attitude, just as extraversion is the "style" of the West.[176]

To the West, the palpable and objective world is the only real one. What cannot be measured and explained physically is not to be taken seriously. This attitude has led to the conflict between science and religion, which is to Jung a misunderstanding of both. Science and religion are experiences of the mind, interpreted by it, and therefore equally real and equally uncertain:

[175] Carl G. Jung, "The Difference between Eastern and Western Thinking," *The Tibetan Book of the Great Liberation*, edited by W. Y. Evans-Wentz, London 1954, p. xxxiv.

[176] Carl G. Jung, "The Difference between Eastern and Western Thinking," *The Collected Works of C. G. Jung*, volume 11, transl. R. F. C. Hull, New York 1958, p. 481.

Whether you call the principle of existence "God," "mat-
ter," "energy," or anything else you like, you have created
nothing; you have simply changed a symbol.[177]

The East, though, regards the mind and its subjective perception of the world as the higher reality. Only by pursuing the inward exploration, man can become whole. That is the Eastern route to "the self-liberating power of the introverted mind."[178] It is also the core difference in religious perspectives:

With us, man is incommensurably small and the grace of
God is everything; but in the East, man is God and he re-
deems himself.[179]

Jung sees this division as one between the conscious and the unconscious. The West tends to deny the existence, or at least the importance, of the unconscious. But to the East, the unconscious is everything, and the conscious should be ignored. Thereby the mind joins with what Jung perceives as the collective unconscious: "Thus our concept of the 'collective unconscious' would be the European equivalent of *buddhi*, the enlightened mind."[180]

The Eastern idea of this higher state contains the characteristic manifestations of the unconscious, "archaic thought-forms imbued with 'ancestral' or 'historic' feeling, and, beyond them, the sense of indefiniteness, timelessness, oneness."[181]

Although Jung is eager to stress the vast importance of the unconscious, he does not praise the way of the East as the one

[177] Ibid., p. 477.

[178] Ibid., p. 484.

[179] Ibid., p. 480.

[180] Ibid., p. 485.

[181] Ibid., p. 491.

true solution, especially not for Westerners, who seem increasingly to turn to the East for new spiritual revelations:

> *I have serious doubts as to the blessings of Western civilization, and I have similar misgivings as to the adoption of Eastern spirituality by the West.*[182]

The West and the East make similar mistakes by neglecting the other side of the psyche. Just as the Western mind gets lost by refusing to grasp how the unconscious interacts with the conscious, the Eastern mind is unaware that the unconscious cannot be completely controlled by any mental effort, but has to be understood in relation to the conscious.

Self-liberation may or may not be produced by the unconscious. It can't be produced at will. The unconscious has its own dynamics, mainly incomprehensible to the conscious mind. So, the Eastern path is little more than a roll of the dice. This insufficiency, the Eastern mind has missed:

> *It is a curious thing that Eastern philosophy seems to be almost unaware of this highly important fact. And it is precisely this fact that provides the psychological justification for the Western point of view.*[183]

Christianity versus Buddhism

Of course, some measure of generalization is needed when speculating about differences or similarities. But there must be reasonable cause for the generalization. So, is there reason for talking about the West and the East as two clearly definable cultures, and to presume that each has homogeneity within it?

Mere geography is surely not enough. All the continents of our planet have a multitude of different populations within them, with more or less separate cultures, languages, histories,

[182] Ibid., p. 487.

[183] Ibid., p. 491.

and so on. Finding trustworthy generalizations from just splitting the world into West and East is as difficult as to decide exactly where to put the dividing line.

But Jung's division seems to be based on religions. If we define the West as the countries which have for hundreds of years or more been formed by Christianity, then that might constitute a somewhat homogenous culture — at least in aspects connected to that religion and its ideas. But there are substantial differences within Christianity and its many churches. For example, Jung has frequently in his writings pointed out the vast differences between Catholicism and Protestantism, also regarding what is of such importance to him — the unconscious and its workings.

The East is no less complicated. Jung seems to base his claims about the East exclusively on Buddhism, the influence of which is certainly spread over great parts of Asia. But it has far from a monopoly on that continent, and it is far from homogenous. Although stemming from the same Indian prince, Buddhism has developed into interpretations, teachings and practices that are quite far apart.

So, generalizations about Christianity and Buddhism also run the risk of missing most of their respective characteristics and inner discrepancies.

When Jung moves on to state that the West has turned from religion to science whereas the East has not, he compares the present Western world to the ancient Eastern one. The East has also adapted modern science and its technology, which was definitely obvious in the 1950s, if not long before that.

What remains, then, is a comparison between Christianity and Buddhism, and the ideas they contain regarding the psyche and its tendencies. Jung claims that one is extroverted and the other introverted. That, too, needs to be examined.

Christianity may well be called extroverted in that you are judged by your actions towards others, but also introverted in the sense that the purity of your soul is what really counts at the end. The ideal is to fill your psyche with faith and erase any immoral urges — in other words a cultivation of the soul. The carnal and the spiritual are regarded as incompatible opposites, where the latter is deemed good and the former bad.

In other texts, Jung has discussed this Christian tendency to dismiss and suppress what is natural to the human species, in order to promote the idea of a perfectly moral psyche. To the pious Christian, the body is all but condemned and the soul is all.

Buddhism can be seen as introspective in as much as it propagates dismissal of all material values in order to reach detachment from all things worldly. The unattached mind is one free from the influence of longings, fears, and ambitions. Optimally, it leads to a final farewell to worldly existence, or at least complete detachment from it.

On the other hand, Buddhism also contains several extroverted conditions about behavior towards the outside world. This is expressed in the eightfold path, where several of the conditions deal with how to act in the world with the right intention, speech, action, and livelihood.[184] Karma is created by both action and thought.

The Buddhist path to detachment from the world focuses on worldly matters, but not to be replaced by some inner enrichment. Actually, the inner world of one's mind should also be dissolved. Emotions and any mental aspirations are illusionary and need to be dismissed. The Buddhist process is one of letting go of the outer and the inner world, as if they are essentially one and the same. Introversion is just as much of a trap as extroversion. Both need to be overcome.

When dividing Christianity and Buddhism according to extroversion and introversion, there is just as much reason for both to be one or the other. It is a question of subjective interpretation.

There is one significant difference between Christianity and Buddhism, though, which surely has an impact on the

[184] Edward J. Thomas, *Early Buddhist Scriptures*, London 1935, pp. 94f.

minds of their practitioners. One has an elevated deity in firm control of all, whereas the other makes so little use of deities in any shape or form that it is really questionable to call it a religion in any mythological sense of the word.

Buddhism's lack of significant deities also sets it apart from Hinduism of the same national origin. But it shares this with Taoism from China, which is frequently but mistakenly categorized as a religion. The fact that Buddhism all but lacks deities, whereas Christianity is totally dominated by one, makes it questionable indeed to compare them as if they were somehow relatable phenomena.

Now, the central idea of an invisible and impalpable deity suggests a mentality of prioritizing the imaginary over physical reality. That would indeed make for introversion. A tradition lacking this element, then, would come closer to focusing on what is observable. Thereby, the Buddhist would more readily accept science over belief, and the Christian would not.

Jung described Christian mentality as he saw it in his own time, roughly the first half of the 20th century. But doing so, he ignored the many centuries when Christian churches fought hard against scientific thinking and discoveries. Buddhist countries have definitely not taken that long to accept and adapt Western science, which reached them much later.

The difference is still visible today, as fundamentalist Christians insist on denying major scientific discoveries already established a hundred years ago or more. The Buddhist world, to my limited knowledge, shows little of the same reaction.

Satori Without an Empty Mind

Jung's significant writing on Eastern traditions was in the form of forewords or commentaries in books by others, as in the above case. For example, he also wrote a psychological commentary to *The Tibetan Book of the Dead* in 1935, a foreword to the Chinese classic *I Ching* in 1950, and a foreword to D. T. Suzuki's *An Introduction to Zen Buddhism* in 1939.

Since Jung's treatment of Eastern thought has little to do with mythology and mythical components, but deals with their ideas of the psyche and its transformation, there is no need to explore all his texts on the subject here. His thoughts on Zen, though, deserve some attention since it is obvious how well his theories on analytical psychology allow themselves to be applied to it. The concepts and aims of Zen translate remarkably to Jung's ideas of the dynamics between the conscious and the unconscious.

Jung's foreword to D. T. Suzuki's book on Zen was originally published in its 1939 German translation. The first edition of Suzuki's book, which was in English, appeared in 1934. In its 1949 edition, an English translation by Constance Rolfe of Jung's foreword had been added.

Jung begins his foreword by stating the importance of *satori*, usually translated as enlightenment, and pursues with this concept in focus all through. In support for this, he quotes Suzuki's words later in the same book: "*Satori* is the *raison d'être* of Zen, and without it there is no Zen."[185]

On the same page from which Jung quotes, Suzuki also writes: "Without the attainment of *satori* no one can enter into the truth of Zen. *Satori* is the sudden flashing into consciousness of a new truth hitherto undreamed of." But already on the next page he points out that "there is also such a thing as too much attachment to the experience of *satori*, which is to be detested."[186]

There are, of course, many different schools of Zen with differing focus. They all acknowledge satori, but this sudden moment of enlightenment or insight is rarely described as the goal of Zen. It is merely an event, though spectacular, after which things go on pretty much as usual. This usual may be seen in a very different light from that point on, as Jung is also

---

[185] Carl G. Jung, "Foreword," transl. Constance Rolfe. D. T. Suzuki, *An Introduction to Zen Buddhism*, New York 1964 (first edition 1949), p. 9.

[186] Ibid., p. 96.

aware, "It is not that something different is seen, but that one sees differently."[187] Nonetheless, the exercises of Zen go on and they essentially have no goal. They need to be without goal, or what can be reached is only what was imagined beforehand.

That said, Jung's interest in satori is understandable, since it has evident similarities with his theories of the interaction between the conscious and the unconscious. That is also how he describes it in his foreword.

Any path towards a spiritual whole must reach the unconscious, since "the conscious is only a part of the spiritual, and is never therefore capable of spiritual completeness: for that the indefinite expansion of the unconscious is needed."[188] He compares it to his concept of the individuation process, which he describes as "becoming whole" (*Ganzwerdung*). This implies that he talks about the collective unconscious, partly or exclusively.

Jung quotes the view on satori as an insight into the nature of self, but points out that this self is not the same as his concept of the ego. Expressed in his own terminology, satori can be described as "a break-through of a consciousness limited to the ego-form in the form of the non-ego-like self."[189]

He finds that this spiritual experience is not unknown in the West, presenting the medieval theologian Master Eckehart (also spelled Eckhart) as an example, quoting from his Sermon 87:

> *But in the breakthrough, when I wish to remain empty in the will of God, and empty also of this will of God and of all his works, and of God himself — then I am more than all creatures, for I am neither God nor creature: I am what I am, and what I will remain, now and forever!*[190]

[187] Ibid., p. 17.

[188] Ibid., pp. 27f.

[189] Ibid., p. 14.

[190] Ibid.

Indeed, Master Eckehart's bold statement is not far from the empty mind of Zen and its rooting in the very fundamental experience of "I am," whatever that is.

As another example of a Western experience similar to satori, Jung turns to one of his foremost literary favorites, appearing frequently in his writing: Nietzsche's *Zarathustra*. There Jung sees a transformation process "which has completely swallowed up intellect." The result is:

> *A new man, a completely transformed man, is to appear on the scene, one who has broken the shell of the old man and who not only looks upon a new heaven and a new earth, but has created them.*[191]

Jung sees satori as first of all a psychological problem, and that makes it irrelevant if the experience is a real enlightenment or not. It is a spiritual reality, whatever outside conclusions would be: "The man who has enlightenment, or alleges that he has it, thinks in any case that he is enlightened."[192] Because of its psychological nature and the modern tendency of the West to dismiss such experiences, Jung concludes:

> *The only movement within our culture which partly has, and partly should have, some understanding of these aspirations is psychotherapy. It is therefore not a matter of chance that this foreword is written by a psychotherapist.*[193]

The second ingredient in Zen that catches Jung's attention is the traditional method by which satori is reached — *koan*, the paradoxical question of the master, pushing the student to the

[191] Ibid., p. 18.

[192] Ibid., p. 15.

[193] Ibid., p. 25.

mind-altering experience. This seemingly nonsensical riddle by which the teacher challenges the student is a well-known favorite of the Zen curriculum.

Jung describes it as a destruction of the rational intellect, creating an almost perfect lack of supposition of the consciousness. What is not erased, though, and never can be, is unconscious supposition:

> *It is a nature-given factor, and when it answers — as is obviously the* satori *experience — it is an answer of Nature, who has succeeded in conveying her reactions direct to the consciousness.* [194]

This leak of unconscious content into the conscious, almost to the point of replacing it, changes the psyche so that it "corresponds better to the whole of the individual personality, and therefore abolishes fruitless conflict between the conscious and the unconscious personality."[195]

However, Jung doubts that the Zen method is accessible to Western people. The necessary trust in a superior master's incomprehensible ways exists only in the East, he claims. Already the belief in such a paradoxical transformation, demanding years of pursuit, is beyond us.

In the West it would even be hard to find someone willing to lead others through such a heterodox transformation. Not that there are no satori experiences happening to Westerners. Jung is sure of it.

> *But they will keep silence, not only out of shyness but because they know that any attempt to convey their experiences to others would be hopeless.*[196]

[194] Ibid., p. 20.

[195] Ibid., p. 23.

[196] Ibid., p. 25.

Jung ends his foreword by dismissing the false hope of Europeans that the spirit of Zen can be obtained by sitting and by breathing. He insists that Zen demands intelligence and will-power, "as do all the greater things which desire to become real."[197]

His final remark is amusing, considering how Zen teaches the fundamental importance of breathing and ever more so of sitting. A typical Zen school teaching is to sit (*zazen*) not for reaching any goal, but just to sit. Both will-power and intelligence are distractions, not methods to reach the state of empty mind. The Zen disciple is encouraged to expect nothing and think of nothing. If there is one mental capacity it takes, it is patience.

Still, Jung's theories of the psyche apply well to Zen practice. The conscious mind can be said to succumb to the unconscious — or whatever it is that is left when the conscious is switched off. The experience that there is something replacing the conscious and renewing it, as if out of nowhere, must indeed be a sensation of enlightenment.

In the psyche of Jung's description, what would appear from the collective part of the unconscious should be archetypes, since they are ever-present and shared by all humanity. But he makes no mention of it in this text. He says little about the exact nature of the satori experience, beyond what causes it.

He does mention a sense of oneness or completeness, which may have an archetypal quality to it. But can that really be the only thing emerging from the unconscious, when the conscious has been drained? If so, Zen practice must have the ability of erasing a lot of the unconscious, too.

Jung's theory does not allow it, stating that the content of the unconscious always remains. So, either Zen is an anomaly in Jung's psychology, or he has missed some aspect of it in his presentation.

[197] Ibid., p. 29.

In the case of the latter, what he seems to neglect is the important Zen concept of empty mind — maybe because it would be difficult to accept without thereby confessing to the anomaly.

The Elusive Unconscious

Jung's theories, as well as their application to mythology and religion, raise questions that his voluminous writing does not answer clearly or adequately. Mostly with his claims, we are to trust his words without further proof than that he speaks from a long therapeutic experience.

First and foremost, he bases his whole psychology on the existence of an unconscious, hidden from and unreachable by the conscious mind. But is there such a thing in the brain?

It is a strange idea that the brain should have compartments isolated from one another, as if the left hand really doesn't know what the right one does. You would think that this takes something like a lobotomy. Certainly, there are lots of mental activities that need no conscious initiative, such as reflexes and instincts.

We dream at night, inventing complicated stories full of details without any scriptwriting, which is something Jung connects to the unconscious. But we daydream when awake, if we let our minds go, which indicates that the mental process might very well be similar to dreaming asleep. And when we wake up from dreaming, we are usually able to follow its tracks backwards at least partially. We can even surmise how the dream will move forward if we close our eyes and let it. So, neither dreams nor daydreams are completely out of reach of the conscious.

Furthermore, there is the *hypnagogic* state, right before falling asleep, when we can use our conscious imagination to direct at least the start of the dreaming process.[198] Its counterpart is the *hypnopompic* state, when waking up from a dream and

---

[198] The term hypnagogic was introduced by Louis Ferdinand Alfred Maury in an 1848 text about hypnagogic hallucinations. Maury, "Des hallucinations hypnagogiques ou erreur des sens dans l'état intermédiaire entre la veille et le sommeil," *Annales médico-psychologiques*, Paris 1848, volume XI, pp. 26-40.

still aware of it.[199] Another term for dreaming while being consciously aware of it is *lucid dream*.[200]

Jung was aware of both hypnagogic and hypnopompic hallucinations, as well as the works of those introducing the terms. He regarded them as expressions of the same phenomenon, i.e., the imagination taking over as conscious reasoning fades towards sleep. He also recognized their ability to influence dreams:

> *It is highly probable that hypnagogic pictures are identical with the dream-pictures of normal sleep — forming their visual foundation.*[201]

Dreaming seems not to be a definite isolated state, but an ability of our brain not only when it is completely unconscious. It is the same with other so-called unconscious processes. They need not be. Reflexes can be controlled and conditioned to change. Instincts can be suppressed. We are even quite able to consciously alter something as fundamentally unconscious as our breathing.

So, solid borders between the conscious and the unconscious might not be that easy to find.

Another example is automaticity, the automatic behavior we can go through without consciously focusing on it, which can sometimes be quite complex. Every driver has experienced driving a familiar route without being aware of it until reach-

[199] The term hypnopompic was introduced by the psychical researcher Frederic W. H. Myers in a book published 1903, two years after his death. Myers, *Human Personality and Its Survival of Bodily Death*, volume I, New York 1903, p. xvii.

[200] The term lucid dream was introduced by the Dutch psychiatrist Frederik van Eeden in 1913. Eeden, "A Study of Dreams," *Proceedings of the Society for Psychical Research*, volume 26, Glasgow 1913, pp. 431-461.

[201] Carl G. Jung, *Collected Papers on Analytical Psychology*, London 1916, p. 62.

ing the destination. It even has a name: *highway hypnosis*.[202]

This state of mind is similar to daydreaming. The mind wanders off, while the body completes the task. But the conscious mind is never shut off. As soon as something out of the ordinary happens on the way, the conscious control is back in an instant. It was never really gone.

The above examples don't suggest a separate entity in the mind, isolated from the conscious, but a multi-tasking consciousness that is able to move its focus between tasks, though never completely losing contact with any of them. It is less comparable to a team of individuals with separate tasks, than to the ability of the eyes to focus on separate parts of the view. We take it all in, but vary effortlessly what we give our attention.

And we are quite aware of what makes our focus shift. It is according to importance. What we regard as the most important at the moment is what catches our attention, and it can differ from one second to the next. The shift is instant.

Although the grading of importance is complex, its mechanics are evident in instances of drastic change of focus. For example, while driving the car we snap out of any daydream, whatever its topic may be, immediately when we perceive the threat of an imminent accident.

We do the same when conversing with passengers in the car. They have our attention only between the moments when safety demands that we focus on the driving. Self-preservation overrides just about everything else.

But these priorities of importance go the whole scale, from

---

[202] The term highway hypnosis was introduced in 1963 by the psychologist Griffith Wynne Williams, "Highway Hypnosis: An Hypothesis," *International Journal of Clinical and Experimental Hypnosis*, volume 11:3, Philadelphia 1963, pp. 143–151. Already in 1921, though, the phenomenon was discussed as road hypnotism in a *Literary Digest* article (volume 69, pp. 56-57). Griffith Wynne Williams & Ronald E. Shor, "An Historical Note on Highway Hypnosis," *Accident Analysis and Prevention*, volume 2:3, New York 1970, p. 223.

lethal to just a trifle uncomfortable. It is not even sure that threats always have a priority over pleasures, or Romeo would never have gotten his Juliet.

The computing involved is impressive, though not infallible. When we have trouble focusing on a certain task for any amount of time, it may be because we fail to see its superiority over other simultaneous influences. But we are never unable to figure out the reason for our lack of concentration when we examine the circumstances. It all makes sense to us, even when our choices are questionable. We can even sort of negotiate with ourselves and force our attention on something less attractive or threatening, for very conscious reasons.

Our conscious is never really out of charge, except for momentarily — before it notices the dilemma.

Surely, like the eyes never stop seeing, the mind is never a blank, but keeps going with or without conscious attention to it. But is it possible for some of the thinking to hide when we consciously search for it? And if so, wouldn't we at least be aware of that border? Freud and Jung, the latter in particular, would answer yes to the first question and no to the second. What we know about the structure and workings of the brain suggests the opposite answers.

Notice that I speak of an unconscious completely out of reach for the conscious mind, and not the simple fact that a lot of thinking can go on in our minds without us being consciously aware of it. There is a huge difference between a part of the mind to which the conscious is denied access and not even aware of, and one that we can reach by conscious effort but otherwise does its thing more or less unnoticed.

The difference can be described by grammar. The unconscious of Freud and Jung is a noun, representing an entity separated from other parts of the mind. But there is also an adjective unconscious, as in unconscious action or unconscious thought. That is temporal unconsciousness, which might or might not be noticed by the conscious. We have plenty of those, as exemplified above. Similarly, there is the adverb unconsciously. We do indeed frequently think or act unconsciously. Again, though, this is accessible to the conscious and not hidden from it. We need only to put our attention to it.

So, what I discuss here is Freud's and Jung's idea of a separate hidden unconscious, and not all those more or less unconscious thoughts and actions that we have plenty of every day.

The writings of Freud and Jung indicate a view of the mind as something different in nature from the biochemistry of the body, including its brain. That is in line with the traditional conception of the psyche, since long before the two analytical psychologists. It was believed to differ in essence from everything carnal, as if made of other stuff. Something spiritual, ruled by laws different from those of the physical. That view was also advocated in Schelling's and Eduard von Hartmann's pioneering works on the unconscious, mentioned earlier.

When the psyche is regarded as something basically different from the substance it occupies, then it can easily be postulated to have different entities or processes isolated from one another. Such a psyche does not need to obey any physical law, whereas thinking done only by synapses and such in the brain must. But the brain, as we know it, shows little support for the traditional view. It is part of the body, and made of the same stuff. So, the idea that a very important and decisive part of it should be hidden from the rest is in dire need of substantial evidence, given by neither Freud nor Jung.

There are additional problems with the concept of a separate unconscious. Freud and Jung define it so that it becomes inaccessible to prove or disprove. They really try neither. Instead, they just make a number of claims that can at best be called speculations. What they say could be true or not. There is no way of deciding. That is, to them, a consequence of the nature of the unconscious as something hidden and impenetrable.

But can something unprovable exist — outside the world

of religion? The unconscious of Freud and Jung is a matter of belief instead of evidence. All their examples reveal it. They never show how their interpretation surpasses alternative explanations. They have even defined the unconscious so that it rejects comparison to other models. Actually, they never try any other explanation, as if none were fathomable.

As a science, this is a dead-end. If it can't be proven or disproven, it cannot be advanced. It is just a list of claims, which can be extended but not meaningfully revised and improved. Essentially, it is nothing more than a "what if?"

So, how about this what if? Does it still have value worth exploring? Things don't need to be true to be interesting, even in some way rewarding. This, some would say, makes a case for religion. And it is definitely true about fiction, as our fascination with it through the ages has shown.

Indeed, there is something intriguing, even spooky, about the idea of the human mind held captive by a greater hidden mind, like an island surrounded by the deep sea. It would be a good premise for the start of a horror story. And it has its modern parallel in the persistent myth of us using only 10% of our brain — or just not knowing what the other 90% is up to. This misconception might have been inspired by the iceberg metaphor of the mind being 90% unconscious and 10% conscious, falsely accredited to Freud. It was expressed by Stefan Zweig in his 1931 book *Die Heilung durch den Geist*, published in English the following year.[203]

We are all excited by a wondrous mystery, whether we find it likely or not. Like Aristotle said about a good story, "Things probable though impossible should be preferred to the possible but implausible."[204]

---

[203] Stefan Zweig, *Mental Healers: Franz Mesmer, Mary Baker Eddy, Sigmund Freud* (Die *Heilung durch den Geist. Mesmer, Mary Baker-Eddy, Freud*, 1931), transl. Eden and Cedar Paul, New York 1932, p. 292.

[204] Aristotle, *Poetics*, 1460a, transl. Stephen Halliwell, Loeb 199, London 1999, pp. 123f.

It is not at all implausible that we should have secret compartments in our minds, steering us away from catastrophe — or towards it. Just like we often feel victims of our emotions, a hidden influence on our conscious can seem real when what pops up in our minds bewilders us. Such a circumstance would have the wonderful attraction of suggesting that there is more to us, much more, than what we normally perceive.

In a sense, it would make us mythological.

It would also be a wonderful excuse when we acted otherwise indefensibly. The idea of the free will is much more of a burden on our responsibility than, say, that of an angel whispering in one ear and a devil in the other. The unconscious is within us, but still not us. So, we are not really to blame for what it makes us think or do.

But what might appear from that unknown sea of the unconscious is upon examination not much of a surprise to the conscious. As Miss Frank Miller concluded about her fantasies and poetry, discussed in Jung's *Psychology of the Unconscious*, their strange ingredients were really easy to trace as earlier memories and such. Nothing hidden, nothing invented in some secret corner of her mind, just impressions her conscious had come across before and already regarded as significant.

Just the Will

Since the existence of a separate unconscious is doubtful, this leads to a need to examine if the conscious is also misconceived. Without an unconscious counterpart, what is really so conscious about the conscious mind?

The psyche is a heap of things constantly going on simultaneously. There are new and old memories appearing and disappearing, countless impressions from the five senses in need of interpretation, instincts struggling to act while restraint is struggling to stop them, diverse or even opposite emotions bubbling in the body, thoughts colliding and competing — all in a veritable chaos. It is a wonder that our minds can make any sense of it all.

In Zen, a major object is to calm down this calamity of the mind, ideally so far as to reach what is called empty mind, a stillness wherein no thought grabs control of our attention. In *zazen*, seated meditation, one should learn to think about nothing. Not an easy task.

I had a Japanese aikido teacher who explained how to accomplish this. He said that there is no point struggling to keep thoughts off. They just become more persistent. But when you sit there and a thought appears, just acknowledge this, and tell yourself that it is not important right now, so you can let it go. When another thought comes, do the same, and so on and on and on. The thoughts will become less intrusive and the distance between them will increase, until finally they cease completely. But that, he admitted, takes years and years.

Although difficult to follow, it is good advice. The key is the importance. The less important we regard our thoughts, the less they bother us. Our attention is the decisive factor.

That brings a clue to what the conscious might be at its core: the will. It is by will we navigate the chaos of the mind and make some sense of it. Without this will, the noise of the mind produces all kinds of impressions and impulses, making us either erratic or apathetic.

The will is an intriguing concept that has attracted the attention of philosophers through the ages, sometimes calling it desire. It is the prerequisite for action. Without it nothing happens.

That is why ancient thinkers regarded it as the initial impulse in the very creation of the world. It is what Aristotle points to in his principle of the prime mover, the first cause in the never-ending chain of cause and effect, "something that moves without being moved."[205] It is also suggested by the "Let there be" formula of creation in *Genesis I* of the Bible. God creates by wishing it. Plenty of other creation myths indicate the same. The world would not be if no one willed it.

[205] Aristotle, *Metaphysics*, 1998, 1072a, p. 373.

In human beings it is obvious: we do what we will to do, or we do nothing. We think what we will to think, or our thoughts take us nowhere.

The body moves a lot inside itself without the impulse of our will, with blood flowing through our veins, air inhaled and exhaled, heart beating, and so on. But it takes our will to stand up and walk somewhere. Similarly, the mind is constantly doing a lot of thinking, noticing, learning, probably even deductions in some way, all on its own. But it is by will that we become aware of it and make use of it. Wisdom without willful access to it is not different from ignorance.

Of course, our will is not any first cause in the sense of stemming from itself only, nothing preceding it. Any theory of a first, in psychology as well as cosmogony, runs into the problem of the chicken or the egg. This was pointed out already by Plutarch in the first century CE:

> *Which was first, the bird or the egg? And my friend Sylla, saying that with this little question, as with an engine, we shook the great and weighty question (whether the world had a beginning), declared his dislike of such problems.*[206]

What we will depends on just about all that moves around inside our brain, and how it relates to the outside world. It is not one single will, marching steadily towards one goal. Instead, it changes on a whim by impulses from what we have experienced, what we crave or fear, how we relate to our ever-changing surroundings. The will may take charge of the chaos of the mind, but it is still a victim of all that goes around in there.

The mind is thereby an example of the utter difficulty to

[206] Plutarch, *Essays and Miscellanies*, volume 3, transl. William W. Goodwin, Boston 1909, p. 242. Plutarch's answer to the question (pp. 245f) is the bird: "For we never see an egg formed immediately of mud, for it is produced in the bodies of animals alone." That is debatable, too.

decide cause and effect in complex interaction. The cause is not uninfluenced by the effect, and the effect is not just a passive servant of the cause. In the brain, the effect can be the cause and the cause can become an effect. It is a spiral process, where the effects are the causes of following causes.

That means the existence of the will can also be questioned. At least, it can't really be seen as an entity, a noun, any more than the unconscious can. It exists when it appears and not when it doesn't.

It is not the constant I of the human being, in charge of all the rest. It is merely one of the ingredients interacting with the others, among them instead of above them, but with the ability to take charge at times.

It is nothing but the ability to take charge of the being.

The I

So, next we have to ask if there is an I of the human being, and what that might be if there is. We certainly experience one, some of us even more than one at times. We have names and regard ourselves as individuals, unique from all the other individuals. No psychological theory would make any sense if that were not the case. But how to define it? Who or what am I?

Examining our own minds, we are not likely to come up with more than that we recognize a sense of identity, of being me, whatever that encompasses or originates from. As is indicated by the classic statement of Descartes — "I think, therefore I am" — there is something that thinks about being, and that something, whatever it is, must in some sense be.

Since this is reasoning, what must exist according to Descartes is reason.

He also finds it to be a proof of the existence of god:

And the total force of the argument lies therein that I would recognize that it cannot happen that I would exist of such a nature of which I am, namely, having the idea of God in me, unless God did also really and truly exist.[207]

God of the Old Testament had something similar to say when asked by Moses about his name:

And Moses said unto God, Behold, when I come unto the children of Israel, and shall say unto them, The God of your fathers hath sent me unto you; and they shall say to me, What is his name? what shall I say unto them?

And God said unto Moses, I Am That I Am: and he said, Thus shalt thou say unto the children of Israel, I Am hath sent me unto you.[208]

In modern Bible translations God says, "I am what I am."

Both Descartes and Yahweh may have spoken the truth, but it's not of much help. Our sense of an I is still an enigma. When we make an inward search to find the answer, we discover nothing but new questions. Maybe the real object of empty mind in Zen and Nirvana of Buddhism is to finally put that question to rest and just be, without worrying why. It might also be at the core of monotheism: I don't know what I am, but god does. He is.

We find it so much easier relating to others and who they are. Each person is what fills that particular body, and nothing outside of it. We don't know them enough to read their minds, but that doesn't matter much. Whatever goes on in their heads is meaningless to us. What counts is what they express — their words and deeds. So, that is how we perceive them. They are what they do.

Returning to Aristotle and his *Poetics*, he compares the functions of the plot and the characters, repeatedly stressing

---

[207] René Descartes, *Meditations on First Philosophy*, transl. George Heffernan, Notre Dame, Indiana 1990 (originally published in Latin 1641), p. 149.

[208] Exodus 3:13-14, *King James Bible*.

the superior importance of the former. The tragedy (drama)[209] is about action and not persons. Characters make a difference because of how they act, not how they are: "It is in virtue of character that people have certain qualities, but through their actions that they are happy or the reverse." The characters are included in the play for the sake of their actions. Aristotle also points out, "Without action there could be no tragedy, but without character there could be."[210]

As for what he means about character, Aristotle says:

> *Character is that which reveals moral choice — that is, when otherwise unclear, what kinds of things an agent chooses or rejects (which is why speeches in which there is nothing at all the speaker chooses or rejects contain no character).*[211]

In other words, it is only by action a character is revealed and makes a difference. It is doubtful that Aristotle meant this to be true outside the stage as well as on it, but the comparison is not uncalled for. As Shakespeare famously had one of his characters say: "All the world's a stage, and all the men and women merely players."[212]

We perceive others very much like Aristotle's players in a drama. They are what they do and what their actions lead us to believe they might do next. We may be curious about why they do what they do, but such speculation, again, is mainly to understand or predict their actions. We don't hope to discover

---

[209] Aristotle reasoned about only two forms of plays – the tragedy and the comedy, but his rules for the former would apply to any drama. His text about comedy is lost to us, as made famous by Umberto Eco's 1980 novel *The Name of the Rose*.

[210] Aristotle, *Poetics*, 1450a, transl. Stephen Halliwell, Loeb 199, London 1999, p. 51.

[211] Ibid., 1450b, p. 53.

[212] William Shakespeare, *As You Like It*, Act II scene VII.

how they perceive themselves as individuals, what they believe is the nature of their I, and it is not something bothering us much.

As for how we look at ourselves, though, it is far more complicated. It is a constant itch in our minds that we are unable to complete Yahweh's I am what I am, but reach only halfway through, making it a question: I am what?

Along with Aristotle's claims above, we are often left to read ourselves the way we read others — by our actions, which often come as surprises to us. In particular, we tend to be frustrated by what we do not do, although it would make more sense to us. We make choices, but the reasons for them are frequently only accessible in hindsight.

But the reasons for our choices are accessible, and upon examination show to have been predictable. We can know the traits of our behavior without knowing what it is that we are. We read ourselves by what we do. Like Aristotle's characters, that's what we are.

So, the answer to the question is: I am what I do. There is no fixed personality. We change constantly as our actions affect us. The famous Heraclitus quote about the river is equally true about human beings:

> *Heracleitus is supposed to say that all things are in motion and nothing at rest; he compares them to the stream of a river, and says that you cannot go into the same water twice.*[213]

The Heraclitus principle that everything flows, *panta rhei*, is as true for the human mind as it is for the cosmos. Everything changes — certainly the mind, by what flows through it. Just as the unconscious is more adequately described as an adverb or an adjective than as a noun, this is just as true about the

[213] Plato, "Cratylus," 402, *The Dialogues of Plato*, volume I (of 5), transl. Benjamin Jowett, Oxford 1892 (first edition 1871), p. 344f.

whole mind and any aspect of it. There are mental aspects and processes that can be comprehended, but they don't reveal the complete nature of the mind — they don't even confirm that there is one.

Strictly speaking, it is about verbs rather than nouns. Instead of asking what is, we should ask what is happening. If nothing happens there is nothing to consider.

But we tend to favor the idea of things that are presumed to somehow stay the same while going through events—as if the brain had any significance even without its myriad of processes, as if a human being had a personality without ever expressing it.

Freud and Jung claimed that there are fixed patterns in the human mind, regardless of who or when or where. To them, the psyche is a machine, which forever works in the same way whenever it is turned on, like a tram stuck to its tracks. It would be more adequate to liken the psyche to the passenger of the tram, stepping off at any point to take a walk, or get into a car, or sit down at a café and get involved in a conversation with some strangers there.

Our thinking is not significant for what rules by which it might be bound, but for what rules it breaks. The remarkable thing about it is not what stays the same, but how much it always changes. The mind continuously reinvents itself. It is never what it is, because in a moment that is merely what it was.

So, a psychology searching for what in the mind stays the same will see but a fraction of it, and that fraction is most likely obsolete immediately after being observed.

The Collective Unconscious

What is said above about the unconscious is even truer for Jung's idea of a collective unconscious, which carries the traits of an illusion within an illusion. It supposes another secret entity within the psyche, even less accessible to the conscious and therefore also to empirical study.

Of course, this goes for Freud's similar idea of the archaic heritage, too.

To Jung, the collective unconscious is the domain of the archetypes. His idea of archetypes hidden and yet remaining in the human mind through generations, independently of time and place, calls for an explanation similar in kind to Freud's theory of an archaic heritage. Freud compared it to animal instincts and claimed that events being significant enough and happening often enough would be added to the archaic heritage.

That was also what Jung started with, but he continued by developing a solution of his own — the collective unconscious, which is not that different at all from Freud's concept.

According to Jung, each person has an unconscious, part of it very personal indeed and part of it is the same for all human beings. The latter is the collective unconscious, where the archetypes are stored. It is simply the part of the unconscious, which does not come from personal experience. The personal unconscious contains such material as actual personal memories and experiences that have been forgotten or repressed. The rest belongs to the collective unconscious.

Jung did not see this as any sort of telepathic dimension with the ability to reach outside a person's mind.[214] To him it was more like an imprint, something inherited by all, along the line of animal instincts — just like Freud explained the archaic heritage.

The instincts progress and adapt in animals, as they change by evolution and their needs alter according to changes in their environment. Otherwise, their instincts would soon be their doom instead of their support in survival. Therefore, some kind of evolution of instincts must be mandatory. Jung

[214]Not that Jung was opposed to the possibility of ESP, extrasensory perception, "which medical psychology should on no account ignore." He regarded the phenomenon of ESP as one of the very few established psychological facts. Carl G. Jung, *Fundamental Questions of Psychotherapy*, quoted in Segal, *Jung on Mythology*, pp. 65f.

imagined a similar development of the human brain, as the means by which the collective unconscious appeared and was filled with archetypes. To Jung, the complexity of the human mind allows for that additional and more refined set of instincts which is the collective unconscious.

> *The hypothesis of the collective unconscious is, therefore, no more daring than to assume there are instincts.*[215]

The archetypes give examples of this, since many of them obviously relate to phenomena that all people have in common — such as the mother, the child, life, and death. Jung insisted that archetypes are shared by all, and not just by people of one culture or one time period. Therefore, he must have meant that what cannot be grasped or recognized by every human being is not an archetype.

So, the idea of the collective unconscious creates a definite border for what are archetypes and what are not. They must relate meaningfully to all human beings. That is not so obvious with some of the archetypes Jung specified — they are rather limited to his own European and Christian background. Still, if he made mistakes in applying his theory, it does not necessarily mean that the theory is faulty.

To Jung, the collective unconscious had little else to do than store the archetypes, which are the instruments for any person to reach self-realization in the individuation process. Archetypes are essentially all of what the collective unconscious consists. Everything kept there is in the form of archetypes, which suggests that it is the way for the collective unconscious to code itself.

Myths, according to Jung, are born out of the collective unconscious, and therefore they are made up of archetypes.

[215]From a lecture in London 1936. Carl G. Jung, "The Concept of the Collective Unconscious," *The Collected Works of C. G. Jung*, volume 9 part 1, Princeton 1969, p. 44.

The myths are expressions of that part of the psyche. He regarded the whole of mythology as a kind of projection of the collective unconscious.

Dreams, on the other hand, come from the personal unconscious, and cannot become myths, because of their personal nature. While the personal unconscious is unable to influence the collective unconscious, the reverse is possible:

> *The collective unconscious influences our dreams only occasionally, and whenever this happens, it produces strange and marvelous dreams remarkable for their beauty, or their demoniacal horror, or for their enigmatic wisdom — "big dreams," as certain primitives call them.*[216]

Methods of Proof

Such "big dreams" are the main evidence Jung presents for the existence of archetypes hidden in all our minds. Not all dreams, though, and not all the content in them. He explains in a short chapter with the title "Method of Proof" in an edited 1936 text from a lecture he gave in English:

> *We must look for motifs which could not possibly be known to the dreamer and yet behave functionally in his dream in such a manner as to coincide with the functioning of the archetype known from historical sources.*[217]

But how to decide that those archetypes are inherited and not learned, especially if they are known from historical sources? And how to decide that they are not known to the dreamer? Jung does not say.

[216] Jung, "Analytical Psychology and Education," *The Collected Works of C. G. Jung*, vol. 17, transl. R. F. C. Hull, Princeton 1970, p. 117. The original German text was published in 1946.

[217] Carl G. Jung, "The Concept of the Collective Unconscious," *The Collected Works of C. G. Jung*, volume 9:1, Princeton 1969, p. 49.

The second method he mentions has the same problems. He uses "active imagination," by which he means fantasies seeming significant to the patient, explored by conscious effort. He points out that it is not to be compared to Freud's "free association" in dream-analysis. Then Jung wards off any further inquiry by stating: "This is not the place to enter upon a technical discussion of the method."[218] So much for proof.

He also finds sources of archetypal material "in the delusions of paranoiacs, the fantasies observed in trance-states, and the dreams of early childhood, from the third to the fifth year."[219] Then he gives an example of a paranoid schizophrenic he met in 1906, and wrote about already in his *Wandlungen und Symbole der Libido* from 1912, published in English 1916 as *Psychology of the Unconscious*.

The patient claimed to see the sun's penis, and four years later Jung found an ancient mythological reference to something similar, "hanging down from the disc of the sun something that looks like a tube."[220] Jung goes on with somewhat similar imagery in medieval paintings of Mary being fructified by a tube from God's throne. Jung is aware that as evidence his example is weak, to say the least. His defense is not convincing:

I mention this case not in order to prove that the vision is an archetype but only to show you my method of procedure in the simplest possible form.[221]

He continues by sketching how such research should be done — mainly by examining a series of a few hundred dreams to follow the development of "typical figures" in them, which must mean just a single patient examined. As for the figures, "You can select any figure which gives the impression of being

218 Ibid.

219 Ibid., p. 50.

220 Ibid., p. 51.

221 Ibid., p. 52.

an archetype by its behaviour in the series of dreams or visions."[222]

So, you prove the existence of archetypes by searching for
figures that give the impression of being archetypes. Well, that
way you are sure to find what you are looking for, if just persistent enough and lenient enough about what seems like what
you are looking for.

Jung ends his text by pointing to another text of his: "I
have described the method of investigation elsewhere and
have also furnished the necessary case material."

The text he refers to is an essay with the title "Dream Symbols of the Process of Individuation," which was originally
published in German in 1936. There, Jung examines the process of individuation through following how one archetype,
the mandala, develops over ten months through 400 dreams
and daydreams of a "youngish" man who is scientifically ed-
ucated in history, philology, archaeology, and ethnology. Still,
Jung claims, "The bearing of his dreams upon the subject matter of these fields was almost wholly unknown to him."[223]

Then Jung gives a number of examples of those dreams in
comprised forms, spending significantly more words explaining their meanings. So doing, he allows himself a tremendous
amount of far-fetched speculation. For example, this is how he
explains the first dream in which the dreamer is simply putting
on another hat than his own:

*What is the significance of this dream? To begin with, the
hat, as the covering of the head, has in general the meaning
of something comprising the head. As in the act of subsum-
ing we "bring all ideas under one hat," so the hat, like a
universal concept, covers the whole personality and shares
its meaning. Coronation lends to the ruler the divine na-*

---

[222] Ibid., p. 53.

[223] Carl G. Jung, "Dream Symbols of the Process of Individuation," *The
Integration of the Personality*, transl. Stanley Dell, London 1940, p. 97.

ture of the sun, the mortarboard bestows the dignity of a scholar, a strange hat imparts a strange nature. Meyrink employs this theme in The Golem, where the hero puts on the hat of Athanasius Pernath and, as a result, is translated into a strange experience. It is clear enough in The Golem that it is the unconscious that entangles the hero in fantastic experiences. (Let me call attention right here in a hypothetical way to the significance of the Golem parallel: it is the hat of an Athanasius, of an immortal, of a timeless being, by which we are to understand a universally authentic, perpetually existent human being in contradistinction to the individual who happens but once and is, so to speak, accidental.) The hat, which embraces the head, is round like the sun-disk of the crown and therefore contains the first allusion to the mandala. The ninth mandala dream, discussed on page 132, will confirm the attribute of imperishable duration, and the thirty-fifth, given later on page 179, the mandala nature of the hat. As a general result of the exchange of hats, then, we may perhaps expect in this case a development similar to that in The Golem, namely, an emergence of the unconscious. The unconscious with its figures already stands like a shadow behind him and presses into consciousness.[224]

Or it could just mean that the patient dreamed about putting on the wrong hat.

The dreams that follow become increasingly odd and seemingly symbolic, for the most part, which is of no surprise. Over the ten months with hundreds of dreams recorded, the patient would have had a hard time avoiding increased complexity. That is how the mind works, whether unconsciously or not. It is like a total novice by the piano, gradually playing more elaborate patterns, searching for melodies.

To Jung, proof of the mandala appearing in the dreams is

[224] Ibid., p. 102.

mostly nothing more than that there are round objects in them
— like the hat. That persists to the 59th and last of the cited
dreams, which Jung calls a "great vision," indicating that it is
more of a daydream or fantasy:

> *There is a vertical and a horizontal circle, having a common centre.*
>
> *This is the world-clock. It is supported by black birds. The vertical circle is a blue disk with a white edge, divided into 4X8=32 parts. On it revolves a pointer. The horizontal circle consists of four colours. Upon it stand four little men with pendulums, and around it lies the ring that was formerly dark and is now golden (previously carried by the four children).*
>
> *The "clock" has three rhythms or beats:*
>
> *The small beat: The pointer of the blue, vertical circle advances 1/32.*
>
> *The middle beat: A complete revolution of the pointer.*
>
> *At the same time the horizontal circle advances 1/32.*
>
> *The great beat: 32 middle beats make a revolution of the golden ring.*[225]

The dreamer described it as an "impression of the greatest
harmony." Jung calls it a three-dimensional mandala, "one,
therefore, that has attained substantiality and realization." The
doctor-patient privilege hinders Jung from revealing the details, but assures us that the realization did take place.

As usual with Jung, the bottom line is that we have to take
his word for it.

Stone Age Mind

So, Jung's collective unconscious is an inherited part of the
psyche, a fundamental driving force, a container of great

---

[225] Ibid., pp. 189f.

truths, and the only trustworthy guide to self-realization. Yet, it is hidden in the depth of the mind, unknown to man. Dreams and myths are the instruments to discover and to utilize it.

Jung's theory raises many questions, several of which have been treated above. Apart from the questionable idea of an unconscious completely out of reach of the conscious mind, already discussed, Jung states about the collective unconscious that its content is identical for all mankind. That is problematic in several ways.

Excluding, as Jung does, a telepathic explanation, the content of the collective unconscious would have been formed in some manner similar to our instincts and how they evolve. That is also what Jung suggests — the content of the collective unconscious must be biologically inherited. But then, if it is globally identical, the same for all of us, it must have been completed in the time of our most recent common ancestor.

That would suggest the time of Mitochondrial Eve, around 150,000 years ago in Africa, who was the earliest common matrilinear ancestor found so far. The corresponding Adam is generally assumed to be older. But DNA is reproduced through both sexes and finds its way between them in a manner sort of similar to how information flows through the World Wide Web — there are many alternative routes.

Therefore, the true most recent common ancestor for humankind is considerably less ancient. Research with mathematical models suggests this ancestor might be as recent as 3,000 years ago. There is also the concept of the identical ancestor point, before which all our ancestors are exactly the same. That, too, might be no longer ago than 5,000 to 10,000 years.[226]

Of course, this does in no way mean we are identical to these distant ancestors. Genes mix and transform in the process of reproduction. But it can't be stated that human capacities present at the identical ancestor point were not transmitted

---

[226] Douglas L. T. Rohde et al., "Modelling the recent common ancestry of all living humans," *Nature*, volume 431, London 2004, pp. 562-566.

to the following generations. A lot of them certainly were, such as instincts and numerous mental abilities. Some sort of collective unconscious could, theoretically, be one of them.

But if identically shared by all mankind, such a collective unconscious cannot contain material more recent than some 5,000 to 10,000 years ago — and it would be a marvel if things of that specific era could have been genetically included in the following generations. Genes don't work that fast. It would be much more plausible with remnants of experiences far older than that. A plausible collective unconscious would consist of Stone Age experiences and hardly anything closer to our time.

That era spanned millions of years, when people's lives were pretty much the same hunter-gatherer reality all through. That must be enough to make its mark in the genes. So, any kind of common collective unconscious content would just about exclusively be formed by human experiences of the Stone Age. And only to the extent that people all over the world share the same experiences, can additional content ever be added to the collective unconscious while keeping it identical for all humankind.

In the past century or so, the human world has started to become as homogenous as it was in the Stone Age, due to industrialization, global communication, and world politics. Still, human life is far from as conform as it once was, and it is unlikely that it ever can be. The complexity of modern society opens for so much unforeseen diversity. Also, genetics takes its time programming future generations with new inherited codes, especially if they are to be identical in us all. Homogeneity comparable to that of the Stone Age probably cannot ever be repeated.

So, a collective unconscious of the kind Jung describes can only contain material which was relevant to people of the Stone Age. Since Jung stated that the content of the collective unconscious is nothing but archetypes, they all have to be such that they had significant meaning to those distant ancestors of ours.

Certainly, several of the archetypes he suggested would be relevant also in the Stone Age. It is true for the ones he regarded as the most important — anima and animus, i.e., the female and the male entities in the human mind. Our genders and their significance have been with us since long before the Stone Age. This is equally true for the mother and the father, as well as the child, an archetype Jung has written extensively about.[227] They have forever been with us and always been of great importance.

The same might be said about the archetype of the hero. There were tremendous challenges and ordeals that Stone Age people had to face, demanding both courage and commitment of heroic kind. Another central archetype is the sage (the old wise man), who may very well have been a frequent figure in society — at least since methods to express wisdom, by language or any other means of communication, were developed.

Celestial symbols, like the sun and the moon, were of course present all through our history, and human fascination with them is documented as far back as we have any sources. They also had crucial functions in human life, one bringing daylight and warmth, and the other giving some visibility to the dangerous night. They would need to be archetypes.

Jung regarded several animals as archetypes, each with its symbolic meaning in the collective unconscious. All of those animals were certainly around in Stone Age days, and maybe others that have become extinct since. Even trees, rivers, mountains, and other parts of nature have been with us all through the existence of our species.

But Jung has mentioned other archetypes, who were not that obviously relevant to Stone Age life. The trickster is a character popping up in many myths, but would that be a recognizable character in the Stone Age? In myths preserved by

---

[227] For example, "The Psychology of the Child Archetype," *The Collected Works of C. J. Jung*, volume 9 part 1, transl. R. F. C. Hull, Princeton 1968, pp. 151-181. The original text is from 1940.

hunter-gatherer societies today, the trickster often appears. That does not necessarily indicate a Stone Age origin, but it shows that the trickster can be a familiar concept within such a culture.

The maiden, the chaste young woman, on the other hand, is something that would probably have little relevance to the Stone Age. It is an ideal of much later date. On the other hand, if we see it simply as a prepubescent girl, then our distant ancestors could relate to the concept.

The important figure of the king was unheard of in Stone Age times, though a leader of the tribe was not, and that might be sort of the same in an archetypal perspective.

So, applying generous criteria, the bulk of Jungian archetypes could probably fit the Stone Age mind.

It should also be noted that Jung was persistent in pointing out that the words and images used to describe the archetypes are not the actual archetypes, but representations of them. The actual ones should be understood as symbolical principles, which need to take concrete forms in order for us to perceive and relate to them consciously. Accordingly, the child archetype is a representation of childhood as such, with its combination of innocence and potential. The anima is not the woman, but the concept of the female quality, whatever that is. And so on.

Seeing by Symbols

It is not by these archetype representations Jung commits an anachronism. It is by how he describes the underlying principles of the archetypes, what they are supposed to really mean. There, he is alarmingly stuck to his own European Christian background of the late 19th and early 20th century, as several examples earlier in this book show.

Still, that is no ground for dismissing his theory. He may be right about his basic principle, although he is mistaken when applying it.

It is Jung's claim of universality of the content of the collective unconscious that is the foremost weakness of his theory. If he allowed for the collective unconscious and its archetypes to be evolving and changing over time as well as in different cultures, like so much else of the human mind, his theory would be much more readily applicable. It would also open for alternative explanations to mechanisms behind it.

What he sees, which also the rest of us can observe, is a tendency in the human mind to make symbols out of significant experiences and pass them on, often making these symbols commonly recognized by the community we live in — sometimes shared by a whole civilization. It may be essential to how our minds work. We translate perceptional input into elements that tend to be generalized into symbols. Without this ability, we would drown in the constant flood of details from our senses. It is our way of sorting the world.

We can't meaningfully relate to every degree on the thermometer, but tend to divide temperatures into categories that worked already before the thermometer was invented — from freezing cold, through could, cool, warm, hot, to burning hot. We have always observed that there is a multitude of different animals in the world, but we grouped them according to our needs into pets, livestock, game, predators, and so on. As for other people, we have called them family or tribe or strangers.

No doubt, a primary intent with these generalizations has always been to identify useful and useless, and quickly decide what is harmless or harmful. We still show this behavior like a reflex, in the midst of our technologically complex society: is this useful or not, is it harmful or not? In children already at infancy, we see reactions based on experiences of pleasure and pain, or security and fear.

From these fundamental opposites, complexity has by time increased, but the basics remain — pain or pleasure, threat or asset. The symbols we create and share may be ever more numerous and varied, but that is still at the core.

Among Jung's archetypes is a hero but also a villain, a sage and a trickster, a self and a shadow. Jung often allows them to have both beneficial and detrimental traits, but this division is just another example of the basic need to sort the world into assets and threats.

When he speaks about their function as one of promoting a person to self-realization, he is jumping past the primary function of self-preservation. Everything instinctual, be it a bodily or a mental reflex, is first of all aimed at survival. Anything else can be regarded as a luxury in comparison, and must therefore be secondary.

Of course, by time the secondary can swell both in quantity and importance. That is one more reason for the need of allowing the content of Jung's collective unconscious not to be fixed, but evolving. Everything about every living creature is affected by the mechanics of evolution.

New Symbols Learned

One thing remains, though. Jung showed no convincing evidence for the archetypes being genetically inherited instead of adapted in social interaction. Except for a number of instincts governing bodily survival and procreation, what moves in our mind is what it learns from the surroundings and the experiences gained through life. There is no reason to assume that the archetypes were created in another way, far back in the past.

If we allow for significant symbols to be learned instead of inherited — as both Jung and Freud admit they had to be in the very beginning — there is no anomaly in the fact that we continue to adapt new such symbols as the world around us changes.

We have had a bundle of new symbols since the Stone Age ended, such as the prophet, the king, the martyr, the knight, the maiden, the executioner, the philosopher, the lawyer, the tyrant, and the genius, to name but a few. Also, non-animate symbols like the castle, the throne, the sword, the prison, the tomb, money, the temple, the tower, and the bridge. We keep on adding symbols filled with meaning, like the bomb, the ro-

bot, the rocket, the space alien, the celebrity, the oligarch, the
terrorist, the expert, the laboratory, the morgue, the detective,
the computer, and so on.

The way we relate to these post-Stone Age symbols is in
no significant way different from how Jung described the influence and functions of the archetypes. Actually, many of the
archetypes Jung mentioned in his writing connect more readily
to agrarian society, even specifically to Medieval Europe, than
to the Stone Age.

Certainly, several of the symbols introduced after the
Stone Age can be described as merely new forms of old archetypes. For example, the king is a larger version of the tribal
chief. The prophet, the philosopher, the genius, and the expert
can be called versions of the sage. The martyr, the knight, and
the detective are easily compared to the hero. But there are significant differences between the ancient archetypes and the
later versions.

Compared to the tribal chief, the king is elevated on his
throne, far away from his subjects, almost as a god of sorts.
That would be unfathomable to the members of a Stone Age
tribe.

And to the tribe, the sage would be the one with sound
advice for anyone so wishing, whereas the prophet demands
departure from the ways of the present, the philosopher becomes all but incomprehensible and drifts away from reality
into theory, like the expert, and the genius has no interest in
either giving or receiving advice, consumed instead with
whatever quest that person's talent suggests.

Although the sources to the later symbols might be found
also in Stone Age reality, the differences are often so extensive
that it is hardly meaningful to treat them as identical. And several of the later symbols simply do not have any counterparts
in the Stone Age, such as the prison, money, the robot, the
bomb, and the computer.

Obsolete Archetypes

Now, if there are new archetypes appearing as the world changes, the question that follows is if old ones disappear from our minds. If archetypes losing their meaning to us fade away, then the obvious conclusion must be that they are learned instead of genetically inherited.

It is hard to test, though. The world has indeed changed since the Stone Age, but by adding and not by subtracting. There is still the cyclic shift between night and day, with the moon and the sun parading in the sky. There are still women and men and children, people we know and those who are strangers, trees and seas and mountains. The world seen in the Stone Age is still here, though covered to a large extent by things our ancestors could never have imagined.

None of the archetypes Jung mentioned in his writing have become completely obsolete. Our minds can still relate meaningfully to them. That is in itself no surprise. Jung could not have mentioned archetypes no longer relevant at the time of his writing, or he would by that have contradicted his own thesis. He would not make that mistake, but if he had made it, his theory would have been dismissed and soon forgotten.

So, to test Jung's claim of the archetypes being forever planted in our minds, which means they must be transmitted genetically, we should search for symbols not mentioned by Jung, but significant enough to Stone Age humans to qualify as Jungian archetypes. Such symbols would be the anomalies in Jung's paradigm.

As discussed above, the most obvious ones would be those that dealt with longings or fears, assets or threats. Symbols of those kinds would have been the most deeply engraved in Stone Age minds, and therefore unquestionable archetypes. And of the two, symbols connected to fear would have been the most insistent, since they represented imminent threats to survival — real or imagined.

Some fears we definitely share with our Stone Age ancestors, such as those of natural catastrophe, big predators, or the outbreak of fire. They are still dangerous to us. But we have new fears, unimaginable in the Stone Age, and there are things we have stopped fearing due to measures eliminating the threats or to learning that they were no threats to begin with.

The Chapman University conducts an annual survey on the fears of USA inhabitants. More than a thousand adults are asked to grade each item on a long list of different kinds of fear. The results vary considerably from year to year. Comparing 2015 results to those of 2020-2021, shows this clearly.[228]

At the top of both is the fear of corrupt government, but only 58% of Americans held that fear in 2015, whereas 80% did so in 2020-2021. After that, the lists have little in common. In 2015, several of the top fears dealt with Internet threats to integrity and personal economy, whereas the list of 2020-2021 to no surprise is topped by health fears related to Covid-19. The fear of global warming rose from 31% to 49%.

In the 2015 list, a fear that would have been recognized and shared by people of the Stone Age, that of illness, comes at the 14th place (feared by 34%). Already at the 2nd place in the later survey, is a fear known also in the Stone Age — that of loved ones dying (59%), surely due to the pandemic. The 2015 survey lacks this alternative, but in 2017 it was on the 17th place with 40%. The fear of one's own dying rose modestly from 22% in 2015 to 29% in 2020-2021.

People worry about their health more than their death, but they worry significantly more about the health of their loved ones. Human beings are compassionate, which is something far too often underestimated or even ignored.

Although we will definitely all die, the risk of it happening before old age is so reduced that the Reaper is nowadays a figure of comedy rather than horror. But it would be vastly premature to dismiss death and its symbolic representation as an obsolete archetype. When we are reminded of it, it speaks

[228] *The Chapman University Survey of American Fears*, chapman.edu, 2015 and 2021.

to us loud and clear — as in the case of the Covid-19 pandemic.

In the 2020-2021 survey, apart from the health-related issues, fears that would have been recognized in the Stone Age include those of heights (31%), reptiles (25%), spiders and other insects (23%), strangers (11%), and animals (5%). Percentages might have differed in the Stone Age, but these fears were definitely not absent back then. The question here, though, is what fears of that distant past have disappeared since.

To find completely obsolete fears of the Stone Age, we must look for threats that we have eliminated or those that were based on superstition.

In the latter category, there is one spectacular celestial phenomenon that terrified our ancestors, but does not worry us in the least — the solar eclipse. Historically, it was seen as an ill-boding omen, and before that it must have created a sense of imminent doom. Nowadays, it is merely an amusement.

The eclipse has lost just about all of its ghastliness, which was considerable in the past. Celestial phenomena left people in awe, since they were as incomprehensible as they were spectacular. The latter they still are, as entertainment we are prepared to travel long distances to experience. The archetype of it is not extinct, but it has lost all its potency. We keep it as sort of a museum piece, reminding us of the fear out of ignorance it induced in our ancestors.

To a lesser extent, this might also be said about lunar eclipses.

The comet, though, is a different story altogether. Its appearance frightened our ancestors and continued to do so into modern times. As late as 1910, Halley's Comet created quite some panic when spectroscopic analysis found that its tail, which the earth passed through, contained toxic gas. The New York Times reported that the French astronomer Camille Flammarion was "of the opinion that the cyanogen gas would impregnate the atmosphere and possibly snuff out all life on the planet."

The article also mentioned that most astronomers did not agree with him.[229]

Comets still induce awe in us as visible reminders of the many meteors, hidden in the dark space, which may collide with earth and really "snuff out all life." This is a possible catastrophe that science has discovered, which was unknown in the Stone Age. The superstition has become real.

As for celestial phenomena closer to the ground, such as thunder and lightning, they can be scary today, too, but not to the extent they were before we found their explanations. They still function as archetypes, symbols to which we attach a lot of meanings, but they have lost their ability to terrify us like in the past, and therefore also most of their symbolic significance. Dark clouds covering the sky do not make us crouch, thunder is no overture to doom, and lightning is diverted by a rod. Today, most threats that appear in the sky are man-made.

Returning to the subject of death, there is one alternative suggested by the folklorist James George Frazer — the fear of the dead. He devoted a book to it in 1933, where he claimed that this fear was a prime source in primitive religion.[230]

Its importance can be discussed, but as Frazer shows in his book there are numerous indications in mythology and ancient beliefs, especially those of hunter-gatherer cultures, of the dead being highly revered and also feared. Ancestor worship was widespread.

As Sigmund Freud suggested, it might even have been the beginning of the belief in deities. He claimed it to be the result of guilt feelings after a patricide, but that addition is not necessary. With or without such a drama, the dead were very much present in the minds of our ancestors.

To what extent this should be primarily regarded as a fear is another matter, but it is frequently occurring in mythologies,

[229] "Comet's Poisonous Tail," *The New York Times*, 1910 (nytimes.com).

[230] James George Frazer, *The Fear of the Dead in Primitive Religion*, London 1933, p. v.

old and new, that the ones worshipped should be feared for what they might cause if not pleased. The worship often had the character of being a manner of pleasing the deities in order to appease them. Sacrifices and such were acts of fear instead of adoration.

Ancient attitudes towards the dead were similar in many cultures. Deities or not, they were to be feared. Maybe that might even have been a reason for burying them, which was practiced already in the Stone Age. It could have been an effort to imprison the dead, so that they could not hurt the living. The funeral pyres of some cultures might have had the same original intent. That is, of course, pure speculation.

But the fear of the dead has been persistent. We know it in the Western world as fear of ghosts, which still remains with a few of us. In the Chapman University survey discussed above, it holds the 88th position with 9% confessing to it. The fear also has a modern version in the zombie of Haitian folklore, popularized in fiction. It has the same percentage as that of ghosts. Nowadays, though, fictional zombies tend to be created by biological warfare or some kind of plague, rather than by waking the dead.

It is still safe to say that the fear of the dead, indicated by ancient mythology and rituals, is something we have left behind. Wandering skeletons, ghosts, and roaming undead have joined the solar eclipse in becoming entertainment. The archetype of the dead, which would most definitely have fit Jung's concept not that very long ago, has lost its gravity and thereby also its significance — at least for most of us.

The above is not evidence solid enough to dismiss Jung's theory of genetically inherited archetypes, but the variation of fears through time very strongly suggests that symbols of them are upheld and communicated consciously by people, and not rooted in a hidden and inaccessible unconscious. It is a solution closer at hand, and supported by observable facts.

Stone Age Individuation

Jung's collective unconscious and its content of archetypes have a defined purpose — that of individuation, which is self-realization. Although this unconscious is explicitly collective, the definitions of the archetypes zoom in on the personal. Within each psyche they speak to that particular individual.

This focus on the personal makes Jung's psychological cosmos very individualistic indeed. The human being may share fundamental parts of the psyche with all the others of the species, but its function is to extract and define what is individual — it works to strengthen the sense of I as opposed to we.

But would that be relevant and desirable, even at all understandable, to people of the Stone Age?

A common present-day strife is to be unique, but also to belong. Our names are clear symbols of this. We have a first name, which is given us by our parents but still points out our personal uniqueness, and a family name, showing that we belong to a defined group. It creates a basis for our two-sided worldview — the inner identity with its continuous processing of emotions and thought, and the outer environment to which we relate but are still always separate from. Each modern human is at the very center of their own universe.

Jung's model speaks relevantly to this perception of existence. We can relate to the principle of examining ourselves in order to define our uniqueness, i.e., the needs and abilities of our own personalities, not to get lost in what is expected of us and thereby becoming little more than identical puppets, as if we were all clones from the same genetic donor.

But Jung's claim that the content of the collective unconscious is constant and shared by all demands that this individualistic urge was true already in the Stone Age. Otherwise, it would have been irrelevant at the time of its formation, and could hardly remain. Evolution is not clairvoyant.

It is hard, maybe impossible, to prove if Stone Age people had a strong individualistic urge or not. At least it is rather safe to assume that in the tribal life of the hunter-gatherers of that era, belonging was far more important than standing out.

Again, the instinct of self-preservation gives a hint. In those days, the individual had little chance of survival outside the group. Exposed to all the life-threatening dangers in the surroundings, the tribe was a much better protection than anyone could muster on his own, no matter how capable and fierce. Also, hunting was not easily done alone.

If we assume that Stone Age hunter-gatherer societies were similar to those studied in our time, the strength of the collective was expressed in the structure of tribal life. A major example of this is the habit of reciprocity, the equal sharing of food and other necessities. It is almost universally present in hunter-gatherer societies.[231] Those who deviated from the reciprocal sharing, the freeloaders, were despised and cast out if they persisted.

Given the vital importance of individual adaption to the tribe in Stone Age life, it would be more likely for the content of a collective unconscious formed in those times to lead the individual towards higher identification with others, increasing the sense of belonging, than the opposite. Individuation, as a path of differentiation from fellow humans, would have been detrimental to the chance of survival. So, it would have little chance of being inherited in humankind.

It also means that an instinctual behavior towards blending and identifying with others to increase a mutual sense of belonging is likely. Certainly, also our modern world shows many signs of it.

What Jung describes as the individuation process is much more relevant to the last few centuries, especially in the Western world, than ever before. The idea of the genius is an illustration of this. The present meaning of the word genius for an individual talent, standing out remarkably from others, ap-

---

[231] Richard B. Lee and Richard Daly, ed., *The Cambridge Encyclopedia of Hunters and Gatherers*, Cambridge 1999, p. 4.

peared in the 18th century. The *Encyclopédie* writes this about the genius in 1757:

> *The man of genius is he whose soul is more expansive and struck by the feelings of all others; interested by all that is in nature never to receive an idea unless it evokes a feeling; everything excites him and on which nothing is lost.*[232]

What follows is a long praise of the uniqueness and exceptional ability of the genius, and it ends with this humble remark by the writer:

> *Its definition is best left to the person himself to speak of himself and this article which I should not have written should have been the work of one of these extraordinary men who honor this century and to recognize genius would only have had to look at himself.*

The word existed long before the days of the Enlightenment, but it did not stress a difference of one individual from all others. There was no sense of humans at the very core of their being standing out from others. Rather, it was seen as a resource or ability within all. The Roman origin of the term is mythological, signifying a generative and protecting spirit of which every man had one from birth. Women had the counterpart Juno.[233]

In German Romanticism of the 19th century, the concept of the genius as someone outstanding, elevated above normal human capacity, was adapted and propagated. The major inspi-

---

[232] Jean-François de Saint-Lambert (ascribed), "Genius," *The Encyclopedia of Diderot & d'Alembert Collaborative Translation Project*, transl. John S.D. Glaus, Ann Arbor 2007 (umich.edu). From *Encyclopédie ou Dictionnaire raisonné des sciences, des arts et des métiers*, volume 7, Paris, 1757, pp. 582-584.

[233] *The Encyclopædia Britannica*, 11th edition, volume XI, New York 1910, pp. 594f.

ration to this view was Immanuel Kant. In his book *Critique of Judgement* (*Kritik der Urteilskraft*) from 1790, he described the character and modus operandi of the genius. It is not hard to see how his description attracted the German romantics.

According to Kant, only artists can be geniuses. Not scientists, since they are bound by reason, and anything they conclude can be explained completely to others, as can the process to that conclusion. The genius, on the other hand, "does not know himself how he has come by his Ideas." The genius needs to be free of boundaries. It is even Kant's primary definition, "genius is a talent for producing that for which no definite rule can be given."[234]

Kant states firmly that "beautiful Art is only possible as a product of Genius." Such art cannot be repeated by others, not even completely appreciated by anyone but another genius. This was also what the text in the *Encyclopédie* humbly admitted.

Such conditions separate the genius all but completely from the rest of humankind. It does, though, approach Jung's idea of the individuation process of finding oneself and one's own uniqueness, no matter what social norms dictate. Jung showed in his writing a fondness for larger-than-life characters that would qualify as geniuses. Two stand out: Johann Wolfgang von Goethe, especially his *Faust*, and Friedrich Nietzsche, especially his *Also sprach Zarathustra*. They are mentioned and discussed numerous times in many of Jung's texts, always with profound praise.

He also expressed a view on the genius particularly interesting in this context:

*One might expect, perhaps, that a man full of genius could
pasture in the greatness of his own thoughts, and renounce
the cheap approbation of the crowd which he despises; yet*

[234] Immanuel Kant, *Kritik of Judgment*, transl. J. H. Bernard, London 1892, p. 189.

*he succumbs to the more powerful impulse of the herd in-
stinct. His searching and his finding, his call, belong to the
herd.*[235]

Clearly to Jung this is a tragedy. The individual succumbs
to the herd. Jung would have it the other way around, which
is precisely what his individuation process is supposed to accomplish. But it would be just about as far as one could get
from the Stone Age mind.

[235] Jung, *Psychology of the Unconscious*, p. 16.

Archetypes Beyond Jung

According to Jung, the archetypes are clues to self-realization in myths and many other cultural phenomena, as well as in the depth of the individual mind. Although the term is not his own invention, he used it in an elaborate way in his theories on psychology and culture, giving it his own specific meaning.

The word is from the Greek *arkhetupon*, which means first mold or model, in the meaning of being the initial version of something later multiplied. That would nowadays be called a prototype.

The word is made up of *arkhos*, meaning beginning, origin, or first, which also implies a ruler, and *tupos*, meaning mold, model, type, or imprint.

Although the term would fit Plato's theory of Forms splendidly, he never used the word archetype specifically. Nor did Aristotle, as far as I have found. Others have certainly done so, when discussing Plato's theory.

The first one to make substantial use of the word in his philosophy was Philo of Alexandria in the 1st century CE. As a Hellenized Jew, he compared the cosmology of *Genesis* to that of Plato. When commenting that man was created after the image of god and in his likeness, Philo wrote:

> *Let no one represent the likeness as one to a bodily form; for neither is God in human form, nor is the human body God-like. No, it is in respect of the Mind, the sovereign element of the soul, that the word "image" is used; for after the pattern of a single Mind, even the Mind of the Universe as an archetype, the mind in each of those who successively came into being was moulded.*[236]

[236] Philo, "On the Account of the World's Creation," *Philo I*, transl. F. H. Colson and G. H. Whitaker, Loeb 226, London 1929, p. 55.

The following century, Irenaeus, who was bishop of Lyon, wrote about a cosmogony where the world was not created by god but by the demiurge who copied an archetypal world, called the *Pleroma*. He discarded the idea as fiction, and traced this thinking to Democritus and Plato:

For Democritus first says, that many and various figures, copied from the Universe, descended into this world. But Plato again speaks of Matter and the Archetype, and God. And they, following them, have styled his Ideas and his Archetype, Images of the things on high: under this change of name boasting themselves to be inventors and framers of the aforesaid imaginary fiction.[237]

Yet another century later, the 3rd, we find the Neoplatonist philosopher Plotinus, who used the term archetype frequently. Primarily, he saw it as the perfect shape by which the world took its form. Therefore, it belongs in the realm of thought and not in the imperfect material world. Actually, the world is really one of thought:

This universe is a living thing capable of including every form of life; but its Being and its modes are derived from elsewhere; that source is traced back to the Intellectual-Principle: it follows that the all-embracing archetype is in the Intellectual Principle, which, therefore, must be an intellectual Cosmos, that indicated by Plato in the phrase 'The living existent'.[238]

Plotinus spoke of different archetypes, or aspects of the archetypal, in a manner slightly approaching that of Jung. He

[237] Irenaeus, "Against Heresies," *Five Books of S. Irenaeus*, transl. John Kemble, Oxford 1872, p. 130.

[238] Plotinus, *The Enneads*, transl. Stephen MacKenna, revised by B. S. Page, London 1956, p. 440.

even insisted that there was an ideal archetype of evil.[239] He also expressed a wish for us humans to become archetypes, by which we would be practically divine:

> *To me, moreover, it seems that if we ourselves were archetypes, Ideas, veritable Being, and the Idea with which we construct here were our veritable Essence, then our creative power, too, would toillessly effect its purpose: as man now stands, he does not produce in his work a true image of himself: become man, he has ceased to be the All; ceasing to be man — we read — 'he soars aloft and administers the Cosmos entire'; restored to the All he is maker of the All.*[240]

Jung's use of the term may be less aloft, but still comparably fanciful.

Acted Archetypes

Archetype is a term also used for something much profaner than the fabric of the cosmos and the manner of its emergence. In fiction of all kinds, archetypes are basic stereotype characters easily recognizable by the audience. They are also with a modern term called stock characters.

With these prototype figures of the stage and the story, there are many similarities to the archetype content of Jung's collective unconscious. Even more so, the patterns can be found in the characters peopling mythology.

We are quite familiar with them as they appear in plays, novels, and movies. It is like we know them at the moment they are introduced, which is exactly the intention of the writer. Through these archetypes, the plot has a flying start. It is sort of like chess, where the 32 pieces and their abilities are known from the start. The game can commence immediately.

Any story, especially when performed by actors, needs

[239] Ibid., p. 440.
[240] Ibid., p. 428.

easily recognizable characters that generally behave as expected in any given situation. Without them, the story would be as complicated for the audience to grasp as it would be for them to adapt to a strange land and connect with its people.

We are all quick to spot the protagonist and the antagonist, who are usually — but not always — the hero and the villain of the story. Still, they are not exactly archetypes in this meaning. But if the protagonist is gallant and compassionate, whereas the antagonist is traitorous and malevolent, then they approach the archetypal. It is not the function in the plot that makes a stock character, but how recognizable the traits of that character are.

In comedy, they are often exaggerated to the point of being caricatures, but in drama the character traits can be subtler and their complexity increase as the story unfolds. The stock character is a starting point, an introduction. As the drama deepens, so can the characters.

Aristotle was the first one to write a significant text on the theory of drama, which was in his *Poetics*, mentioned earlier. Although well aware of the importance of the characters in the play, he never used the word archetype nor presented any examples of what we would call stock characters. To him, action was what mattered. Characters were defined by the choices they made, especially those of moral kind.

Therefore, he really recognized just two kinds of characters — the vicious and the virtuous, "it is through vice and virtue that the characters of all men vary."[241] This variation is in comparison to us, so that they represent "people better than our normal level, worse than it, or much the same."

Yet, he regarded a drama as superior if the characters in it acted out of necessity, making the only choices that were accessible to them. In that, they should follow the same rule as that of a good plot:

[241] Aristotle, *Poetics*, 1448a, p. 33.

*With character, precisely as in the structure of events, one
should always seek necessity or probability — so that for
such a person to say or do such things is necessary or probable, and the sequence of events is also necessary or probable.*[242]

Thereby, their characters were formed by what happened
to them, and not by some fixed qualities of their psyche. It is a
wise principle, since we can all recognize it in our own lives.
So much of what we do is not optional, but forced upon us by
circumstance. We rarely have the free choice we would wish,
especially not in times of crisis.

In our actions, we are frequently victims of circumstance.
That is how Jeppe defends his drinking in the 18th century com-
edy *Jeppe on the Hill* by the Danish playwright Ludvig Holberg.
Jeppe's major but far from only gripe is his wife:

*Folks around here say that Jeppe drinks, but they don't say
why Jeppe drinks; why, I never got so many poundings in
the ten years I was in the army as I get every day from that
awful woman. She pounds me, the overseer drives me to
work like a beast; and the sexton pays court to my wife.
Mustn't I drink, mustn't I use all the means nature has
given us to drive away sorrow?*[243]

Theophrastus, the philosopher taking over the Lyceum
when Aristotle had to flee Athens, wrote extensively about
character, famously so in *Characters*, a text devoted to the subject. Like his teacher, he did not use the word archetype,
though in his treatment of the subject it would have made
sense. In his descriptions of different kinds of personalities, he

---

[242] Ibid., 1454a, p. 81.

[243] Ludvig Holberg, *Jeppe on the Hill*, transl. Waldemar C. Westergaard &
Martin B. Ruud, Grand Forks 1906 (originally written in Danish 1722), p.
18.

presented a number of what we would call stock characters and this has inspired others in his posterity to do the same.

The dramatist Menander, who was one of his students, used such character types in his many comedies. He may even have participated in the creation of the text.

Theophrastus was not talking about characters of fiction, but about real people. Still, his text had a significant influence on the emergence of stock characters in drama and other storytelling. His text goes through 30 such characters, which are mainly described from a moral standpoint, "the manners of each several kind of men both good and bad."[244]

Upon inspection, all the 30 characters definitely belong to the bad kind. This has led to disputed speculations about a second part of the text, dealing with good characters, to be sadly missing.

If so, it has a parallel to Aristotle's text on comedy being lost, whereas the one on tragedy remains. It would seem that misfortune is more persistent than the opposite.

It is a colorful gallery of types that Theophrastus has assembled. To name but a few: arrogance, backbiting, buffoonery, cowardice, dissembling, nastiness, pretentiousness, stupidity, superstitiousness, and unconscionableness (shamelessness). The descriptions of the characters are vigorous and straightforward.

There is also a sense of humor over the whole text project. This is said about the oligarch, a character not unknown to us in present days: "The one and only line of Homer's he knows is this: 'Tis ill that many rule; give one man sway.'"[245]

Here is how Theophrastus starts his description of loquacity (talkativeness):

[244] Theophrastus, *The Characters of Theophrastus*, transl. J. M. Edmonds, Loeb 225N, London 1929, pp. 37f. The translator also suggests "of either kind of men."

[245] Ibid., p. 109.

*Loquacity, should you wish to define it, would seem to be
an incontinence of speech; and the Loquacious man will say
to any that meets him, if he but open his lips, 'You are
wrong; I know all about it, and if you will listen to me you
shall learn the truth.'*[246]

Not only for the talkative does Theophrastus give examples of what they would say. He does so with each character, and it is quite amusing. A playwright would absolutely enjoy getting ideas and inspiration from this text. It is sure to have happened. Many of those character quotes sound familiar, indeed.

The descriptions of behaviors are also recognizable and amusing. Arrogance is defined as "the despising of all the world but yourself," and the arrogant "will go speak to no man before the other speak to him."[247] This is what to expect of the coward:

*When he is serving on land and the troops are going into
action, he will call his messmates and bid them all first stop
and look about them; it is so difficult to tell which is the
enemy; and then when he hears cries and sees men falling,
he remarks to the men next to him that in his haste he forgot to take up his sword, and runs to the tent, and sending
his man out with orders to reconnoitre, hides it under his
pillow and then spends a long time pretending to seek for
it.*[248]

It continues with the coward happily tending to a wounded friend, so that he needs not return to battle, later showing off the friend's blood on his shirt and claiming to have saved his life at personal peril.

[246] Ibid., p. 57.
[247] Ibid., p. 103.
[248] Ibid., p. 107.

Surely, to many writers *The Characters* has been a splendid source of ideas. To Theophrastus it was probably mainly done in jest. That would explain why he might not have gotten around to writing about good characters. They are not as much fun to portray as the bad ones. Every writer knows.

The sketches of Atellan fables in ancient Rome, where the subject was given in advance but the dialogue was improvised, contained a set of stock characters: "There was the old man (Pappus), the old woman, the comic slave (Centunculus), the country booby (Buccus), the arrogant soldier (Manducus), the pompous doctor (Dossenus), and the sharp-tongued hooked nosed hunchback (Maccus)."[249]

The Roman playwright Plautus of the late 3rd and early 2nd centuries BC used stock characters inspired mainly by Greek comedy. They included *senex iratus*, the grumpy old man, *adulescens amator*, they young lover, *servus callidus*, the clever slave, *parasitus*, the parasite flatterer, *meretrix*, the courtesan, and *miles gloriosus*, the boasting soldier.[250]

In Renaissance Italy, commedia dell'arte used a partly similar set of stock characters: the greedy old Pantalone, the skillful servant Arlecchino (Harlequin), the boasting Capitano, the two young Innamorati (lovers), the pompous Dottore, the cunning servant Colombina, among others.[251]

William Shakespeare made some use of stock characters, especially in his comedies but also in comedic roles of his tragedies. But he not only deepened and expanded these characters — he could also reverse their behaviors, so that the fool showed profound wisdom, the vicious villain revealed compassion of sorts, and the lovers could burst into moments of

---

[249] Michael Byrom, *Punch and Judy: Its Origin and Evolution*, London 1978, p. 4.

[250] George E. Duckworth, *The Nature of Roman Comedy: A Study in Popular Entertainment*, Princeton 1952, pp. 237ff.

[251] Winifred Smith, *The Commedia Dell'Arte: A Study in Italian Popular Comedy*, New York 1912, pp. 5ff.

hate. Hollywood movies, though, often regress to the flat stock characters of ancient comedies and Theophrastus.

The basic role of the stock character is not to represent a certain personality, but to serve a function in the plot. The old miser stands in the way of the union of the lovers, and the clever servant helps them solve the problem since they are themselves all too obsessed with their love to think straight. That brings us back to Aristotle and his principle of the characters being subordinate to the story.

This is a structure easily found also in mythology. *Servus callidus*, the clever slave of Plautus, and Colombina of commedia dell'arte are cousins to the trickster in many myths, who is the one fooling even the gods for one or other purpose — often to the gain of humans. And gods are frequently behaving much like *senex iratus* and Pantalone, sabotaging human fortune. Yahweh has been known to do the same.

Looking at the easily recognized stock characters of theater and myth, where they carry distinct functions in the development of the plot, the term archetype makes sense — also from a Jungian perspective. Jung described the archetypes as symbols in the process of individuation. That is not so far from the tours and detours before the lovers in a play finally can embrace. The archetypes are means towards a goal.

And Then Some

Jung's use of the term archetype is similar at first glance to the stock character. He repeatedly refers to such fictional type-roles as archetypes, the hero being the one most frequently used. But to Jung they are far more than recognizable characters. In fact, they are not at all characters, essentially, but something as fancy as symbolic keys to truths about human condition and to the path of personal enlightenment.

Jung's archetypes can reveal the workings of the world as to how it affects the human psyche, and what man should do to accomplish something or for that matter ward something off. They are learning tools, lessons from primordial time, answers included. And they do more than that, as stated in the last essay Jung wrote, *Symbols and the Interpretation of Dreams* from 1961:

> *Archetypes create myths, religions, and philosophical ideas that influence and set their stamp on whole nations and epochs.*[252]

Jung's archetypes are not limited to characters. There are also animal archetypes, like the serpent and the lion, and objects functioning as archetypes, like gold or a castle or a forest. There is a multitude of archetypes — some known, many others yet to be discovered. Jung allows for an unlimited number of them, stating in a 1936 lecture, "There are as many archetypes as there are typical situations in life."[253]

It might be best compared to mathematical components, such as *pi* or the *x* of an equation. An archetype is like *pi* in the sense that it has a fixed value, but its applications are just about endless. It is like the *x* of an equation in the way that it is the solution to a given problem — if that problem is significant enough.

Archetypes carry meanings for the human mind to decipher and utilize. Jung, too, associates the concept to formula:

> *The archetype is a symbolical formula, which always begins to function whenever there are no conscious ideas present, or when such as are present are impossible upon intrinsic or extrinsic grounds.*[254]

[252] Carl G. Jung, *The Undiscovered Self: with Symbols and the Interpretation of Dreams*, transl. R.F.C. Hull, Princeton 2010, p. 118.

[253] Carl G. Jung, "The Concept of the Collective Unconscious," *The Collected Works of C. G. Jung*, volume 9:1, Princeton 1969, p. 48.

[254] Carl G. Jung, *Psychological Types*, transl. H. Godwin Baynes, London 1923, p. 476.

In a text from 1938 he compares the archetypes to "the axial system of a crystal, which, as it were, preforms the crystalline structure in the mother liquid, although it has no material existence of its own."[255] This shows a resemblance to Plato's world of Ideas and theory of Forms, where physical manifestations are but inferior copies of the ideal forms, which are the only things completely real, giving meaning to everything in this world.

Since the archetypes are symbolic components rather than objects or persons, they are discovered by their function instead of their attire. A symbolic element that reappears in many a myth from separate cultures or time-periods, and seems to contain some kind of significance in those stories, is in the Jungian perspective most certainly an archetype:

An image can be considered archetypal when it can be shown to exist in the records of human history, in identical form and with the same meaning.[256]

Not only that, but in Jung's world, an archetype contains such potency that it is archetypal, wherever it appears. Its symbolic function emerges, even when that was not intended by its user in that specific case. It is also this primordial potency of the archetypes that makes them attractive and exciting, wherever they appear. People are drawn to archetypes, often obsessed by them, whether they know of their Jungian function or not. They feel a resonance from their unconscious, recognizing and being stimulated by the archetype.

So, where do archetypes come from? How do they appear and remain? Jung is not very talkative about it, but his expla-

[255] Carl G. Jung, "Psychological Aspects of the Mother Archetype," transl. R. F. C. Hull, *The Collected Works of C. G. Jung*, volume 9:1, Princeton 1969, p. 79.

[256] Carl G. Jung, "The Philosophical Tree" (1954), transl. R. F. C. Hull, *The Collected Works of C. G. Jung*, volume 13, Princeton 1983, p. 323.

nation is quite identical to that of Freud about how memories get incorporated into the archaic heritage — by repetitious experience. Jung imagines the same for archetypes:

> *It seems to me that their origin can be explained in no other way than by regarding them as the deposits of the oft-repeated experiences of humanity.*[257]

List of Jungian Archetypes

Jung made it clear that it is impossible to make a complete list of archetypes, since many of them are yet to be discovered. He never even suggested a listing. The closest I have seen him come to one is in the essay "Archetypes of the Collective Unconscious," originally published in 1935, discussed earlier in this book.

It is far from complete, but it goes through a number of archetypes and their respective roles in the individuation process.

Not only are the archetypes countless, but some of them can be seen as examples of more fundamental ones, or a sort of mix of other archetypes. It is not a very orderly universe.

So, here are just some of the archetypes mentioned by Jung and his followers, together with my own attempts at shortly explaining them:

- *The hero*, who pursues a great quest to realize his destiny;
- *The self*, the personality striving towards its own complete realization;
- *The shadow*, the amoral remnant of our instinctual animal past;
- *The persona*, the mask and pretense we show others;

[257] Carl G. Jung, "The Unconscious in the Normal and Pathological Mind," transl. H. G. and C. F. Baynes, *Two Essays on Analytical Psychology*, London 1928, p. 71 (footnote).

- *The anima and animus*, our female and male roles and urges;
- *The mother*, primarily in the sense of our need of her;
- *The father*, primarily an authority figure often inducing fear;
- *The child*, our innocent beginning with all our potential in front of us;
- *The sage*, or wise old man, one who has the profound knowledge;
- *The god*, the perfect image of the Self;
- *The goddess*, the great mother, or Mother Earth;
- *The trickster*, a rascal agent pushing us towards change;
- *The hermaphrodite*, the joiner of opposites;
- *The beast*, a representation of the primitive past of man;
- *The scapegoat*, suffering the shortcomings of others;
- *The fool*, wandering off in confusion and faulty directions;
- *The artist*, the visionary and inspired way of approaching truth;
- *Mana* and other concepts of spiritual energy;
- *Mandala*, symbol of self-realization;
- *The journey*, a representation of the quest towards self-realization;
- *Life, death and rebirth*, the cyclic nature of existence;
- *Light and dark*, images of the conscious and the unconscious;
- *The tree*, the growth towards self-fulfillment;
- *Water*, the unconscious and the emotions;
- *The wizard*, knowledgeable of the hidden and of transformation needed.

In addition, Jung has mentioned several animals as representing archetypes for different stages of transformation, such as the bird, frog, horse, wolf, bull, lion, spider, and the serpent, the last of which is akin to the dragon of myths.

There are also numerous inanimate archetypes, like the

crossing, cross, circle, wheel, square, star, egg, sun, and the prison.

The foremost of archetypes is the hero, who bravely overcomes great difficulty in order to realize his destiny. He could be described as a role-model, urging each of us to go ahead and pursue our own quest. Freud, too, put significant emphasis on the hero of myth and lore.

Jung's hero meets with certain characters, events, and obstacles on his quest. Those are often recognizable from one myth to another, and they are archetypes as well. The hero myth is the ultimate formula of self-realization, wherefore it is central in Jung's treatments on myth.

Other myths — even such of seemingly greater magnitude, like those of creation, the flood, or apocalypse — could more or less be seen as components of the hero myth, symbolizing certain premises or necessary processes of the hero quest.

Nothing Mysterious

One thing about the list above is noteworthy. There is nothing mysterious about those archetypes and their meanings. Whether this should be interpreted as support for Jung's theory or dismissal of it is another matter.

What is sure is that it takes no hidden unconscious to come up with a protective mother, an authoritarian father, an innocent child with its future ahead of it, an old person who has attained wisdom, a king who is to be feared, a brave hero who is the model for us all, a mask of pretense to make us look good, the beast inside us that might run amok, and so on.

The same goes for how we perceive and relate to different animals, objects, and natural phenomena. These images and the values we attribute to them can easily have been formed by our conscious minds. No obscure process is needed to explain them.

Actually, if they were the creations of hidden archaic remnants, should they not be less obvious to us? A secret compartment in our minds should contain bigger secrets than that mothers are usually protective and fathers usually demand obedience. We already know that. Much of what Jung's collective unconscious keeps in its vault is trivial, in no need to be kept from our conscious. It is already there.

The archetypes would be so much more intriguing — and charged — if they were less obvious and more mysterious, even contradictory to our conscious understanding.

At least, there should be the idea of a threatening mother and a devoted father. Our conscious minds know that they exist, as well. Or, to approach Jung's idea of the individuation process, the mother as the straitjacket, though cozy, hampering that process, and the father, though aggressively demanding, encouraging it. Jung was certainly aware of these alternatives.

As so often with the human nature, there are multiple possibilities, and they may differ tremendously. Our psyche is one of contradictions. We are neither that very rational nor completely irrational. Maybe we are best described as rationally irrational or irrationally rational. Somehow, our thoughts, emotions, and actions make sense to us, but the route to that conclusion is winding.

Still, the whole voyage needed to find it out can be traveled in the conscious mind, just as the archetypes Jung spoke of can have taken their shape there. Otherwise, they would not be so readily comprehensible to the conscious.

What some of Jung's archetypes represent might be more of a challenge for the conscious to grasp, even thought the symbols of them are no strangers. In those cases, it is evident that the symbols could even more readily be explained without the use of a hidden unconscious.

For example, *the self* is a term with a lot of implied meanings in Jung's psychology, but it boils down to the age-old human awareness of existing as an individual, the "I am" of Yahweh as well as Descartes. What I am, precisely, might be a mystery to me, but not that I am. Without that awareness, we would be objects instead of subjects, unreachable to others as well as to ourselves.

The *anima* and *animus* are curiosities if we regard humans as either men or women, and nothing in between. But biology has proven that this is not the case. We are humans, firstly and mainly. Gender is not just binary in our biology, and a lot of it is socially formed. To his credit, these two of Jung's archetypes point out a complexity in gender that science has gradually revealed in just the last few decades. But they are better explained by biological diversity and social conformity, than by some unconscious entities. The tensions these factors can create in the human psyche are completely accessible to the conscious mind, though for many still a struggle.

Another pair of opposites, *light* and *dark*, which to Jungians represent the conscious and the unconscious, is a very widespread couple in all kinds of cosmologies. It can be compared to the Chinese yang and yin, to heaven and earth in so many mythologies, or the upper world and the netherworld. Mainly, it is the imagery of day and night, and how they forever interchange. In the psyche it is represented by being awake and being asleep. And that, in turn, leads to the true separate expressions of the mind — the one awake and the one dreaming.

Earlier, I have discussed Jung's theory of dreams as expressions of the hidden stuff in the unconscious. Dreams are indeed not consciously created. It happens spontaneously in our minds when we are asleep. But that doesn't mean they convey intentional messages to our conscious. Research strongly suggests they don't. They are still enigmas, as is the process in which they form, but neither Jung's nor Freud's explanations hold.

There is no archetypal symbol that cannot have been created by the conscious mind.

Dramaturgical Archetypes

The hero is a central and familiar figure in countless myths, as well as in all kinds of fiction. It is also what the main character of a movie is usually called. Typically, movies have a hero who is challenged by a villain, and the movie doesn't end until the former has utterly defeated the latter.

They are the *protagonist* and the *antagonist* of the story. That is much older than cinema. It has been the pattern at least since the plays of Ancient Greece. The struggle of the protagonist to overcome the troubles introduced by the antagonist is what makes the plot exciting and keeps the audience in their seats until the end of it.

Strictly speaking, though, the protagonist is not necessarily a hero, and the antagonist must not be a vicious villain. That may be the most common situation, but there are many exceptions.

A hero, like Achilles or Hercules, is heroic from start to finish. It is just who they are. But the protagonist can just as well start off as a frightened coward or simply a normal person like anyone of us. Heroism may be what is needed to finally succeed, and if so, the protagonist has at this moment transformed into a hero. That is quite different from being born one. In other words, it is not heroic of heroes to be heroic. That is just natural to them. No one in the audience would raise an eyebrow. But for anyone else to rise to heroism in a moment of crisis — that is indeed heroic.

Here, I use the perspectives of *dramaturgy*, which deals with stories performed by actors on stage or screen, and not *narratology*, which applies to written texts. The former fits mythology better, since most of that material began with oral transmissions, even in some cases with ritual enactments, and not as texts. The form of myths has kept those oral traits, also in writing.

In modern film dramaturgy the hero is often someone other than the protagonist. It is a character with the stature and ability to solve all the problems and swiftly end the battle with the antagonist, but something happens that prevents this from happening. The hero is absent in the time of crisis, maybe even dead, so the protagonist just has to do it. In this case, the hero is the model the protagonist should try to live up to, and finally does by the end of the story. The hero inspires the protagonist to make the change and face the challenge. It is about how to become a hero.

Also, the antagonist needs not be a villain, a forceful enemy with a drawn sword. There are so many other ways in which one can be an obstacle and a provocateur. It is enough to be a boring but persistent bureaucrat, or simply a tease. The antagonist is the one who triggers the protagonist, mildly or brutally. In romantic comedies since Ancient Greece, the antagonist can be nothing fancier than a stubborn father refusing to accept a young man's proposal to his daughter. In tragedies, though, the antagonist tends to be both grimmer and more forceful. Then, everybody suffers at the end.

The function of the antagonist is to be a driving force, who pushes the protagonist towards the change — or else.

The Drama of Psychoanalytical Therapy

Jung did not declare the protagonist and the antagonist to be archetypes. He was not even keen on mentioning them in his treatment of myths and other legendary stories. I have not found him mention "antagonist" in the dramaturgical sense even once in his texts. The term "protagonist" I found him mentioning briefly three times, all of them in relation to religion.[258]

His disinterest in these concepts is peculiar, since the combination of them describes a process towards realization and

---

[258] Jung speaks of "protagonists of the sacrificial drama" in "Transformation Symbolism in the Mass" from 1954, *Collected Works* 11, p. 228. In "Answer to Job" from 1952 Jung writes: "Job's final declaration is so formulated that one can assume with some certainty that, for the protagonists, the incident is closed for good and all." *Collected Works* 11, p. 384. About the struggle between good and bad in Christian dogma, Jung writes: "Into this as yet unresolved conflict the Christian is cast as a protagonist of good, a fellow player in the world drama." "Introduction to the Religious and Psychological Problems of Alchemy" from 1944 and revised 1952, *Collected Works* 12, p. 22.

personal growth, which is at the core of his individuation theory. But he wanted that process to be exclusively personal, not in some dynamics with other people. He regarded it as utterly internal.

Of course, in drama the process is also internal although it is by necessity shown externally. The protagonist has to make the change by going beyond personal shortcomings, which must be an intense internal struggle. But every drama makes the claim that it cannot be done without exterior forces pushing in that direction.

So, dramaturgy is based on the idea that major personal change is possible only through active outer interference. It can't be done solely by introspection. It takes two to tango, preferably also a few musicians playing.

Any psychoanalyst or analytical psychologist would hesitate to accept that, since it means that individual introvert therapy must be insufficient. Group therapists, on the other hand, should applaud it.

One of the pioneers of group psychotherapy, Trigant Burrow, was a student of Jung and a psychoanalyst, who in 1921 expressed that the failure of analysis was due to its "exclusive emphasis on the personal to the utter neglect of inherent social factors."[259] His social conception of human mentality led to him being expelled from the American Analytical Association in 1932.[260]

One might argue that a psychoanalytical session involves two — the patient and the therapist — and their interaction can be compared to that of the protagonist and the antagonist, with the therapist as the latter, pressing the patient towards the change. That would make sense and could even be a play on stage, a chamber drama with minimal setting and cast.

It is doubtful, though, that either Freud or Jung would

---

[259] Pertegato & Pertegato, ed., *From Psychoanalysis to Group Analysis: The Pioneering Work of Trigant Burrow*, London 2013, p. xxiii.

[260] Ibid., p. xlii.

have agreed on that comparison. They insisted that the therapist was and should be detached and neutral, almost just an observer, as the whole process was taking place inside the patient. To them, if they would allow the terms, both the protagonist and the antagonist were contained within the patient's mind. Then the conscious would be the protagonist in need of change, and the unconscious the antagonist pushing towards it. The therapist would be absent from the actual drama.

That is not how dramaturgy would describe it, since the therapist is there and influences the proceedings. Nor is it accurate for therapy in reality. The therapist definitely plays a role in it. That might be the main reason for Freud and Jung refusing to see it so. Otherwise, they would have to admit that they interfered in the patient's personal process with their own preconceived notions and aims — which was certainly the case.

It is evident from their writing that both had a goal they regarded as more important than the cure of their patients: proving their psychological theories to be accurate and their therapies to be successful. Instead of using therapy for the benefit of their patients, they used the patients to prove and promote the theories behind their therapy.

What stands out in their own descriptions of therapy sessions is their manipulation of the patients towards accepting and perceiving the perspectives of the therapist, no matter how alien they may seem at first. The patients are guided, sometimes quite forcefully, into the paradigm of the therapist's psychology, until that is how they see it, too. No wonder, then, that such psychotherapy can take a lot of sessions.

It is strange that Jungian analytical psychology, using myth and all kinds of fiction with the highest regularity, if not to say reveling in them, would ignore their fundamental premise: the progression of the conflict between the protagonist and the antagonist.

Although not fond of these two basic concepts, Jung did put his own definitions on other dramaturgical terms, such as the hero discussed above. Another one is the *persona*. His use of it as the mask we show others, what we pretend to be, does not deviate much from its original meaning in Antique drama, where it signified the character that the actor was playing. There was even an actual mask used in some such traditions. And Jung was far from the first one to claim that we are all actors, as if on a stage.

Several Jungian archetypes are easily recognized as dramaturgical characters, though the terminology may differ slightly. The *sage* or wise old man of Jung is quite the same as the *mentor* of many plays and movies, assisting the protagonist with words of wisdom. More often than not, it is indeed a wise old man. The *fool* of Jung fits the role of the *comic relief*, creating some release from the tension of the drama by just being silly, often unintentionally so.

Emergence of the Trickster

In mythology, the antagonist pushing the protagonist towards challenge and change is often the role of the *trickster*, which is also one of Jung's archetypes, although the term is of much older date than his psychology.[261] Its use as a term for a rascal kind of mythological creature, though, approaches his time and may well have been additionally advanced by his writing on the subject.

The 1883 English translation of Jacob Grimm's *Deutsche Mythologie* translates *troner* of medieval German as trickster, but it is without any indication of it being an established term in mythological theory.[262] The German original does not expand on the term *troner* at all.

---

[261] The first known English mention of trickster is from 1711: "The other, he said, was such a Lubbard Trickster, so aukward at Mischief, that he deserv'd only to be laugh'd at." Joseph Addison et al., *The Medleys for the Year 1711*, no 39, London 1712, p. 420.

[262] Jacob Grimm, *Teutonic Mythology*, volume 3, transl. James Steven Stallybrass, London 1883, p. 958.

The American 19th century ethnologist Daniel Garrison Brinton is sometimes referred to as being the first to apply the term to its mythological meaning. He may have touched on such mythological figures in his book *The Myths of the New World* from 1868, but without mentioning the term even once.[263]

He did use the term, though, in a three-page article for *The American Antiquarian* in 1885, "The Chief God of the Algonkins, in His Character as a Cheat and Liar." Brinton reports that the Crees call one of their deities "*Wisakketjak*, which means 'the Trickster,' 'the Deceiver.'" He ends his short text by wishing for a literary and psychological study comparing this deity with similar European mythical figures, like the "wily Ulysses" and Reynard the Fox in Medieval literature: "The same Spirit breathes in all of them."[264]

It is doubtful, though, that Brinton was instrumental in establishing the present use of the term, or it would have appeared earlier in literature on mythology. Edward Tylor did not use the term "trickster" in his *Primitive Culture* from 1871, nor Andrew Lang in *Myth, Ritual, and Religion* from 1887, or James G. Frazer in *The Golden Bough* from 1894 and its abridged 1922 edition.

The extensive *Encyclopædia of Religion and Ethics* in twelve volumes by James Hastings, published between 1908 and 1927, lacks the term trickster in its index volume.[265] But the term is used about a dozen times through the volumes, beginning with the third volume from 1910, saying about Californian Native American importance of "myths dealing with culture-he-

---

[263] Daniel G. Brinton, *The Myths of the New World: A Treatise on the Symbolism and Mythology of the Red Race of America*, New York 1868.

[264] Daniel Garrison Brinton, "The Chief God of the Algonkins, in His Character as a Cheat and Liar," *The American Antiquarian*, May 1885, p. 137ff.

[265] James Hastings, *Encyclopædia of Religion and Ethics*, Index vol. (13), Edinburgh 1926.

roes, more or less of the trickster type familiar from so many other parts of North America."[266] Almost all of the tricksters mentioned in the *Encyclopædia* are Native American, but parallels to similar figures elsewhere are mentioned, such as the similarity between the Raven and "the European Reynard the Fox."[267]

Still, the term is never discussed at any length, just presented as a concept adequate to its original linguistic meaning.

That may be the problem of the term. The word has a meaning that is quite sufficient in itself, also for mythological applications. Its use in mythology seems to have grown mainly out of texts on Native American tales and beliefs.

An early source mentioned in the *Encyclopædia* is *Myths of the Cherokee* from 1902, by the American ethnologist James Mooney. He used the term five times, always about the mythological figure the Rabbit:

> *First and most prominent in the animal myths is the Rabbit (Tsistu), who figures always as a trickster and deceiver, generally malicious, but often beaten at his own game by those whom he had intended to victimize.*[268]

Interestingly, Mooney did not use the term trickster in his 1891 book *The Sacred Formulas of the Cherokees*.

Not even Mircea Eliade's *The Myth of the Eternal Return* from 1955 uses it.[269] On the other hand, in Joseph Campbell's *The Hero With a Thousand Faces* from 1949, the trickster is mentioned seven times, as a trickster-divinity or -god, or -hero, or just trickster. But he gives neither an explanation of the term

---

[266] Ibid., vol. 3, 1910, p. 144.

[267] Ibid., vol. 12, 1921, p. 592.

[268] James Mooney, *Myths of the Cherokee*, Washington 1902, p. 262.

[269] Mircea Eliade, *The Myth of the Eternal Return* (*La Mythe de l'éternel retour: archétypes et répétition*, 1949), transl. Willard R. Trask, London 1955.

nor any reference as to from where he got it.[270] Campbell uses seven of Jung's texts as sources, but none of them contains the term trickster in any edition accessible to Campbell at the time of writing his book.

The particular use of the trickster term in relation to Native American mythology is confirmed by the prominent social anthropologist E. E. Evans-Pritchard, who in 1967 called it "the excellent term employed by American ethnologists for the hero of Amerindian tales (e.g. Paul Radin, *The Trickster*, 1956)."[271]

Now, the American cultural anthropologist Paul Radin is interesting in this context for two reasons — his importance in establishing the trickster as a fixed concept in mythology, and his connection to Carl G. Jung. Radin's book, mentioned by Evans-Pritchard, was originally published in German in 1954 as *Der göttliche Schelm*, where both Jung and the classical philologist Károly Kerényi, with whom he cooperated on several projects, wrote additional chapters. *Schelm* is the German word for trickster, as explained in the book: "Trickster (englische Bezeichnung der Schelmenfigur)."[272]

The English version was published two years later. The book has proven to make a lasting impression, not the least due to the weights of its three contributors. It would not be an exaggeration to claim its significance in promoting the concept of the trickster in mythology thereafter.

Jung begins his contribution to the book by indicating that his first knowledge of the trickster figure, "many years ago," was through *The Delight Makers* from 1890 by the American ethnologist and archaeologist Adolf F. Bandelier.[273] I have not

[270] Joseph Campbell, *The Hero With a Thousand Faces*, Princeton 1972 (first edition 1949), pp. 44, 45, 90, 132, 145, 196, 248.

[271] Edward Evan Evans-Pritchard, *The Zande trickster*, Indiana 1967, p. 28.

[272] Paul Radin et al., *Der göttliche Schelm: Ein indianischer Mythen-Zyklus*, Zürich 1954, p. 186.

[273] Carl G. Jung, "On the Psychology of the Trickster Figure," transl. R. F.

found this reference in any other text by Jung, nor the use of the term trickster in its archetypal sense in any text of his preceding this one.

Actually, as late as 1952, he used "jester" when writing about the demiurge of Gnosticism: "The corresponding archetype is probably to be found in the *cosmogonic jester* of primitive peoples."[274] That may have been either *Schelm* or *Narr* in Jung's original German manuscript.

Bandelier did not use the term trickster, but already the title indicates that kind of figure. His recount of the traditions and myths of the Pueblo Indians of New Mexico is in novelistic form: "The plot is my own. But most of the scenes described I have witnessed."[275] He lets one of his characters explain about the *koshare* (translated as delight-makers):

> *Their task it is to keep the people happy and merry; but they must also fast, mortify themselves, and pray to Those Above that every kind of fruit may ripen in its time, even the fruit in woman's womb.*[276]

The koshare were traditional Pueblo clowns who induced both laughter and fear in their audience. They were also instrumental in rituals, in disciplining of children as well as adults, and in rain-making.[277] Although they had ceremonial func-

C. Hull, in Paul Radin, *The Trickster: A Study in American Indian Mythology*, New York 1956, p. 195.

[274] Carl G. Jung, Introduction to: Raphael Jehudah Zwi Werblowsky, *Lucifer and Prometheus: A Study of Milton's Satan*, London 1952, p. xi. Jung's German manuscript was translated by R. F. C. Hull, not credited in the book but in a slightly edited reprint of the text in *Collected Works* 11, New York 1958, p. 311.

[275] Adolf F. Bandelier, *The Delight Makers*, New York 1916 (1st edition 1890), p. vi.

[276] Ibid., p. 34.

[277] Elsie Clews Parsons and Ralph L. Beals, "The Sacred Clowns of the

tions, they were not tricksters in the mythological or archetypal meaning. Still, their role in Pueblo society was not far from the jester-type found in many cultures.

Jung compares the North American trickster of Radin's description to "the alchemical figure of Mercurius," poltergeist, shamanism, and even "the daemonic features exhibited by Yahweh in the Old Testament." He sees in this figure, "transformation of the meaningless into the meaningful."[278] He finds another parallel in the medieval festivities where a child was the bishop or a fool was the pope for a day. Jung sees the trickster as "a 'psychologem', an archetypal psychic structure of extreme antiquity," and continues:

In his clearest manifestations he is a faithful copy of an absolutely undifferentiated human consciousness, corresponding to a psyche that has hardly left the animal level.[279]

This explains the trickster's odd behavior, since "the older the archaic qualities are, the more conservative and pertinacious is their behaviour." He goes on to compare it to another archetype, that of the shadow, which has a role in the personal psyche as a reason for slips and faux pas, but the personal shadow is in part descended from a numinous collective figure:

This collective figure gradually breaks up under the impact of civilization, leaving traces in folklore which are difficult to recognize. But the main part of him gets personalized and is made an object of personal responsibility.[280]

Pueblo and Mayo-Yaqui Indians," *American Anthropologist*, volume 36:4, 1934, p. 507.

[278] Radin 1956, pp. 195f.

[279] Ibid., p. 200.

[280] Ibid., p. 202.

As the trickster progresses from malicious to beneficial, so can its myth stimulate a civilizing process within the human mind. Like many myths it has a therapeutic function: "It holds the earlier low intellectual and moral level before the eyes of the more highly developed individual, so that he shall not forget how things looked yesterday."[281]

Jung sums it up: "The trickster is a collective shadow figure, an epitome of all the inferior traits of character in individuals."[282] It is not a very flattering view of the trickster, and far from adequate for its role in myth and ritual. Jung's perspective is mainly moral, which may stem from his idea of individuation as a civilizing process, and his bitter thoughts on mankind after World War II. He clearly points to the latter in this passage about modern man:

> *He never suspects that his own hidden and apparently harmless shadow has qualities whose dangerousness exceeds his wildest dreams. As soon as people get together in masses and submerge the individual, the shadow is mobilized, and, as history shows, may even be personified and incarnated.*[283]

The Shadow of Jung in Recent Dramaturgy

Discussing the trickster, as seen above, Jung compares it to or even combines it with another archetype of his, which is the *shadow*. It is the amoral remnant of our instinctual animal past, hidden within us but far from disarmed. That makes it similar or even identical to his archetype the *beast*, representing the primitive past of man. The similarity to the trickster, on the other hand, can be discussed. It may be a question of implications more than of likeness.

[281] Ibid., p. 207.

[282] Ibid., p. 209.

[283] Ibid., p. 206.

As for his shadow archetype, Jung writes that "the same idea can be found in the Church Father Irenaeus, who calls it the 'umbra'."[284] He must be referring to these sentences of *Against Heresies* from the 2nd century CE, which was a criticism of Gnostic ideas of a Demiurge:

> *But he who was of the Demiurge was a spirit of ignorance, and decay, and error, and the offspring of a shadow; how could there be in one and the same, perfection and decay, knowledge and ignorance, error and truth, light and darkness?*[285]

The shadow is a translation of *umbra* in the original Latin text. In a footnote the translator suggests gloom as an alternative.

Jung's interest in the Gnostic Demiurge has been touched on above, and the polarity of extremes in one single character is something he found in both the trickster and the shadow. To Irenaeus, though, it would be an absurdity. His god would not mix perfection and decay, not put "new wine into old bottles."[286]

Returning to modern dramaturgy, there is a shadow to be found in it, too. But as a movie character, the shadow is something quite different from Jung's archetype. It is someone who has a similar situation as that of the protagonist of the story, but is unable to solve the problem. It is the one who fails at what the protagonist must accomplish, often in such a way as to show the dangers ahead. It can also be someone joining the protagonist all the way to the final outcome, like an ally.[287] But the solution must be caused by an act of the protagonist.

[284] Ibid., p. 202.

[285] Irenaeus, "Against Heresies," *Five Books of S. Irenaeus*, transl. John Kemble, Oxford 1872, p. 419.

[286] Matthew 9:17, Mark 2:22, and Luke 5:37.

[287] Kjell Sundstedt, *Att skriva för film*, Stockholm 2000, p. 194.

Again, it stresses the difference between Jung's model of the personal psyche and the social dynamics of the drama. Jung's shadow is internal, however blatantly it might be expressed by the individual, whereas the dramaturgical shadow is a mirror in which the protagonist can see an alternative outcome. It is like the saying ascribed to the 16th century preacher John Bradley, "There, but for the grace of God, go I."[288] The protagonist, though, cannot trust a *deus ex machina*, but has to solve the problem without the interference of any god.

Jung's ideas have made a lasting impression on all kinds of thinking — also regarding dramaturgy. His archetypes have snuck in and their definitions have altered those of the old theatrical types. The shadow is a clear example of this. Many writers on dramaturgy and scriptwriting have adapted Jungian terminology to some extent, but the main source repeatedly referred to is a book by the American screenplay story analyst Christopher Vogler.

It started in 1985 as a seven-page memo to fellow writers at Disney, with the title "A Practical Guide to *The Hero with a Thousand Faces*," referring to Joseph Campbell's book from 1949.[289] In 1992 Vogler had expanded it to a book titled *The Writer's Journey*. Vogler's admiration for Joseph Campbell is evident already in the title. A TV documentary about mythology narrated by Campbell was called *The Hero's Journey*. It premiered in 1987.

Vogler suggests that the hero's journey is what the writer should follow in the story. In the introduction, Vogler states that his concepts of storytelling are "shaped by the patterns of mythology and the thinking of Joseph Campbell and Carl Jung."[290] Campbell is present on almost every page, but Jung appears scarcely and with no reference to source. No text of his

---

[288] For more on the saying, see quoteinvestigator.com/2014/07/06/grace/.

[289] Christopher Vogler, *The Writer's Journey: Mythic Structure for Writers*, 3rd edition, Saline Michigan 2007 (1st edition 1992), p. xxix.

[290] Ibid., p. x.

is listed in the one-page bibliography, but two of Campbell's. It seems that Vogler's impressions of Jung are from the Campbell texts.

Vogler uses *The Hero With a Thousand Faces* as a veritable bible for his theories on script writing. In particular, he follows the pattern of the hero's journey in a number of stages from outset to end as described by Campbell, calling it "nothing less than a handbook for life, a complete instruction manual in the art of being human."[291] He also appoints it "one of the most influential books of the 20th century," and stresses its importance in Hollywood:

> *Filmmakers like George Lucas and George Miller acknowledge their debt to Campbell and his influence can be seen in the films of Steven Spielberg, John Boorman, Francis Coppola, and others.*[292]

Here, though, I focus on Vogler's use of archetypes. He explains them as Jungian concepts: "Jung employed the term archetypes, meaning ancient patterns of personality that are the shared heritage of the human race."[293] This definition leads him directly to the idea of the collective unconscious, a concept for which he expresses support:

> *Fairy tales and myths are like the dreams of an entire culture, springing from the collective unconscious. The same character types seem to occur on both the personal and the collective scale. The archetypes are amazingly constant throughout all times and cultures, in the dreams and personalities of individuals as well as in the mythic imagination of the entire world.*

[291] Ibid., p. xiii.

[292] Ibid., p. 3.

[293] Ibid., p. 23.

He adds a perspective on the archetypes introduced by Joseph Campbell: "Joseph Campbell spoke of the archetypes as biological: as expressions of the organs of the body, built into the wiring of every human being."[294] Vogler repeats this strange claim by the end of his book, explaining it with the physical reactions we tend to have to archetypes at play. Tears emerge when we watch a tragedy, we feel a strong sense of protectiveness toward an infant, laugh at fools, and so on.[295]

In addition to the Jungian idea of the archetypes, Vogler mentions another, "not as rigid character roles but as functions performed temporarily by characters to achieve certain effects in a story." This he extracts from *Morphology of the Folktale* by the Russian folklorist Vladimir Propp.[296] But it is the Campbell approach he mainly applies in his own book — with certain adaptions to the perspective of the screenwriter.

Although Vogler admits a multitude of archetypes, "as many as there are human qualities to dramatize in stories," he lists the eight he regards as the most common and useful for storytellers: the Hero, the Mentor (Wise Old Man or Woman), the Threshold Guardian, the Herald, the Shapeshifter, the Shadow, the Ally, and the Trickster.[297]

The foremost of them is of course the hero, whose story is always a journey. To Vogler it has to be none other than the protagonist: "The protagonist of every story is the hero of a journey."[298] The journey can be an introspective one or the development of a relationship, but it still follows the steps Campbell suggested, "the way stations" with Vogler's words. This is indeed in line with the Jungian view of the hero as the archetype of the individual on a quest to self-realization.

[294] Ibid., p. 24.

[295] Ibid., p. 355.

[296] Ibid., p. 24.

[297] Ibid., p. 26.

[298] Ibid., p. 7.

It is also the term very often used for the main character of the story, who is usually — but not always — the protagonist.

But as discussed earlier, making the hero identical with the protagonist creates a dramaturgical problem. The protagonist is not necessarily heroic, nor is the most prominent hero of the story necessarily the protagonist. Vogler agrees with the basic principle of modern dramaturgy that the main character is "the one who learns or grows the most in the course of the story."[299] That is also the typical trait of the protagonist, but lots of stories have spectacular heroes who are as heroic from their entry on the scene as on their exit. They certainly exist in myths as well. Such heroes cannot be protagonists, since they don't change through the story.

The influence of Jung and Campbell has created this alternate terminology, identifying the protagonist as the hero, but for dramaturgy it would be more adequate to simply stick with the term protagonist. It has worked well for very long.

But Vogler also mentions heroes more akin to the dramaturgical one, calling them catalyst Heroes. They are not protagonists, but characters "who do not change much themselves because their main function is to bring about transformation in others."[300] They are often mentors to the protagonist. That is the dramaturgical hero spot on.

As for the shadow, Vogler makes it similar or even identical to the antagonist, the villain of the story — more precisely the one creating the obstacle that the protagonist has to overcome: "The function of the Shadow in drama is to challenge the hero and give her a worthy opponent in the struggle."[301] It is evident that Vogler's use of the shadow archetype is more psychological than dramaturgical, the Jungian interior darkness we need to heed:

[299] Ibid., p. 31.

[300] Ibid., p. 37.

[301] Ibid., pp. 65f.

> *It is a force that accumulates when you fail to honor your gifts, follow the call of your muses, or live up to your principles and ideals. It has great but subtle power, operating on deep levels to communicate with you, perhaps sabotaging your efforts, upsetting your balance until you realize the message these events bring — that you must express your creativity, your true nature, or die.*[302]

Again, this is an unnecessary confusion of terms. The role described by Vogler is that of the antagonist. The shadow in modern dramaturgy is rather a character that meets with the same challenge as the protagonist, but fails at it. It is a shadow in the meaning of standing in the shadow of the protagonist, trying the same without shining at it.

Actually, Vogler hints at such a definition of the shadow later in his book, where he speaks about a common figure in fairy tales, who enters late in the story to claim that he, and not the hero, made the big feat. This false claimant Vogler calls "the pretender (the Shadow)."[303]

Vogler also discusses the trickster, but he seems to give it less of archetypal gravity than Jung did. To Vogler the trickster is one of mischief and comic relief: "All the characters in stories who are primarily clowns or comical sidekicks express this archetype."[304] He mentions the Norse god Loki as an example, but such epithets would make Loki rattle his chains more than from the drops of snake venom on his face. He was much too vicious for a clown.

There are, of course, also trickster-heroes. Vogler mentions the many clever rabbits in folktales, Coyote and Raven of Native American mythology, as well as Charlie Chaplin and the Marx brothers in movies. There are also many myths and

[302] Ibid., p. xxiii.

[303] Ibid., p. 208.

[304] Ibid., pp. 77f.

other stories where the trickster is an antagonist, whom the protagonist has to learn to outsmart. Strangely, this is all but ignored by Vogler, probably because it is hard to fit with his idea of the shadow being the antagonist.

Archetypal Literary Criticism

Just as there is a Jungian influence on the structure and components of drama and other storytelling, there is one on how these works should be interpreted. Since the 1930s, Jung's archetypes and analytical psychology have been used in literary criticism, at least in theory. To what extent it has entered the literary reviews is another matter.

The line of thought is called archetypal literary criticism, and it has two main sources — Maud Bodkin and Northrop Frye, whereof the latter made significantly more of an imprint, although Bodkin preceded him with more than twenty years.

Maud Bodkin

The English classical scholar and literary critic Maud Bodkin is regarded as the first one to discuss archetypal criticism. She did so in a 1930 article for the *British Journal of Psychology*,[305] where she focused on tragic poetry, and then with the 1934 book *Archetypal Patterns in Poetry: Psychological Studies of Imagination*, in which also the article from 1930 was included.

Her commitment to Jung is evident already on the introductory quote, which is from Jung:

> *Philosophical criticism has helped me to see that every psychology — my own included — has the character of a subjective confession... it is only by accepting this as inevitable that I can serve the cause of man's knowledge of man.*[306]

---

[305] Maud Bodkin, "Archetypal Patterns in Tragic Poetry," *British Journal of Psychology*, volume 21:2, 1930, pp. 183-202.

[306] Maud Bodkin, *Archetypal Patterns in Poetry: Psychological Studies of Imagination*, London 1934, p. vi.

The quote is from Jung's 1933 book *Modern Man in Search of a Soul*, in a chapter where he explores the contrasts between him and Freud. Bodkin left out quite a lot, mainly where the three dots are, but also at the end. This is what she substituted with the three dots:

And yet I must prevent my critical powers from destroying my creativeness. I know well enough that every word I utter carries with it something of myself — of my special and unique self with its particular history and its own particular world. Even when I deal with empirical data, I am necessarily speaking about myself.[307]

And the last sentence is incomplete. This is how it ends: "—the cause which Freud also wished to serve, and which, in spite of everything, he has served."

Bodkin may have wanted to exclude Freud from the picture, although she refers to him frequently in the book, and to soften the blow of Jung's confession to allow himself creative freedom in his scientific work — what in the world of literature is called poetic license.

In the very beginning of her text, she gives credit to Jung for having set forth a hypothesis in regard to the psychological significance of poetry,[308] with his essay "On the relation of analytical psychology to poetic art" published in 1928 in *Contributions to Analytical Psychology*. Her aim is to test this hypothesis.

She does so by comparing the Oedipus myth and the fate of Hamlet. Both express the conflicting relations of hate and love towards parents, which is also the basis of Freud's theory

[307] Carl G. Jung, *Modern Man in Search of a Soul*, transl. W. S. Dell and Cary F. Baynes, London 1933, pp. 135f.

[308] Bodkin 1934, p. 1.

of the Oedipus complex.[309] In it, Bodkin sees a more general
conflict between generations, and that can be explained as the
process repeated by each generation of maturing from the free-
spirited child to the civilized adult:

> *In infancy and in the later years of those who remain child-
> ish, a comparatively feeble imaginative activity together
> with an undisciplined instinct of self-assertion may pre-
> sent a fantasy self — the image of an infantile personality
> — in conflict with the chastened image which social con-
> tacts, arousing the instinct of submission, tend to en-
> force.[310]*

In other words, it is the agony of the free spirit of the
growing child having to conform to social upbringing. She
uses Jung's analogy of a sacrifice, "a childish self that must be
sacrificed, if the libido is to move forward into active life."[311]
Bodkin finds the same pattern in the story of Orestes and
Shakespeare's *King Lear*.[312] She concludes:

> *Thus the archetypal pattern corresponding to tragedy may
> be said to be a certain organization of the tendencies of self-
> assertion and submission.[313]*

When defining archetypal patterns, she paraphrases the
classical scholar Gilbert Murray about that within us which
leaps in response to the effective presentation in poetry of an

[309] Ibid., p. 11. In claiming Hamlet as an example of the Oedipus complex,
Bodkin refers to Ernest Jones, *Essays in Applied Psycho-Analysis*, London
1923, p. 1-98.

[310] Bodkin 1934, p. 23.

[311] Ibid., p. 18. She refers to the chapter "The Sacrifice" in Carl G. Jung,
The Psychology of the Unconscious, New York 1916, p. 479.

[312] Bodkin 1934, pp. 14f.

[313] Ibid., p. 23.

ancient theme. In her own words, the archetypes are "themes having a particular form or pattern which persists amid variation from age to age, and which corresponds to a pattern or configuration of emotional tendencies in the minds of those who are stirred by the theme."[314]

Although expressing great respect for Jung's psychology and its applicability to drama theory, Bodkin is hesitant about his idea of the collective unconscious:

> *Jung believes himself to have evidence of the spontaneous production of ancient patterns in the dreams and fantasies of individuals who had no discoverable access to cultural material in which the patterns were embodied. This evidence is, however, hard to evaluate.*[315]

Still, Bodkin makes the claim that there is such a thing as a biological inheritance from our ancestors, making us relate intensely to the above-mentioned themes in *Hamlet*, *Oedipus Rex*, and *King Lear*, so that "all those systems or tendencies which appear to be inherited in the constitution of mind and brain may be said to be due to racial experience in the past." She also calls it the community consciousness,[316] which may not be the same for all humanity but "the common nature lived and immediately experienced by the members of a group or community."[317]

The above is from the chapter reprinting Maud Bodkin's 1930 article. In the following chapters she explores other poems and dramas from the archetypal perspective. She uses Co-

---

[314] Ibid., p. 4. Murray's wording (also quoted by Bodkin) is, "Yet there is that within us which leaps at the sight of them, a cry of the blood which tells us we have known them always." Gilbert Murray, *The Classical Tradition in Poetry*, London 1927, p. 239.

[315] Bodkin 1934, p. 4.

[316] Ibid., p. 23f.

[317] Ibid., p. 20.

leridge's poem *The Ancient Mariner* to reexamine the rebirth archetype, the heaven and hell archetypes in the same poet's *Kubla Khan* and in Milton's *Paradise Lost*, the images of the devil, the hero, and god in Shakespeare's *Othello* and Goethe's *Faust*, and so on. One chapter examines the image of woman in the *Iliad*, Dante's *Divine Comedy*, *Faust*, Greek dramas, and several other sources.

Regarding the dramaturgical character of the shadow, discussed earlier, Bodkin has this to say when examining the "Devil-figure" of Iago in Shakespeare's play *Othello*: "Iago is the shadow-side of Othello,"[318] by which she means that he is the necessary dark opposite to the noble hero, representing the dark forces inherent in the hero.

This is closer to Jung's idea of the shadow than to that of dramaturgy, with the important exception that in the drama, Iago is most definitely another character than Othello. He may express something hidden within Othello as well, but it would be in the spectator's imagination and not in Shakespeare's manuscript.

Northrop Frye

The most prominent book on archetypal literary criticism is *Anatomy of Criticism* from 1957, by the Canadian critic Northrop Frye. He only mentions Maud Bodkin in a note, together with others he deems relevant to the theory of archetypal approach in criticism — Kenneth Burke, Gaston Bachelard, Francis Fergusson, and Philip Wheelwright.[319]

Jung is mentioned frequently through the book, and three of his books are referenced in the end notes: *Wandlungen und Symbole der Libido* from 1912, *Psychology and Alchemy* from 1953, and *On a Science of Mythology* from 1949 (with Kerényi). Freud is mentioned, too, but mainly his analysis of *Oedipus Tyrannus* as a dramatization of the Oedipus complex.

[318] Ibid., p. 245.

[319] Northrop Frye, *Anatomy of Criticism: Four Essays*, Princeton 1957, p. 358.

Also, Joseph Campbell's *The Hero With a Thousand Faces* from 1949 is used.

Frye makes his own definition of the archetype as "a symbol which connects one poem with another and thereby helps to unify and integrate our literary experience." The archetypal critic studies these patterns to "fit poems into the body of poetry as a whole."[320]

Some of the archetypes are so deeply rooted in how we think about them that they unavoidably bring a certain association, for example "the geometrical figure of the cross inevitably suggests the death of Christ."[321] That does not mean Frye subscribes to Jung's idea of the collective unconscious as a constant storage of archetypes. He flat out discards it, at least for literary criticism:

> *This emphasis on impersonal content has been developed by Jung and his school, where the communicability of archetypes is accounted for by a theory of a collective unconscious — an unnecessary hypothesis in literary criticism, so far as I can judge.*[322]

Still, Frye recognizes that there is a "center" of archetypes, a group of universal symbols, common to all, such as food and drink, the quest or journey, light and darkness, and sexual fulfillment. Their communicable power is potentially unlimited. But he points out that he does not mean any "archetypal code book which has been memorized by all human societies without exception."[323]

Frye does not base his ideas of archetypal criticism on Jung alone. He sees Jungianism as particularly useful when analyzing literature of the romance genre, but for comedy he pre-

[320] Ibid., p. 99.

[321] Ibid., p. 102.

[322] Ibid., pp. 111f.

[323] Ibid., p. 118.

fers Freud and for tragedy "one naturally looks to the psychology of the will to power, as expounded in Adler and Nietzsche."[324]

As for romance, though, he finds good use of Jung, mainly because of its method of characterization:

The romancer does not attempt to create "real people" so much as stylized figures which expand into psychological archetypes. It is in the romance that we find Jung's libido, anima, and shadow reflected in the hero, heroine, and villain respectively.[325]

Comparing the shadow archetype to the villain of the story takes it far away from the dramaturgical function described earlier of the shadow as a failed version of the protagonist, someone who may go along but is not instrumental in the solution.

However, on another page Frye writes, "The faithful companion or shadow figure of the hero has his opposite in the traitor."[326] That is much closer to the dramaturgical shadow than to Jung's archetype.

Jung's Poetics

Carl G. Jung's own approach to Jungian poetics was with his essay "On the Relation of Analytical Psychology to Poetic Art." The original text was published in 1922, with an English translation in the *British Journal of Psychology* the following year. It was also included in his book *Contributions to Analytical Psychology* from 1928, which is the source used here.

Jung begins his essay by pointing out that it is the practice and form of art that can be investigated by psychology, but not its essential nature, what art is in itself. This can also be said

---

[324] Ibid., p. 214.

[325] Ibid., p. 304.

[326] Ibid., p. 196.

about religion.[327] He goes on to argue strongly against the Freudian habit of trying to understand the art by exploring the childhood and such personal circumstances of the artist:

> *The school of medical psychology inaugurated by Freud has certainly tended to inspire the literary historian to bring certain qualities of the individual work of art into relation with the personal and intimate life of the poet. But in so doing nothing more has been said than what the scientific treatment of poetic works had long since revealed.*[328]

Jung even finds it offensive: "A slight touch of scandal often flavours a biography, but a little more becomes a nasty inquisitiveness." His main objection is that this path discovers nothing that is not true for everyone. So, it reveals nothing essential about either the artist or the art. He compares it to the statement that every artist is a narcissist: "Every man who pursues his own line to the limit of his powers is a 'narcissist'."

Jung is not holding back in dismissing Freud's approach, and in doing so expands his disapproval beyond its use in the treatment of art and artists: "The reductive method of Freud is purely a method of medical treatment that has for its object a morbid and unsuitable structure." He even accuses Freud of rigid dogmatism.[329]

These strong words may have been triggered by Freud's most famous analysis of an artist — his 1910 essay about Leonardo da Vinci, where he searched the artist's childhood to find what, so to speak, made him tick.[330] That would be twelve

---

[327] Carl G. Jung, "On the Relation of Analytical Psychology to Poetic Art," transl. H G. and Cary F. Baynes, *Contributions to Analytical Psychology*, London 1928, p. 225.

[328] Ibid., p. 228.

[329] Ibid., pp. 230 and 232.

[330] Sigmund Freud, *Leonardo da Vinci: A Psychosexual Study of an Infantile*

years before Jung wrote his essay, but the book had an edited second edition in 1919 and a third in 1923. Freud's text was very much still around when Jung wrote his essay on poetry.

In his own sketch of a poetics, Jung defines two forms of art — one consciously produced in a controlled process by the artist, and the other flows more or less spontaneous and perfect from the author's pen.[331] Works of the latter kind "positively impose themselves upon the author." He calls the former introverted, whereas the latter is extraverted:

> *The introverted attitude is characterized by an upholding of the subject with his conscious ends and aims against the claims and pretensions of the object; the extraverted attitude, on the contrary, is distinguished by a subordination of the subject to the claims of the object.*[332]

In other words, the latter kind of poetry is the one that writes itself, as the saying goes. It is art of this kind that Jung gives his main attention. There, he states, consciousness is not only influenced by the unconscious, but is actually led by it.[333] A creative process of this kind, Jung calls an autonomous complex, and explains it as "a detached portion of the psyche that leads an independent psychic life withdrawn from the hierarchy of consciousness."

Here, of course, Jung indicates the collective unconscious and its primordial images — the archetypes, which appear particularly in the artwork he calls symbolical, the source of which "is not to be found in the personal unconscious of the author, but in that sphere of unconscious mythology, the primordial

Reminiscence (*Eine Kindheitserinnerung des Leonardo da Vinci*, 1910), transl. A. A. Brill, New York 1916.

[331] Jung, "On the Relation of Analytical Psychology to Poetic Art," pp. 234f.

[332] Ibid., p. 236.

[333] Ibid., p. 237.

contents of which are the common heritage of mankind."[334] Because of the ancient significance of those symbols, they take the forms akin to mythology whenever they appear in art:

> *The primordial image or archetype is a figure, whether it be a daemon, man, or process, that repeats itself in the course of history wherever creative phantasy is freely manifested. Essentially, therefore, it is a mythological figure.*

The roots of these symbols and their allegories give them "a peculiar emotional intensity" and has a "stirring" effect. The one who speaks with primordial images "transmutes personal destiny into the destiny of mankind." In so doing, the artist shapes the archetype into a form that relates to the present, which indicates what that particular age is most lacking. That is what makes the artwork relevant to the audience of that time. The archetype emerging is the one "best fitted to compensate the insufficiency and one-sidedness of the spirit of the age."

Except for brief mentions in passing of Schiller, *Faust*, and *Zarathustra*, Jung does not illustrate his ideas with examples from the world of art. It is nontypical for him, who otherwise filled his writing with countless references to myths as well as poetic fiction. He is aware of this, ending the essay by suggesting it happened instead in the mind of the reader:

> *But I may perhaps hope that what I have been obliged to omit, namely, the concrete application to poetic works, has been furnished by your own thoughts, thus giving flesh and blood to my abstract intellectual frame.*[335]

It is a strange excuse, sounding suspiciously much like negligence. It would have been particularly interesting to read

---

[334] Ibid., p. 245.

[335] Ibid., p. 249.

some examples of what symbols in artworks of different time periods would have expressed what needs of those times. Not that it is a very bold claim. Poetry irrelevant to the time of its writing tends not to make enough noise to survive it.

On the other hand, Jung also claims in his essay that some artworks have been given a renaissance long after their creation, because they were suddenly relevant to another later age:

> *It happens moreover quite frequently that a poet long dead is suddenly rediscovered. This may occur when our conscious development has reached a higher level, from which standpoint the ancient poet can tell us something new.*[336]

Again, that is something with which we are familiar. There are several instances of it in the history of art and literature, such as the paintings of El Greco and even the praise of Shakespeare's plays. Still, some examples from Jung would have been helpful.

Also, he would need to explain how these past artists could come up with symbols irrelevant to their age, which is contradictory to what he says in his text about what archetypes emerge from the mind of the artist. It would take a clairvoyant artist.

Anyway, Jung's omissions may have been what inspired the continued pursuit of the subject by such writers as the above-mentioned Maud Bodkin, Northrop Frye, Joseph Campbell, and Christopher Vogler.

[336] Ibid., p. 241.

Myth as Self-Realization

According to Jung, myths emerge from the unconscious and contain archaic truths about existence. They are "psychic manifestations that represent the nature of the psyche."[337]

Although Jung emphasized the myths as stories, a series of related events from a beginning to an end, he showed no interest in the satisfaction of relief that Aristotle called *catharsis*, a mental or emotional cleansing appearing in the audience after a good drama.

I have not found any text in which Jung discusses the term in relation to the Aristotelean meaning. His only use of the word is in reference to psychotherapy, as an early method of "putting the patient, with or without hypnotic aid, in touch with the hinterland of his mind."[338]

The goal of the treatment is the release of suppressed emotions.

Jung did point out the emotional attraction of those mythical stories, but explained it as a resonance from within the human mind, an inner recognition of the hidden truth those stories contained.

In that way, the myths served as inspiration. The hidden truth was a number of keys to self-realization, and the inspiration was one of getting people started on that path.

> *Myth is the primordial language natural to these psychic*
> *processes, and no intellectual formulation comes anywhere*
> *near the richness and expressiveness of mythical imagery.*
> *Such processes are concerned with the primordial images,*

---

[337] Carl G. Jung, "Archetypes of the Collective Unconscious" ("Uber die Archetypen des kollektiven Unbewussten," 1934), *The Integration of the Personality*, transl. Stanley Dell, London 1940, p. 54.

[338] Carl G. Jung, *Modern Man in Search of a Soul*, transl. W. S. Dell and Cary F. Baines, London 1933, pp. 40f.

*and these are best and most succinctly reproduced by fig-
urative language.*[339]

The most obvious example is that of the hero myth, where
the hero's struggle to overcome his fear and other obstacles to
reach his goal, serves as an instigation for every person to do
the same — get free of inhibition, and find the courage to pursue the path that leads to the realization of one's own potential.
That makes the myth a kind of self-therapeutic manual, and
the final outcome for the successful use of it is an enlightened
mind, someone who truly knows himself.

This self-realization is what Jung calls the *individuation
process*. It mainly consists of joining the unconscious with the
conscious, by having the knowledge of the former rise to the
latter. When man is completely aware of his unconscious and
what is stored therein, especially in the collective unconscious,
he has reached self-realization.

Jung's theories have certainly been applied to the study of
myth — abundantly so. But not in their entirety. The collective
unconscious and the process towards self-realization are psychoanalytical components with little meaning to historians of
religion or anthropologists, and dreadfully difficult to work
with when examining mythological material. The archetypes,
on the other hand, have flourished in interpretations of myths.

Joseph Campbell, Mircea Eliade, and others have not exactly adapted the Jungian archetypes as such, although several
of those scholars of mythology admit to their existence and importance, but they have used the idea of extracting symbolic
elements from the myths, and comparing these across cultural
borders.

Myths do have lots of similarities, no matter what culture
or time they stem from, and these similarities can easily be de-

[339] Carl G. Jung, "Introduction to the Religious and Psychological Problems of Alchemy" (originally from *Psychologie und Alchemie*, 1944), transl.
R. F. C. Hull, *Collected Works*, volume 11, London 1968, p. 25.

scribed in a manner approaching that of the Jungian archetypes. There are certain character types appearing and reappearing in countless myths — such as the hero, the sage, the god, and the child — often with recognizably similar character traits. Also, significant ingredients that are neither human nor anthropomorphic seem to pop up and look just about the same in myths without any cultural connection — such as the flood, the journey, and certainly life as well as death.

Of course, this can easily be explained by the existence of these phenomena in any human life, wherever it is lived, but that is also one of the points Jung makes — the universality of those symbols. If they were not universal human experiences, they would not be archetypes.

Then the question is, are they symbols carrying additional meaning, or are they just heroes, sages, floods, journeys, and so forth? I have not found that Jung gives any method of proving the one or the other, nor have I seen it done by any other writer on myth.

It is understandable, since this is not easily accomplished. If myths are stories of no other meaning than to entertain and excite, they would still need to contain elements of what people have vivid ideas about. Otherwise, they could not make any sense at all.

So, how to prove that a myth is more than just a story?

Historians of religion, anthropologists, and other scholars point to how myths are used. Some of the myths, those dealing with creation in particular, are acted out in ritualistic ways, and integrated into a religious apparatus. These myths are definitely regarded as more than just stories, by the people keeping them alive.

It should be noted that myths of the highest significance to Jung, those of the hero, are normally not treated that reverently in the cultures where they belong. This might imply an anomaly in Jung's paradigm.

If he is correct about the archetypes and the function of individuation, would not the myth that is the most accurate portrayal of this be worshipped and cherished the most?

Even in the mythological tradition closest to Jung himself — that of the Old and New Testament — the hero marching triumphantly towards his self-fulfillment is much harder to find than figures of a less triumphant fate.

In *Genesis I*, God creates the world in six days, and upon completion he does nothing more spectacular than take a rest — as if that quest was just a regular week's work. Adam does the very opposite of rising to self-realization, when spending a long life in misery after being expelled from Eden. It was actually knowledge — that of good and bad — getting him expelled. Jesus has a few years of increased success, only to be painfully executed at the end, complaining that his god has forsaken him, and his glorious return is yet to happen after two thousand years.

Most of the other characters in the stories of the Bible also struggle with misfortune and a god hard to please. It is not often that they end their days in any kind of bliss.

The same is true for many myths around the world. Hardships and tragic endings are to be found everywhere — even for heroes. The ancient epic of *Gilgamesh* has its hero go through all kinds of ordeals, even in the underworld, only to find that life is a tragedy with no hope of a happy ending. The formidable hero Achilles meets his end in a humiliating way when an arrow pierces his heel. Again, the lesson is far from cheerful.

There sure are hero tales that end happily, but it is questionable if they are the ones making the deepest imprints in our souls. It seems we cherish the tales of those who suffer more than the ones that end in triumph. Actually, most myths are closer to tragedy than to any kind of success story. If that is indeed what our collective unconscious has to teach us, then there is reason to despair.

Furthermore, death is regarded with awe in most cultures and myths. Also, the dead are feared in many cultures, which regard them as malcontent and malevolent. The pie in the sky when you die is offered to few others than the Christians. And the religion most connected to the idea of incarnation, Buddhism, preaches that this is a rotation one should do the utmost to end, by utterly and finally disappearing.

Upon examination, the myths really don't say much more than that life is tough and then you die — something of which our conscious minds are already quite aware.

Jung's interpretation of myth and its meaning is rather utopian, almost like a salvation doctrine for the modern man. It may be possible to extract something that positive from at least some of the old myths, but it is quite another thing to regard it as the standard.

Other writers on myth have found the need to limit the application of Jung to using the idea of the archetypes as a means of sorting and classifying them, to some extent also in pointing out archetypal elements in the meaning extant before Jung — that of type-characters and type-events. Even when they repeatedly refer to Jung in pointing out archetypes, what they actually do is much nearer to just finding the recognizable components of a story. That is just about the opposite of cryptic symbols from a hidden unconscious.

These components represent basic concepts or characters with the specific quality of being immediately recognized as such by any audience. The types used in myth and drama are not echoes of patterns in the depths of our minds that we react to without understanding why. They are standard ingredients that our conscious minds understand and relate to immediately. They are not mysterious, but evident.

The universality that Jung demands of myths and their components is precisely what makes applying his theory halt. That which is universal is immediately recognizable by all, otherwise it would not be universal, and therefore it cannot contain anything that is hidden from the conscious mind. We react to those universal elements of myths and other stories, because we recognize them and can relate to them. If not, they would leave us indifferent.

Yet, there is truth in the strange and complex attraction some of the Jung archetypes emit. They do ring a bell, deep in our minds. We need to ponder what in the myths makes them so fascinating to us, and what — if anything — they may tell us with those stories that we just can't let go.

Most definitely, there are universal truths about the human being to be found in such an exploration. I do not think that this truth only can be found in the stories we call myths, but they are a good place to start.

And, again, they are all accessible to the conscious mind or they would be of no significance to us.

Personal Myth

Although both Freud and Jung made their major contributions in the field of individual psychology, they have jumped to conclusion in assuming a collective psyche — the former in his idea of the archaic heritage, the latter in the concept of the collective unconscious and its archetypes.

They both admit to having little proof for those assumptions, mainly referring to impressions from patients they have treated. In therapy sessions, several patients have revealed concepts and images that neither Freud nor Jung could imagine to have come out of personal experience. Thereby, in spite of their specialty, they actually underestimated the complexity of the human psyche.

The human mind is quite able to absorb a multitude of impressions from its surroundings — even unawares — and make its very personal stew of it all, one that it can itself fail to interpret or at all understand. We do not need to have first hand experience of everything we load into our minds, but fill it also with hearsay, things implied, misunderstandings, rumors, vague impressions, and whatnot. The brain's input is so vast that there is simply no way of saying what it cannot have amassed.

And it starts long before we are able to talk, some of it even before we are born. There is fetal perception, especially that of hearing, so that the fetus learns to identify different voices.[340]

Freud and Jung took support for their theories in the fact that they received complex, seemingly mythological images also from children. Well, those children were obviously able to talk about these things, or they would not have been understandably transmitted — and by the time you have learned to talk, you have learned a lot of other things as well.

It is also odd that the two pioneers of psychological dream interpretation neglected the possibility of personal dreams mixing with social awareness, and finding a collective frame of reference in which to translate them. This is what every artist does — inner fantasies are translated to a form conceivable to other people.

A writer needs to do this when putting a story into words, since words are instruments for communication between people. The mere writing down of a story, then, equals translating it to a socially understandable form. Painters do something similar when reproducing an inner image with the tools of brush and colors, musicians with their instruments, and dancers with their body movements. If inner images are at all to be presented to the outside world, they have to be transformed and adapted to it. The very process of bringing them out from the individual mind for others to perceive is a process of translation.

Dreams are pure dreams only as long as they are not retold in any way. When they are, they become interpretations of dreams, representations of them, but not dreams at all. So, what is true for the artist is true for the dreamer — if those images, impressions, and sentiments are at all to be presented, they have to adapt to socially understandable forms. If not, the conscious mind would simply be unable to transmit them.

In the translation of inner images to the outside world,

[340] Ferris Jabr, "Study of Fetal Perception Takes Off," *scientificamerican.com*, 2015.

concepts familiar to the latter are bound to be used. What cannot be translated into such a concept is simply not presented. It either leaves a gap, or it is ignored, or it is substituted by something socially recognizable.

We all know it. When did anyone of us manage to present a dream exactly as we experienced it? So, instead of the dream there is a combination of elements familiar to all, or at least to most of us. Anything else, the social forms of communication do not have tools for. There is no word for something that people are unable to recognize.

We are approaching Wittgenstein's theory of *language-game* (*Sprachspiel*), which states that the meanings of words depend on the context in which they are uttered — even if the basic understanding of those words is shared by all, and that is rarely the case.[341] When one person tells a story to another, it is done by words representing familiar concepts, but it is very difficult indeed to ascertain that the concepts are identical for the narrator and the listener. This is certainly true for all the concepts that Jung calls archetypes — such as mother, god, tool, child, journey, and so forth.

The same confusion is likely to take place within a person's imagination. The social concept of the mother corresponds to a multitude of images in one's mind — the countless impressions of each person's own mother, as well as those of other mothers, the mother one would like to have, the mother one dreads to have, and so on almost infinitely.

So, we have a mind that has the same difficulty both ways — translating the complex inner images into socially understandable concepts, and also interpreting such concepts when taking them in. In this cobweb, all kinds of generalized structures and symbolic forms are bound to appear. We have no need for an inherited storage of them. They are learned by each individual, step by step, much like the ability to walk. Every

---

[341] Ludwig Wittgenstein, *Philosophical Investigations*, transl. G. E. M. Anscombe, New York 1953.

person creates their own set of archetypes and other tools of generalization. These tools are as sure to have much in common with the corresponding tools of other people, as they are to also differ significantly from them.

Take the image of the clown. Not so few people find it scary, although for most of us it is a character we associate with amusement and laughter. The difference may stem from childhood experiences or what impression Stephen King's horrific clown in *It* made, either through the novel or the screen versions. The same archetype is experienced in vastly different ways.

It is a pity that the two pioneers of penetrating the individual mind did not explore its ability to create its own universe of symbols, before yielding to a solution giving much less credit to it.

Each man has his own mythology, some of it similar to that of other people and some of it not, some of it rather constant through a lifetime because of its relevance to early personal experience and aspirations, and some of it evolving with the additional impressions received through the years. That personal mythology relates tightly to personal beliefs, as well as to personal anxieties and frustrations. It is the framework from which we as persons present ourselves and things of our imagination. Also, it is the framework to which we adapt impressions from outside. We utilize it in reading and writing, listening and talking, watching and showing.

Any myth or other story entering this personal framework of one's own mythology will transform to fit it. If such a fitting is impossible the person will reject the myth, or maybe alter their framework slightly to adapt to it, if rejection is not possible. If it is an easy fit, the person will cherish it as confirmation of the personal mythology. The bottom line is that any myth, no matter how universal, becomes utterly personal to each one who hears it.

In that way, myths as well as any other stories can be instruments towards self-realization. Probably, the myths that fascinate its audience the most are not the ones which easily fit into their personal mythologies, but the ones that seem to make a lot of sense in that framework and still have some anomalies, demanding the personal mythology to adapt.

Fascinating stories challenge the personal mythology slightly, so that the process of making them fit disturbs the mind somewhat, and then reforms it. Nice stories caress the mind, but good stories tickle and tease it.

Myths Are Stories

Myths are stories, often very good ones, and as such they have a certain power to affect and stimulate their audience. In that sense, they are not different from other stories. Any story can promote self-realization or be used to support ritual and tradition.

Every story affects the minds of its audience, more or less. The human psyche is influenced by all it takes in, as well as all it does itself produce. When stories engage, the impression they make is deeper and lasts longer. For the audience, that is done from the outside inwards, which means the experience has to pass through their conscious minds. For the creator of the story, the process can be described as reversed — from the inside of the author's mind, through the translation of the conscious and then onto the audience. For both, it is a conscious process, in no need of the hidden activity of an unconscious.

Myths and their effects need primarily to be regarded and examined as consciously produced and consciously consumed stories, whatever themes and components they have. There is no mystery in that process.

The stories engaging the author as well as the audience are those that relate to their lives, their experiences, and needs. As discussed above, the basic emotional triggers are fears and longings, losses and gains. Any story must play on these opposites to get the attention of an audience.

The audience does not have to feel threatened or tempted. Their empathy will be evoked by watching characters in a story subjected to these things. We care when characters risk losing something or have a chance of gaining something. That is the first and foremost premise. If we humans lacked the ability of empathy there would be no stories.

So, every story needs to contain the threat of losing something and the hope of gaining something. Strictly speaking, it could be enough if there is just a threat of losing something, or just the hope of gaining something. But such a story would lack the excitement brought on by the polarity. No other gain than avoiding loss is just status quo, and so is no other loss than the opportunity to gain. It really just means that nothing significant has happened at the end of the story. The situation is just as it was in the beginning.

A good story needs to up the ante, as explained already by Aristotle in the 4th century BC, and demonstrated by the great Greek playwrights of the century before that. An engaging story approaches the extremes — the risk of losing everything versus the hope of gaining everything. That will keep an audience on its toes.

There is no need for an unconscious urge towards self-realization, not even for catharsis, the sense of relief after the story has ended. It is just how we are triggered, like the dog chasing a stick or the toddler staring at all the plates with food at the dinner table. When we hear of someone — fictive or real, stranger or family — being involved in, say, a car accident, we want to know how that person fared. If a pole-vault athlete rushes with his pole towards the bar way up high, we don't turn our eyes away before we see how the jump went.

That athlete could be anybody. If it is a world champion, a failed jump would be more of an excitement for the audience than if he succeeds as expected. If it is a total beginner, the opposite is true. For those two — as well as, to a lesser extent, for anyone in between — we would watch the jump to the end. That is the basic force of a story.

The story can be extended both backwards and forward. We can follow the jumper through years of training and ordeals before that jump, and we can see what happens to him afterwards, whether his jump was successful or not. But in order to get the audience's attention already in the beginning of the story, that particular jump must be indicated, as must the consequences of it be for the audience to remain after the jump.

The story can be extended quite a lot at both ends, by the use of all kinds of complications. But the general pattern is the same. As long as we want to see that jump, we remain attentive.

Of course, once we have seen it, the story cannot extend very long without the promise of something like a new jump, even more spectacular. If there is none ahead, the story might as well end shortly — and it will only keep us to the end if we feel it is imminent.

The Hamlet Story

Now, let us move from the pole-vault athlete to arguably the greatest play ever written, that of Shakespeare's *Hamlet, Prince of Denmark*, for comparison.

Very early in the play it is evident what jump will come. The ghost of Hamlet's father informs him of having been poisoned by his own brother Claudius, who is now not only the new king but also the husband of Hamlet's mother, the widow of the assassinated king.[342] Hamlet has to avenge the murder of his father. Between royalties in a drama, it can only mean killing him.

That is quite a dramatic event to expect, so we can wait for it. And we do, through the long play of formidable monologues, dialogues, and intricate complications. We know the vengeance, the jump, will come. Otherwise, the play would not have survived its opening night.

The attraction of the play has little to do with the moral demand for Claudius to be punished, although that helps pro-

---

[342] The name of Hamlet's father is also Hamlet, which surely tickles the imagination of every psychoanalyst.

voke the feelings of the audience. An injustice needs to be corrected, whereas a simple struggle for power would leave the audience indifferent. If Claudius had not killed Hamlet's father and Hamlet still wanted to kill him, it would be for gaining the crown. As the prince, he might feel entitled to it, but the audience would not approve.

That is at the bottom of the moral component in stories containing one, and most stories do. It enhances the empathy of the audience, which is precisely why a story needs a moral setting. It is not to promote moral values — although that is often claimed — but for the audience to be additionally engaged.

The main magnet of the play is the awaited vengeance, which must mean the death of Claudius to counterweigh that of Hamlet's father. It has been strongly indicated at the outset. Actually, it is so inevitable that we keep on watching the play in increased frustration over why it has not happened yet. Frustration is also an excitement. Why has Hamlet not killed Claudius yet? Why does it take him so long?

Moral dilemmas, existential perspectives, and other sophisticated additions may enrich the experience for the audience, also in contemplations after the play has ended. But they are little more than distractions, compared to the audience's expectation of the vengeance, the jump. There is no way the audience would be inspired to discuss such matters, if the traitorous king were still alive when the curtain fell. That would be an end in disappointment, which is a feeling we don't like to dwell on for long. And we certainly would not recommend others to see the play.

Regarding the characters of the play, few are really needed. Except for Hamlet and Claudius, who must be there at the moment of the jump for it to happen, any additional character is superfluous. They just serve the purpose of extending and complicating the drama — with one important exception.

In dramaturgy, all the way back to Aristotle and the playwrights he studied to reach his conclusions, the necessity of a protagonist and an antagonist has been pointed out. These are not necessarily the so-called hero and villain of the story. The protagonist is the one who needs to change in some way or do something beyond their normal abilities, whereas the antagonist is the one both triggering and hindering it. What the protagonist must do is exactly what the antagonist doesn't want, and the latter's actions to prevent it from happening make it ever more imperative for the former to succeed. It is a war of opposing needs.

The protagonist is not necessarily the main character of the story and the villain not necessarily the antagonist, though that is very common. But there is nothing common about Shakespeare.

Hamlet is indeed the main character of the play given his name, but we should not assume it means that he is the protagonist. And his uncle Claudius, the assassin king, is certainly the villain of the story, but is he the antagonist, forcing whoever is the protagonist to that which in cowboy movies is called the showdown, i.e., the jump?

Hamlet may be frustrated to the point of what Freud and Jung would call neurotic, but he is on a mission from the beginning to the end. He is set on avenging his father and does not deviate from that conviction for a moment. He just has trouble finding the proper opportunity for it. Killing a king is not to be taken lightly, even when the king is a villain of Claudius's caliber. When Hamlet finally does kill the king, it is done as swiftly as if blowing out a candle. He shows no hesitation or transformation. It is simply time, and he is quick to use it.

King Claudius is certainly a villain, comparable to the worst of them through the history of literature. His actions are focused on Hamlet, and they are confusingly inadequate until the showdown, when he poisons both the sword of Hamlet's dueling opponent and the cup from which he wants the prince to drink. A king of long-gone days would not have hesitated to be both quicker and more drastic when feeling threatened.

The most plausible explanation for the king's hesitancy is that he feels genuine fondness for Gertrude, his queen who is also the mother of Hamlet. That would make him reluctant to whisk away the inconvenient prince in a kingly manner, which would be to quickly have him killed, like his father. King Claudius obviously refrains from that, more or less, until the end of the play.

For Hamlet, too, his mother the queen is a complication. She has no awareness at all of Claudius's dreadful deed to his own brother. When Hamlet tries to imply it to her, she does not even comprehend. There is a moment in act III scene IV, where Hamlet confronts his mother about her inability to see King Claudius for what he is. Then the ghost of Hamlet's father suddenly appears and scolds him, demanding him to comfort the queen whom the ghost regards as innocent:

Do not forget: this visitation is but to whet thy almost blunted purpose. But, look, amazement on thy mother sits: O, step between her and her fighting soul: Conceit in weakest bodies strongest works: Speak to her, Hamlet.[343]

The ghost then appears no more in the play, which shows how significant this sudden reappearance is. The ghost of the dead king will not have Hamlet accuse and upset Gertrude. And his son complies.

It is all about the queen. Were it not for her love of her son, King Claudius would have killed Hamlet at his first sign of accusation. Were it not for her commitment to her new husband, Hamlet would have killed Claudius immediately after learning the truth from the ghost in the beginning of the play. Both Claudius and Hamlet hesitate for the queen's sake.

Queen Gertrude is the protagonist of the play. She is the one who has to come to a realization, a tremendously difficult

[343] William Shakespeare, *Hamlet*, edited by John Livingstone Lowes, New York 1914, p. 96.

one since it means she has to admit that she married the assassin of her former husband, the father of her son. It takes this whole play, the longest one Shakespeare wrote, to reach that conclusion. As soon as she does, when she accidentally drinks the poison intended for Hamlet, and calls it out to him, her son can kill the king and the play has arrived at its ending.

There would be no additional jump the audience would hang on to witness. This is enough. So, all of the principal characters die right there and then.

Contrary to his mother, Hamlet knows all along what has passed and what needs to be done. But he cannot force the queen to be convinced of the same. She has to find it out. That makes her the protagonist. Hamlet should be seen as the dramaturgical role of the hero. He already understands what his mother needs to figure out, and he is determined about what needs to be done. He is where the queen needs to be.

In her innocent ignorance, the queen is not able to live out the frustration that the situation calls for, so this task goes to Hamlet. Her frustration, instead, is the distress she feels about her son's increasingly odd behavior. He signals again and again that something is wrong, but she thinks that wrong is with him. Until her moment of realization, when tasting the poison of the cup: "No, no, the drink, the drink, — O my dear Hamlet, — the drink, the drink! I am poison'd."[344] At that moment she dies.

Hamlet is already dying from a poisonous wound, his combatant Laertes informs him. But he has time to finally take his revenge and kill the king. He does so by twice using the king's own potion — stabbing him with the poisoned blade and forcing some of the remaining poisoned drink down his throat. The last he says to him is "Follow my mother."

His greeting to his mother in the following speech is different: "Wretched queen, adieu!" Surely, he means wretched as unfortunate and pitiable, but he may also feel a touch of the

[344] Ibid., p. 151. Act V, scene II.

word's derogatory connotation. The queen's slowness to learn
has cost them both dearly.

It is possible to see, as many do, Hamlet as the protagonist, struggling to make himself avenge his dead father. His
main obstacle is his mother. Finally, when she dies, Hamlet is
able to overcome his hesitation and complete his task. But
there are two problems with this way of understanding the
drama.

One is that the death of his mother, then, would be a *deus
ex machina*, a solution by divine interference — or more precisely, a chance occurrence, when she happens to drink the poison meant for Hamlet. Like Aristotle in his *Poetics*, Shakespeare
was not fond of such solutions, and rightly so. It is a lousy way
to end a play.

The second argument against Hamlet as a hesitant protagonist, is that he actually already did kill the king without hesitation midway through the play. Well, he thought that he did.
In Act III, scene IV, he stabs Polonius hiding behind a tapestry,
thinking it is King Claudius.[345] Although it turns out to be the
wrong one dead, Hamlet has shown that he already has the
resolution and ability. He just waits for the right moment.

Even earlier in the play, Hamlet sneaks up on the king
with the intent of killing him. But he chooses not to, since the
king is involved in solemn prayer, and Hamlet does not want
to set the king's soul free at a moment when it shows unusual
piety:

*Now might I do it pat, now he is praying; and now I'll do't.
And so he goes to heaven: And so am I revenged. That
would be scann'd; a villain kills my father; and for that, I,
his sole son, do this same villain send to heaven. O, this is
hire and salary, not revenge.*[346]

[345] Ibid., p. 93.

[346] Ibid., p. 91. Act III, scene III.

The king, unaware of Hamlet's presence, is indeed sincere in the struggle with his conscience. He finishes his lament famously: "My words fly up, my thoughts remain below: Words without thoughts never to heaven go."[347] So, he most definitely is the villain of the piece, but not an ice-cold psychopath unable of remorse. He does struggle with his guilt. Not that it stops him from using tricks and violence to keep what he has wrongly gotten, but it makes him human.

Is he the antagonist of the play? If Hamlet is the protagonist, then he surely is. Their battle, sometimes in the open and sometimes in the hidden, goes on all through the play. But if Queen Gertrude and not Hamlet is the protagonist — then the king is not much of an antagonist. He is occupied with Hamlet all through, and never once challenges the queen in any way.

For Gertrude, then, the antagonist is none other than Hamlet. He is the one confronting her repeatedly, insisting that she needs to open her eyes and face the truth. That is why the queen shouts to Hamlet, when realizing that she is poisoned. That is how she confesses to him that he was right all along.

For those three main characters of the play, the most convincing setting is with the queen as the protagonist and Hamlet the antagonist. But that is not the only dramaturgical possibility.

Another character in the play can be the protagonist. Not Horatio, Hamlet's friend and confidant, who has the role of his companion. But there is another, with a significant role to play all through, and coming to a spectacular realization at the end. It is Laertes, Hamlet's other foe whose father he killed, and the one willingly using the poisoned blade against him.

Right before he does so, he mumbles to himself: "And yet 'tis almost 'gainst my conscience."[348] This "almost" disappears at the moment he is wounded by his own poisonous blade: "I am justly kill'd with mine own treachery." And he is the one to

---

[347] Ibid., p. 92.

[348] Ibid., p. 150. Act V, scene II.

reveal that the king is to blame. He repents with his dying breath:

> *Exchange forgiveness with me, noble Hamlet: Mine and my father's death come not upon thee, nor thine on me!*[349]

That is the progression of a protagonist. It would, of course, make Hamlet the antagonist, the one always challenging and enraging Laertes. Blaming Hamlet for the deaths of his sister Ophelia as well as his father, and not without cause, he has to overcome a lot of resistance within himself to realize the truth of the matter.

It is the trait of the master playwright Shakespeare at work. He knew and followed the dramaturgical principles of his ancient Greek colleagues and Aristotle, but did so in clever and mysterious ways.

Writing his play, he had no need of the hidden workings of unconscious archetypes. He consciously created the characters and made them interact as those characters would. The patterns to be found in this play and, I dare say, all the others, are dramaturgical. They are not cryptic clues from a collective unconscious, but simply calculated measures to make a drama excite and please an audience. It is all very conscious — the ingredients as well as their brilliant application.

The king is an archetypal figure of might and authority, but that does not mean Claudius should be interpreted as one. Shakespeare chose to make the stage one of a royal court in order to increase the gravity of the situation, and probably also to give the drama what today would be called extra bling, to please the audience.

It has always been a simple storytelling trick to make the characters additionally fancy, bringing a sense of importance to the characters and what they go through. Royalty is as high as you can go on the human scale. Mythological tales often use

[349] Ibid., p. 152.

the only higher authorities imaginable, the gods, to create the same effect.

In *Hamlet*, the choice of royalties also simplifies how the death of a man automatically leads to his brother taking over his position, which is something the plot needs. The king is not there as an archetype forcing itself onto the play by the medium of an unknowing playwright. He is a piece of the puzzle for the playwright to make a functioning whole of the story.

Actually, also the roles of the protagonist and the antagonist are more or less arbitrary. They are not necessary as such in a story, and if present they do not need to follow the usual patterns. That is evident from the structure of *Hamlet*, where these roles are not that easy to find and define with certainty. They are just commonly used as ingredients in a story to move it forward in an exciting way. Other tricks may very well accomplish the same.

Stories Are Self-Explanatory

Aristotle states famously in his *Poetics* that the drama has to have a beginning, a middle, and an end. This denotes that something has to have changed significantly from beginning to end. If not, the audience will feel utterly cheated.

Jung might have called that change a transformation, and why not? But in essence, it is just a change — in a character's mentality, in the prospects from then on, in what could have happened into what did happen. A change of whatever kind has to be there.

All the ingredient in a play — setting, events, and characters — primarily serve that purpose. A plot is simply a description of a change. That goes for myths as well as plays and other stories. It can be as subtle as a couple realizing that their love will last, which makes a huge difference from when they worried that it might not. Or it can be as bombastic as Armageddon. The change is the story.

Something I find disturbing with Jung's theories, and the reason for the above look at the structure of *Hamlet*, is that he supposed hidden mechanics and messages other than those of the author's conscious effort. While there may be such things, there is nothing in myths or other stories proving any of it. They are completely explainable and understandable without it.

So, Jung is doing the opposite of Ockham's razor. He introduces additional lines of explanation that are not called for. Even with stories that have obvious messages of moral or other kind, the idea of them stemming from a hidden collective unconscious is just not necessary to explain them.

For example, there is certainly a moral to the story of *Genesis 3* of the Bible, where Adam and Eve are expelled from the Garden of Eden. They committed the original sin by eating of the forbidden fruit, and as punishment they are both made mortal and thrown out of that sweet garden. Countless myths about primordial times have similar themes to explain the world of hardship in which we live. There is nothing unconscious about it. The story makes perfect sense as a composition of a conscious mind.

This is also true for Jung's idea of the archetypes. Certainly, ingredients in the myths can be described as archetypes in the meaning of representing concepts or traits of a familiar kind. But there is no necessity of going beyond the principle of stock characters in dramaturgy — the easily recognizable figures of a story to get it going without too much explanation. Those characters, then, demand the conscious understanding of both the author and the audience. They would not work equally well if they depended on unconscious reactions, in which case they would still confuse.

Yahweh in the story about the forbidden fruit is the almighty god. That means disobeying him is sure to be revealed and result in a terrible punishment. Adam and Eve are the very first humans, which means that their fate will be the fate of all humankind thereafter. The story works because these premises are understood consciously by the audience.

The snake is a figure introducing temptation, a human

weakness known by all to be the cause of so much suffering. Well, pleasure too, to be honest. It is a snake because that is often a poisonous animal, slithering silently, which makes it a threat to begin with. The story would not be as compelling if this rascal were, say, a fluffy white rabbit.

The fruit of which Adam and Eve have a bite, usually pictured as an apple although it is not specified in the Bible, is a medium by which the sin is committed. It is comparable to the magic potion of so many fairy tales. But again, it is not the emergence of an archetype with hidden origin and meaning. It is simply an instrument by which to move the action forward.

It is the pole-vault jump of this story. With those bites of the fruit catastrophe is bound to come. The fruit is a way of making it concrete, and the moment exact, to increase the excitement of the audience. It is the moment for us to shout "No!" as if believing our sentiment could somehow influence the actions of the characters. We know it will not, but still we are tempted to cry out.

Mythology as well as fairy tales and legends have myriads of similar stories. One single mistake and everybody suffers forever after. In Western society, for almost two thousand years, the Adam and Eve version has been the most famous of them. It could be called the archetype of such stories, although other versions preceded it. And the figures in it have come to be archetypes, much in Jung's sense — except for their place in the human mind. We are most definitely aware of them, and we know from where we got them. They are powerful symbols, but we all know why.

Jung made some interesting observations about the human use of symbols and the emotional response they trigger. But he jumped to conclusions about the nature of those things. He took them as evidence of his own claims about the structure of the psyche. They are not.

His whole theory complex was based on prejudice, which is hard to explain as something other than his urge to make his very own psychological doctrine and justifying it. He created a mythology, pretending it to be science. Instead of being so quick to conclude that the patterns he found in myths and other stories indicate an origin in a hidden collective unconscious storing ancient archetypes, he should at least have experimented with the idea that all those myths and stories were the ones creating and cementing the archetypes.

For thousands of years, we have been a storytelling species, and those stories have by time found a common mold, increasing their effect and memorability. It is definitely more likely that our long tradition of stories and their components have created the archetypes, than the other way around.

At the very least, there is no proof of the one explanation being more likely than the other. But really, Jung's model is harder to prove, since it calls for additional components not necessary in the alternative model. Stories do not need a collective unconscious of mysteriously charged archetypes to explain their structures and ingredients. The needs of the stories in themselves explain all that just fine.

The easily recognizable characters in most myths and stories can be called archetypes, in the meaning of being with us for quite long, but it would really suffice to call them types. That also allows us to include figures and symbols of later dates, since there are new types emerging in our culture over time.

The art of storytelling may follow ancient customs, but it is also innovative — or it would gradually lose its relevance to the audience. To both the writers and the audiences, stories are self-explanatory. All their components are accessible to conscious minds. They may be dependent on a more or less specified context, such as the time and society of their setting, but that is also something the conscious mind is equipped to grasp.

Jung's archetypes cannot encompass a specific context, since they are by definition archaic and unchanging. Nor can they explain the appearance of new types of archetypal dignity. That makes the concept inadequate for the explanation of myths and stories. They contain types, but not archetypes in

the Jungian sense. There is in no story any need of the latter —
except for in the story of Jung's own invention.

Granted, it is a good story, which is why it has attracted
so many psychologists, mythologists, artists, and others. But a
story it still is, and not a validated scientific theory. It stems
from Jung's imagination instead of from facts assembled in his
research. He seems to have hinted at it in the Prologue to his
autobiography, which was published posthumously. There he
explains:

> *I speak chiefly of inner experiences, amongst which I in-
> clude my dreams and visions. These form* the prima
> materia *of my scientific work.*[350]

As such, i.e., closer to fiction than to empirical science, his
theories make much more sense. He created a world of "what
if?" and it has proven to be inspiring, especially but not exclusively to other fiction.

The mysteries of it are intriguing, the symbols fascinating,
and the perspective on the human mind thought-provoking.
His conclusions may not be correct, but they are interesting.
They have led artists to new motifs, and they have also triggered psychologists as well as mythologists to come up with
innovative perspectives.

So, his dreams and visions certainly bore fruit. That is
worthy of praise, even though many of his scientific claims are
not.

[350] Jung & Jaffé 1965, p. 4.

Jungians

The following selection of Jungians consists of those who have written about myth and religion. Due to the nature of Jungian psychology, that would be most of them. Mythology is so intertwined with Jung's conception of the psyche that the latter is inadequately applied without the former. Therefore, I have needed to limit the selection to the most prominent or otherwise significant writers on the subject.

Surely, this selection can be questioned regarding who are included as well as who are not. I trust, at least, that the most obvious names are, especially regarding the first several decades of the emergence of Jungian analytical psychology.

In my previously released book about Freudian theories about myth and religion,[351] the corresponding selection was noticeably easier. The Freudian collective is overall much more homogenous, by their persistent loyalty towards Freud and his theories, and far from all of them have written about mythology. Mostly, they have been practicing psychoanalysts, often with a medical education, and a limited interest in subjects outside of the treatment of patients.

Although Sigmund Freud wrote a few books on the subject of mythology and how his psychology could be applied to it, few of his followers did the same. Most of those who did were his direct students.

Not so with the Jungians. Their number did by time get greater, and they shared Carl G. Jung's fascination with myths and religion. The influence of his ideas spread way beyond the discipline of psychology, particularly into anthropology and

---

[351] Stefan Stenudd, *Psychoanalysis of Mythology: Freudian Theories on Myth and Religion Examined*, Malmö 2022.

the history of religion, as well as studies of the arts, dramaturgy, esoteric literature, and more. Also, to a greater extent than with Freud, Jung's theories have survived past his own lifetime and not only among his direct students. Therefore, some writers treated here had little or no contact with Jung. Intellectually, though, they followed in his footsteps.

That following has been less faithful than was the case with Freud's disciples, who mostly remained almost religiously committed to Freud's thoughts. Jung's ideas might have lent themselves easier to individual interpretation and innovation, because those are noticeable traits in the texts of his followers. Already the complexity of Jung's theories and the vagueness of his definitions allow for it, maybe even demand it.

Not that it led to anarchy. The basic principles of Jung's understanding of mythology — the collective unconscious, individuation, and archetypes — remained. But these concepts are such that they give plenty of room for personal speculation, and that was exploited to different degrees by his followers.

As with Carl G. Jung, the thoughts on myth and religion of the following selection of Jungians are explored through the texts they wrote about those subjects.

Erich Neumann

German-born Erich Neumann (1905-1960) was a PhD in philosophy, but also got a medical education before he moved to Tel Aviv in 1934 to escape the Nazi persecution of Jews. That remained his home for the rest of his rather short life as a practitioner of analytical psychology.

In 1933, he attended a seminar held by Carl G. Jung in Berlin, and later the same year went to Zürich for seven months to be analyzed by him.[352] Jung held Neumann in high regard, which is evident in the foreword he wrote in the latter's book *The Origins and History of Consciousness*, praising his achievement, "he arrives at conclusions and insights which are among the most important ever to be reached in this field."[353]

Before meeting with Jung, he had developed an interest in Judaism, in particular Hasidism and its mysticism connected to the Kabbalah, which stayed with him through his life.[354] His attraction to mystical thought was evident already in his 1927 dissertation in philosophy, about the early 19th century philologist Johann Arnold Kanne, who had used a very speculative etymology to find a primordial mythology.[355]

New Ethics in the Shadow

Neumann's early literary projects were within fiction and poetry, but in 1949 he published two books with psychological themes, both containing respectful forewords by Jung. The first, *Tiefenpsychologie und neue Ethik* (*Depth Psychology and a*

---

[352] Lance S. Owens, *C. G. Jung and Erich Neumann: The Zaddik, Sophia and the Shekinah*, PDF 2017, p. 4.

[353] Erich Neumann, *The Origins and History of Consciousness*, transl. R. F. C. Hull, New York 1970 (originally published in German 1949), p. xiv.

[354] Owens 2017, p. 4.

[355] Erich Neumann, *Johann Arnold Kanne: Ein Beitrag zur Geschichte der mystischen Sprachphilosophie*, University of Erlangen 1927.

New Ethic), dealt with the horrifying evil exposed in World War II, which he related to the Jungian idea of the shadow, the dark side of the personality. When this entity within us is ignored, a reaction is unavoidable, and we fall much like Icarus after flying too high:

> *It is this lower element, the part disregarded by man's hubris and sinful pride, which is responsible for his downfall in the end; the repressed element, overlooked in the arrogance of the flight, ultimately takes its revenge.*[356]

The solution lies in recognizing this inner evil instead of conforming to the "old ethic" of the collective, which is to insist on being good according to its values. Facing one's inner darkness is not easy:

> *To be obliged to admit that one is infantile and maladjusted, miserable and ugly, a human animal related to the monkeys, a sexual beast and a creature of the herd is in itself a shattering experience for any ego that has identified itself with the collective values.*[357]

The shadow can only be tamed if recognized and dealt with. Its needs cannot be suppressed, "it becomes necessary for the ego to enter into some kind of gentleman's agreement with the shadow." That is what Neumann's new ethic proposes.

Certainly, society's moral demands on its citizens, some outspoken and some not, can be a straitjacket strapped so tightly that people nearly suffocate. Conformity can easily go too far, allowing no room for personal deviation, not even accepting that the human being is equipped with any urges re-

---

[356] Erich Neumann, *Depth Psychology and a New Ethic*, transl. Eugene Rolfe, London 1969 (the original was published in 1949), p. 43.
[357] Ibid., 79f.

garded as immoral. As if perfect adaption to social demands is human nature. That won't work, and the cost for insisting on it is high for individuals as well as society. It leads to discomfort, unrest, and brutality.

Whether that has anything to do with a shadow entity residing in an unconscious, though, is questionable, and so is basing a cure for society and its people on such a concept.

People have needs. Some of them are unacceptable to society, but others might just as well be allowed or at least disregarded. In every society, there is continuous interaction between what is expected of people and with what they are unable to comply. There is compromise everywhere. It is not unconscious. People know when they are suppressed, and what causes their inhibitions as well as the instances when they act in spite of them.

Since these processes are known and considered in any society, there is little hope that introducing an unconscious shadow into the mix will fix things. The delicate balance between social demands and personal needs will still be continuously recalibrated.

Consciousness through Mythology

The second book of the same year, which made much more of an impression on Jungians, was *Ursprungsgeschichte des Bewusstseins* (*The Origins and History of Consciousness*), where he used a number of mythological components to describe stages in the evolution of consciousness, both in mankind as a whole from primeval times and in each person's development from infancy and on, since "the individual ego consciousness has to pass through the same archetypal stages which determined the evolution of consciousness in the life of humanity."[358]

Before this process begins, the human mind is unconscious, or as Neumann puts it, "the ego is contained in the un-

[358] Erich Neumann, *The Origins and History of Consciousness*, transl. R. F. C. Hull, New York 1970 (originally published in German 1949), p. xvi.

conscious."[359] The awakening of consciousness comes in stages, shown by archetypes. Since the archetypes reside in the collective unconscious, that must be the engine in this process. Neumann refers to the content of the collective unconscious as transpersonal, as opposed to individual.

The archetypes and their meanings are rooted in us all, but Neumann firmly denies that historical events can be inherited, no matter how unique or recurrent they are, "for up to the present there has been no scientific proof of the inheritance of acquired characteristics."[360] He uses this argument to dismiss a central theory of Sigmund Freud, without mentioning his name. He doesn't need to, since it is obvious:

> *The castration motif, for instance, is not the result of the inheritance of an endlessly repeated threat of castration by a primordial father, or rather by an infinity of primordial fathers. Science has discovered nothing that could possibly support such a theory, which moreover presupposes the inheritance of acquired characteristics. Any reduction of the castration threat, parricide, the "primal scene" of parental intercourse, and so on, to historical and personalistic data, which presumes to paint the early history of humanity in the likeness of a patriarchal bourgeois family of the nineteenth century, is scientifically impossible.*

That raises the question, though, of how the many transpersonal archetypes can remain from generation to generation. As Neumann describes them, they are indeed inherited. So, where is the scientific proof of that?

There are additional peculiarities with Neumann's theory about the origins of consciousness. Starting all the way back to primordial times, he finds relevant archetypes in creation myths. He compares the development since that distant begin-

[359] Ibid., p. 5.

[360] Ibid., xxi.

ning with the child growing up, but it is strangely unclear if he refers to the actual past or just the transpersonal images of it, residing in the unconscious of us all.

He must mean the latter, or his understanding of scientific cosmogony is lacking, indeed. But then, how did the archetypes take form, since mankind did not appear for a few billion years after our world was formed? From where did they get a symbolic imagery describing the creation of the world?

Neumann doesn't discuss this in his book, but the plausible answer would be that the archetypes are in no way about the creation, only about human growth of consciousness. Still, he suggests that primeval man was wondering about the mysteries of the world:

> *The symbolic story of the beginning, which speaks to us from the mythology of all ages, is the attempt made by man's childlike, prescientific consciousness to master problems and enigmas which are mostly beyond the grasp of even our developed modern consciousness.*[361]

Admittedly, that was a conscious effort, and yet Neumann insists on the same page that answers to the questions about origin were to be found in the unconscious:

> *The mythological answers to these questions are symbolical, like all answers that come from the depths of the psyche, the unconscious.*

So, conscious questions were answered symbolically by the unconscious, to which the conscious had no access. That would not do for the conscious mind. It would come up with its own answers, and as the creation myths show — it sure did. Denying this is sadly underestimating and simplifying what thoughts were involved in the formation of the creation myths.

[361] Ibid., p. 7.

Our ancestors based them on conscious speculations about how the world might have begun. It is evident in those myths, also in the ones that Neumann refers to.

For example, he mentions Egyptian creation texts where the sole primordial deity gives birth to offspring by masturbating into his mouth and spitting it out. Neumann interprets it symbolically, but to ancient Egyptians it was a reasonable explanation to how the first deity all alone could multiply — by self-impregnating. Nothing unconscious is needed to explain the myth.[362]

Mythology is full of clever solutions to the problem of origin, what was first and how the rest of the world came into being. It was something our ancestors enjoyed contemplating, as we still do. Neumann does not allow for this, claiming about early man that "abstract questions of this kind were wholly alien to his consciousness."[363] According to Neumann, it is still not much the "primitive" understand, not even the basics of procreation: "Many primitive peoples do not recognize the connection between sexual intercourse and birth." He gives no source to this absurd claim.

As for his archetypes at the dawn of creation, there is a primary one — the circle, which is "allied" to the sphere and the egg, but Neumann links it mainly to the *ouroboros*, the circular image of a snake biting its own tail. To him it stands for "the Primal Deity who is sufficient unto himself," but it also represents the maternal womb, the union of masculine and feminine that are the world parents, and even the primal ocean.[364]

Thereby, Neumann combines ingredients from several different creation myths into one. That is hard to find in mythology. A primal entity can be a world egg, or the womb of one deity who gives birth to the world, or an initial couple be-

362 Ibid., p. 19.

363 Ibid., p. 13.

364 Ibid., pp. 11, 13, 23.

ing its parents, or a primordial sea out of which the world emerges — but not all in one myth. And the ouroboros is utterly rare in creation myths, if there is even one where it is the primal being. There are similarities in creation myths, but also many differences. They cannot be molded into one.

Neumann's creation process towards consciousness goes through several steps, represented by archetypal deities that seem to be essentially the same one in stages of metamorphosis. There is the Great Mother, about whom he would soon publish a separate book, the separation of the World Parents, then the Hero slaying his mother and father, whereby he gets his treasure.

This treasure is a captive liberated by the hero killing a dragon of some sort, like the valiant knight saving the princess in many fairy tales. But this captive is to be understood symbolically, as "something within — namely the soul herself." By freeing the captive, the hero is really freeing his own soul. The puzzle of the archetypes at play shows the way for anyone to accomplishing this, since "the hero myth is never concerned with the private history of an individual, but always with some prototypal and transpersonal event of collective significance."[365]

Neumann's view on the soul is peculiar. He claims its reality is felt by all, but completely misunderstood by primitive man:

> The reality of the soul is one of the basic and most immediate experiences of mankind; it permeates primitive man's whole view of life, naturally without his being aware that it is an inner experience.[366]

Naturally? One has to wonder what he means by the soul, if there are people who experience it only as something outside

[365] Ibid., pp. 196f.
[366] Ibid., p. 209.

themselves. He doesn't define it, but his text suggests that he sees it as synonymous to the psyche, which is set free by being discovered:

> *This discovery of the reality of the psyche corresponds mythologically to the freeing of the captive and the un-earthing of the treasure.*[367]

By this discovery the psyche's creative powers, which Neumann calls primordial, are accessible and expressed. That is the goal of the process:

> *The self-generating power of the soul is man's true and final secret, by virtue of which he is made in the likeness of God the creator and distinguished from all other living things.*

He continues by describing at length the myth of Perseus as a paradigm of the hero myth and turns to Osiris as the symbol of the final self-transformation of the hero.[368]

Accessing the whole world of mythology, it is easy to find similarities or patterns when picking a few. Many anthropologists have been known to do the same, especially in the 19th and early 20th centuries. In the vast mythological material assembled, anything could be argued about the meaning and function of mythology as a whole, by selecting examples carefully. But there are always deviations from the suggested norm, and usually they are in majority. It is a hopeless task trying to prove any theory that claims all mythology to be basically the same, since that is just not the case.

The same problem is obvious in Neumann's writing. It does not hold up to close inspection, nor do the sources he uses to prove his case. Jung was the source that Neumann leaned

---

[367] Ibid., p. 210.

[368] Ibid., pp. 213ff, 221ff.

on the heaviest, referring to his texts as proof of claims about the archetypes and the human psyche. But Jung did not present any solid evidence of his theories. They were just speculations, and the patterns he saw were indeed questionable.

As for mythology and its interpretation, Neumann frequently used the writing of Swiss 19th century anthropologist Johann Jakob Bachofen, who had theories about early stages of society and linking them to certain significant deities. In his book *Das Mutterrecht* (*Mother Right*) from 1861, he claimed that in the distant past there had been a stage of matriarchy, basing much of society as well as religion on motherhood, later replaced by patriarchy.[369] An interesting theory, certainly, but again speculation, lacking convincing evidence.

As for Neumann's theory about archetypes from the collective unconscious gradually giving people consciousness, it needs first of all to show that they lacked it previously. It is a strange presumption.

We are biological creatures, and the brain has been formed by the same slow evolutionary process as the rest of the body. Consciousness, as in self-awareness, is a consequence of how our brains have evolved, and it may have been with us for very long. After all, it is an essential resource in keeping ourselves alive. And as long as we have had that resource, we have used it. Otherwise, we would not have it. Babies might not be self-conscious already at birth, but it is sure to come — without the need of archetypal stimulation.

Still, comparing creation myths with human development, the species as well as the individual, is an interesting thought experiment. They share some elementary components, such as describing a birth of sorts, and a growth in both size and complexity. Well, that's about it.

But the claim that creation myths are about humans and not at all about the world is erroneous. It is indicated already

---

[369] Erich Fromm also referred to Bachofen and the matriarchy, in *The Forgotten Language* from 1951.

by the fact that there are many creation myths where humans enter very late, and often fail to play any significant role. Most of all, the cosmogony of those myths makes it quite clear that they primarily express speculations about how the world began and why it is as it is. The perspective is one of humans as spectators instead of main players. So, it is not really about us.

Woman as an Archetype

Neumann's other major book is *The Great Mother*, which he wrote in German (*Die große Mutter. Der Archetyp des großen Weiblichen*) but its first publication was the English translation of it in 1955.

As the title states, the book is about the archetype of the Great Mother, who was also treated at length in *The Origins and History of Consciousness*. But here the subject is expanded, and so are the examples and different appearances of this archetype. He explains its vast importance:

> *The effect of this archetype may be followed through the whole of history, for we can demonstrate its workings in the rites, myths, symbols of early man and also in the dreams, fantasies, and creative works of the sound as well as the sick man of our own day.*[370]

He gives examples of female deities from numerous mythologies, which are certainly not hard to find. The book also contains a lot of illustrations on the same theme. As in the previously treated book, his analysis follows Jung's theories and claims support in Bachofen, although altering the perspective of the latter:

> *Bachofen has brilliantly shown this elementary character to be typical of matriarchy; and if understood psychologi-*

[370] Erich Neumann, *The Great Mother: An Analysis of the Archetype*, transl. Ralph Manheim, Princeton 1972 (first edition 1955), p. 3.

cally rather than sociologically, his discoveries have lasting value.[371]

Although the title of the book specifies the mother, Neumann widens the scope to treat the archetype of the woman. He finds the central symbol of her being the vessel as the essence of the feminine:

> *The basic symbolic equation woman = body = vessel corresponds to what is perhaps mankind's — man's as well as woman's — most elementary experience of the Feminine.*[372]

That must largely be based on her womb and what it can contain, which is quite a limited representation of the gender, as if the meaning of her existence is to carry for nine months the offspring. If so, the corresponding symbol of the masculine should be the ejaculation, but that is hardly what Neumann or anyone of his Jungian colleagues claim.

Woman is described as an intricate, mysterious being of vast archetypal importance, whereas man is little more than synonymous to humankind, as if only he belongs to the species and she is a mythical creature, a superhuman deity. A flattering description at first, but excluding at length.

Neumann widens the symbol of the vessel to point to the human body's interior, what it carries inside, which is "archetypally identical with the unconscious."[373] So, in this sense both men and women are vessels. Still, it applies particularly to woman:

> *For obvious reasons woman is experienced as the vessel par excellence. Woman as body-vessel is the natural expression*

---

[371] Ibid., p. 25.

[372] Ibid., p. 39.

[373] Ibid., p. 40.

*of the human experience of woman bearing the child
"within" her and of man entering "into" her in the sexual
act.*[374]

He frequently refers to mythology for examples of the female archetype in her different appearances and roles, constructing an elaborate schema of the dynamics of those roles. This schema, he explains, is a compromise between the conscious effort and the uniqueness of the material it is based on. He admits this weakness, but defends it in words that have a tone similar to religious dogma:

*Thus it will always be possible to criticize the schema for
being far from reality, and to criticize the material chosen
to illustrate the schema for being accidental. Both criti-
cisms may be true to a certain extent. But they will be pow-
erless to alter the fact that psychic reality evades our desire
for schematic exposition.*[375]

It seems that he thereby argues against the possibility and utility of at all making a schema. As for his mode of interpreting the myths, it doesn't differ from what he applied in the previous book discussed above, so there is not much point in dwelling on it here.

Neumann first writing was within fiction and poetry. This passion might explain his interest in the fantastic landscape of Jungian psychology, and his way of treating the subject in his books — like fantastic stories, full of fantastic creatures steering humans in hidden ways, some towards tragedy and some towards a happy ending. Neumann turned depth psychology into a fairy tale. He might even have approved of this analogy.

[374] Ibid., p. 42.
[375] Ibid., p. 83.

Károly Kerényi

The Hungarian classical scholar Károly Kerényi (1897-1973) was not a Jungian, strictly speaking, although he had a similar understanding of mythology and was invited by Jung to lecture repeatedly on the topic in Switzerland.

The main reason for including him here is that he co-wrote a book on that very subject with Carl G. Jung: *Einführung in das Wesen der Mythologie* (*Introduction to the Essence of Mythology*) in 1942.

It this book they take turns. Kerényi presents mythological themes, *mythologems*, and Jung adds psychological aspects to them. There are two main themes, the child-god and the Kore. According to Kerényi, the latter is not only Persephone who is usually associated with the name, but the maiden goddess in general. Kore simply means maiden.[376]

In spite of their elaborate ways to analyze mythology, Kerényi insists that one does justice to it, "not by interpretation and explanation but above all by letting it alone and allowing it to utter its own meaning."[377] He adds:

> *In a true mythologem this meaning is not something that could be expressed just as well and just as fully in a non-mythological way.*

It stops neither of them from trying, but Kerényi does so with evident knowledge of and admiration for the Greek myths, which constitute the vast majority of his references. He claims that mythologies always refer to a primordial time, which is true in a general sense. At least they usually start

---

[376] Carl G. Jung & Károly Kerényi, *On a Science of Mythology: The Myth of the Divine Child and the Mysteries of Eleusis*, transl. R. F. C. Hull, New York 1949 (originally published in German 1942), p. 147.

[377] Ibid., p. 4.

there, and remain in a distant past. What he says about the divine child, though, can be debated:

> *The mythologies speak in the image of a divine child, the first-born of primeval times, in whom the "origin" first was; they do not speak of the coming-to-be of some human being but of the coming-to-be of the divine cosmos or a universal God.*[378]

A primordial child-god is not typical in mythology. Really, most creation myths are strikingly devoid of children. Deities emerge as adults. Even humans do when it is time for their appearance. Not a word about an initial childhood. This is in itself worthy of pondering. Why is childhood so rare in creation myths, although we know from ourselves that it inevitably follows birth?

Kerényi's statement can only be understood symbolically. When gods are born, they must do that as children although it is not mentioned in the myths. He seems to regard it as implied, but that is a weak basis for a theory of the mythological meaning.

When discussing Kore, the maiden goddesses, he readily admits that they are "far more typical of Greek religion than boy-gods."[379]

As for Kore, he sees her as a female counterpart to the boy-god, representing the woman's fate in a budlike form:

> *The Kore-goddess throws light on the old mythological idea of the bud in its capacity to unfold and yet to contain a whole separate world in itself. The idea can also be likened to a nucleus.*[380]

---

[378] Ibid., p. 12.

[379] Ibid., p. 148.

[380] Ibid., p. 147f.

He goes on to state that divine maidens are so typical of Greek religion that it can be called neither a "Father religion" nor a "Mother religion" or a combination of the two:

> *It is as though the Olympian order had thrust the great Mother-Goddesses of olden time into the background for the sole purpose of throwing the divine Korai into sharper relief.*

As with the child-god, Kerényi may have exaggerated the importance of Kore in Greek mythology. It is voluminous, which means all kinds of patterns can be extracted from it. The question is if they are the most adequate ones. He seems to be guided by a wish to find archetypes fitting his — and most likely Jung's — idea of a nucleus of mythology.

Contrary to his co-writer, though, Kerényi is rather reluctant to use the term archetype. He mentions it only three times in passing. To compare, his use of the concept *monad*, as understood by the ethnologist Leo Frobenius, is much more frequent. He explains the concept:

> *Frobenius names such factors, which are not amenable to further explanation, "monads" and sees in them the "structural principles" of the various views of the world in various cultures.*[381]

Primordial image

Generally in his writing, Kerényi seems hesitant to apply the term archetype — or even to mention Jung. In *The Heroes of the Greeks*, written more than a decade after the above discussed text, he just mentions Jung once, and that is in the preface. He doesn't dwell on the archetypes at all, although the hero is the most central of them in Jungian thought.

Also in his last book, *Zeus and Hera*, he mentions Jung

[381] Ibid., p. 26.

once, in the introduction, but the term archetype appears several times, also in the subtitle, *Archetypal Image of Father, Husband, and Wife*. But that is in the English translation.

The German subtitle uses "*Urbild*" (primordial image) instead of archetype. They are often treated as synonymous, although the word "*Archetyp*" exists in the German language. Kerényi uses it a few times in the German version of the book. At one instance he connects it to Urbild, and there the English translator chose "prototype" for the German word, which is neither wrong nor optimal.

Anyway, while comparing the two words, Kerényi explains why he is reluctant to use archetype: "The Greek word *archetypos* — from the language of the philosophers — is adjectival and I like to use it substantively only when greater intelligibility can be achieved."[382] That grammatical condition was respected by the translator in the subtitle, and there are plenty of instances of the adjective archetypal in the text.

It is harder to understand the title *Asklepios: Archetypal Image of the Physician's Existence*, since neither archetype nor prototype or anything like it is in the German title: *Der Göttliche Arzt. Studien über Asklepios und seine Kultstätte*. But Kerényi explains in the preface that he was the one insisting on that translation in the subtitle for this and the other monographs on Greek deities. He did so to "stress the possibility of convergence with modern psychology."[383]

Still, he insists on the previous page that he does not attempt to apply the methods of Jungian psychology. He refers to other writers for that. The word is not used elsewhere in the book.

[382] Károly Kerényi, *Zeus and Hera: Archetypal Image of Father, Husband, and Wife*, transl. Christopher Holme, Princeton 1975 (originally published in German 1972), p. xii.

[383] Károly Kerényi, *Asklepios: Archetypal Image of the Physician's Existence*, transl. Ralph Manheim, New York 1959 (originally published in German 1947 and revised in 1956), p. xxvi.

His reluctance to use archetype as a noun separated him distinctly from Jung, who definitely regarded the archetypes as entities in the collective unconscious. Kerényi stayed with the adjective, indicating that he did not agree with Jung on that.

What he described with the word was an attribute, and not a thing in itself. To him, then, the father was not an archetype, but some mythological fathers could be archetypal, and the same for the mother, the maiden, and so on. He also allowed for the archetypal significance of a deity to change as its role shifted in the mythology.

Jung's view was much more rigid.

In the introduction to *Eleusis: Archetypal Image of Mother and Daughter* Kerényi discusses Jung at some length, and points out that it was not he who turned to Jung, but the opposite. Jung found support for his own theories in Kerényi's writing.[384]

Kerényi is clear about not always agreeing with Jung's interpretations, for example when it comes to the archetypal:

From my point of view, I speak of archetypal facts of human existence, of realities which cannot be mere realities of the psyche and which, of course, are also not concrete in the manner of tangible objects.[385]

[384] Károly Kerényi, *Eleusis: Archetypal Image of Mother and Daughter*, transl. Ralph Manheim, New York 1967 (originally published in 1960), pp. xxiv ff.

[385] Ibid., p. xxxii.

Joseph L. Henderson

The most remarkable thing about the American analytical psychologist Joseph L. Henderson (1903-2007) might be the age he reached, which was 104, and continuing his practice in San Francisco until just a couple of years before that. In 1929, he spent a year in analysis with Carl G. Jung and Toni Wolff in Zürich.[386]

His writing through the years consists mainly of articles in Jungian journals and chapters in anthologies, but there are two books of his own: *Thresholds of Initiation* from 1967 and *Cultural Attitudes in Psychological Perspective* from 1984. Together with Maud Oakes he wrote *The Wisdom of the Serpent* in 1963, where his contribution was the introduction of some 70 pages. He also wrote a chapter of about 50 pages in Jung's *Man and his Symbols* from 1964.

Henderson devoted much of his writing to the subject of initiation in the light of analytical psychology, which would bring him closer to rite than to myth, but in Jungian tradition the two are mainly understood as expressions of the same psychological processes.

Reading Dreams

Before his death in 1961, Carl G. Jung invited Henderson to write a chapter in *Man and his Symbols*, an honor only three others shared with him. The book was published in 1964 and has been in print ever since, in several languages. Jung was the editor of the book and his own chapter in it was the last text he wrote before his death.

Henderson's chapter, "Ancient myths and modern man," treats the hero myth as a symbolical representation of the steps people need to take for their psychological development to-

[386] Thomas B. Kirsch, *The Jungians: A Comparative and Historical Perspective*, London 2000, p. 80.

wards complete adults. He has quite a specific description of the hero tale, which he regards as universal:

> *Over and over again one hears a tale describing a hero's miraculous but humble birth, his early proof of superhuman strength, his rapid rise to prominence or power, his triumphant struggle with the forces of evil, his fallibility to the sin of pride (hybris), and his fall through betrayal or a "heroic" sacrifice that ends in his death.*[387]

There are many hero tales around the world that fit this structure, more or less, but there are others that certainly do not. For example, the story doesn't always end with the hero's death, at least not in any other sense than that we all die, given time. In some tales the hero is a deity, blessed with immortality, so death is out of the equation. Nor is every hero born in humble circumstances or a victim of hybris.

Henderson's description is far too specific, applicable to some but not all heroes. What they may all have in common is some extraordinary capacity, not necessarily strength, and a grand quest that may or may not include the victory over some mighty foe, who does not have to be evil. That is enough of a definition for hero tales: remarkable persons on spectacular quests. Like Jung, Henderson has twisted the definition to fit the archetypal patterns he wants to find.

Doing so, he sees the hero tale show a process in which "the image of the hero evolves in a manner that reflects each stage of the evolution of the human personality." There are four such stages, or cycles, which he labels according to Paul Radin's study of Winnebago hero myths: the Trickster, Hare, Red Horn, and Twin cycle.[388]

[387] Joseph L. Henderson, "Ancient myths and modern man," Carl G. Jung & Marie-Louise von Franz (ed.), *Man and his Symbols*, New York 1964, p. 110.

[388] Ibid., p. 112.

In the book Henderson refers to, *Winnebago Hero Cycles* from 1948, Radin has the following definitions, all relating to the concept of libido: the Trickster represents the undifferentiated libido, the Hare the partially and imperfectly differentiated libido, the Red Horn the well differentiated libido, and the Twins the integrated libido. He calls the four periods "the primordial, the primitive, the Olympian and the Promethean."[389]

He goes on to state that the Trickster is totally non-moral and non-purposive, the Hare only secondarily moral and purposive, the Red Horn almost completely moral and purposive, and the Twins symbolize man's mastery of the world.

Radin doesn't define libido, but his use of it strongly suggests that he refers to Jung's rather than Freud's application of the term, i.e., not just a sexual urge but urge as such, the passionate longing. In his introduction, Radin discusses the theories of both Freud and Jung, with particular respect for the latter. He insists that the new lines of inquiry they have initiated should be utilized, although he personally disagrees fundamentally with the viewpoints, the methods and the conclusions of Freud and Jung as well as their followers.[390] That did not stop him from later spending a few years in Switzerland and cooperating with Jungians.

Henderson applies the four Winnebago cycles to his definition of the hero tale stages, and does so by interpreting dreams patients of his have described. He sees the same pattern there, which he takes as evidence of its existence. To him, as to all his fellow analysts, dreams are keys to the psyche and to its needs:

The individual may feel that his dreams are spontaneous
and disconnected. But over a long period of time the ana-
lyst can observe a series of dream images and note that they

[389] Paul Radin, *Winnebago Hero Cycles: A Study in Aboriginal Literature*, Baltimore 1948, p. 8.

[390] Ibid., pp. 7f.

have a meaningful pattern; and by understanding this his
patient may eventually acquire a new attitude to life.[391]

But dreams are elusive by nature, and even more so when retold instead of personally experienced. Normally, the dream quickly fades away when the dreamer awakens, and even before that it is usually fragmentary, meaningless to the dreamer. Henderson also points this out:

The dreamer is not usually presented with clear images by the unconscious. He has to puzzle out a meaning from a succession of contrasts and paradoxes.[392]

So, the meaning of the dream as it actually appears is unclear. It has to be interpreted by the conscious mind — and in a therapy session this effort is guided, to say the least, by the analyst. The dream only gets a meaning by this conscious process in a dialogue steered by elaborate preconceptions about what can be found and how it is to be understood. More than that — after repeated sessions, the patient is inclined to search for dreams of a certain kind already when waking up. For all we know, this compliance may even happen in the formation of them.

What is certain is that dreams extracted in this manner can't prove any theory navigating the search for them. The very idea of someone's dream making no sense until explained by another person is close to preposterous. It makes dream analysis unfalsifiable, which also means it is improvable. That may seem like a haven for the analyst, but it is at the cost of credibility.

Already the first dream Henderson presents displays this flaw. In it, a guide explains things to the dreamer, and Henderson concludes that this guide is presumably his analyst. But he

[391] Jung & von Franz (ed.) 1964, p. 107.
[392] Ibid., p. 116.

fails to consider how this may have influenced the dream or the patient's recollection of it. Since all the dreams he uses in his reasoning are from his patients, they share the same weakness.

To Henderson, the transformation process described by the four stages ends in death and rebirth, after which it is completed. That is what he sees as the function of initiation rites:

> *The ritual takes the novice back to the deepest level of original mother-child identity or ego-Self identity, thus forcing him to experience a symbolic death. In other words, his identity is temporarily dismembered or dissolved in the collective unconscious. From this state he is then ceremonially rescued by the rite of the new birth.*[393]

Using the fairy tale of Beauty and the Beast, he comments on the psychological process necessary for women, and his perspective is quite dated, to say the least. Jungians, as well as Freudians, have mostly expressed rather conservative ideas of gender and sexuality. Often quite bluntly, they have insisted on the heterosexual norm as the natural state of things, and any deviation from it is a sign of some kind of malfunction in the psyche of the patient. Henderson is no exception.

He claims that "the sacred marriage as an archetypal form has a particularly important meaning for the psychology of women, and one for which they are prepared during their adolescence by many preliminary events of an initiatory character."[394] That could definitely be discussed also at the time of his writing. As for the Beauty's commitment to the Beast, he told a woman having a dream which he connected to the tale:

> *I explained to her that this meant she was ready to give up the habit of "living in her head"; she must learn to free her*

[393] Ibid., p. 130.
[394] Ibid., p. 136.

body to discover its natural sexual response and the fulfill-
ment of its biological role in motherhood.[395]

He explains that she had to sacrifice the "masculine" hero role, and as she heeded his advice, he assures us:

> *She did then improve her love-life and became the mother of two very satisfactory children.*

So, the children were even satisfactory. There seems to be no limit to what analysis can accomplish.

The dream of the woman, leading to Henderson's advice, he relates in the following way:

> *She dreamed she was in a line of young women like herself, and as she looked ahead to where they were going she saw that as each came to the head of the line she was decapitated by a guillotine. Without any fear the dreamer remained in the line, presumably quite willing to submit to the same treatment when her turn came.*

If dreams are at all possible to interpret, there are other less elaborate ways to understand this one. Henderson's advice seems to be that she should go ahead and let herself be beheaded, since that is demanded of her gender. Indeed, something similar has been demanded of women for centuries. The symbolism is striking — her head is to come off, as if the body would do better without it.

Repeated Initiation

The subject of initiation in the light of analytical psychology was one Joseph L. Henderson returned to repeatedly, describing it as a process of consecutive archetypes. The above-mentioned text was published in 1964, but existed at least as a draft

---

[395] Ibid., p. 137.

in 1961 when Jung approved it.[396] Already in 1939, he wrote a paper on the subject for the Analytical Psychology Club of New York City, titled *Initiation Rites*, and in his introduction to the 1963 book *The Wisdom of the Serpent*, co-written with Maud Oakes, he treated initiation as a theme in myths. In 1967 his book *Thresholds of Initiation* was published.

His view on initiation was consistently that of the ritual as death and rebirth. The old personality needs to die for the transformed person to emerge, as in childhood replaced by adolescence, the most significant of the rites of passage, which is often performed with ingredients of both pain and blood. So far, Henderson's analogy makes sense.

It gets less convincing when he applies Jungian theory to it all. Mainly, the archetypes are superfluous in explaining the form and function of initiation.

Henderson's perspective is that of a therapist, not an anthropologist. He is focused on how the concept of initiation can be applied to the treatment of patients, and his major method is dream analysis. This does inevitably turn his attention from a social to an individual understanding of initiation, although as a rite it is obviously socially upheld and performed. But he removes the rite of it and replaces it with an individual process towards increased maturity, akin to a school with only one pupil — and one teacher, being the analyst.

That is expressed in the idea of its goal being individuation, a tell-tale term for this perspective:

> *What is important for our study is to seek to discover in all these materials specific thresholds of initiation, the rites of passage which make possible the transition from childhood to adolescence, from adolescence to early maturity, and from maturity to the experience of individuation.*[397]

[396] Ibid., p. 11.

[397] Joseph L. Henderson, *Thresholds of Initiation*, Middletown 1979 (first edition 1967), p. 19.

It may be an unavoidable consequence of the discipline of depth psychology, another tell-tale term. The truth is sought internally, deep within the individual mind — and through dreams, which are as personal as it gets since they are invisible to anyone else.

The Jungian concept of the collective unconscious gives the impression of a social perspective, but that is misleading. This hidden part of the mind is supposed to share material common to us all, but its function is again strictly personal. It speaks internally to the individual, its symbolic language giving clues to the self-realization of individuation.

The Jungian idea of the psyche is at the core solitary, in spite of its features being common to us all. But by devaluing the social aspects, only half of what we are remains.

Fear of Death

There is one sentence by Henderson that demands attention. It is from the book *The Wisdom of the Serpent*, which he co-wrote with the ethnologist Maud Oakes in 1963, wherein a number of myths are presented as examples of initiation. As the subtitle specifies, the initiation pattern is explained as a process through death to a new life: *The Myths of Death, Rebirth, and Resurrection*.

In the introduction, Henderson discusses the fear of death, which to him is "at bottom the ego's fear of the unknown."[398] That is one way of describing it, though hardly the whole truth. It is not necessarily what might be on the other side of death that scares us, but the unavoidable prospect of dying. We want to keep it off as long as we can. Only a small minority welcomes it — and that is not because they look forward to death, but because they find life miserable.

---

[398] Joseph L. Henderson & Maud Oakes, *The Wisdom of the Serpent: The Myths of Death, Rebirth, and Resurrection*, Princeton 1990 (first edition 1963), p. 3.

So, our attitude towards death is not as much about the unknown as it is about the life we know.

Still, those words by Henderson are not the ones standing out the most. It is what ha says on the next page, to explain why the fear of death is not at all about death:

> *Viewed from the only absolute standpoint we have, that is, of being still alive, we can therefore regard fear of death as being fear of change, or fear of growing up, or fear of becoming independent of the claims of the material world, or a mixture of all three.*[399]

The fact that we are still alive does not mean that we can't fear death. Actually, the opposite is true: it is because we are alive that we fear death. We could not fear it if we were not alive, since we would already be dead.

Of course, that does not mean we don't fear change, growing up, and thousands of other things. But the fear of death is definitely one of them — the big one — and has been so for as far back as recorded history takes us, and in every known culture. It is what lies at the core of most religions, and the gnawing frustration that frequently muddles our emotions and actions.

Not long after we are born, we learn that we will die, and there is no way around it. We don't even know when. It is hard to enjoy life fully, when knowing it can be snatched away from us at any moment.

It may be that the great lesson to be learned in life is to come to terms with the fact that it ends. But that is far from Henderson's idea of archetypes setting off a series of initiations leading to individuation. Even if such a process is successfully completed, so that the conscious is aware of the unconscious and at peace with it, the prospect of death is unchanged — and so is the fear of it.

[399] Ibid., p. 4f.

Joseph Campbell

Joseph Campbell (1904-1987) was born in White Plains, New York. He traveled in Europe with his family, where he met and befriended the Indian philosopher Jiddu Krishnamurti, before studying at Columbia University. In 1927 he received an M.A. in English and comparative literature. After that, he went to the universities of Paris and Munich to study Arthurian romances.

That was when he got familiar with the work and ideas of Carl G. Jung, but they did not meet until the 1940s, when both were editing texts by the Indologist Heinrich Zimmer after his death in 1943. It seems they met only once, having tea in the Bollingen tower Jung had built for himself.[400]

In 1934, Campbell started teaching at Sarah Lawrence College in Bronxville, New York, and remained there until the early 1970s. In 1987 he was elected into the American Academy of Arts and Letters. He died the same year, which was one year after Mircea Eliade.

He reached wide popularity with the television series *The Power of Myth*, which was made in 1985 and 1986 but aired in 1988, after his death.

In writing, he started as a literary critic, co-authoring a study of James Joyce's *Finnegan's Wake* in 1944. In 1949 he published *The Hero With a Thousand Faces*, comparing hero myths from around the world and finding a Jungian process through rites of passage in the hero archetype. The book became an international bestseller. In 1959 to 1968 he published the four volumes work *The Masks of God*.

Campbell's appreciation of Jung and use of his theories is evident in his work, and in his comments on the matter. Late in life, Campbell explained in an interview, "I think the longer

---

[400] Joseph Campbell, *An Open Life: Joseph Campbell in Conversation with Michael Toms*, New York 1988, p. 122.

you live, the more Jung can say to you."[401] But he also pointed out that Jung is not the final word, and he firmly denied being a Jungian:

I'm not a Jungian! As far as interpreting myths, Jung gives me the best clues I've got. But I'm much more interested in diffusion and relationships historically than Jung was, so that the Jungians think of me as a kind of questionable person. I don't use those formula words very often in my interpretation of myths, but Jung gives me the background from which to let the myth talk to me.

If I do have a guru of that sort, it would be Zimmer — the one who really gave me the courage to interpret myths out of what I knew of their common symbols.[402]

Another indicator of Heinrich Zimmer's influence on Campbell is that he edited four books with texts by Zimmer translated into English, as mentioned above. He also edited one book with texts by Jung, *The Portable Jung* from 1971, where he in the introduction expresses profound respect for Jung, also in the fields relevant to this book:

Jung was not only a medical man but a scholar in the grand style, whose researches, particularly in comparative mythology, alchemy, and the psychology of religion, have inspired and augmented the findings of an astonishing number of the leading creative scholars of our time.[403]

Monomyth Hero

Campbell's first book on the subject of myth and how to interpret it, *The Hero With a Thousand Faces* from 1949, made an im-

---

[401] Ibid., p. 121.

[402] Ibid., p. 123.

[403] Carl G. Jung, *The Portable Jung*, edited by Joseph Campbell, New York 1971, p. vii.

pression on Jungians as well as Freudians, scholars of mythology, and the general public. To this day, it remains his most recognized and popular book.

The Jungian delight in his text is no surprise, since his way of understanding myth is largely based on the theories of Carl G. Jung, but that makes its impression on several Freudians all the more surprising. They were generally impatient with any thinking approaching that of Jung.

The explanation might be that Campbell starts his book with a long quote from Freud's *The Future of an Illusion* in the preface, showing his respect for the father of psychoanalysis, adding that for understanding the symbols in mythology "I know of no better modern tool than psychoanalysis."[404] And he returns to Freud repeatedly through the book. Not as much as he leans on Jung, but clearly with similar respect.

Campbell's aim with the book is to compare a number of myths and folk tales from around the world in order to show their similar patterns, assuring the reader that "the parallels will be immediately apparent."[405] He is far from the first to have this approach to myths, and he is aware of the inherent risk to underestimate the diversity. But it doesn't discourage him in the least:

There are of course differences between the numerous mythologies and religions of mankind, but this is a book about the similarities; and once these are understood the differences will be found to be much less great than is popularly (and politically) supposed.

That is an odd defense of his method. Since he sets out to find similarities, it is no wonder that he finds them, especially considering the vast material at his disposal. There are so many

---

[404] Joseph Campbell, *The Hero With a Thousand Faces*, Princeton 1972 (first edition 1949), p. vii.

[405] Ibid., p. viii.

myths. If he had instead went on a search for differences, he would easily find at least as many examples of those, too. Nothing can be proven by either method.

This mistake has been made by so many others searching for patterns in mythology — psychologists as well as anthropologists, folklorists, and historians of religion alike. They have failed by ignoring anomalies to their theories, in the eagerness to have them confirmed. It has also often led them to interpret the material quite elaborately, in order to find similarities where they are not apparent. Other chapters of this book describe many such instances, as does my book about Freudian theories on mythology.[406]

Joseph Campbell is as bold about what his exploration has found as he is about what myth entails:

> *It would not be too much to say that myth is the secret opening through which the inexhaustible energies of the cosmos pour into human cultural manifestation. Religions, philosophies, arts, the social forms of primitive and historic man, prime discoveries in science and technology, the very dreams that blister sleep, boil up from the basic, magic ring of myth.*[407]

That doesn't leave very much out.

James Joyce Once

As for Campbell's dissection of myths, he claims that it reveals a structure almost all of them share — at the very least all those that can be described as hero myths — as if they are basically one and the same myth. He calls this shared structure the *monomyth*, a term taken from the novel *Finnegans Wake* by James Joyce.[408]

[406] Stenudd 2022.

[407] Campbell, *The Hero With a Thousand Faces*, p. 3.

[408] Ibid., p. 30.

Indeed, the word is there — just once in the well over 600 pages long novel Joyce spent 17 years writing, and in a context no less cryptic than famously the whole text:

Ah, dearo! Dearo, dear! And her illian! And his willyum! When they were all there now, matinmarked for lookin on. At the carryfour with awlus plawshus, their happyass cloudious! And then and too the trivials! And their bivouac! And his monomyth! Ah ho! Say no more about it! I'm sorry! I saw. I'm sorry! I'm sorry to say I saw![409]

What Joyce might have meant with the term, which seems to be an invention of his, is far from clear. I have not found him using it in his other books. Nor is it explained in the book about the novel written by Joseph Campbell and Henry Morton Robinson, *A Skeleton Key to Finnegans Wake*, which was published in 1944 — right between the release of Joyce's book and that of *The Hero With a Thousand Faces*.

Since the release of the latter, it is Campbell's application of the term monomyth that has spread and become widely adopted. Joyce is merely referred to as the source to the word, but not to its meaning and definitely not Campbell's use of it.

As for Joyce's own idea about it, we can only speculate. It is significant that he writes "his" monomyth, indicating just one person's myth, whereas Joseph Campbell speaks of "the monomyth," suggesting one basic myth behind them all.

The context where the word appears in *Finnegans Wake* is one of intercourse. In the sentence right before the above quote, Joyce writes "*mens conscia recti*, then hemale man all unbracing to omniwomen." The Latin expression means a mind conscious of rectitude, which is a not-so-subtle way of indicating an erection, and together with the following words coitus is obviously intended. So, the quote above describes the excited state of it. Then, it may be simply so that monomyth is a word-

[409] James Joyce, *Finnegans Wake*, London 1939, III:4, p. 581.

play on *monolith*, implying an erection of mythical proportion — at least in the eyes of the one confessing to have seen it. Joyce's twisting of words and their meaning are evident all through his book.

Still, about this one can only guess. Joyce was as prone to confuse as he was reluctant to explain.

The Acts and Scenes of a Myth

Contrary to James Joyce, what Joseph Campbell means with monomyth is quite clear. It is sort of a one-size-fits-all formula describing the structure and content of a myth — presumably just about every hero myth, and those exist in abundance. To Campbell, they alone are proper myths, and convey a message, a meaning, which is their function.

In essence, the hero myth is "a magnification of the formula represented in the rites of passage: *separation—initiation—return*."[410] And he continues with a comprised synopsis of the hero story structure:

> *A hero ventures forth from the world of common day into a region of supernatural wonder: fabulous forces are there encountered and a decisive victory is won: the hero comes back from this mysterious adventure with the power to bestow boons on his fellow man.*

Campbell gives a number of examples myths where this pattern can be found, such as that of Prometheus stealing fire from the gods and giving it to the humans, Jason getting the Golden Fleece and thereby the throne, Aeneas descending to the underworld to meet his deceased father, and Prince Gautama struggling on his path to become the Buddha, which he compares to the stories of both Moses and Jesus.

The structure of the hero myth, summarized in the above quote, Campbell expands by specifying a number of compo-

---

[410] Campbell, *The Hero With a Thousand Faces*, p. 30. The italics are his.

nents, as chapters of the story or rather acts and scenes in a play.

Like in many traditional plays, there are three acts. In the first act the adventure begins by departure from the present situation, in the second act the hero has struggles leading to revelations and growth, and in the third act the hero returns to accomplish an important change, which is the solution.

That is indeed a very common plot in myths as well as plays. Campbell makes additional divisions of the story, very much like the scenes of a play, to form this synopsis:[411]

Separation or departure
(1) The Call to Adventure, or the signs of the vocation of the hero;
(2) Refusal of the Call, or the folly of the flight from the god;
(3) Supernatural Aid, the unsuspected assistance that comes to one who has undertaken his proper adventure;
(4) The Crossing of the First Threshold;
(5) The Belly of the Whale, or the passage into the realm of night.

Trials and victories of initiation
(1) The Road of Trials, or the dangerous aspect of the gods;
(2) The Meeting with the Goddess (Magna Mater), or the bliss of infancy regained;
(3) Woman as the Temptress, the realization and agony of Oedipus;
(4) Atonement with the Father;
(5) Apotheosis;
(6) The Ultimate Boon.

Return and reintegration with society
(1) Refusal of the Return, or the world denied;
(2) The Magic Flight, or the escape of Prometheus;

---

[411] Ibid., pp. 36f.

(3) Rescue from Without;
(4) The Crossing of the Return Threshold, or the return to the world of common day;
(5) Master of the Two Worlds;
(6) Freedom to Live, the nature and function of the ultimate boon.

As components of a monomyth, the acts are more convincing than the scenes. Myths may have things in common, but not necessarily when going into elaborate specifics. There are so many myths and so many different kinds of heroes. It seems that with the scenes, Campbell has slipped from a straightforward reading of the myths into the psychological cosmologies of Freud and Jung.

But he persists, claiming every ingredient to be essential and even in a way present also where it is absent:

> *If one or another of the basic elements of the archetypal pattern is omitted from a given fairy tale, legend, ritual, or myth, it is bound to be somehow or other implied — and the omission itself can speak volumes for the history and pathology of the example.*[412]

That is like claiming his theory is proven whether a story conforms to it or not. I beg to differ. Several of the scenes specified above are absent from many hero myths, and there is nothing significant about them missing in those stories. They are still complete adventures.

Many heroes never refused the call to adventure nor the return from it, or had any encounter with either a great mother goddess or a female temptress, never went through an atonement with the father, and so on. Certainly, there are many hero myths that contain all the stages Campbell suggests, but at least as many that definitely do not, if they are allowed to

411 Ibid., p. 38.

speak for themselves and not be twisted by far-fetched assumptions about what might be implied.

He even warns against such distortions of myths, himself:

The outlines of myths and tales are subject to damage and obscuration. Archaic traits are generally eliminated or subdued. Imported materials are revised to fit local landscape, custom, or belief, and always suffer in the process.[413]

Such and other changes of the original myths lead him to conclude that "secondary interpretations are invented, often with considerable skill."[414] It does not strike him that he contributes with yet another example of just that.

The instances of Campbell's own far-fetched interpretations of the myths fill his book. They mostly consist of elaborate symbolic explanations that go way beyond what meets the eye. Just to give one typical example, this is how he explains the phenomenon rather common in myths and fairy tales with food endlessly replenished:

The motif (derived from an infantile fantasy) of the inexhaustible dish, symbolizing the perpetual life-giving, form-building powers of the universal source, is a fairy-tale counterpart of the mythological image of the cornucopian banquet of the gods.[415]

Or it could just be the pleasant fantasy of never going hungry. It would make mouths water in any audience. The constant and vital struggle for food has always been known to all people everywhere. No universal force or god is necessary to explain it.

[413] Ibid., p. 246.

[414] Ibid., p. 247.

[415] Ibid., p. 173.

Dramaturgy Suffices
Another major issue with Campbell's monomyth theory is that the many specifics about its plot are insufficiently argued for, i.e., the why of each of them. He may have found a pattern applicable to many myths, though far from all, but that in itself is mere statistical correlation. The causation of it all needs to be demonstrated. Why do all these ingredients of the story need to be there?

He makes some general references to Freudian and Jungian theories, more of the latter than the former, but he neglects to present plausible reasons for each of the acts and scenes of his scheme. He claims that they have to be in the monomyth, albeit with some variations, but doesn't state why they do.

Why a refusal of the call, why a supernatural aid, and so on? Campbell is remarkably vague about it. For comparison, a purely dramaturgical analysis of those scenes would easily present plausible reasons for their functions and necessity in the story, without the need of Freudian or Jungian psychology.

Then, this type of myth is simply an adventure story with a main character becoming heroic through the process of the adventure. The three acts are essentially the beginning of the adventure, followed by the ordeal of it, and finally the return from it. That is simply the progression of the story Aristotle in his *Poetics* described as the beginning, the middle, and the end. Without these three parts, there would be no story.

So much for the acts. The scenes in Campbell's list can also be explained by dramaturgy. Far from all of them are needed, but if they are present there are easily found dramaturgical reasons for them.

The Call to Adventure is the start without which there would be no adventure and no story to tell. *Refusal of the Call* emphasizes how big of an adventure is ahead, or our hero would not hesitate. *Supernatural Aid*, if there is one, makes the adventure rise in wonder and dignity, way above everyday matters. *The Crossing of the First Threshold* and *The Belly of the Whale* are challenges met along the way. So is *The Road of Trials*.

Without them, the adventure would not be very adventurous.

Then come a few scenes with which Campbell points clearly at Freudian and Jungian psychology, but they are definitely not present in every hero story: *The Meeting with the Goddess (Magna Mater)*, *Woman as the Temptress*, and *Atonement with the Father*. If they are described simply as the mother, the lover, and the father, they are easier to find in myths, since relations familiar and important to us all engage the audience more than random strangers.

Their roles in the story can vary considerably, but their basic function is to make the adventure more emotionally charged for the hero and thereby also for the audience. Any story needs to evoke the audience's empathy, or it will be quickly forgotten.

Next in Campbell's scheme comes *Apotheosis*, the deification, which is when the hero transforms into a heroic being, becoming able to complete the demanded feat. The protagonist overcomes previous weaknesses and saves the day. It is the climax of the drama, when catastrophe is avoided and peace restored. *The Ultimate Boon* is the ability the hero has gained and the blessing it can bring to all the others. The hero has become a savior. It may be, as the word suggests, a gift from the powers that be, but not until the hero is worthy of it. Otherwise, it would be a phony hero.

In modern adventure stories, especially in the movies, this climax is very close to the end — for the very reason that afterwards, the audience doesn't have much excitement to expect. Mere minutes remain to "The End." But Campbell suggests several additional scenes, having them form the third and final act, which is that of the return.

There are indeed many hero tales that have this extended ending, where new problems are faced and need to be solved before the adventure is over. This often happens on the hero's return after a glorious victory, which everybody thought would have solved it all. What it implies dramaturgically is that a great adversary remains, the real antagonist of the story is not yet defeated. It is commonly used as a surprising turn of the story in action movies, but also in many tales of old.

Still, it cannot be prolonged. A new battle, coming as a surprise after the victory that seemed to solve all, may be spectacular but is quickly over. It has to be, since it strains the audience's patience. They rightly feel somewhat deceived.

Nonetheless, there is a good reason for the hero's return meeting complications. Through the previous adventure, the protagonist has changed considerably, so a return to what things were beforehand is really impossible. The difference is that now, the hero is capable of dealing with it. That makes all the difference in the world — for protagonist and antagonist alike.

Campbell divides this last act into six scenes, through which the hero struggles to bring the boon back to where it was needed from the beginning. In his understanding, they represent the last stages of the hero's transformation. But that would just mean he has not yet transformed and remains in the middle of the adventure. His previous victory was incomplete or even illusionary, and the major threat remains.

As for Campbell's *Refusal of the Return*, it happens that some heroes, after their great feat, wish to remain to savor the victory and the transformation making it possible. A battle between their complacency and their conscience ensues, ending with duty calling them to return. That call of duty may well be uttered by another character in the story.

A version mentioned also by Campbell is where mighty powers oppose and hinder the hero's departure. *The Magic Flight* is the escape, which doesn't necessarily involve any magic but often enough trickery of some sort. In some stories, the hero gets help to escape by others arriving, which is what Campbell calls *Rescue from Without*.

Both the refusal and the flight are minor and swiftly passing events in the story, which is why many stories do without them. Their main dramaturgical function is to create a pause between the recent victory and what adventure comes next. After a very intense event, the hero as well as the audience need a moment of relief and calm before getting excited anew.

If there is no more grand feat ahead, this is where the story ends, with a final pensive scene in tranquility. No audience is at peace with a story that ends immediately after great calamity. We need some time to settle our emotions and reflect.

In a story where the hero has more to do upon returning, there may well be additional adventures on the way. But the bigger the hero's first victory was, the less time there is for the rest of the story. And if events that follow overshadow that first victory, then it was neither the climax of the story nor the major transformation of the hero. If there are several crescendos in a symphony, the last one has to be the loudest.

It is a question of emphasis, which has several functions in a story. Any story moves towards a climax, the major emphasis. But elements of the plot must participate to raise that emphasis and thereby intensify the climax. So, the hero has to start off weak and insecure, to make the transition into heroism all the more impressive. The challenges the hero has to face must be overwhelming, even seemingly insurmountable.

But these measures are relative. In everyday realism, the challenges can be rather ordinary as long as the situation makes them intense to the protagonist. In myths, the hero is up against gods and battles to save the world. The emotional value is equivalent. Campbell deals with the latter, but dramaturgically there is no difference.

For example, the scene he calls *The Crossing of the Return Threshold* is the leap from the fantastic world of gods and magic, which was where the hero victoriously transformed, back to the much less splendid human reality from where the adventure started. This return to normality doesn't have to be such a leap for the transition to be demanding, but in myths the monumental is preferred. It makes the audience gasp. Still, the dramaturgy is the same in every kind of story, big or small, as is the effect on the audience.

And heroes don't need to be gigantic to be heroic.

Campbell's *Master of the Two Worlds* is the one who has reached the ability to handle both the divine world, in which the hero transformed, and the human world from which the hero came. Having gained a divine quality, the hero can still remain human. If the hero's divinity had been lost, the whole quest would have been for a fleeting moment, and the story would have lost its relevance as soon as it ended. On the other hand, if the hero had by the transformation ceased to be and feel like a human, the story would have lost relevance to us all. It would be a monster.

Actually, that is almost unthinkable since gods, too, have human traits and emotions or we would be unable to relate to them. That is as true for myths as it is for religions.

This is so self-evident that most stories don't dwell on it. Campbell implies the same: "The myths do not often display in a single image the mystery of the ready transit."[416] Any compassionate hero would manage it, and it would be very difficult to find a myth where the hero is not compassionate at heart. Nobody would like it.

The final scene in Campbell's synopsis is *Freedom to Live* It is the end of the story and therefore its conclusion. He calls it "the result of the miraculous passage and return" and calls the goal of the myth "a reconciliation of the individual consciousness with the universal will."[417] He continues:

And this is effected through a realization of the true relationship of the passing phenomena of time to the imperishable life that lives and dies in all.

Campbell's wording has a religious inclination, which would not be required by dramaturgy. The protagonist needs to arrive at some kind of revelation, accomplish something previously out of reach to solve the problem at hand, before the

---

[416] Ibid., p. 229.

[417] Ibid., p. 238.

story can end. Only then can the hero live happily ever after —
or die tragically, which is not that rare. The conclusion of the
story is within it. A mighty foe is defeated, a war is won, a
kingdom is saved, and so on. Involving gods or not, the obstacle is concrete and so is the solution.

It is for the audience to contemplate further implications
and applications of the story. That goes for myths as well, or
they would be sermons.

I speak repeatedly about the audience, although Joseph
Campbell treats the myths without much consideration of that.
Still, also to him the audience is implied or the tale would lack
any meaning. But he seems to take it for granted, in spite of the
strange content and the cryptic meaning he claims that myths
carry. No one would get it or even care, if they could not relate
to the story.

In dramaturgy, though, the audience is everything. Aristotle made that very clear in his *Poetics*. What makes a drama
work or not is how the audience relates to it. And the myths
show evident traces of applied dramaturgy, though many of
them are older than this concept. The dramaturgical considerations come naturally as a story develops, much like a stand-
up comedian learns to skip the jokes that get no laughs and
enhance the ones that do, so that the audience laughs even
more.

Only stories that attract will prevail, no matter how laden
with profound meaning they might be. Campbell should have
started with what have made myths remain through time, before trying to extract some hidden meaning in them.

Joseph Campbell states one thing, though, on which I am
prepared to agree, when comparing myths to fairy tales:

*Typically, the hero of the fairy tale achieves a domestic, mi-
crocosmic triumph, and the hero of myth a world-histori-
cal, macrocosmic triumph.*[418]

[418] Ibid., pp. 37f.

Indeed, fairy tales may involve some magic but still deal with rather down to earth matters, where failure or fortune befalls just the human beings directly involved. Not so in most myths, where the main characters are superhuman and the outcome affects the whole world.

I discuss the particulars of fairy tales elsewhere, especially in the chapter about Marie-Louise von Franz.

Adolescent Adventure

It may seem that one role is missing in Campbell's monomyth. The mother, the lover, and the father are there, but what about the child?

That is the hero.

Tales of heroic quests have every sign of dealing with adolescence. The essential process described is akin to that of a child becoming an adult. The adolescent leaves the security of childhood behind to face the challenges of adulthood. The hero myth is a coming-of-age story.

It is easy to see in Campbell's scheme of the monomyth. The young protagonist is both excited and hesitant when the call to adventure arrives. It means leaving the comfort and security of the childhood home, which is scary but also a longing that keeps on growing until it is irresistible. Then out into the world, yet mostly unknown, and a future that is completely unpredictable. The voyage is one from childhood to adulthood, and the quest is to find one's role in the adult world.

It is an adventure, indeed, with ups and downs, problems and solutions, struggles and rewards, dreams and disappointments. Mistakes are made, of course, but by learning from them they tend to get sparser and less costly. The process is one of adapting to adult life, which was what childhood partly prepared for — but here is the real thing.

When that is accomplished, the protagonist settles in a home much like the one of childhood, but now as an adult. So, it is a return, albeit to a new setting.

What this also implies is that the hero myth would be particularly popular among children, because they see it in their future, and even more so among adolescents, because they live it. Adults, on the other hand, would not feel as touched by those stories. They have already lived them. I have the impression that this is indeed the case, but must admit that it is mere speculation.

A parallel to the hero myth as a coming-of-age story is the rite of passage at puberty. Joseph Campbell mentions it in his book.[419] This rite exists in most cultures, but takes on different forms. In hunter-gatherer cultures it can be quite severe. When the children reach their teens, or thereabout, they are taken away from parental care and have to go through some ritualized ordeals, often painful, after which they return and are regarded as adults. And by suffering through the rite, they have proven themselves heroic.

Myth and ritual are connected. Just as many rites are explained by myths, many myths have ritualistic ways of performing them. Those going through the passage rite to adulthood thereby enact the hero myth, as many others have done before them for countless generations. In that way, the hero does indeed have a thousand faces.

Primeval Mythology

The above discussed book, *The Hero With a Thousand Faces* from 1949, continues to be Joseph Campbell's best known and most recognized written work. But it is not the most voluminous one. Ten years later, in 1959, he published the first book in a series of four with the common title *The Masks of God*, the last of which was released in 1968. Their titles are rather self-explanatory: *Primitive Mythology, Oriental Mythology, Occidental Mythology,* and *Creative Mythology*. The last of the four concerns individual experiences and expressions of the mythical.

Campbell's perspective on mythology is recognizable

---

[419] See for example ibid., pp. 10ff.

from what he wrote in *The Hero With a Thousand Faces*. Already the title of this book series indicates it. The hero has a multitude of faces and God has a number of masks. What this suggests is that all hero myths are basically the same, just as all gods of different forms fundamentally express the same phenomenon.

In the prologue to the first book in the series, Campbell concludes from his comparative study of the mythologies around the world, "an honest comparison immediately reveals that all have been built from one fund of mythological motifs."[420]

The Evolution of Mythology

Although Joseph Campbell sees sort of the same divine principle behind all the masks, he recognizes that there are huge variations to the theme. He compares it to the division of the human psyche into the personal and the collective unconscious, so that mythology has a local character although the foundation is shared by all.

Carl G. Jung would agree and maybe also Sigmund Freud, whom he refers to as much or even more.

Campbell spends a substantial part of the first book in the series, *Primitive Mythology*, describing the development of religious ideas through time as akin to human growth from childhood to old age. He sees three distinct periods of growth, each making its own impression on us:

> *(1) childhood and youth, with its uncouth charm; (2) maturity, with its competence and authority; and (3) wise old age, nursing its own death and gazing back, either with love or with rancor, at the fading world.*[421]

[420] Joseph Campbell, *The Masks of God: Primitive Mythology*, New York 1959, p. 4.

[421] Ibid., p. 60.

The very first imprint on our psyche comes at the moment of birth and the "sense of suffocation experienced by the infant before its lungs commence to operate," causing a birth trauma and an unconscious longing back to the security of the womb.

Otto Rank had written a book about the subject in 1924, *The Trauma of Birth*,[422] where he claimed it to be the first and foremost influence on the human psyche — dethroning the Oedipus complex from that position. It quickly led to his expulsion from the Freudian community. Joseph Campbell must have known about both him and his book, but mentions neither.

Campbell also compares the development of mythology and religion to the evolution of all of nature. That is what he proposes to demonstrate in his book. He explains:

> *For, as in the visible world of the vegetable and animal kingdoms, so also in the visionary world of the gods: there has been a history, an evolution, a series of mutations, governed by laws; and to show forth such laws is the proper aim of science.*[423]

As he sets out to explain the psychology of myth, he uses quite a lot of biology. That is refreshing to find in a writer connected to psychoanalytical theories. Things like the prolonged infancy and childhood of the human species, the experience of puberty as well as the deterioration at old age, are all closely considered when he sketches an evolution of mythology.

Make-Believe

Campbell begins his account on the psychology of myth by considering the mask in the title of his book series, referring to primitive festivals where it was worn to signify a deity. Even

[422] Otto Rank, *The Trauma of Birth* (originally published in German 1924), London 1929.

[423] Campbell 1959, p. 5.

though everyone knew that a man had made the mask and a man was wearing it, during the ritual the one with the mask was identified as the deity: "He does not merely represent the god; he is the god."[424]

It is a make-believe like that of a theatrical play, an "as if." Campbell associates it with childhood, where fantasy can become quite real. That is very much what happens with myth, which concerns "the phenomenon of self-induced belief."[425] He connects it to the *Homo Ludens* (human playing) theory of Johan Huizinga.[426] First of all, it is the fun of play, just like how children create their imaginary adventures. The participants do not necessarily believe it, but pretend to do so while they are playing the game.

Indeed, that is a major ingredient in myth as well as ritual. Whether it is fictional nor not, it brings excitement and engagement. So much in mythology and religion is dependent on this factor, though most historians of religion as well as Freudians and Jungians have tended to underestimate or even ignore it. We need to be entertained, and a prerequisite of that is our pretending to believe, or we would be indifferent. In film and theatre, it means that we accept the premise in order for the story to stir our emotions.

Religious rites also demand that we accept the premise for us to care about the rite at all. It is the mystery of faith, making us pretend, for example, that with the bread and wine in the Communion we are actually served the body and blood of Christ.[427] This pretense is far from meaningless. The experience of it is real and Campbell insists that it brings a reward to the participants:

[424] Ibid., p. 21.

[425] Ibid., p. 22.

[426] Johan Huizinga, *Homo Ludens: A Study of the Play-Element in Culture*, Boston 1955 (originally published in Dutch 1948).

[427] Campbell 1959, p. 24.

> *The opaque weight of the world — both of life on earth and of death, heaven, and hell — is dissolved, and the spirit freed, not from anything, for there was nothing from which to be freed except a myth too solidly believed, but for something, something fresh and new, a spontaneous act.*[428]

This is equally true about mythology. However grim its content may be, "the paramount theme of mythology is not the agony of quest but the rapture of a revelation, not death but the resurrection: Hallelujah!"[429] All is well that ends well, at least in the emotions of the audience. Aristotle said something quite similar about tragedy in his *Poetics*. The drama and bitter end of the play causes an emotional release, a cleansing of sorts, *catharsis*, in the spectators. Campbell also points out this parallel.[430]

A Biological Archetype

Joseph Campbell presents an interesting way to explain the Jungian concept of archetypes from a biological perspective. He compares them to *innate releasing mechanisms* (IRM), which are instinctual behaviors linked to certain events or forms. It is what makes sea turtles hurry towards the sea as soon as they are hatched, and chicks at the same early stage of their lives dart for cover when a hawk flies overhead, but not when non-predator birds do. They are programmed to behave this way, already before birth.[431]

Discussing this phenomenon, Campbell refers primarily to the Austrian ethologist Konrad Lorenz, otherwise most famous for his book *On Aggression*, originally published in German 1963.

Carl G. Jung's theory about archetypes contained within

[428] Ibid., p. 28.

[429] Ibid., p. 56.

[430] Ibid., p. 50.

[431] Ibid., pp. 30f.

the collective unconscious of us all is intriguing, but difficult to prove. There is really no room in biology for complex symbols to be genetically inherited, and no other way for complex information to be transmitted between generations without a cognitive process after birth. Either it is inherited as instinct or learned by experience.

But with IRM, Campbell finds a biological explanation for human response to certain stimuli, which does indeed suggest something similar to the archetypes and the effect they are supposed to have on us. That would, of course, make the unconscious similar or identical to the instincts.

On the other hand, it is implausible bordering on the absurd that we should have the multitude and intricacies of the Jungian archetypes and our responses to them instinctually innate in us. That is just too much for our genes to amass and carry along between generations.

Campbell adds another phenomenon from ethology, applying what he calls "biological psychology" to it, and using it to shed light on his take on the archetypes: *supernormal sign stimulus*. It is when instinctual reactions are led astray by enhanced signals, making the response behavior meaningless or even detrimental.[432]

He gives the example of the male grayling butterfly, which prefers to mate with females of a darker hue, and therefore cannot help but pursue something even darker, whether it is a female of the same species or not. When the signal is strong enough, it is irresistible.

Campbell sees this supernormal sign stimulus at work among humans, too. He mentions women's age-old use of cosmetics, as well as men dressed in gladiator vestments or kingly robes, and "every other humanly conceived and realized improvement of nature." He even regards the gods as such stimuli, which is something he claims to present evidence for in his "natural history of the gods."

---

[432] Ibid., pp. 42f.

Certainly, the gods of most mythologies are vastly enhanced versions of humans. They are what we dream to be, and we are strongly attracted to those who show some signs of such grandeur. They are idols, worshipped by many. So, it is fathomable that we have imagined characters with extremely exaggerated features of the kind we admire the most, and become so attached to those images that we made them gods — even though they were nowhere to be found. Their existence was enforced by our longing for them.

That would be a process possible to describe as the interaction between the ethological principles of innate releasing mechanisms and supernormal sign stimulus. Still, Campbell willingly admits that none of it is yet proven scientifically:

> *However, the human psyche has not yet been, to any great extent, satisfactorily tested for such stereotypes, and so, I am afraid, pending further study, we must simply admit that we do not know how far the principle of the inherited image can be carried when interpreting mythological universals. It is no less premature to deny its possibility than to announce it as anything more than a considered opinion.*[433]

That is the trap of exploring psychology biologically. The science of the latter demands hard evidence of clearly defined hypotheses. None of that can be said for the theory of archetypes in a collective unconscious. The archetypes are vaguely defined, and so are their effects on the psyche.

That would be fine for something transmitted by culture, which is a continuously changing entity, but not if it is to be innate. Biology demands a sharply and narrowly formulated hypothesis of what to find in an explicitly given situation, for the result to serve as evidence. What was expected, and did that occur?

[433] Ibid., pp. 44f.

The ethological examples mentioned above have that distinct clarity. The sea turtles hurrying to the sea right after hatching, the chick hiding from the hawk, and the grayling pursuing the darkest hue — they leave little room for speculation. It is just a question of if they do or don't, and they do. Equally strict experiments are hardly possible with the archetypes or other claims specific to Freudian and Jungian psychology.

Already Freud's fundamental principle of the Oedipus complex would fail, since it is definitely not so that every son kills his father and copulates with his mother, or even longs to do so. Finding and proving an archetype common to all humans is just as hopeless. They come in all kinds of shapes and mean all kinds of different things, which is also what Jung and his followers have stated about them.

Even the basic archetypes *anima* and *animus*, the female entity in men and the male one in women, are experienced and expressed in very different ways from person to person. That is true also for the hero archetype treated by Campbell in his previously discussed book on the subject. It is a character with so many different faces and fates. How to formulate what to expect, and how to determine if it occurs?

Not That Primitive

Campbell's idea of an evolution of mythology analogous to human mental development from infancy to old age is also difficult to assess, mainly because he doesn't present a developed model of what kind of mythology each stage would produce. He mentions some ingredients typical for each age, but they are not applied to a complete whole. It is not clear what mythological structure is to be expected at each stage of development.

In his first book in the *Masks of God* series, *Primitive Mythology*, where he presents this theory of evolution, one would expect a sketch of the most primitive form, the infancy of it. What would the very oldest mythology be like, according to his theory? It is hard to confirm, since we have little or no evidence to support it, but with his theory he should at least be able to propose some general characteristics, the basic content of mythology at the infancy of the human species.

Instead, he begins his closer examination of myths with those of the primitive planters, the beginning of agriculture, although that just gets us something like 10,000 years back or less. The first elaborate myth he quotes, about a tradition of regicide, was recorded in 1912 by the German ethnologist Leo Frobenius, on whose writing he leans heavily in this book.[434] The myth may, of course, have had a long history — but not far enough back to be regarded as primitive, not even in the time scope of agriculture. That is also true for the next legend examined, that of Scheherazade, famous from *Arabian Nights*.[435] There is nothing primitive about it.

The following part of the book deals with the primitive hunters, which takes us substantially farther back. Humans were hunters and gatherers already at the emergence of our species. That is millions of years ago. In search for the dawn of mythology, this is the place to go.

This part of the book starts by comparing North American Indian planter and hunter tribes, both existing at the same time. This means it cannot be assumed that the mythologies of the former are more recent than those of the latter. If mythologies evolve, which is indeed likely, they must be expected to do so regardless of what form of culture they exist in.

So, a hunter society mythology can change just as a planter mythology can, albeit probably in different directions. What counts is when their mythologies were recorded. The principle of evolution is not exclusive to some cultures, just as it doesn't happen only to some species. It applies to all.

Eventually, Campbell does approach truly primitive mythology, when speculating about its content in the Paleolithic

---

[434] Ibid., pp. 151ff.

[435] Ibid., pp. 161ff.

Age, which began more than three million years ago and ended around the time when agriculture was introduced, roughly 10,000 years ago. Very little is known about human culture for most of that era, but by the end of it, let's say from around 100,000 years ago, there are archeological findings giving significant clues to cultural phenomena. They show the advancement of human thought and creativity, but are not easy to interpret with any certainty.

Campbell starts off with comparing a Blackfoot legend about bull hunting to a cave drawing at Trois-Frères in France of a man dressed in bull gear as he is hunting the animals. It is estimated to have been drawn around 13,000 BC. To Campbell, this is "a very strong suggestion" to the legend being at least as old.[436] Not really. It just implies the use of buffalo disguise when hunting them. That is not myth, but method.

He uses another paleolithic art work as argument for his interpretation — Venus of Laussel, a bas-relief of a naked woman with what is probably a bison horn in her hand, approximately 25,000 years old. Again, he is jumping to conclusions, even describing it as part of a hunting shrine.

It has been a habit of archaeologists and others to interpret such objects of Stone Age art as religious and ritualistic expressions, but other explanations are closer at hand. They may simply be artistic representations of life at that time, no magic or mythology intended. Trying to find evidence of a mythology cannot be done by elaborately interpreting objects as mythological, without also trying other explanations for them.

It is the same problem when paleolithic graves are taken as proof of belief in an afterlife. We still bury our dead, even though our belief in an afterlife has withered, to say the least. For starters, we can't just let the corpses lie where they fell, and we do mourn our deceased without needing a mythology to justify it.

An amusing example of Campbell's jump to conclusions

---

[436] Ibid., p. 286. The Blackfoot legend was collected c. 1870. Ibid., p. 288.

is when he mentions the handprints on the walls of paleolithic caves, stating that they were made by "participants in the rites," without mentioning what circumstance made him draw this conclusion.[437] No, they were much likelier just cavemen having fun and making their marks, as a sort of paleolithic graffiti.

Campbell continues by presenting bits and pieces of myths from various recent or present cultures, much like laying a big jigsaw-puzzle, but that is no way to ascertain a primeval mythology. Such a puzzle could end up with any image, depending on the choices made along the way. Since he presents a distinct idea about mythology evolving from a kind of childhood, he should have started with a sketch of what mythology that would be, and then compared it to the clues we have — however minute — about paleolithic beliefs.

There is yet another problem with his theory about a childhood mythology. Since he bases it on childhood emotions and perceptions of reality, it would mean that children formed this mythology. But surely, adults did it. The sentiments of childhood cannot have been decisive in the process. There is no reason to assume that adults of primeval times were seeing the world as the children of their time. They had grown out of that, and so must their conceptions have done.

A primeval childhood of mythology was not formed by children, but by adults of that time.

Reason Before Religion

Campbell shares a basic misconception with most of those who have interpreted ancient myths and rites. They tended to regard our distant forefathers as superstitious and religious by nature, seeking supernatural explanations to explain phenomena around them and trying to control them by magic.

But the ideas of deities and invisible forces ruling everything cannot have been the first ones to emerge in the minds of

[437] Ibid., p. 288.

paleolithic humans. They would have started with the most near-at-hand concepts, based on sight, sound, smell, and touch. Their world would have been one of what was actually there, long before they started to speculate about what was not. Like all animals, they were practical creatures.

Religious beliefs and rituals must have taken quite some time to appear, and it should not be taken for granted that their emergence replaced practical and rational thinking. Both moods of relating to life and the world coexisted, as they still do to a large extent. The balance between them may have fluctuated, but not enough for one of them to completely take over.

So, when Campbell takes for granted that cave art must have had ritualistic, magical, and even religious meanings, he forgets what Johan Huizinga said about *Homo ludens*, the playing human, although he mentions it earlier in his book. People play, and have most certainly done so for about as long as our species has existed. Other animals surely do.

Art is primarily playing, where both the artist and the audience participate in the game. That can also be said about myths. Fundamentally, they have been meant to entertain. The religious and ritualistic functions of them were later developments, but their basic entertaining values were never abandoned. Again, that is still true today.

Instead of searching for what could be interpreted as signs of religious beliefs in paleolithic culture, which is completely in the eyes of the beholder, what should be pursued at first is how the practical and rational minds of primeval humans developed ideas of the immaterial, with invisible powers in control. It must have been a process of rational thinking to have begun at all, although it eventually led to what often seem to be very irrational conclusions.

Considering that we have had this big brain of ours for very long, we should not assume that our forefathers didn't know how to use it. In other words: Even in the very distant past, people's worldviews must have made sense to them, or they would have been dismissed.

East Versus West

The second volume of the *Masks of God* series is *Oriental Mythology*, published in 1962. As the title states, it deals with mythologies of Asia, but Campbell treats the subject with frequent references to Occidental mythologies, which is the theme of the third book. He introduces *Oriental Mythology* by comparing the two mythological traditions, where he shows an affection for the Oriental ones shared by Carl G. Jung, basing it on a similarly rather romantic understanding of them.

Jung's perception of Asian mythology and spirituality has been discussed previously. He was an express admirer of the Chinese classic *Tao Te Ching* and the Japanese tradition of Zen Buddhism. Campbell discusses the two, but adds the Indian mythology predating Buddhism, with its ancient literary sources of the Vedas and other texts.

To explain the difference between Western and Eastern religion, Campbell uses the two trees in the Garden of Eden — one with fruits giving eternal life and the fruits of the other bringing knowledge of good and evil. The former is the path of Oriental religion, whereas the latter is characteristic of the Occidental.[438]

It is a clever analogy, and not that far-fetched. Looking at the Abrahamic religions, they definitely have a leniency towards a moral worldview, as Genesis shows. Adam and Eve ate of the fruit giving knowledge of good and evil, but were thrown out of Eden before having a bite of the fruit of life. Our path, then, is one of moral obligations until our dying days, after which we will be judged.

On the other hand, whether we pass or fail the test, there is eternal life awaiting us, as if we finally get a bite of that fruit. Granted, this eternity is a blessing for some and a curse for others. But eternal it still is.

[438] Joseph Campbell, *The Masks of God: Oriental Mythology*, London 1962, p. 9.

As for the Oriental religions, it would be a gross oversimplification to state that they put no emphasis on moral demands. They certainly do, all of them. Buddhism has plenty of rules to live by, and so does Hinduism. Even Taoism, which deviates the most from what is usually meant by religion, is full of dictates about how we should and should not live. Its major text, the *Tao Te Ching*, makes it clear already in the title. The word *Te* can be translated as virtue, which is explained as living in accordance with the principle of *Tao*, the Way.

Shinto, too, as presented in its two major texts from the 8th century, *Kojiki* and *Nihongi*, points out moral standards that even the gods have to obey.

It is simply so that morality is a prominent ingredient in every religion, which is to no surprise considering the role religion plays in societies. It establishes and enforces behavioral norms by giving them supernatural origins. That is not the only function of religion, but certainly a very important one — in several religions clearly the most important one.

Still, it is doubtful that the level of morality can be decided by geographical longitude. The religions originating in the Bible certainly emphasize morality, but it can hardly be said that they have established only in the West. In particular, the missionary religions Christianity and Islam have millions of devoted followers also in the East. That would not be the case if they were particularly alien to the Eastern mindset.

Also, there have been plenty of Western religions in the West with little focus on morality, such as Greek and Roman mythology, where the gods often behaved in deplorable ways. The Norse gods were quite violent and the myths about them were scarcely concerned with moral aspects. The fact that these and many other religions were replaced by Christianity had much less to do with the morality of their content than with the military and economic power of the latter.

Those old religions were not deserted due to their moral inferiority. They were conquered by the invading superior force of Christian societies. Although the intent of the invaders was often described as missionary, it had little to do with religion. That was just part of the appropriation.

So, Campbell's distinction between Oriental and Occidental religion based on moral content is questionable. It is not that simple.

A Cyclic World
Campbell presents another model, which might be more fruitful. He describes it as the myth of the eternal return, "which is still basic to Oriental life."[439]

It is the belief in the cyclic nature of the world and everything in it, with no absolute beginning or end, just an eternity of returns. Much of what we have always been able to observe conforms to it. The sun's daily disappearance and return, the phases of the moon, the rhythm of the seasons, the succession of generations of people as well as animals and plants, and so on, are all evidently cyclic. It must have seemed obvious to our ancestors that if this much is cyclic, then maybe everything is — forever: "There never was a time when time was not."

Campbell points out the existential consequence of this worldview:

There is therefore nothing to be gained, either for the universe or for man, through individual originality and effort.

Nothing can change the course of history, since everything is forever on repeat. Because of this, individual strife to stand out and make a difference is pointless. Instead, the only meaningful attitude is one of adaption:

The first duty of the individual, consequently, is simply to play his given role — as do the sun and moon, the various animal and plant species, the waters, the rocks, and the stars — without resistance, without fault.

[439] Ibid., p. 3.

This ideal is clearly promoted in Taoism, with its principle of *wu-wei*, non-action. The natural order is disturbed by human interference, which should therefore be minimal. Striving for greatness leads to failure, whereas the sage succeeds without action and without receiving praise, as if having nothing to do with the accomplishment. Similar ideals can be found in Hinduism and Buddhism.

Western ideals are different. Individual accomplishments are energetically pursued and cherished. We yearn for standing out and living a life that makes for a spectacular biography, our personal hero myth. Our religions promote it, too.

In Christianity and Islam, the ultimate success story is a virtuous life leading to Paradise, whereas the unworthy end in Hell. In Norse mythology it was a courageous life as a warrior that led to eternal festivities in Valhalla. The Greek and Roman mythologies were more ambiguous. An end in success was not guaranteed any hero, nor was it always clear what behavior would be rewarded. But their stories were spectacular and so were their endings.

Certainly, in Western religion and culture the individual's fate is valued far above that of the collective. We are not celebrated for conforming to others, but for deviating. In several Eastern cultures this is seen as improper and shameful.

In Western cultures, even when an ideology is forthright collectivistic it points out the role of the individual. That is indicated already by the names they are given, such as Marxism and Leninism. Also the dominating Western religion, Christianity, is named after a person, although it preaches piety and humility. The three religions Judaism, Christianity, and Islam are called Abrahamic, and a name commonly given by the West to Islam is Mohammedanism, though never used by Muslims.

It is a generalization, but a fairly plausible one, to regard the Western ideals as individualistic, praising those who stand out, while the Eastern ideal is not to stick out from the group, but humbly conform to it. Of course, these are ideals, not necessarily followed by all. The individual strife to gain recognition is not unheard of in the East, nor is modest adjustment to the group in the West. But they are exceptions rather than norms in those cultures.

Still, it is not only in Western mythology that a timeline from beginning to end is found. Creation accounts exist in practically every mythology, also those in the East. *Tao Te Ching* describes a primordial chaos from which Tao emerges and introduces order.[440] In Indian mythology there are several creation myths, whereof the most intriguing one is Rig Veda 10:129. The short text describes how The One awakens in the nothingness and starts creation out of desire, but it ends with the following reservation:

> *Whence this creation has arisen — perhaps it formed itself, or perhaps it did not — the one who looks down on it, in the highest heaven, only he knows — or perhaps he does not know.*[441]

The uncertainty admitted by the author is understandable, but there is no doubt about the world having once begun. The Japanese mythology also contains a beginning of the world. Both *Kojiki* and *Nihongi*, the two classics, describe a primordial state where neither heaven nor earth existed as separate entities, which implies a chaos of the same kind as in *Tao Te Ching*, to no surprise. There was, at the time of their writing, a substantial influence of Chinese thought on Japanese culture, including ideas about cosmogony.

While mythical ideas about the emergence of the world are common around the world, ideas about its end, *eschatology*, are much rarer.

Tao Te Ching mentions nothing about it, nor do the two

[440] *Tao Te Ching*, chapters 25 and 42.
[441] Wendy Doniger, *The Rig Veda: An Anthology*, London 1981, pp. 25f.

Japanese classics. Hinduism states that the world has ended countless times and will continue to do so, always with a new beginning. In classical Buddhism, neither a beginning nor an end of the world is mentioned, but there are later Mahayana ideas about it. Judaism speaks of a coming Messianic age, but not an end of all. Similarly, Christianity speaks of a second coming of Christ and the Last Judgment, leading to a new world. Islam has a comparable concept. Norse mythology has *Ragnarök*, the final war where even the mightiest of gods perish, but it is followed by a resurrection of the god Balder and a splendid new world. Greek mythology contains no end of the world.

It is worth pondering why ideas of a beginning have been so common, but those of an end have not. What is born will also one day die. That is true for humans, animals, and plants alike, and this has been known since primeval times. So, the thought of an end for the whole world — if it was once born — would seem to be apparent.

There is, of course, the reluctance to consider death, as opposed to the joy of birth, but that is hardly the whole explanation. Humanity has been accustomed to the grim realities of life since we got the brain capacity to contemplate them. What is more difficult to comprehend, though, is how something can become nothing, how a world once born can cease to exist. This paradox is additionally implied by the fact that creation myths very rarely begin with nothing turning into something. There is always something present beforehand, be it a god, a primordial sea, an abyss, or a combination thereof. The world was created out of something. So, it may change but not turn into nothing.

The cyclic nature of which Campbell speaks is one that may have had a beginning, but once it began there is no apparent reason for it to ever stop. The sun clocks the days and the moon the months, seemingly without end. People and animals continue to procreate since it is in their nature, and they even multiply. To our ancient predecessors it was as difficult to imagine the end of it as it is to us. Individuals perish but life goes on.

Nevertheless, Campbell's observation about Eastern mythology pointing to the collective and the Western one to the individual makes sense. As far as these kinds of generalizations go, the one he proposes is valid.

There are certainly deviations and variations to be found, in the East as well as the West, and they may upon closer examination be found in abundance. Still, these two main perspectives can be meaningfully applied as categories of mythology from whatever part of the world. The myth of the hero, divine or human, certainly shows an individualistic emphasis. What myths would belong to the other category, though, is not as obvious. In its purest form it may not take the shape of a story at all.

Comparing the texts of the Eastern and Western religions, the former tend to be more abstract and philosophical, whereas the latter come closer to fables ending with a moral conclusion. Campbell shows this difference as seen in Indian and biblical texts: "The Indian point of view is metaphysical, poetical; the biblical, ethical and historical."[442] Although both have exceptions to this rule, they follow it more than they deviate from it.

The reason for this may to a large extent lie in the fact that the Western world has a long tradition of separating religion and philosophy, which is not equally true for Eastern texts — at least not in Western eyes. For example, the presumed author of *Tao Te Ching*, Lao Tzu, would be more adequately described as a philosopher than a prophet, and ancient Taoism is far more of a philosophy than a religion. This could also be said about Siddhartha Gautama Buddha, as well as many of the unknown contributors to the Veda texts of India.

Many of these were not religious but philosophical writings, which have in spite of that been categorized as the former by Western minds. To compare, Plato, Aristotle, and other

---

[442] Campbell 1962, p. 11.

Greek philosophers speculated about gods, the cosmos, and spiritual subjects, without us ever thinking of them as prophets of a religion.

Four Ages of Western Mythology

The third book in Campbell's *Masks of God* series, *Occidental Mythology* published in 1964, presents Western mythology as a development through four "ages" — the age of the goddess, the heroes, the great classics, and the great beliefs. The first age was the primeval one, before 1500 BC, when a mother goddess of fruition was worshipped, the second between 1500 and 500 BC, which included the oldest biblical and Greek myths, the third between 500 BC and 500 CE, with Persian, Greek, and Roman mythologies, and the fourth after 500 CE until the present, with Byzantium, the emergence of Islam, and the changes within Christianity in Europe.

This chronology can be questioned, as could any strict division of mythological development through time. The main problem would be the difficulty of ascertaining how old certain myths and mythological ingredients might be. About this we can do little more than speculate.

It is not enough to sort them by the age of textual sources, since these are probably based on traditions dating much farther back. Mythologies certainly did not begin to take shape with the introduction of writing, but somewhere along the way of the development of speech, which was long before 1500 BC.

Furthermore, the Occident in not homogenous enough to serve as a base for a chronology of mythology. It contains areas and cultures with quite disparate histories of religion. A geographical and cultural area where a timeline is significantly easier to apply is Europe, at least for the last 3000 years or so. Then the first period, until the 4th century CE would be one of diverse polytheistic mythologies, such as those of the Greek, Roman, and Germanic people. That was followed by the spread of Christianity and its monotheism, still to a large extent dominant on the continent.

The era of Christianity can also be divided into rather distinct periods, starting with its emergence and slow growth in the 1st to 4th centuries CE, until in the year 380 it became the Roman state religion by the Edict of Thessalonica. The next major event was the split between the Catholic and the Eastern Orthodox churches, becoming definite with the Schism of 1054. Almost 500 years later, in 1517, Martin Luther published his Ninety-five Theses that became the start of the Reformation and Protestantism.

Still, these changes of Christianity were in practice and organization, not so much in its mythology. The major source remained the Bible with the New Testament, and the core principle was that of the trinity established in the 4th century. What made a profound change to Christianity was not within its mythology, but outside of it.

The scientific revolution from the Renaissance and onward put Christian dogma into question, until scientific discoveries had all but dismissed it. The most important challenge was astronomical — the change from a geocentric to a heliocentric worldview in the 16th to 17th centuries. When earth was pushed from the center of the universe, so was God. Next came Newton's celestial mechanics, showing the movements of the celestial bodies having no need of a divine force. And when Darwin's theory of evolution made God redundant even in the creation of man, there was very little left for which to praise the Almighty.

Campbell sees this development as a return to reason:

Within Christianized Europe itself, furthermore, the absolute authority of the One Church was dissolved through the irresistible return to force of the native European principles of individual judgment and the worth of rational man.[443]

[443] Joseph Campbell, *The Masks of God: Occidental Mythology*, New York 1991 (first published in 1964), p. 5.

Reluctantly at first, Christian doctrine had to adapt, not by changing its sources but how they were interpreted. Also, the tremendous power of the church waned, since it could no longer make believable claims about the high power they represented. As God lost control of the world, so did his church.

Accordingly, the Christian mythology has not changed substantially through its 2000 years, not even during the last centuries of scientific progress — but it has increasingly moved towards being interpreted symbolically. This idea was not new. Already in the 4th century, Augustine pointed out that much of what the Bible says must be understood as symbolic, and not strictly factual, so that the six days of creation were no ordinary days and so on. Other Christian commentators through the centuries have had similar approaches, especially regarding the creation as described in Genesis 1 and 2.

Returning to Campbell's four ages, additional questions arise regarding the first age in particular. The mother goddess of that age is little more than speculation, since it goes back to a time before the introduction of writing. That does not stop him from making bold claims about that primeval goddess:

Now in the neolithic village stage of this development and dispersal, the focal figure of all mythology and worship was the bountiful goddess Earth, as the mother and nourisher of life and receiver of the dead for rebirth.[444]

Campbell mainly uses elements of biblical and Greek mythology to suggest what previous beliefs might have been and how ancient artifacts should be interpreted. Many other interpretations are just as possible or even more so. We simply can't say for sure, and there is no evidence of a past when goddesses were regarded as superior to gods, though that has been claimed among Freudians as well as Jungians.

[444] Ibid., p. 7.

In the chapters on the age of heroes, he deals mainly with the Pentateuch of the Bible, especially Genesis and the story of Moses. As for the latter, he refers frequently to Sigmund Freud and his book *Moses and Monotheism*, but points out, "I am not going either to defend or to attack the views of Freud."[445] Still, in the same paragraph he calls Freud "one of the bravest creative spirits of our day."

To the same age he connects early Hellenic mythology and its traces in Homer's *Iliad* and *Odyssey*.

As for the age of the great classics, Campbell begins with Zoroaster and *Avesta*, followed by Hellenism from the 4th century BC and on, ending with the Roman era in which he includes the development of Christianity.

The age of the great beliefs introduces Islam and explores the Irish and Germanic mythologies, as well as the continued development of Christianity.

Four Functions of Mythology
In the concluding chapter of the book, Campbell presents what he calls "four essential functions of mythology."[446] Indeed, those four aspects cover most, if not all, of what mythologies have meant to the societies committed to them.

The first function is the "sense of awe before the mystery of being," with which he refers to Rudolf Otto's idea of the *numinous*, also emphasized by Mircea Eliade. Without it the other functions would not be reached, simply because the mythology would lack attraction and bewilderment. Nobody would care about myths that did not amaze and intrigue, nor could any religion assemble followers if it lacked wonders.

The second function is a cosmology that also brings a sense of awe. Still, it has to make some kind of sense and be believable:

445 Ibid., p. 127.
446 Ibid., p. 519.

*The cosmology has to correspond, however, to the actual
experience, knowledge, and mentality of the culture folk involved.*

This is compatible with what was discussed above regarding science dethroning religion. When the cosmology in question can no longer be supported by reason, it collapses. Ideas
of how the world works must fit how the world is perceived,
at least not oppose it, since this is an element of mythology
which can be tested against reality. What is stated about the
observable world needs to match what is observed. To Campbell, this is where religion today fails the most:

*And here we touch upon a crucial problem of the religions
of our time; for the clergies, generally, still are preaching
themes from the first to fourth millenniums B.C.*[447]

As an example, he mentions that no one of "adult mind"
would today turn to Genesis for explanations about the origins
of the earth and its living creatures, including mankind. Since
his book was published in 1964, though, it has become increasingly clear that numerous adults persist with the biblical cosmology and reject scientific discoveries to the contrary. The
minds of the so-called creationists must still be regarded as
adult, at least in the biological sense.

But for them, too, the need of a cosmology fitting the per-
ceivable world is evident, or they would not bother to make
elaborate alternative theories about the world to make it conform to the description in Genesis. At the failure of that, they
grasp what they regard as anomalies in scientific claims, in an
effort to make all conflicting theories equally a matter of belief,
only. Their persistence demonstrates that they have other priorities than that of reason, but of course, that makes sense to
them — as long as they are able to convince themselves.

[447] Ibid., p. 520.

The third function, according to Campbell, is social. The mythology serves to "support the current social order, to integrate the individual organically with his group." This has been emphasized by many anthropologists. Certainly, there are countless examples of it in how mythologies are treated in societies and the rites connected to them. A mythology can hardly exist without a community keeping it in place and committing to it as a common understanding. Campbell explains:

> *The social function of a mythology and of the rites by which it is rendered is to establish in every member of the group concerned a "system of sentiments" that can be depended upon to link him spontaneously to its ends.*[448]

In other words, mythology is used as an instrument to make the members of a society conform to its demands and to accept its doctrine. That is not necessarily a case of oppression, since it may very well be supported by almost all in that society, and in order for it to last it needs at least a clear majority willingly committed to it. But it has been known to happen in history as well as the present, that when willingness faded it was replaced by force. The authoritarian component in religion, with its invisible deities ruling from above, lends itself easily to an authoritarian regime.

Campbell's fourth function is the least obvious one. While the previous three are easy to confirm and have so been done in abundance by ethnologists, anthropologists, historians of religion, and others, this last function raises several questions. Campbell describes it, "to initiate the individual into the order of realities of his own psyche, guiding him toward his own spiritual enrichment and realization."[449]

That has a Jungian ring to it, approaching his idea of individuation, the self-discovery connecting the conscious with the

[448] Ibid.

[449] Ibid., p. 521.

hidden unconscious mind. What it actually means, though, is less clear outside of the depth psychology paradigm. Campbell's wording raises a bundle of questions. What initiation, what realities, what spiritual enrichment, and what realization?

It seems that he points to some kind of personal satori, a revelation of a mystical kind, reforming the individual psyche into an enlightened one. But what he speaks about is instead the victory of the rational mindset, "the informed, rational faculty of responsible judgment."[450]

He describes it as a humanistic individualism, and states that it is of European origin:

For it was in Europe alone that the principle of individual judgment and responsibility was developed in relation not to a fixed order of supposed divine laws, but to a changing context of human actualities, rationally governed.

This opening of the eye of the European man led to "the vanishment thereby of all the earlier masks of God, which now are known to have been of developing man himself." This is what he sets out to demonstrate in the last book of the series, *Creative Mythology*.

Individual Mythology

Joseph Campbell's fourth and last book in the *Masks of God* series, *Creative Mythology*, was published in 1968. Here he focuses on the mythology of sorts created by great individual minds, especially in the last couple of centuries, as opposed to the traditional mythologies upheld by societies where all their members were expected or even forced to commit to them.

He sees it as a release of mankind, mostly but not solely accomplished by the advances of science and its methods of research. Those were accomplishments by "the minds of al-

[450] Ibid., p. 522.

ready self-reliant individuals,"[451] with the courage to think freely. This affected society way beyond the confines of science:

> *Moreover, not only in the sciences but in every department of life the will and courage to credit one's own senses and to honor one's own decisions, to name one's own virtues and to claim one's own vision of truth, have been the generative forces of the new age, the enzymes of the fermentation of the wine of this great modern harvest — which is a wine, however, that can be safely drunk only by those with a courage of their own.*

Obviously, in Campbell's mind these are the heroes, much more so than the mythical figures he discussed in *The Hero With a Thousand Faces* from 1949, discussed earlier. He praises those outstanding persons — scientists, philosophers, authors, and artists — to the point where it is as if he is writing a Gospel of Individuality: "The masters of these works, then, are the prophets of the present dawn of the new age of our species."[452] He calls them a pantheon of actual individuals, and their works are the mythology of our time:

> *The arts of Shakespeare and Cervantes are revelations, texts and chapters, in this way, of the actual living mythology of our present developing humanity.*[453]

Among the other great minds that he mentions are James Joyce, his lifelong favorite author, Spinoza, Giordano Bruno, Einstein, Newton, Schopenhauer, Thomas Mann, and to no surprise Friedrich Nietzsche, whom he quotes: "The goal of

[451] Joseph Campbell, *The Masks of God: Creative Mythology*, New York 1976 (first published in 1968), p. 30.

[452] Ibid., p. 34.

[453] Ibid., p. 36.

mankind is not to be seen in the realization of some terminal state of perfection, but is present in its noblest exemplars."[454]

Campbell's praise is certainly not without cause, but it is strange that he would separate these great minds and their accomplishments from the social setting in which they lived and worked. They were hardly alone and their contributions were not only products of their own minds. There was always a context, always a fellowship, without which they would not have been able to perform so splendidly.

For example, William Shakespeare worked in a theater among other actors who surely inspired and cooperated with him, and his plays were founded on those of Ancient Greece as well as on Aristotle's *Poetics*, among many other influences of his time and the tradition transmitted to it. Not that it takes away any of the brilliance of his plays, but it connects them to his surroundings.

Accordingly, the radically original prose of James Joyce had grown out of the literary tradition with which he was very familiar, Einstein stood on the shoulders of Newton who stood on those of Copernicus and Kepler, and so on. Geniuses, like everyone else, wither without company and their thoughts don't ascend if not carried by the thoughts and contributions of others.

Furthermore, outstanding individual accomplishments are nothing new, nor the lasting respect for them. The Greek philosophers are well known to us and have been cherished since their own time. The same is true for many artists and authors through the ages. Several religions have remarkable individuals worshipped for their deeds, such as Zarathustra, Jesus, and Mohammed. Nor is it anything exclusive to the Occidental or European cultures. For example, there is Buddha of India, Lao Tzu and Confucius of China, and so on.

Remarkable individuals have always existed and been recognized as such. Equally true is that some of them have

454 Ibid., p. 41.

been persecuted for deviating from the social norm more than the powers of their society tolerated. This, too, has not changed in our present days. Nor was it different for the Western world in the politically charged year of 1968, when Campbell's book was published.

Again, the Functions of Mythology

Campbell returns to his idea of four functions of mythology, which he presented in the previous book, *Occidental Mythology*, but this time with slightly altered definitions of those functions.

The first function, previously described as the sense of awe induced by mythology, is now "to reconcile waking consciousness to the *mysterium tremendum et jascinans* of this universe *as it is*."[455] Although the words differ, what is implied is surely the same *numinous* of which Rudolf Otto spoke.

The second function, though, deviates considerably from the cosmology he previously assigned to it. Now it relates directly to the previous function of perceiving the universe, in order to "render an interpretive total image of the same, as known to contemporary consciousness." That is quite cryptic and not cleared up much by his explanation:

> *It is the revelation to waking consciousness of the powers*
> *of its own sustaining source.*

Actually, it seems to be little more than a repetition of the first function. Where he previously spoke of two separate functions — the sense of awe and the structure of a cosmology — he now blends them into one. By that, both are obscured. The experience of the numinous loses its emotional significance and the cosmology loses its rational clarity. Campbell should have stayed with his earlier definitions, which made more sense.

[455] Ibid., p. 4.

The third function, that of supporting the social order and conforming the individual to it, is in its new wording the same, but sharpened: "the enforcement of a moral order." That is indeed how a social order is usually established and defended. It is proclaimed a necessity of a higher dignity, not to be questioned by individuals. Society and its norms are declared to be as they must. A social order is open to alteration, but a moral order is not.

Before turning to Campbell's fourth function of mythology, the first three call for additional consideration. They form a complete whole, regarding not only the functions but also perspectives of mythology.

Most if not all mythologies contain a mixture of three separate perspectives, which can be described as modes of thought: artistic, scientific and moral. They correspond quite precisely to the first three functions in Campbell's model.

The scientific perspective is the intention to explain — the origin of the world and its inhabitants, the forces of nature, the fate of men, and so on. The moral perspective is the intention to discipline the members of the community by establishing higher causes for the rules of that society and thereby imprinting them in people's minds. The artistic perspective is what creates the sense of awe mentioned by Campbell. It is the intention to entertain, without which the other two perspectives would fall flat. A boring mythology gets no devotee.

Creation myths are usually very clear examples of this triangle of perspectives and how they appear with shifting emphasis within myths as well as between them. For example, Genesis 1 with its six days of creation has a clear emphasis on the scientific side of the triangle, whereas Genesis 2 with the story of Adam, Eve, and the forbidden fruit leans heavily to the moral side. Both are artistically enhanced for effect — Genesis 1 with the grand cosmic spectacle and Genesis 2 with the drama striking its main characters, who are portrayed as all too human, so that we feel their desperation and pain.

There is nothing mysterious about the three sides of this

triangle, neither with the intentions behind them nor with how they are expressed in mythology. Together, they cover just about all significant ingredients in mythology, which is also implied in Campbell's treatment. It is with the fourth function he complicates matters unnecessarily. Still, he calls it the "most vital, most critical" of them, and explains that its aim is "to foster the centering and unfolding of the individual in integrity."[456]

This centering and unfolding are done in accord with a foursome relating to the four functions, and therefore with letters signifying their order:

d) himself (the microcosm), c) his culture (the mesocosm), b) the universe (the macrocosm), and a) that awesome ultimate mystery which is both beyond and within himself and all things.

This creates kind of a loop, where the fourth function contains all of them, including itself. That is rather close to mumbo jumbo. Campbell is carried away by his urge to make depth psychology of it all, and doing so implies a purpose that is hard to imagine being incorporated in the formation of mythologies. The ancient sages, or individual geniuses if you will, who developed the mythologies were hardly aiming at a psychoanalytical strategy by which to lead each person to some kind of self-realization.

Campbell is simply projecting his own conviction onto the ancient material. So, of course he can show no substantial evidence for it.

Mythologies are socially adapted and upheld. They are not concerned with the personal psyche, other than that they need to be at least partially convincing to the minds towards which they are directed. Certainly, they can still induce sensations of self-discovery in those who adhere to them, but that is

456 Ibid., p. 6.

more of a side effect than an intended function of them. Persons with that experience are much likelier to have made their own interpretations.

Of course, there are exceptions. Some mythologies explicitly include elements of self-realization, such as shamanistic paths to discover and express personal characteristics and powers, and the alchemist method of using the transmutation of lead into gold as a metaphor for personal refinement. Still, the main object of mythology has always been social, and not personal, however some individuals may have found to use it.

Campbell's excuse, in this last volume of *Masks of God*, is that here he deals with the creations of individual and independent minds. He asserts, "the mythology of which we are treating in this volume springs from individual experience, not dogma, learning, political interests, or programs for the renovation of society."[457] But that is not a valid argument, for two reasons.

Firstly, there is no contrariety between individual experience and dogma, learning, et cetera. They are not mutually exclusive. Quite the contrary. Most literary works contain what must be described as dogmatic or political messages, aimed at improving society. Otherwise, they would be pointless — only words, words, words. No author of any dignity just tells a story. There is a point to it, something of importance that the writer wants to address.

Secondly, it cannot be stated that mythologies of old were not the results of individual experience. The author's identity may be lost to us, but there surely was one — or several, which makes no difference. Mythologies were born out of minds with their individual experiences. Just as mythologies do not appear without people forming them, minds do not operate without experiences influencing them.

The difference Campbell claims is not one of content, but of use. That use is likely to have reshaped mythologies over

---

[457] Ibid., p. 84.

time, though more in how they were interpreted than how they were altered to fit this or that purpose.

This is evident in how the words of the Bible have been treated through the centuries. The writing remains unedited, but the explanations of it have differed considerably through time and in various cultural settings. That can also be said for the Greek mythology, which was once in Ancient Greece regarded as a reality, but later became no more than fairy tales.

So, when Campbell condemns mythologies of old, he does so because of their use, but mistakenly claims it is due to their content.

The Gospels should have enlightened him, if he were not so opposed to how Christian churches have misused them by twisting their meanings. The many atrocities of the authoritarian and intolerant churches have no support in the teachings of Jesus, as the words of the Gospels transmit them.

Considering this, the truly baffling thing is that those words have remained unaltered throughout, although they exposed the hypocrisy of those churches. Still, the clergy evidently did not dare to change the texts, since they had founded those churches on declaring the scriptures sacred, of divine origin. They were trapped by the very thing that gave them their power.

Campbell, too, is not altering the texts he discusses, but he picks the ones that fit his theory and interprets them accordingly. It is his right, of course, but he does it with such bias that his conclusions are neither surprising nor convincing.

Mircea Eliade

In the history of religion during the mid-20th century, Mircea Eliade (1907-1986) was one of the main academics. He was born in Romania, commencing philosophy studies in 1925 at the University of Bucharest, specializing on Renaissance humanism. In 1928 he went to India to study Sanskrit and Indian philosophy for four years. Back at Bucharest, he received his PhD in 1933 with a dissertation on yoga and the origins of Indian mysticism.

In 1945 he moved to Paris, where he got acquainted with comparative mythology scholar George Dumézil, and started teaching comparative religion at the Sorbonne. His first meeting with Jung was in 1950, as Eliade started to attend the annual Eranos conferences in Switzerland. He gave lectures there regularly until 1967.[458] In 1958 he was appointed to head the University of Chicago History of Religions department, where he remained until his death in 1986.

In addition to his teaching and extensive writing (mainly in the 1950s and 60s), he started the journals *History of Religions* and *The Journal of Religion*. His extensive work *Histoire des croyances et des idées religieuses* in three volumes was published between 1976 and 1983. An English translation, *A History of Religious Ideas*, followed shortly. He was the editor in chief of the *Encyclopedia of Religion* in 17 volumes, published in 1987, the year after his death. Eliade also wrote a number of novels, often with erotic and mythological components.

Other Archetypes

In 1949, while still in Paris, Mircea Eliade published *Le mythe de l'éternel retour: Archétypes et répétition* (*The Myth of the Eternal Return: Archetypes and Repetition*), which was widely spread

---

[458] *Welcome to Eranos*, a yearbooks PDF list (daimon.ch/Eranos.pdf), Daimon Verlag, p. 28.

and appreciated. The English edition was published in 1954, without the subtitle.[459] Its slightly revised 1959 edition was titled *Cosmos and History: The Myth of the Eternal Return*, and the 1965 edition *The Myth of the Eternal Return or, Cosmos and History*. In the preface of the 1959 edition, Eliade writes that he considers it "the most significant of my books."[460]

Although the term archetype disappeared in the English title, it is prominently used in the text. But Eliade points out in the 1959 preface that he is not referring to the Jung archetypes. Instead, he compares his use of the term to that of the Spanish essayist Eugenio d'Ors, as a synonym for "exemplary model" or "paradigm," which he means is the Augustinian sense of the term. He notices that Jung's use of the term has become so established, other uses of it need to be explained or even avoided:

> *But in our day the word has been rehabilitated by Professor Jung, who has given it a new meaning; and it is certainly desirable that the term "archetype" should no longer be used in its pre-Jungian sense unless the fact is distinctly stated.*[461]

The archetypes Eliade discusses are symbols given an elevated value in archaic societies, which traced them back to a primordial time. They refused to accept time as linear. Instead, they saw it as cyclic, which was "their revolt against concrete, historical time, their nostalgia for a periodical return to the mythical time of the beginning of things."[462]

Accordingly, archaic man linked things and events to their archetypes in order to make them "real" in the sense of

---

[459] Mircea Eliade, *The Myth of the Eternal Return*, transl. Willard R. Trask, New York 1954 (originally published in French 1949).

[460] Mircea Eliade, *Cosmos and History: The Myth of the Eternal Return*, transl. Willard R. Trask, New York 1959, p. ix.

[461] Ibid., p. ix.

[462] Ibid., p. xi.

having a lasting significance, since "for archaic man, reality is a function of the imitation of a celestial archetype."[463] In other words, the archetypes were deemed sacred, a concept Eliade was to explore more in later books. By regarding them as sacred, archaic man could trust their endurance:

> *Hence the outstanding reality is the sacred; for only the sacred is in an absolute fashion, acts effectively, creates things and makes them endure.*[464]

Eliade gives several examples of such archetypes and argues for their function by referring to a number of myths and rituals. There is no shortage of those, so it would be surprising if he found no confirmation of his theory, especially since his definitions of the archetypes include more than they exclude.

For example, when discussing the archetype of the center of the world, such as the sacred mountain where heaven and earth meet, he states: "Every temple or palace and, by extension, every sacred city or royal residence is a Sacred Mountain, thus becoming a Center." Also, it is regarded as "the meeting point of heaven, earth, and hell."[465]

Places given this significance can be found, but so can numerous temples and palaces that are not. Eliade is applying his own symbolism, not necessarily that of the people who built and inhabited those places. He speaks of the center of the world as "the earth's navel, the point at which the Creation began,"[466] which leads him to this questionable reasoning:

> *1. Every creation repeats the pre-eminent cosmogonic act, the Creation of the world.*
> *2. Consequently, whatever is founded has its foundation at*

[463] Ibid., p. 5.

[464] Ibid., p. 11.

[465] Ibid., p. 12.

[466] Ibid., p. 16.

Eliade hurries to generalize. There are indeed creation myths that more or less specify a center for the creation, which in itself has little symbolic value. A creation begins somewhere, which does not mean it begins from a center. There could not have been a center before the creation.

Not only that, but so many creation myths lack a central point for the beginning of creation, and simply could not have one. There is often a primordial sea, in which a center is hard to find, and then there is heaven, also lacking a center. The earth is rarely described as created from a central point. Usually, the whole of it appears at once. It is definitely more common that no specific place for the beginning of creation is pinpointed.

It is not even the case in Genesis of the Bible. God begins by creating light in the primordial darkness, then day and night, then the firmament, and so on. No center, no certain spot from which the world grows. Nor can the Garden of Eden be called a center from which creation took place, since its appearance is late in the process.

Eliade includes rituals in the pattern he proposes. They all have a divine model, an archetype, and "all religious acts are held to have been founded by gods, civilizing heroes, or mythical ancestors."[468] Again, that is far from certain about them all, even considering the very broad definition of who would have done it. Many rituals around the world have no fixed origin, but are performed because of tradition.

He includes dance in the same reasoning: "All dances were originally sacred; in other words, they had an extrahuman model." By extrahuman he means they were presumed to have been created "in the mythical period, by an ancestor, a

---

[467] Ibid., p. 18.

[468] Ibid., p. 22.

totemic animal, a god, or a hero."[469] But every dance is not a sacred ritual, just as every song is not a hymn — nor is there reason to assume that archaic man believed so. People must have danced and sung before they started using such expressions in religious acts justified by mythical explanations. Claiming that it was all sacred ritual to archaic man makes no more sense than saying the same about the dancing and singing of modern man.

Eliade takes his theory into the absurd, making our ancestors unable to relate to their world in any other way than religiously:

We must add that, for the traditional societies, all the important acts of life were revealed ab origine *by gods or heroes. Men only repeat these exemplary and paradigmatic gestures* ad infinitum.[470]

That can only be true if by "important" acts he solely mean those that fit his criterion.

Still, there is truth to his model. We do tend to sort of glorify aspects of our lives as well as ourselves. Life and its components are given theatrical effects that make us appreciate and remember them. History is made up of extraordinary events and people, whereas the everyday things in between have faded away, as did the vast majority of anonymous persons never mentioned in history books. We do the same thing today, paying attention to places and persons we regard as remarkable, while the rest is little more than a blur.

So, it can be said that we make some types into archetypes, ascribing particular importance to them. It is a completely conscious process, and it does not signify a longing back to some legendary primordial time. Nor does it mean that those archetypes are more real than other types — just fancier. It is ques-

---

[469] Ibid., p. 28.

[470] Ibid., p. 32.

tionable to assume that archaic societies were different from ours in this sense. They just had other explanations for it.

It can be compared to how the word *idol* changes meaning when used for the present instead of the past. Traditionally it represented the worship of a deity, whereas today's idols are worshipped but still regarded as human. The common denominator is the worship. It doesn't need to be based on a religious belief, so we should not take for granted that it was to archaic man.

The same can be said for rituals. We uphold many of them, even when they have no religious significance to us. They are, and were also for archaic man, first of all celebrations.

To Eliade, rituals connected to the new year were expressions of the eternal return to the time of creation, whereby the world was created anew. But the cyclic behavior of nature was as evident to archaic man as it is to us. It happened with or without a ritual. Yet, it was something to celebrate, especially when taking place at the spring equinox, as it did in many cultures. Eliade's explanation is more elaborate:

> *What is important is that man has felt the need to reproduce the cosmogony in his constructions, whatever be their nature; that this reproduction made him contemporary with the mythical moment of the beginning of the world and that he felt the need of returning to that moment, as often as possible, in order to regenerate himself.*[471]

Our New Year is in the dark of the winter, soon after the winter solstice, when the days start getting longer again. That, too, is a reason to celebrate, and we do, without thinking that it would help the daylight to return. We fondle the idea that it will regenerate us, in some small way, but enjoy the festivity even if we discard that possibility. Archaic man might very well have had the same sentiment about it.

---

[471] Ibid., p. 76f.

What Eliade's theory implies is that archaic man was an unknowing victim of superstition and in need of religious comfort, which formed his perception of the world. Eliade is far from alone in assuming this. Most texts about ancient religion and mythology have expressed similar views.

They are not without reason. There are many examples that indicate such beliefs and customs in the distant past. But the texts describing them tend to take it too far. The mind of archaic man was not unable to think rationally.

Returning to the subject of archetypes, Eliade's conception of them is not that far from Jung. To both, the archetypes are archaic mental objects by which to reach an improved state of mind, be it Jung's individuation or Eliade's cyclic renewal. Also, both work symbolically, through myths and rituals, and both are shared collectively as well as experienced individually.

Without a microscopic perspective, Eliade's and Jung's archetypes are not easy to tell apart.

The Sacred

In the preface to his book *The Quest* from 1969, as well as in that of *A History of Religious Ideas*, Eliade describes religion as closely connected to the experience of the sacred. This is a consequence of the conscious mind: "In short, the 'sacred' is an element in the structure of consciousness and not a stage in the history of consciousness."[472] He continues:

> *On the most archaic levels of culture,* living, considered as being human, *is in itself a* religious act, *for food-getting, sexual life, and work have a sacramental value. In other words, to be — or, rather, to become — a man signifies being "religious."*

[472] Mircea Eliade, A *History of Religious Ideas*, vol. 1, transl. Willard R. Trask, Chicago 1978 (originally published in French 1976), p. xiii.

To Eliade, the sacred is not something that has evolved through history, but it is a trait of the human consciousness. It is by the sense of the sacred that man experiences what is real and significant in the turmoil of existence. What is religious, then, is to be human, with all that it entails. It is simply how we relate to our world.

Already in the 1950s, Eliade wrote a book specifically on the subject of the sacred: *The Sacred and the Profane*, which repeats several of the ideas from *The Myth of the Eternal Return*. As the title reveals, he describes a polarity between the sacred and the profane, where he sees the latter gaining influence in modern society at the cost of the former.

He regards this as unfortunate, robbing modern man of a sense of meaning of life and a place in the world. He explains it through the cyclic work of agriculture:

> *Emptied of religious symbolism, agricultural work becomes at once opaque and exhausting; it reveals no meaning, it makes possible no opening toward the universal, toward the world of spirit.*[473]

In the introduction, Eliade refers the idea of the sacred to the German theologist Rudolf Otto and his 1917 book *Das Heilige* (*The Holy*), presenting the holy as an essential component in religion.

Otto focused on it as an experience of the divine, going beyond reason. It is a mental state:

> *This mental state is perfectly* sui generis[474] *and irreducible to any other; and therefore, like every absolutely primary and elementary datum, while it admits of being dis-*

---

[473] Mircea Eliade, *The Sacred and the Profane: The Nature of Religion*, transl. Willard R. Trask, New York 1959 (originally published in French 1957), p. 96.

[474] Of its own kind.

cussed, it cannot be strictly defined.[475]

Eliade's view of the sacred does not involve any divine influence, and he makes no claim of either gods or the sacred existing outside of human minds. But he does stress the religious nature of man in archaic societies, calling him *homo religiosus*, and points out the benefits the religious experience brings. The modern profane worldview, on the other hand, leaves man unfulfilled. This is something new:

> *It should be said at once that the completely profane world, the wholly desacralized cosmos, is a recent discovery in the history of the human spirit.*[476]

This profane world modern man finds himself in, lacks any comforting quality, such as purpose and a designated place in it:

> *Properly speaking, there is no longer any world, there are only fragments of a shattered universe, an amorphous mass consisting of an infinite number of more or less neutral places in which man moves, governed and driven by the obligations of an existence incorporated into an industrial society.*[477]

That could not suffice for those of a religious mindset. Instead, "religious man can live only in a sacred world, because it is only in such a world that he participates in being, that he has a *real existence.*"[478]

[475] Rudolf Otto, *The Idea of the Holy: An Inquiry into the non-rational factor in the idea of the divine and its relation to the rational,* transl. John W. Harvey, 1943 (originally published in German 1917), p. 7.

[476] Eliade, *The Sacred and the Profane,* 1959, p. 13.

[477] Ibid., pp. 23f.

[478] Ibid., p. 64.

The consecration of the world is done through myth and ritual, so that the world creation described in the myth is symbolically repeated in the ritual. Since the religious perspective of time is cyclic, such rituals are performed annually, for "each year the world must be created anew."[479] Religious man makes his world sacred by ritually recreating it.

This ritual recreation is done for the whole world, but also for cities, temples, even single abodes. Thereby, they all become symbolical centers of the world, which causes no problem: "The multiplicity, or even the infinity, of centers of the world raises no difficulty for religious thought."[480]

Eliade applies a narrow definition of myth, which he seems to claim is the only proper one:

> *The myth relates a sacred history, that is, a primordial event that took place at the beginning of time, ab initio.*[481]

He calls myth a paradigmatic model, peopled by gods or culture heroes, and it is "always the recital of a creation; it tells how something was accomplished, began to be." That would exclude a number of traditional tales usually regarded as myths, for example many of those so popular among Jungians — the hero myths. They do far from always tell how things began to be.

That is a minor issue regarding Eliade's theory. He is free to use the definition of his choice in order to fit his approach to myth, although he goes too far by claiming it to be true for all myths.

What is more disturbing is that he applies this kind of generalization to several components in his theory. He assumes homogeneity in archaic societies, among religious people, among those who are non-religious, regarding the meanings

---

[479] Ibid., p. 49.

[480] Ibid., p. 57.

[481] Ibid., p. 95.

of rituals, and so on, presenting no other evidence than chosen examples from the very vast source of myths and rites around the world. He even confesses to his bias in choosing them, such as here, when discussing sacred space:

> *From the thousands of examples available to the historian of religions, we have cited only a small number but enough to show the varieties of the religious experience of space.*[482]

But it is not the variety he wishes to demonstrate with the examples. It is the very opposite. He aims to show their similarities, which he declares on the following page:

> *But for our purpose it is not the infinite variety of the religious experiences of space that concerns us but, on the contrary, their elements of unity.*

Hence, it comes as no surprise that he neglects discussing examples that contradict his theory, although they are certainly easy to find. He searches for a distinct pattern and chooses examples accordingly. That is not a proper scientific procedure. But in this approach he is in good company with both Freudians and Jungians.

To what extent is Mircea Eliade a Jungian? He definitely does not stick to Jung's dogma so to speak religiously. In this book, Jung is not mentioned even once, and the only book of his listed in the bibliography is the one co-written with Kerényi.[483] As for the term archetype, it is used much less than in the previously discussed book, solely in the sense of a paradigmatic model, without the expanded unconscious dynamics proposed by Jung.

He denies the idea that mythology would be the product of the unconscious, but still sees a link between them:

---

[482] Ibid., p. 62.

[483] C. G. Jung & K. Kerényi, *Einführung in das Wesen der Mythologie*, 1941.

Yet the contents and structures of the unconscious are the result of immemorial existential situations, especially of critical situations, and this is why the unconscious has a religious aura.[484]

Any existential crisis, he explains on the same page, leads to religion: "For religion is the paradigmatic solution for every existential crisis." That means the non-religious are in a dilemma, since they do not have access to this outlet. But their profane mentality is not solid. Their capacity to be religious is hidden in the depth of their unconscious:

From one point of view it could almost be said that in the case of those moderns who proclaim that they are nonreligious, religion and mythology are "eclipsed" in the darkness of their unconscious — which means too that in such men the possibility of reintegrating a religious vision of life lies at a great depth.[485]

Eliade is clearly distancing himself from the Jungian theories about religion and myth. He has his own gospel to preach and it is not that close to Jung's — though also not totally different. His theory is based on what he perceives as mankind's emotional urges and needs, as opposed to rational thinking. In other words, he regards myth and ritual as stemming from what Jungians would call the unconscious instead of the conscious, although he is reluctant to apply those words to his theory.

Eliade refers to religious man, but makes no clear definition of what it is to be religious. The only attribute he describes is the experience of the sacred, which can glorify even something as simple as a stone, and just about everything else:

[484] Ibid., p. 210.

[485] Ibid., p. 213.

*In other words, for those who have a religious experience
all nature is capable of revealing itself as cosmic sacral-
ity.*[486]

So, the religious experience is identical with the experience of the sacred. But what makes something sacred is the religious doctrine, such as its myths and deities. Without that,
there would be no method by which to consecrate anything.
Eliade points out the creation myth as the core model for making things sacred, so that must have been present beforehand.
But then it is odd to present it as a means to fulfill a need. The
means can hardly have appeared before the need.

What Eliade's theory implies is that mythology emerged
to fulfill the urge to make the world sacred, although before a
mythology the concept of the sacred would have no meaning.
So, mythology cannot have risen out of that need, as Eliade describes it. Either mythology existed beforehand and led to the
experience of the sacred, or that experience was originally
something different from what mythology later came to confirm.

The sense of wonder and awe, which the sacred is set to
induce, is likely to have been with us for very long before we
formulated explanations for it. In spite of Eliade's statements
to the contrary, we still feel it, no matter how profane we might
be. The sensation does not need an elaborate religious confirmation. It is much more likely that religion incorporated it,
than that it is something unique to those who have faith in a
religion.

[486] Ibid., p. 12.

Marie-Louise von Franz

Marie-Louise von Franz (1915-1998) was one of the most prominent and loyal followers of Jung during the 20th century, lecturing into her 70s and writing until her death. She was born in Munich to Austrian parents, and the family moved to Switzerland in 1919, after World War I. At the age of 18, in 1933, she met Carl G. Jung, and the next year she began her analytical training with him.

Being of small means but a student of classical philology, she paid by translating Greek and Latin texts related to his research on alchemy. She was to work closely with him until his death.[487]

She stayed committed to Jung's theories. Displeased with the Jung Institute being influenced by non-Jungians in the 1980s, she parted with it and later formed the *Centre for the Research into the Psychology of C.G. Jung,* bringing several analysts and students with her.[488]

The Centre was founded in 1994, its present name being *Research and Training Centre for Depth Psychology according to C.G. Jung and Marie-Louise von Franz.*[489]

Through the years, Marie-Louise von Franz was quite a productive lecturer and writer. Many of her books were transcripts of lectures, which might explain her straightforward writing, unusually accessible compared to many of her colleagues — including Jung.

Since the start of her path within Jungian psychology, a main theme of hers was to examine and explain fairy tales from that perspective, but she also wrote about alchemy, dreams,

---

[487] Kirsch 2000, p. 11.

[488] Ibid., p. 12.

[489] The Centre's website gives no information about a previous name change (centre-dp.org). Presumably, that came after the death of von Franz.

numerology, and other subjects favored by Jung. A decade after his death, her Jung biography was published.[490]

Pure Fairy Tales

In most of her texts on fairy tales, von Franz jumps right at analyzing the psychological implications of specific tales, but in one of the books, *An Introduction to the Interpretation of Fairy Tales* from 1970, she starts by giving an explanation to her fascination with those types of stories:

> *Fairy tales are the purest and simplest expression of collective unconscious psychic processes. Therefore their value for the scientific investigation of the unconscious exceeds that of all other material. They represent the archetypes in their simplest, barest and most concise form. In this pure form, the archetypal images afford us the best clues to the understanding of the processes going on in the collective psyche. In myths or legends, or any other more elaborate mythological material, we get at the basic patterns of the human psyche through an overlay of cultural material. But in fairy tales there is much less specific conscious cultural material and therefore they mirror the basic patterns of the psyche more clearly.*[491]

Jung as well as most of his followers preferred to dig deep into myths of the ancient past, where deities and heroes were involved in fantastic feats. In comparison, her approach is rather humble — but her reason for it is not. She claims that the fairy tales reveal more and truer things about the psyche than elaborate myths can. To her, they are myths stripped bare.

That can be discussed, but what fairy tales tend to show

[490] Marie-Louise von Franz, *C. G. Jung: His Myth in Our Time*, transl. William H. Kennedy, New York 1975 (originally published in German 1972).

[491] Marie-Louise von Franz, *An Introduction to the Interpretation of Fairy Tales*, New York 1970, I p. 1. She states the same on I p. 11.

are stories from outside the temples, close to the lives of common people. They have nothing to do with the creation of the world, or battles between gods risking its destruction. And though they often contain magic, it is not of a very spectacular kind, not something earth-shattering. Compared to mythology, fairy tales are plain, even trivial. They don't tell of big and important things.

This brings them an impression of innocence, of not to be taken seriously. Just for amusement. So, the powers that be have neglected them and what they might have to say. Therefore, they are comparably free of politics and other controlling influences. In that way, they are pure. But it does not necessarily make them simple, nor are they sure to show the basic patterns of the psyche less distorted.

Such assumptions come from prejudice. Human beings are equally complicated, whatever their place in the hierarchy is or what scale there is to their endeavors. The deities and heroes of mythology behave like ordinary people do, with the same personal urges and shortcomings. The size doesn't change the substance. The psychology must be the same. So, analysis of fairy tales can't be much different from that of myths, nor the result of it.

According to von Franz, all fairy tales describe one psychic fact, which is the Self, "the psychic totality of an individual and also, paradoxically, the regulating center of the collective unconscious."[492] It is safe to say that in Jungian theory this is at the core of every myth, and not just in fairy tales.

The basic patterns that fairy tales follow more clearly than myths usually do are those of a story. They have clear beginnings and ends, protagonists and antagonists, obstacles and solutions. Of course, that dramaturgical structure can be traced also in myths, but it is rarely as obvious and direct as in fairy tales. The purity of them is in their storytelling.

Mainly, fairy tales describe the fate of individuals, such as

---

[492] Ibid., I p. 2.

the peasant boy defeating a troll, marrying the princess and becoming a prince. The events affect the lives of the few characters directly involved. They don't change the course of the sun, or separate the land from the sea, or bring the mastery of fire to the people. Contrary to mythology, they alter neither the way the world works nor human conditions. They don't even aspire to explain why snakes have no legs.

Still, there may be general truths about the human psyche found in fairy tales — as well as in myths — and their patterns.

The Answer Within Dramaturgy

The question to ponder first is why those stories all share the same dramaturgical structure. Marie-Louise von Franz and the other Jungians jump to the conclusion that it is because of the archetypal content in the collective unconscious, aimed to guide us all towards individuation.

That jump, though, skips the obvious search for the answer within dramaturgy. If it can in itself explain its presence and homogeneity in just about every story — and it can — there is no need for far-fetched ideas of hidden workings of the unconscious, which have not been proven in the least for the more than one hundred years they have been around. Dramaturgy, on the other hand, has been known and applied successfully since before Aristotle's *Poetics* explained it.

Fundamentally, stories are about getting something that is wanted or unwanted. The former induces delight and the latter dismay, also in the audience since we are empathic creatures.

Aristotle connected the happy ending to comedy and the sad one to tragedy, and the reward for the audience was *catharsis*, an emotional cleansing, sort of what a rollercoaster ride creates. Without that catharsis, the audience is displeased with the story and wants neither to hear the story again nor retell it to anyone else.

No archetypes are needed to explain it, nor an unconscious operating in secrecy within our minds. We want what we want and not what we don't want. That is as basic as being hungry, which is a joy when food is accessible but torment when it is not. It's not a mystery to us. The Jungian explanation, argued also by von Franz, claims that what we really want is something else, which is unknown to us, and yet it urges us on. It is like saying we would not know to eat when we are hungry.

Also, when applied to fairy tales, it would demand that they have an outcome different from what the characters could conceive or even understand they wanted. That's not how it plays out in fairy tales. The characters may have regarded the outcome as highly implausible, but definitely possible and its reward completely comprehendible — also in advance. There is simply no hidden factor involved.

What is intriguing, returning to Aristotle, is that also a tragic ending brings catharsis. They are few in fairy tales, but they do exist. Why would an audience find any kind of satisfaction in that?

In Jungian terms it would be a progression towards failing to reach the self-realization of individuation. That might make sense as a chapter in a story, but hardly as its ending. It would scream out that the story is incomplete, since it has not reached its conclusion, the goal of it. The troll is not killed, the kingdom not won.

Dramaturgically, though, the story is completed also in a tragedy. A story can go from fortune to misfortune, as well as the other way around. It can be about getting the unwanted. Sure enough, that happens in life, so there is recognition and therefore empathy of the audience. Just as we can share the joy of others — real or imaginary — we can grieve their misfortune. That is enough for catharsis.

But also, the plot of tragedies is often more intricate than that of comedies, which might be why Aristotle preferred them. They end with the unwanted, but still an obstacle was overcome, a solution reached. The protagonist's misfortune is not greater than that of the antagonist. The former triumphs over the latter, if not in deed so in character. It is a sacrifice for the greater good. Ours is a social species, so we can agree with that.

In a fairy tale, we accept that it ends with the misfortune of its hero as long as the adversary's end is not fortunate. The hero may fail, but only if less so than the adversary. In this roundabout manner, a bad ending can still be good and the hero's fate is in some way a victory. If the adversary alone succeeds, the fairy tale will be dismissed by the audience and quickly forgotten.

Redundant Explanations

As for how Marie-Louise von Franz interprets fairy tales, it is difficult to stay a patient observer of it, since she does so with a dogmatism surpassing that of Jung. It is this way or the highway.

She spends several pages of the above-mentioned introduction dismissing other researchers of fairy tales and myths, because they showed no sign of incorporating the analytical psychology approach, for which she does not even try to present any substantial arguments. This uncompromising attitude is surely in part due to the fact that the book consists of transcripts from her lectures at the C. G. Jung Institute, i.e., afore allies. Also, her straightforward language reveals her standpoint blatantly.

This does not change when she starts analyzing specific fairy tales. Her first example is *The Three Feathers* from the fairy tale collection of the Grimm brothers, about three sons of a king competing to inherit the kingdom.[493] She turns to alchemy to explain what the king symbolizes, as if this figure would otherwise lack any significance.

A king is a king, in no need of some hidden significance — and was even more so in the days when kings truly ruled

---

[493] Jacob & Wilhelm Grimm, *Kinder und Hausmärchen*, vol. I, Göttingen 1857, pp. 344ff.

the world. If he were a farmer, his three sons would not be that anxious to inherit his position. In the story, there is nothing more to it. But to von Franz, he "represents the divine principle in its visible form; he is its incarnation or embodiment, its dwelling-place."[494] All that amplification of his role is redundant. The story works well without it. She ends up claiming that the king is a symbol of the Self, again something superfluous to the story, not to mention questionable.

The fact that the king and his sons are male is another thing she dwells upon, but that, too, is easily explained. Kingdoms were inherited on the male line — and often still are. Sadly, a daughter would stand no chance, and every audience would know it.

Also, she claims that the king "leaves it to fate to settle who shall inherit the kingdom," but he does no such thing. He puts his sons to the test, albeit with an element of chance, throwing the three feathers to decide where each son will go to complete the task. And what they do shows clearly that their characters are what decide the outcome. Only one of them takes the task seriously.

The fact that what the king throws are feathers makes von Franz discuss the archetypal significance of birds, their bearers. Well, what else could he throw up in the air that the wind would spread in different directions? It needs to be nothing more than a fancy way to introduce an element of chance. The same can be said about the wind sending them out. To von Franz it is a connection to spiritual power, such as that of the Holy Ghost. But that additional meaning is not necessary for the story to make sense, and hinted nowhere in it.[495]

Where we can agree with her is what she sees as the moral of the fairy tale. The least pompous of the sons finds his feather land where he stands, and it is there that he finds what his father asks for. She concludes:

494 von Franz 1970, IV p. 5.
495 Ibid., IV pp. 16f.

Very often we look God-knows-where for the solution of our problem and do not see that it is right before our noses. We are not humble enough to look downwards but stick our noses up in the air.[496]

That is indeed what the fairy tale tells us, but this message is present in the story as it is, without any depth psychology additions.

Preconscious Creation Myths

In spite of her express preference of fairy tales, Marie-Louise von Franz also wrote about myths. One of her books deals exclusively with creation myths. It is based on transcribed lectures of hers from 1961 and 1962, but was not published until ten years later.[497] An edition in German came in 1990, and a revised edition of the English book in 1995, with the title shortened to just *Creation Myths*.[498] The last edition is the one referred to in the following.

Her approach to creation myths is one of personal psychology. That would be a perfectly legitimate take on them, investigating what they might indicate about human thoughts and emotions on the topic, except for her claim that this is the true nature of those myths. In her eyes, they were never about the creation of the world. Instead, "they represent unconscious and preconscious processes which describe not the origin of our cosmos, but the origin of man's conscious awareness of the world."[499]

This is a strange statement, for two reasons. It suggests that creation myths would not come from speculations about

[496] Ibid., IV p. 17.

[497] Marie-Louise von Franz, *Patterns of Creativity Mirrored in Creation Myths*, Zurich 1972.

[498] Marie-Louise von Franz, *Creation Myths*, Boston 1995.

[499] Ibid., p. 5.

the origin of the world and its creatures, although that is just what they describe, and furthermore it firmly states that the myths are not composed by conscious minds, but by unconscious and preconscious processes. She presents no evidence for it, nor does she define these concepts enough for putting them to the test.

Suffice to say that the creation myths around the world certainly give distinct impressions of being about what they profess to be about, and having been composed by minds consciously aware of what they were doing.

It is usually not difficult at all to follow their trains of thought. They make sense, particularly when considering the contexts in which the myths were formed, no matter how contradictory they are to what we now know about cosmology and the evolution of life on earth.

She explains it as a case of *projection*, quoting Jung's definition of it as "the expulsion of a subjective content into an object."[500] So, people have projected internal concerns onto the world as a whole. It is a very Jungian take, making it all about the personal psyche's struggles. And von Franz doesn't confine it to creation myths, but sees it as a general response to anything beyond our understanding, so that "wherever known reality stops, where we touch the unknown, there we project an archetypal image."[501]

Since the archetypes emerge from the unconscious, which works independently of the conscious, so must the concepts they form — such as the creation myths. To von Franz, the unknown belongs to the unconscious:

> *Because the origin of nature and of human existence is a complete mystery to us, the unconscious has produced many models of this event.*[502]

[500] Ibid., p. 3.

[501] Ibid., p. 2.

[502] Ibid., p. 1.

What she claims, then, is that the conscious is unable to deal with the unknown at all. It is obviously false.

We know what it is we don't know. It intrigues us and sets our thoughts in motion — our conscious thoughts. We are aware of thinking about it, and of how we think about it. We come to conclusion, which we can trace back to our process of speculation.

Otherwise, if our conception had just been injected into our conscious from a hidden chamber of our mind, we would dismiss it. It has to make sense to our conscious, or it could not satisfy us. Therefore, it has to be reached involving a conscious effort.

The more important the subject is to us, the more necessary it is that we are familiar with how we reached a conclusion about it. And von Franz is certain, taking support from Jung, that creation myths deal with themes very essential to us. Doing so, she confirms the conscious thought process in this:

> *Despite the fact that we all know that the question of life after death, or of the origin and meaning of life, can never be answered rationally with any final certainty, according to Jung it is of tremendous importance, if not absolutely essential, that we try to form some idea about it. If a person has no myth about such questions, he is psychically dried up and impoverished and is likely to suffer from a neurosis.*[503]

In other words, it is a conscious thought process, and a very important one at that. Accordingly, it is very clear to the conscious that what von Franz states about the role of the unconscious in it cannot be correct.

---

[503] Ibid., p. 11.

The Wording of Father Raven

After the introductory chapter, the first creation myth von Franz discusses is one that "shows more clearly than others how creation is an awakening toward consciousness."[504] She has picked it from a Knud Rasmussen collection of Eskimo myths.

In this one, Rasmussen's informant Apakak[505] tells the story of the primordial creature Father Raven, *Tulungersaq*, who according to this myth "created all life on earth and in human beings and is the origin of everything."[506]

The long excerpt from this creation myth contains some anachronistic anomalies. Tulungersaq, crouching in the primordial darkness, suddenly "awoke to consciousness and discovered himself."[507] That is a suspiciously Jungian wording for a traditional Eskimo myth. So is "a different psychological makeup" two pages down. The expressions "he sank into meditation," "sat in meditation," and "social contact" also seem out of place.[508]

The source used, according to von Franz, is an English translation of Rasmussen, *The Eagle's Gift*, which was first published in 1932, but in a note to the excerpt she states instead that it is from the German version of that book, *Die Gabe des Adlers*, published in 1937. Considering that her mother tongue was German, it is more likely she used that one.

The question is where these anachronisms first appeared — in the English version, in the German one, or maybe she allowed herself some modifications in the quote. I have not been able to check those books, but some things can still be deducted.

---

[504] Ibid., p. 24.

[505] Spelled Apatac by von Franz. Ibid., p. 28.

[506] Ibid., p. 29.

[507] Ibid.

[508] Ibid., p. 30.

The English version is the earliest, translated by Isobel Wylie Hutchison, who spoke Danish as well as several other languages. Normally, German translations of Scandinavian literature are done from those original texts and not from other translations. That would be expected of this book as well, though being of later date than the English one, were it not for the fact that the Danish original from 1929 has a different title, *Festens Gave* (*The Gift of the Feast*).[509] This indicates that the German translation, made by Aenne Schmücker, is based on the English one, and not on the Danish original.

Both translators had met and spent time with Rasmussen on Greenland, before he died in 1933 at the age of 54.

Rasmussen's book gives this myth a title: "The Myth of the Beginning of All Life" ("Myten om alt Livs Begyndelse"). In his Danish text the wordings mentioned above are less questionable. Where von Franz has "awoke to consciousness and discovered himself" he wrote "pludselig kom til Bevidsthed og opdagede sig selv," which strictly translates to almost the same: "suddenly came to consciousness and discovered himself."

What it describes is not exactly an awakening, but a moment when Tulungersaq became aware of his own existence, akin to the famous Descartes statement "I think, therefore I am." It is philosophical rather than psychological, and recognizable from what other creation myths say about a sole primordial being. Before this discovery, the primary deity is unable to act. So, the wording quoted in von Franz's text is not wrong, as long as this is kept in mind.

With the next wording mentioned above, von Franz deviates considerably from Rasmussen. The original Danish version of "a different psychological makeup" is "et andet Sind," which means "another mind" or "another mentality." The term psychological is quite out of place in this context.

[509] Knud Rasmussen, *Festens gave: Eskimoiske Alaska-Æventyr*, Copenhagen 1929.

It has to be remarked that to the English word mind there is not a corresponding term in the Scandinavian languages with the exact same meaning. The word *sind* (*sinn* in Norwegian and *sinne* in Swedish) means something slightly different from mind — closer to the word mentality, or mindset. The text of the myth indicates this, when explaining the difference as "a hot, quick temper and a violent attitude." So, it is about behavior. That could be described as a psychological makeup, but such a wording would indeed be anachronistic.

The English version also adds an "and," which makes it even more misleading. In Rasmussen's text, the character described doesn't have a psychological makeup *and* a hot, quick temper, but a mindset expressed as those traits. The difference is significant. What Rasmussen's wording indicates is not a mind with fixed attributes, but a mentality existing through the behavior. The mentality *is* the behavior.

That is a very old and wide-spread conception about character, expressed in myth and held as a central principle in dramaturgy. Character manifests through action. We are what we do. The myth shows it clearly by describing the activity of the character, leading to Tulungersaq's conclusion about its mentality: from the moment it became alive, it "restlessly, constantly dug in the earth." That is manic behavior. Tulungersaq had reason to worry.

The word "meditation" is in Rasmussen's original simply "thought." This is also the word used in the German version, von Franz informs us.[510] That is academically honorable, but it raises the question: Why, then, would she choose the more elaborate and specific term? The same can be said for her use of "social contact." What Rasmussen wrote was "company" (*Selskab*).

There is another distinct deviation from Rasmussen's text at the end of the von Franz excerpt. Where she finishes, "And so the first man came into being, and later Father Raven cre-

[510] von Franz 1995, p. 34.

ated all other beings,"[511] Rasmussen's text lacks this sentence and instead goes on for a couple of pages describing additional creations. That part of the creation is summarily explained by von Franz, so she must have read the complete version.

There is nothing wrong with making such a summary, but she should not have included that last sentence in the quote, since it is not part of Apakak's account.

The above remarks may be rather petty, but they indicate a problem often found in Jungian retelling of myths — the tendency to adjust them to fit Jungian theory. That calls for watchfulness. One thing important to adhere to, when interpreting myth, is that it has to begin with finding and staying true to the most accurate version of it. Otherwise, nothing trustworthy can be claimed about it.

Marie-Louis von Franz is well aware of it, saying that she tried to find the good translations and still she cannot guarantee the accuracy of "every nuance and every word in each myth." But she continues by still allowing herself the freedom to interpret the material without concern for this uncertainty of it:

> *Because of this, I have planned to put my main emphasis and attention on certain similarities of motif and types of motif and not to go so much into the nuances of a single myth.*[512]

There is no reason to be less particular about details when making generalized claims. Quite the opposite. Only by ascertaining the nuances of each myth is it possible to state something credible about how they compare. Uncertainties increase when added to one another.

As mentioned above, von Franz has selected a myth for the express purpose of proving her theory, which in itself

[511] Ibid., p. 32.
[512] Ibid., p. 26.

weakens her argument substantially, and then she distorts the wording of the myth — albeit in a few details — to bring it closer to her understanding of it.

So, what is it she claims this myth to mean? She says it all in the first paragraph after retelling the story:

> *This is a beautiful story which shows that the mood of the awakening to a realization of reality is something like coming out of an unconscious state. That is projected onto Father Raven, who, as it were, slowly becomes conscious, and in the light of this consciousness reality simultaneously comes into existence.*[513]

Father Raven came out of an unconscious state in the meaning of suddenly being conscious of himself, which should not be confused with the psychological concepts of the unconscious and the conscious. He became aware of existing and then started to explore where he was.

The myth states that heaven and earth had come into existence without the assistance of Father Raven, so he was not the sole creator of the whole world. He appeared after heaven and earth did. Already that circumstance creates an anomaly in von Franz's theory. Part of "reality" was already there before Father Raven became conscious of it.

The notion of Father Raven as a projection of human steps towards consciousness is far-fetched, supported only by him coming into consciousness in the beginning — and that would be the end of it. Once he is conscious, the process is completed. The rest of the story is about his conscious actions.

He was conscious, though not yet enlightened about his role in the world: "all his deeds were completely casual until it became manifest to him who he was and what he should do."[514] The word "manifest" is strange in a mythical tale. Ras-

---

[513] Ibid., pp. 33f.

[514] Ibid., p. 29.

mussen writes "revealed" ("åbenbaret"). Anyway, this passage does indeed suggest a process of self-discovery, but it is not an unconscious process.

In the primordial darkness, he used his hands to explore his surroundings of clay and nothing else, and then his own body. This made him realize that he was not stuck to what surrounded him, but a separate entity, so he started to crawl around to find out where he was.

It is an empathic story about what it must have felt like to be that primordial creature. Many creation myths have the same perspective in the initial stages, not only wondering who was there but also what it must have been like. The story can be explained without the claim that it is about something else.

The Egg

There are several other creation myths discussed in the book, sorted into categories according to the method of creation and the nature of the creators, such as accidental action, from above to below and the other way around, two creators, and *Deus faber*, the manufacturer of the world.[515] Other Jungian writers have also arranged creation myths according to categories, which are more or less alike.

With the plentitude of myths in the world, finding categories or other connections between them is bound to be easy. So, it is tempting to do but it runs the risk of simplifying the complexity of those myths and neglecting the many differences between them. It proves nothing if not the deviations from the norm are fairly and thoroughly examined, which is rarely the case.

The only way to do those myths justice is to investigate them one by one, and only thereafter search for patterns they may share.

What the volume of known creation myths suggests is that those patterns are not to be found in the means that were

---

[515] Ibid., p. 25.

employed in the creation, but what reasoning led their authors to them. Before anything of significance can be said about what people of the distant past believed the creation was like, it is necessary to examine how they came to that conclusion. Then it is easy to follow the conscious reasoning behind it.

Instead, what is often done by von Franz, as well as many other writers on myth, is comparing fragments of myths, single details, to prove a pattern. But that takes the myths out of their own context. Everything and nothing can be proven that way. It is only by considering a myth as a whole that details in it can be correctly comprehended, and possibly compared to those of other myths.

One detail often discussed in writings about creation myths, also in von Franz's book, is the primordial egg. It appears in many creation myths, although it does so in a variety of capacities. To von Franz, presenting a number of mythical examples of it, what it represents is the preconscious state:

> *The image of the golden germ, or the egg, is perhaps not so difficult to understand psychologically as some of the other images, because we can easily recognize in it the motif of the preconscious totality. It is psychic wholeness conceived as the thing which came before the rise of ego consciousness, or any kind of dividing consciousness.*[516]

That's not what first comes to mind when an egg is found in a creation myth. What is easily recognizable is not the motif of a preconscious totality, but the simple fact that the egg is an obvious example of how a complete living creature can come out of a simple single object. It is an obvious parallel to the whole world growing out of one basic primordial state.

This miracle of nature must have inspired ancient speculations about the world origin, searching for explanations.

The symbolic relevance of the egg is still true today. The

[516] Ibid., p. 229.

big bang theory begins with a minimal point in which the whole universe is comprised, before the birth of it in a mighty expansion, which is still going on. Out of a minimal something — everything.

The use of the egg in creation myths is in itself perfectly analogous to the emergence of the world. The conscious reasoning behind it is plain to see. What von Franz wants to add to its significance is superfluous, even irrelevant.

Charles H. Long

Charles H. Long (1926-2020), born in Little Rock, Arkansas, was an American historian of religion, mainly tied to the University of Chicago, where he studied under Mircea Eliade and others, receiving his PhD in 1962 with the dissertation *Myth, Culture and History in West Africa.*

He remained there as a teacher and subsequently a professor. He was also one of the founding editors of the journal *History of Religions*, based at that university.

In 1973 he was elected president of the American Academy of Religion, and in 1987 president of the Society for the Study of Black Religion.[517]

He was neither a psychologist nor expressly a Jungian, but referred frequently to Jung's ideas in his writing, which dealt substantially with mythology and its symbolism. In 1963 he published one of the first anthologies of creation myths around the world, *Alpha: The Myths of Creation*, in which he applied some Jungian principles to the material.

On the other hand, in his 1986 book *Significations: Signs, Symbols, and Images in the Interpretation of Religion*, Jung is not mentioned at all, but Freud is. That may be due to the theme of the former book being myth, while the latter is about religion.

Still, Jung certainly wrote about both subjects, and much more so than Freud.

Long's most renowned contribution to mythology is his writing on creation myths, as in his book *Alpha: The Myths of Creation* mentioned above. He also wrote the article on creation myths in *Encyclopædia Britannica*, which remains on its present

---

[517] Charles H. Long obituary at the University of Chicago/Divinity School website, 2020 (divinity.uchicago.edu/news/charles-h-long-1926-2020).

online version[518] and a corresponding text on cosmogony in Mircea Eliade's *The Encyclopedia of Religion*.[519]

Symbolic Creation Myths

When a mythology contains a creation myth, which is a vast majority of them, that myth is of central importance to the whole mythology and the beliefs of the society adhering to it. Yet, when Charles H. Long's anthology of creation myths from around the world, *Alpha: The Myths of Creation*, was published in 1963, it was — as far as I have found — only the second one in the English language. A few years earlier, in 1956, the American folklorist Maria Leach published *The Beginning: Creation Myths Around the World*, where she retold 62 myths in her own words. Since then, anthologies of creation myths have multiplied and swelled considerably.

Long declares in the beginning of his book's introduction that his approach to myth is that of a historian of religion,[520] but at the end of the same chapter he narrows his scope considerably:

> *In the myths which follow, we shall not place our emphasis on the historical situation in which the myths occur. We shall be interested primarily in pointing up the various religious structures and symbolism in the cosmogonic myths.*[521]

It is surprising that a historian of religion would ignore the historical context and instead focus on finding structures

[518] Charles H. Long, "Creation, Myths and Doctrines of," *The New Encyclopædia Britannica, Macropædia*, vol. 5, Chicago 1976, pp. 239-243 (online at: britannica.com/topic/creation-myth).

[519] Charles H. Long, "Cosmogony," *The Encyclopedia of Religion*, ed. Mircea Eliade et al., volume 4, New York 1987, pp. 94-100.

[520] Charles H. Long, *Alpha: The Myths of Creation*, New York 1963, p. 1.

[521] Ibid., p. 33.

and symbols shared by creation myths. That means he sets out to see their similarities and not their differences. Considering the vast number of creation myths from which to choose, it is not an impossible task to find similarities of whatever kind.

Long regards creation myths as of fundamental importance, since they function as models for all kinds of beginnings: "The cosmogonic myth is the myth *par excellence* precisely because the beginnings of all things within the culture are modeled on the pattern of this myth."[522] His interpretation of those myths is that they are expressions of symbolism:

> *The creation myth expresses in symbolic manner what is most essential to human life and society by relating it to a primordial act of foundation recorded in the myth.*[523]

He admits that creation myths perform an explanatory role to the society believing in them, but he is reluctant to see this as prescientific attempts at understanding how the world works. Instead, he regards mythical thinking as separate from scientific thinking and independent of its findings.[524] It is not very clear, though, what he means by mythical thinking. He states that it is not concerned primarily with logic, but adds: "On the other hand, it is not illogical or prelogical." Actually, it is "at once logical and illogical, logical and magical, rational and irrational."[525] That doesn't clarify much.

He continues with describing it as a type of thinking representing "man's initial confrontation with the power in life," and the beings in the myth, such as gods, animals, and plants, are "forms of power grasped existentially." What he seems to indicate in this roundabout way is the mystified manner in which primeval man regarded the powers of nature. But that

[522] Ibid., p. 30.

[523] Ibid., p. 18.

[524] Ibid., pp. 15f.

[525] Ibid., p. 12.

is no mystery. A rational mind would be just as mystified before science gradually could explain things.

Creation myths are full of examples of rational speculations, which seem irrational only when the very limited understanding behind those speculations is ignored. People did what they could with what little they knew.

When Long suggests that their thinking was symbolic, he is adding complications instead of subtracting them. Symbols are abstractions made by minds aware of what it is they replace with the symbol. Therefore, it cannot be done before some kind of understanding of what is to be symbolized.

The approach of explaining elements of myths as symbolic is used by many mythologists interpreting old myths, but there is no indication that it was done when the myths were formed and upheld. The symbols and their meanings are later inventions by writers on the subject, who have searched for general conditions of the human mind behind the formation of myth as well as religion.

It is obvious when Long states: "The cosmogonic myths express the power, spontaneity, absoluteness, plenitude, and mystery of reality in symbolic forms."[526] Concepts like power and absoluteness are symbolic to begin with, since they are not measurable or palpable. Mystery of reality combines two concepts, both of which resist a non-symbolic definition. What they indicate is the reason why our distant ancestors expressed themselves so differently from us about the world they lived in — reality was a mystery to them. They were not replacing their minimal knowledge of it with symbols, but their confusion made their descriptions confusing. They filled the wide gaps of their understanding with imagination.

They saw powers at work in nature, but not their causes. So, they assumed them to be the doings of invisible beings, which were obviously so powerful that they should be treated with the greatest respect. These entities were not symbols of

[526] Ibid., p. 20.

something else, but the most plausible explanations to what was observed. That plausibility is the main reason why this belief remained for so long. It made sense. A world completely void of invisible powers was unthinkable, since the manifestations of them were evident and plentiful.

They were right, of course. There are invisible powers at work in the world. Contrary to our ancestors, though, we are aware of how they operate and no longer need the existence of invisible masters controlling them.

With Long's symbolic understanding of the myths, the depth psychology of Freud and Jung is near at hand, and he repeatedly refers to both. This is where he sees the source to symbolic thinking:

> *The meanings which emerge from psychoanalysis are not in the conscious literal form, but are symbols expressing the apprehension of the world of the patient in terms of the tensions and resources present therein. This fact is true of both major psychoanalytical schools.*[527]

He embraces the idea of the unconscious, "a psychic reality which, though not conscious, does exert a great influence upon our experiences and expression."[528] The idea of an unconscious hidden from conscious awareness is the very core of Freudian and Jungian psychology. Its existence remains to be proven, which is not an easy task since it is supposed to be consciously inaccessible.

As for Freud's Oedipus complex, he mentions that it has been criticized for being too dogmatic and hardly a total theory of man and religious symbolism, but he also insists that the problem of sexual tension is universal, as can be seen in the rites and beliefs of many diverse cultures. As for Jung's archetypes, he seems to be both reserved and supportive:

[527] Ibid., p. 15.

[528] Ibid., p. 5.

We shall not go into an analysis of the difficult problem of Jungian archetypes. Suffice it to say that his interpretation of the psychic structure enables us to envisage symbolic expressions which are more than expressions of the individual's historical conditioning.[529]

That points to what Jung called the collective unconscious, which he claimed to contain a fixed number of archetypes common to us all and remaining the same through the generations. Without explicitly admitting it, Long connects to this theory with his thoughts about symbols and their function in mythology.

Types of Creation

At the end of the introduction, Long explains how he will treat the creation myths he goes through in the following chapters:

Our commentaries on each type of myth will highlight some of the general ideas mentioned here by pointing to the concrete symbols and structures in the myths.[530]

That perspective is demonstrated already in how he sorts the myths into five categories, according to type of creation, i.e., out of what creation sprung:

Emergence myths, where the creatures of the world emerged from Mother Earth, the Great Mother, who was present from the beginning in the examples he gives of such myths. Most of them are Native American.

World-parent myths, where the world was created by primordial parents. To Long they were symbols of the sky and

[529] Ibid., pp. 22f.
[530] Ibid., p. 33.

earth, the latter being the mother, as in the previous category. Among the examples are the Babylonian primal deities Tiamat and Abzu (also spelled Apsu) of *Enuma Elish* and the Egyptian myth of Geb and Nut.

Creation from chaos and from the cosmic egg, where Long combines creations from a primordial chaos and from an egg, because he often finds both in the same myth, and he wishes to "point out some of the relations existing between these two types of myths."[531] Chaos is described as "confusion, darkness, and water," and not as the gap it originally means, though this is how it appears in several creation myths. A similar notion, also common, is the primordial sea out of which the world emerges.

There is no ambiguity to the egg, though, which is also found in many creation myths. What is dubious is that Long combines them into one category. He may have changed his mind later, since the egg is a separate category and the chaos type is absent in his article on cosmogony in *Encyclopædia Britannica* from 1976.[532]

Creation from nothing, where the world appears out of nothing, *creatio ex nihilo,* which is something extremely rare if existing at all, upon closer examination. Our ancestors were not really able to fathom it, for good reason. As was stated already by Greek philosophers, something out of nothing is impossible. There was always something in the primordial state — a dark sea, a gap, or a deity beginning the process.

The creation from nothing is a doctrine of the Christian church, though Genesis has a primordial sea to begin with, as well as an eternal deity. But Long adds to this category "a sin-

[531] Ibid., p. 109.

[532] Charles H. Long, "Creation, Myths and Doctrines of," *The New Encyclopædia Britannica, Macropædia,* vol. 5, Chicago 1976, p. 241.

gle Supreme Being,"[533] a sole deity responsible for all. This is a strange addition, which he deserted in the *Encyclopædia Britannica* article in 1976, where the supreme being is a category of its own and that of creation out of nothing is omitted.

There is only one of Long's examples that qualifies as a creation from nothing, an Egyptian myth about the first deity Khepri, since also he had a beginning: "I am he who came into being as Khepri. When I had come into being, being (itself) came into being, and all beings came into being after I came into being."[534]

Earth-diver myths, where "a divine being (usually an animal) dives into water to bring up the first particles of earth. The particles of earth are the germs from which the entire universe grows."[535] It is a strangely precise description. Long must have gone through a lot of creation myths to find the ones fitting it. Certainly, none of the more widely known myths serves as an example.

Long finds in this type of myth several important symbols, first of all water, which he interprets as a symbol of the chaotic stage before creation, but also a sign of destruction and renewal, as in the many flood myths. For the descent, Long applies a perspective which is distinctly Jungian:

> *The descent into the water is analogous to a descent into the underworld or a return to the womb. The purpose of such descents into the unformed and chaotic is renewal and stability. The symbolism of baptism is derived from this element in the water symbolism. By plunging into the water the old is washed away and the new creation emerges.*[536]

[533] Long 1963, p. 148.

[534] Ibid., p. 183.

[535] Ibid., p. 188.

[536] Ibid., p. 190.

That is a lot to assume about myths of ancient, maybe even primeval origin. Other explanations are much nearer at hand. The primordial sea often found in creation myths is simply there because it was perceived to be the eternal and limitless entity surrounding the world, out of which the world rose like land does by the shores. The dive into it by a creator was therefore simply the only place to go to find something at all. No additional symbolism is needed to explain it.

It would not work as a symbol of the underworld, since that is always — as far as I am aware — underground, not in the sea. It makes more sense as an image of a return to the womb, but not in a creation story where it happens once and for all. The comparison with baptism and the idea of cleansing in water are not far-fetched, since water has always been used for washing, but not as a means to recreate. Water does not dissolve those dipped in it, and certainly not a creator deity plunging into it. It does nothing more radical than refresh, which is fine in itself.

Long gets carried away by his symbolic thinking, which is a weakness he shares with both Freudians and Jungians. His method of extracting symbols from the creation myths leads him to imagine them where they are not or construct them by combining unrelated items. To primeval man as well as to us, water is simply that very familiar liquid surrounding land, which is also the role it plays in creation myths.

There are similar problems with Long's other types of creation myths. As he admits, there are often mixes of them in single myths, and in others the type of creation is not the initial or significant one. It is not easy to fit the creation myths of the world into those or any other fixed shapes. There will always be deviation and exceptions, which makes such a project rather futile and even misleading.

The uncertainty of it is evident already in the variations of Long's categories in different texts of his. That should have told him he might have been barking up the wrong tree, but still he persisted with it. Here are the types according to *Alpha* from 1963, *Encyclopædia Britannica* from 1976, and *The Encyclo-pedia of Religion* from 1987:

1963	*1976*	*1987*
Emergence	*Emergence*	*Emergence*
World-parents	*World-parents*	*World-parents*
Earth-diver	*Earth-diver*	*Earth-diver*
Chaos and cosmic egg		
		Chaos
	Cosmic egg	*Cosmic egg*
From nothing		*From nothing*
	Supreme being	

The three first types in the table are consistent in Long's three texts on the subject, but after that there are variations. The combination of chaos and cosmic egg is unique to the 1963 text, but both 1976 and 1987 include the cosmic egg as a separate type. Chaos is absent in 1976, but present as a type of its own in 1987. Creation from nothing is missing in 1976, which instead has a supreme being as a type. The supreme being is mentioned in the 1963 and 1987 texts about creation from nothing, whereas the creation from nothing is implied but not explicitly mentioned in the 1976 text about the supreme being.

The existence of a supreme sole creator in a myth, and that is not uncommon, does not necessarily mean the creation was out of nothing. As stated earlier, the idea of a primordial nothing is extremely rare in mythology.

Mircea Eliade, Long's professor and major influence, made his own list of creation myth types in 1967, with four basic categories whereof the third is divided into three subgroups:

> *1. creation ex nihilo (a High Being creates the world by thought, by word, or by heating himself in a steam-hut, and so forth); 2. The Earth Diver Motif (a God sends aquatic birds or amphibious animals, or dives, himself, to*

the bottom of the primordial ocean to bring up a particle of earth from which the entire world grows); 3. creation by dividing in two a primordial unity (one can distinguish three variants: a. separation of Heaven and Earth, that is to say of the World-Parents; b. separation of an original amorphous mass, the 'Chaos'; c. the cutting in two of a cosmogenic egg); 4. creation by dismemberment of a primordial Being, either a voluntary, anthropomorphic victim (Ymir of the Scandinavian mythology, the Vedic Indian Purusha, the Chinese P'an-ku) or an aquatic monster conquered after a terrific battle (the Babylonian Tiamat).[537]

They correspond roughly to Long's types, though adding a few variants and explaining some of them with other words. What both fail to do is argue rationally for using these models at all. They do not promote additional insight into the creation myths treated, but blur their originality by pressing them into these molds.

It is definitely both possible and productive to categorize creation myths as well as mythologies in general, but to avoid misrepresentation it should be done with basic and precise types that are not designed to imply a certain interpretation of them. It should be as neutral as, say, describing the color of garments. Some are blue, some red, and so on. Many of them have mixed colors. When hastening to extract symbols with complex meanings to different creation myths, their content is obscured and distorted.

What is reasonably safe to deduce is, for example, that some creation myths have one creator and the others have several, each doing their part of it. In some there is no deity present before creation, and in the others there is at least one. Some begin with nothing, and they are very rare, while the others start with something already there, the initial something

[537] Mircea Eliade, *From Primitives to Zen: A Thematic Sourcebook of the History of Religions*, New York 1967, p. 83.

being a gap or a sea or something else. In some myths humans are introduced early in the story and in others they are created much later. And so on. The categories should be based on the concrete and not the abstract, what is actually stated in the myths and not what might be implied.

Consequently, it is neither trustworthy nor fruitful to divide creation myths into categories, but to look at their components. A creation myth can have components of different types, and many do. That is only a problem when they are sorted by types. So, it should be abandoned.

James Hillman

James Hillman (1926-2011), born and raised in New Jersey, studied in Paris and Dublin after World War II, until he moved to Zurich in 1953 to enroll as a student at the Jung Institute and at the University of Zurich. He graduated from both in 1959, at the latter as a PhD with the dissertation *Emotion: A Comprehensive Phenomenology of Theories and Their Meanings for Therapy.* The same year, he was promoted Director of Studies at the Jung Institute, a position he kept until resigning in 1969. He stayed in Zurich until 1978, as the editor of the Jungian themed Spring Publications, a position he kept on his return to USA the same year.[538]

Hillman was a prolific writer on the subject of psychology and several of his books were widely read, one of them even reaching the New York Times bestseller list.[539]

As a psychologist, he was rooted in the Jungian principles but allowed himself to deviate with his own interpretations, to the point of forming a separate doctrine in the early 1970's, calling it *archetypal psychology*, in which mythical themes and their functions were emphasized and applied also to the analytical situation as a whole, even to how psychological theories were formed.

In spite of the above, his writing specifically about mythology is limited. His theories about archetypes and myth mainly concern their social influence, whereas their application to mythology is mostly just implied. Still, his widened view on myth and its mechanisms in society definitely justifies his inclusion in this book. In addition, he exposes some fundamental errors in the method of analysis, impairing its ability to cure anything at all.

[538] Kirsch 2000, pp. 20, 22f.

[539] James Hillman, *The Soul's Code: In Search of Character and Calling*, New York 1996.

Inward Search

In 1967, James Hillman published *Insearch: Psychology and Religion*, where he discusses how analytical psychology and theology can mutually improve their cure of souls. His use of the dated or even obsolete word *insearch* (also spelled *ensearch*) in the title points to his intention with the book. It means to search for something, but in Hillman's use of the word this search is inward, into the psyche. He argues for an inward search for the soul, in which psychotherapists and priest alike should participate for the benefit of their counseling.[540]

What he sees in society of the mid-1960s is a clergy shunning away from their role as curers of souls to adapt psychological terminology and practice, instead. The soul has been gradually replaced by the psyche. But that clinical perspective lacks the emotional incentive needed for people to recognize and experience their souls. Instead, they should remain with the religious symbols, which carry that inward connection.

Psychotherapists, too, are in dire need of these instruments and the perspective they contain, and he sees that happening within analytical psychology. While theology tends to demythologize religion, analytical psychology moves toward "re-mythologizing experiences with religious implications."[541]

The soul, although an essential object in counseling, is elusive already in how it should be defined. Hillman states that it cannot be defined, which is why it is not a concept as much as a symbol:

> *The soul is a deliberately ambiguous concept resisting all definition in the same manner as do all ultimate symbols.*[542]

---

[540] James Hillman, *Insearch: Psychology and Religion*, Dallas 1984 (first published in 1967), pp. 6f.

[541] Ibid., p. 5.

[542] Ibid., p. 42.

If this is deliberate, then one must ask who is responsible for the ambiguity and resistance. Hillman says nothing about it, but in Jungian psychology the answer can only be one — the unconscious, that hidden operator behind so much of the human psyche. It is by depth psychology the unconscious, and thereby the soul, can be reached and explored. Since the soul has what he calls "a religious concern," it connects psychology and religion, making both perspectives vital in revealing it:

> *I hope to show as we go on how depth analysis leads to the soul and that this in turn inevitably involves analysis in religion and even in theology, while at the same time living religion, experienced religion, originates in the human psyche and is as such a psychological phenomenon.*

The unconscious is not identical to the soul, but "the door through which we pass to find the soul." Still, the existence of the unconscious and the soul cannot be confirmed by any direct proof. Instead, "We stumble upon it; we stumble upon our own unconscious psyches."[543] That would mean it can only be traced by indications, by experiences hinting at it.

Hillman continues by discussing for several pages such indications of an unconscious in diverse psychological phenomena: forgetting and remembering, habit, slips of the tongue, the word-association experiments done by Jung,[544] multiple personality, mood, symptoms, and last but not least dreams.[545]

All of those indications can be explained by other means than the unconscious, which itself is little more than a term for

---

[543] Ibid., p. 50.

[544] Jung found that with certain words the response took significantly longer than normal, and deduced that their meaning was not fully accessible to the conscious mind.

[545] Ibid., pp. 51-57.

things going on in our brains not solely by a conscious process. That would be fine as sort of a simplified category, but both Freudians and Jungians have claimed that the unconscious is inaccessible to the conscious mind, a separate part of the mind that influences the conscious but cannot be influenced by it. None of Hillman's indications provide evidence of that.

That does not stop him from suggesting a third mental realm, "a sort of conscious unconscious," which he defines by what it is not: "It is rather non-directed, non-ordered, non-object, non-subject, not quite a reality of a concrete kind."[546] He expands on it, but again not very clarifying:

> It is a realm for itself, neither object nor subject, yet both. This third reality is a psychic reality, a world of experiences, emotions, fantasies, moods, visions, dreams, dialogues, physical sensations, a large and open space, free and spontaneous, a realm mainly of "meaningness." In these states of soul we can feel connection to nature and to ourselves.

This conscious unconscious seems to be Hillman's own invention. I don't recall any mention of it in other Freudian or Jungian writing. Nor does he pursue the concept in his book. It may be a mere hunch of his that he felt the urge to put on paper. In any case, the sensation he describes might just as well be part of the conscious. It has the flare of inspiration and a mind caught up in fantasies, which is the nourishment of art. If it is between the dreaming and the awake mind, it might simply be the state of daydreaming.

Dreams, as Always

Hillman leans heavily on the dream as outstanding proof of the unconscious. So have most psychoanalysts since Sigmund Freud published *Die Traumdeutung* (*The Interpretation of*

[546] Ibid., p. 66.

Dreams) in 1899. Indeed, the dream is a sweet mystery of the mind, and so is the process behind its composition. Hillman's explanation of it is not very clarifying:

> *The dream itself is a symbol; that is, it joins in itself the conscious and the unconscious, bringing together incommensurables and opposites. On the one hand, nature: natural, spontaneous, unwilled, objective psychic contents and processes. On the other hand, mind: words, images, feelings, patterns and structures. It is a senseless order, or a structured disorder.*[547]

Dream interpretation has been used by analysts as their major tool in working with their patients, and they have all claimed to be successful with it. That raises two questions, the first one being similar to what was discovered about quantum physics — the risk of influencing the object when it is studied up close. A therapy based on dreams is sure to influence the dreams, or at the very least how the patient remembers them. That way, they both find what they are looking for, which is no guarantee that it was there to begin with.

The second thing to question is the assumption that dreams have a message to the conscious mind. Hillman makes that assumption, too, when he speaks about befriending the dreams, since "they want to be known as a friend would." But they may, as contemporary science suggests, be just dreams. Random combinations of recent or past impressions, like a spread of shuffled playing cards — well, Tarot cards, to approach the Jungian cosmos. The meaning of them is arbitrary, in the eyes of the beholder.

So, who is the beholder? Firstly, it is the dreamer, but in analysis it is an interaction between the dreamer and the analyst, both set on finding something making sense to them. That is always possible, especially if the interpretation is allowed

[547] Ibid., p. 57.

improvisation using vaguely defined symbols from an innumerable supply. Then they can find whatever it is they want to find.

The role of the unconscious, though, is still an enigma — maybe nothing but a mirage. Even if we assume that there is such a thing as an unconscious creating the dreams, it is not the one presenting them to us. They reach us only when we wake up to our conscious state. Dreams are always perceived through the conscious, which means that it is the conscious interpreting and making sense of them. So, it is certainly able to reshape them as well, in accordance with what it expects or even hopes to find. Dream interpretation can be nothing more than a search for confirmation of preconceptions.

Hillman touches on this problem when he warns against giving the dream the meanings of a rational mind, which would just translate it into something known, like a sign or a label.[548] He suggests instead:

The first thing, then, in this non-interpretive approach to the dream is that we give time and patience to it, jumping to no conclusions, fixing it in no solutions. Befriending the dream begins with a plain attempt to listen to the dream, to set down on paper or in a dream diary in its own words just what it says.[549]

That still doesn't solve the problem of the dream only being accessible through the conscious, upon waking up. Furthermore, he doesn't stick to this agenda. He continues by stressing emotional aspects, what the dreamer felt during and after dreaming, as if dreams are mainly emotional. They often appear irrational to the conscious, but it is not the same as being emotional in nature. Of course they consist of thoughts as well as feelings, since that is how our minds always work.

[548] Ibid., p. 59.
[549] Ibid., p. 60.

He also claims that dreams are stories following the Aristotelian structure of beginning, middle, and end. But the beginning is usually hidden in the forgotten past of the dream, and the end is just the moment of waking up. For all we know, had we not woken up the dream would have continued. If we perceive that very familiar structure it is no evidence of dreams adhering to it, but a strong indication of conscious interpretation. We expect such stories, so we search them in dreams, too.

Hillman gets even more specific about what to expect in dreams and how to interpret them in a notably psychoanalytical way:

If for a few nights mainly men come into my dreams, I know that something is going on with the masculine side of myself, that these figures are all different ways to be a man, that each embodies a special set of characteristics, a complexity representing one salient feature of my own personality.

Or they could just be different men I have around me in my daily life. Dreams are certainly known to use people, settings, and events we have experienced when awake.

Hillman seems unaware that he has already broken his own rule by making analytical assumptions about dreams, expecting certain psychological patterns in them. He persists by linking them to the personal myths about ourselves he sees each of us carry:

By encouraging the dream to tell its tale, I give it a chance to present its true message, its mythical theme, and thus get closer to the myths which are operating in me, my real story, the story of my life from within, rather than my case history observed from without.[550]

[550] Ibid., p. 61.

Like other Jungians and Freudians, he can't resist applying those theories to his dream interpretations. If he did not, he might discover the most persistent pattern in them — their randomness. Surely, there are elements in dreams relevant to our psyche, also reappearing themes that relate to things we process when awake. But that is no proof of a willful message from deep within.

Dreams are composed of our conscious experiences, memories from the past as well as things presently on our minds. That is the material they have at their disposal. It also means the messages are not from the dreams, but to them. They are the recipients of a content from the conscious mind, which they shuffle and spread. Sometimes the result is coherent, but mostly it is just a jumble.

The problem of dream interpretation is precisely that it presupposes a certain meaning and message, before even trying the possibility of those things being absent.

Morality

After speculating about the above elusive phenomena, James Hillman turns his attention to morality. That is quite a shift, and a surprising one coming from an analytical psychologist. Morality is a maze. It is not something becoming a therapist, who should stay away from judging the clients, contrary to how priests see the moral guidance of their parishioners as a major task.

Hillman touches on this dilemma, but with a tone of dismissing it:

> *In the popular mind, those in the pulpit are supposed to be identified with morality, while those in the analytical chair are supposed to be on the side of the id, of unbridled desire, and against morality.*[551]

---

[551] Ibid., p. 69.

Unbridled desire, against morality? That is a devious way of putting it. Any therapist would know the difference between observing the patient's character traits, as opposed to praising or condemning them. Those who do not are agitators in disguise. The analyst should not seek to "correct" the patients, but to assist them in self-discovery.

What Hillman suggests is something of an alliance between psychology and theology, as if they have the same goal. That would risk ending with people who don't conform to the ideals of the church being declared mentally ill, in need of drastic treatment. It has been known to happen.

He speaks of it as "analytical ethics," comparing it to legal and medical ethics.[552] But those are quite different — they point to the responsibility of the lawyer and doctor towards the right and protection of the clients, not the moral judgment of them.

Hillman's wish to merge psychology and religion has the major flaw of replacing research with dogma. Then, it is no longer about how things are, but how they should be. Not only does that lead to prejudiced science, but also to intolerant religion. This, too, has been known to happen.

Still, he insists that analysis is a moral procedure.[553] His language gets religious when he states, "Remembrance of sin, remorse, and repentance become the living language of an analysis."[554] That would turn analysis into confession.

Male Femininity

In the last chapter of his book, Hillman treats the Jungian principle of *anima*, the female archetype in the unconscious of men. Jung also spoke of *animus*, the corresponding male archetype in women, but that is something Hillman disregards, as if only the male psyche counts in his psychology.

[552] Ibid., p. 68.

[553] Ibid., p. 71.

[554] Ibid., p. 73.

He is far from alone with this prejudice among Freudians and Jungians, especially the early ones. His book, though, is from as late as 1967, when such an attitude had become quite outdated in Western society. Not that full gender equality was reached — at that time or since — but the exclusion of half the population when dealing with human conditions was certainly not the norm.

Hillman's prejudice is evident also in how he describes the characteristics of anima. They are blatant examples of gender stereotypes. He goes through a number of different roles anima plays in a man's psyche, especially his dreams, like the older woman, who is "school-teacherish, perfectionist, critical"; the positive mother; the one in love with him, "which means nothing other than that he is in love with himself"; the cool, pale blonde; a whore; the old whore, who reflects "a certain impersonality in human affairs, having been through it all and seen so much that nothing perverse astonishes"; and the young and seductive girl, "sometimes tawny-skinned, sometimes nude, often dancing or swimming."[555]

The same kind of stereotypes appear when he discusses what moods, or affects, the inner femininity expresses:

Some affects are particularly feminine in nature — for example, self-pity, sensitivity, sentimentality, the sense of weakness and despondency, depression.[556]

But he continues with an important clarification: "It is not that these affects particularly pertain to women." It is just that those sentiments feel feminine to men, when they experience them. So, it seems that he points out the prejudice of the male mentality, which is also a form of prejudice though not without reason. But when expanding on what these feminine feelings cause, he falls right back into the stereotypes:

[555] Ibid., pp. 96-100
[556] Ibid., p. 102.

*They do not have "go-ahead" in them. They lessen a man's
ability to achieve, just as arguing and fighting often lessen
a woman's ability to connect.*

Hillman sees traces of this inner femininity in religion and
mythology, too. For example, he speaks of shamanic initiations
involving "a ritual and symbolic change of sex, including
transvestism and homosexuality, living as a wife to another
man." There are other explanations to this phenomenon,
nearer at hand than the initiation of a shaman. Hercules after
his feats, Hillman points out, became the servant of a woman
and then went mad — as if that was an unavoidable consequence. But that woman was a queen, and there have been
countless men serving under queens in myths as well as history, without going mad.[557]

And this is how he argues for the Buddha having feminine
features:

*The Buddha's feminine characteristics are obvious: the
heavy, silent, full-bellied, soft-breasted receptivity; the
huge ears, open and taking in; the tree under which he sits
and the lotus posture; compassion.[558]*

He goes on to call the Jewish Sabbath a feminine tradition,
and Jesus feminine in his weakness as revealed by his weeping.
Feminine is also the image of the Holy Ghost as a dove, since
it once belonged to the love goddess Aphrodite, though the
dove bringing an olive leaf to Noah would be a much more
familiar and important symbol in Christianity.

He even claims that the religious experience is necessarily
feminine:

[557] Ibid., p. 105.

[558] Ibid., p. 107.

> *Because the religious moment requires a passive mood to God's intentions, a receptive state to Divine Will, a wounding experience which opens us, it is feminine in nature.*[559]

At the end of his book, Hillman repeats even more firmly that anima is the key to the religious experience:

> *I do not know how better or how else we can prepare for the religious moment than by cultivating, giving inner culture to, our own unconscious femininity.*[560]

Since woman's unconscious is instead equipped with the male archetype animus, that would mean the religious experience is only accessible to men. Obviously, that is not the case.

This utterly binary view on humans has never been confirmed by evidence, either by Hillman or any other depth psychologist insisting on it. The odd thing is that they have still insisted on it, to the point of being blind to other paths of exploring and understanding those issues. Freud and Jung are at least partly excused because of the culture and conventions in which they formed their ideas, but Hillman, being born half a century later than Jung, would have other perspectives accessible to him, had he been perceptive to them.

It is interesting in this context that his book was published in 1967, the year of the summer of love, as they call it, when old ideals were not only questioned, but revolted against. It cannot have passed him unnoticed, especially considering that his profession was one of exploring human mentality.

Archetypal Psychology

James Hillman introduced the concept of *archetypal psychology* in 1970, when he became the editor of the annual Jungian jour-

[559] Ibid., p. 108.
[560] Ibid., p. 126.

nal *Spring* and changed its subtitle from *Contributions to Jung-
ian Thoughts* to *An Annual of Archetypal Psychology and Jungian
Thought*. He explained this change in an editorial postscript,
"Why 'Archetypal Psychology'?"[561]

Hillman is well aware that he enters a minefield by daring
to present an alternative to the established Jungian terminology. He speaks of the hostility of Jungians towards the "non-
Jungians" who promote other psychological theories, but also
"the aggression and destruction released by Jungians against
Jungians in the name of Jungian psychology," which is hardly
resolved by shifting terms.[562]

Jung mainly used the concept *analytical psychology* for his
contribution to the discipline, but also *complex psychology*, with
a slightly different meaning. Hillman sees both as somewhat
insufficient, which is why he feels the need to introduce his
own concept, regarding it as a more adequate representation
of the originality of Jung's psychology, since "the archetype is
the most ontologically fundamental of all Jung's psychological
concepts."[563]

It also has the advantage of widening the perspective from
the strictly analytical approach:

> *Analysis may be an instrument for realizing the arche-
> types but it cannot embrace them. Placing archetypal prior
> to analytical gives the psyche a chance to move out of the
> consulting room. It gives an archetypal perspective to the
> consulting room itself. After all, analysis too is an enact-
> ment of an archetypal fantasy.*

To Hillman, and certainly to Jung as well, the individual
psyche is not the only place where the archetypes manifest.

[561] James Hillman, "Why 'Archetypal Psychology'?" *Spring: An Annual of
Archetypal Psychology and Jungian Thought*, New York 1970, pp. 212-219.

[562] Ibid., p. 213.

[563] Ibid., p. 216.

They can be found just about everywhere in human culture, and therefore:

> *Insights for this approach call for an archetypal eye that is difficult to acquire through focus upon persons and cases. This eye needs training through profound appreciation of history and biography, of the arts, of ideas and culture.*[564]

This leads him to an understanding of the archetypes as expressions of polytheism, which is a deviation from the familiar monotheistic deity he had in mind in the previously discussed book *Insearch*. He states, "The plurality of archetypal forms reflects the pagan level of things and what might be called a polytheistic psychology."[565] He ends the article by saying that this archetypal perspective is the spirit in which he hopes *Spring* will proceed.

Indeed, it is with the archetypes Jung made his most noticeable contribution, not only to psychology but to other fields of cultural pursuits, where the arts were far from the least prominent and popular applications.

In 1988, while Hillman was still editor, the journal's name was changed to *Spring: A Journal of Archetype and Culture*, this time without any explanation of it in the journal. It should not be interpreted as abandoning archetypal psychology, but as an enhancement of the wider application of the archetypes he had already promoted. Hillman left as its editor in 1997, and the journal was discontinued after 2015.

Analysis as Myth

James Hillman's 1972 book *The Myth of Analysis: Three Essays in Archetypal Psychology* consists of three lectures from 1966 to 1969, which he revised and expanded in the book, for the purpose of explaining his ideas behind the concept of archetypal

---

[564] Ibid., p. 217.

[565] Ibid., p. 218.

psychology and how his viewpoint differs from analytical psychology.[566]

That must have been a daring venture within the discipline of depth psychology, as several predecessors — including Carl G. Jung — experienced when deviating from the dogma of Sigmund Freud, which was fiercely protected by him as well as his major disciples. Jung also had devoted followers, forming what Richard Noll in his book about that movement called a cult.[567] Jung's intellectual leadership was unquestionable, and there was certainly intrigue going on among them, but not to the extremes of the Freudians.

Maybe due to his own experience, or his confidence, Jung did not behave as paranoid as Freud, nor did his followers rush to battle in defense of his ideas. Also, his psychology was more of a maze than a formula, which made deviations from it less provocative. His theories left plenty of room for variations, compared to Freud's firm obsession with the Oedipus complex. Furthermore, and maybe most importantly, when Hillman presented his archetypal psychology, Jung had already been dead för almost two decades.

Hillman felt at liberty to question the very fundament of analytical psychology, and he did.

He declares in the introduction that he sets out to free psychic phenomena from "the curse of the analytical mind," which has a predilection for psychopathology, thereby "distorting the psyche into a belief that there is something 'wrong' with it." Psychotherapists and other helping professionals have a direct interest in this perspective: "They must see sickness in the soul so that they can get in there and do their job."[568]

Hillman sees it quite differently:

---

[566] James Hillman, *The Myth of Analysis: Three Essays in Archetypal Psychology*, Evanston 1972, pp. ix and 3.

[567] Richard Noll, *The Jung Cult: Origins of a Charismatic Movement*, Princeton 1994.

[568] Hillman 1972, pp. 3f.

*But suppose the fantasies, feelings, and behavior arising
from the imaginal part of ourselves are archetypal in their
sickness and thus natural. Suppose they are authentic, belonging to the nature of man; suppose even that their odd
irrationalities are required for life, else we wither into rigid
stalks of reason. Then what is there to analyze?*

He questions the model of the unconscious and its psychodynamics, pointing out that it can hardly be the only possible psychological model: "Perhaps the 'unconscious' and
'psychodynamics' are fantasies that could be replaced with
better ones." He suggests that there are some archetypal patterns, as good as those in use for understanding the psyche.
Modesty stops him from saying that they are superior, but that
is certainly implied.

So, in a few sentences Hillman discards the very funda-
ments of both Freudian and Jungian depth psychology, as well
as any other psychological treatment. They have misunderstood what is and what is not an ailment of the psyche.

The damage it may do to their patients is that they try to
suppress what is in their personality in order to fit some clinical norm, as if people are supposed to be the same and never
feel bad or uncertain about where their life is heading.

That is absurd, of course. Life is full of experiences, some
pleasant and some not, and the only way to avoid the latter is
sedation. That is the opposite of a cure. The most it can do is to
postpone.

Hillman is quite rare among depth psychologists by not
only having his own additions to it, which is rather common
among Jungians, but to reevaluate its very basics and coming
to his own conclusions. He says it again, with slightly different
words:

*The psyche can carry its imagination and live from it with-
out professional aid, providing it assumes more confidence*

The problem is not necessarily the agony of the patient, but the prejudice inherent in the therapy.

To Hillman, we are all mythical by nature, in so much as we all regard ourselves and what we do in the light of myth: "We are never only persons; we are always also Mothers and Giants and Victims and Heroes and Sleeping Beauties."[570] The mythic is in our language and observations, also in the theories of science. That includes the "fantasy" of analysis.

He suggests that its three pillars — transference, the unconscious, and neurosis — should be replaced with the erotic, the imaginal, and the Dionysian, in accordance with the mythical perspective.[571] He is also a strong proponent of using the concept of the soul, which he made clear also in the previously treated book. The question is, though, if a change of terminology really changes the dilemma he finds in analytical psychology. The structure remains the same.

Still, he is far from wrong about the mythic nature of the human mind as well as its products. Certainly, analysis is built much more on myth than on empirical science. On the other hand, if the human mind is mythical, maybe a mythical psychology is just what it takes to understand it.

The problem might not be the mythical, but whether those myths are comparable and can be combined to further our understanding. Are the personal and analytical myths analogous enough to be applied to one another? If not, merging them in some kind of therapy would be unfruitful or even detrimental. But if they do correspond, somehow, their meeting could lead to benefits for the patient and analyst alike — although the result might evade clinical scrutiny.

[569] Ibid., p. 5.

[570] Ibid., pp. 5f.

[571] Ibid., p. 8.

What Hillman neglects is that this already takes place in analysis, especially of the Jungian kind. It is based on mythical perspectives and assumptions, as Hillman has also pointed out, so he doesn't really bring anything new to the table. The only difference in his approach, and it is not a small one, is that he objects to regarding the patients as in need of a cure. Instead, the patients should be encouraged along their mythical path. But that, too, is included in the method of analytical psychology, albeit not that outspokenly.

Jung's central idea of individuation shows it. Patients are to discover and come to peace with their true self, by indulging in the archetypal messages from their unconscious. It is by the very acceptance of those signals from the unconscious that they succeed. This is indeed a mythical method applied to a mythical understanding of the self.

Femininity Revisited

The last part of *The Myth of Analysis* returns to the psychology of femininity, which Hillman also treated in *Insearch*, but here it is with firm opposition to misogyny and prejudice. He examines what he calls "the fantasies of female inferiority" through history and their misleading influences on psychology in particular. Therefore, he uses psychology to find out what went wrong: "So we are attempting here to bring psychological, or archetypal, understanding to these errors."[572]

Doing so, he mainly uses two mythological sources: Adam and Eve in Genesis, and the Greek god Apollo. As for the former, the simple fact that God created Adam first, and then Eve out of Adam, made it clear who was the closest to him: "Whatever is divine in Eve comes to her secondhand through the substance of Adam."[573]

Regarding Apollo, Hillman uses a quote from the play *Eumenides* by Aeschylus, where the god states: "The mother is no

---

[572] Ibid., p. 246 and 248.

[573] Ibid., p. 217.

parent of that which is called her child, but only nurse of the new-planted seed that grows. The parent is he who mounts." Apollo even claims, "There can be a father without any mother."[574] Hillman points out that the words of Apollo are of Aeschylus' invention and not necessarily part of the deity's mythology, but he uses it to symbolize this archetypal attitude towards the genders:

> *It is a statement of an archetypal position representing a world-view which can be attributed to Apollo and may be called Apollonic.*[575]

Fair enough. In the play, what Apollo takes as proof of male reproduction is Athene, who is also present in the scene and was born out of her father Zeus. The idea of woman being but a vessel for the seed of man predates even the ancient Greeks, and made some sense before the advances of biology could dismiss it. Misogyny was not necessarily involved.

On the other hand, the belief that the first woman was created out of the first man is more likely a depreciation of Eve's gender compared to that of Adam. It was she who convinced Adam to eat of the forbidden fruit, and therefore God condemned her to give birth in pain and to be ruled by her husband.[576] Surely, too, the biblical myth has had a much greater impact on posterity than the tragedy by Aeschylus.

Greek mythology is not particularly misogynic. Male and female deities were equally immoral, and although Zeus was the ruler of Olympus his might was frequently challenged by female deities, who often got the best of him. The Greek pantheon consisted of both male and female deities, and their level of power was not decided by their gender.

---

[574] Ibid., p. 224. Quoted from Aeschylus, "Eumenides," *Oresteia*, transl. Richmond Lattimore, Chicago 1953, p. 158.

[575] Ibid., p. 225.

[576] Genesis 3:16.

In the Bible, though, the power is definitely male, from God himself to Jesus and just about everybody in between. The only woman of divine significance is Mary, the mother of Jesus, but she was indeed just a vessel of God's offspring, immaculately impregnated by his Holy Spirit.

Hillman goes on to claim that "psychoanalysis found the feminine faulty" and the "urge toward science is governed by the same archetypal background as the tradition of misogyny."[577] That would make science as such male, which is questionable, to say the least.

No doubt, a vast majority of scientists through the centuries have been male, but it doesn't automatically mean that science as such is misogynic. An explanation closer at hand is that the male governed society excluded women from any significant positions, including those of scientific endeavor. Once this started to change, around the turn to the 20th century, women began to participate and make their marks. Not that inequality is completely eradicated, but it is a problem of society as a whole and not just science. Religion is not doing any better on this issue.

Hillman then goes on to the Dionysian aspect, which he regards as opposed to that which Apollo represents, but still they are combined in psychotherapy: "Thus therapeutic psychology has an inherent contradiction: its method is Apollonic, its substance Dionysian."[578]

He explains:

It attempts to analyze the collectivity, the downwardness, the moisture of libidinal fantasies, the child, the theatricality, the vegetative and animal levels — the "madness," in short — of the Dionysian by means of the distance, cognition, and objective clarity of the other structure.

[577] Hillman 1972, p. 288.
[578] Ibid., p. 290.

That would be like applying strictly scientific tools to examine and understand art. Something about the latter might be overlooked, and that is the very essence of it. Therapy strives to diminish the madness in order to make it rationally accessible to the conscious mind, i.e., "transform the unconscious (Dionysian) into consciousness (Apollonic)."

When Hillman speaks of the conjunction of the feminine and masculine, which is what the Dionysian represents to him, he gets rather confusing because he insists on the term bisexuality for it. True, Dionysus had amorous adventures with both men and women, but so did Apollo — and most of the other Greek deities, including their ruler Zeus. Neither Greek mythology nor their culture had any problem with that.

Hillman's use of the term, though, points not to sexual preference but to androgyny or hermaphroditism, where both genders are conjunct in either the body or the mentality, or both. He claims support for his terminology in Carl G. Jung:

In Jung's language, psychotherapy achieves its ultimate goal in the wholeness of the conjunction, in the bisexuality of consciousness, which means, as well, conscious bisexuality, that incarnation of durable weakness and unheroic strength that we find in the image of Dionysus.[579]

So, he speaks primarily about a mentality, someone with both male and female character traits. He sees bisexuality in this sense as the primary human condition to which we should return. Earlier in the text, he states the same, using the more adequate term, "androgynous consciousness, where male and female are primordially united."[580]

In therapy, it is primarily femininity that needs to be raised as equal in importance and value to masculinity, since it is the suppressed one. Therein lies the remedy:

[579] Ibid., p. 293.

[580] Ibid., pp. 282 and 259.

> *We are cured when we are no longer only masculine in psy-*
> *che, no matter whether we are male or female in biology.*
> *Analysis cannot constellate this cure until it, too, is no*
> *longer masculine in psychology.*[581]

Hillman adds, in italics for emphasis: "*The end of analysis coincides with the acceptance of femininity.*" That may seem drastic, but there is no denying the necessity of accepting femininity in whatever body it appears. The question is what that femininity is, exactly. Hillman's description is much more respectful and nuanced here than in his previous book, but it still leans on conventional gender roles that need to be questioned and examined.

After all, the difference is not so great between praising one role and praising two in union. They are still roles, upholding dated conceptions about what we humans are like and how we differ from each other.

Binaries

Hillman's reasoning leads to approaches that easily become absurd. For example, should we all strive for balance between the male and the female inside of us, and are persons without that balance therefore in need of therapy? What signifies persons in such balance, are they both strong and weak, dominant and submissive, rational and emotional, and so on?

People are not purely binary in any sense, not even mixes of different binaries. It is much more complicated. So, a method based on binary concepts will hardly liberate the human soul, whatever that is, but imprison it.

The emphasis on gender is sadly missing one basic fact about us. We are all the same species, and quite a remarkable one at that — for better or worse — and we share so tremendously much more than what separates us, regardless of gen-

---

[581] Ibid., p. 292.

der, sexual preferences, habitat, cultural inheritance, and whatnots. Even in the most misogynic of societies, and there are still plenty of those, a psychology concentrating on gender is ignoring or at least underestimating the very most of what goes on in our psyche. The diagnosis cannot be accurate.

When people are sorted into groups of whatever kind, prejudice is just around the corner. It may be due to the sad fact that so often, the incentive to make that division originates in prejudice, and the dividing is just a method to justify it. That has happened a lot in history and is not over yet.

Hillman is doing a noble effort at getting rid of prejudiced generalizations about the feminine, but fundamentally he is replacing them with other generalizations, and they are not even that different. When a man is emotional or a woman stern, they are not expressing the element of the other gender hiding in their unconscious. It is simply so that he is emotional and she is stern. It happens all the time. So does the reverse. No fundamental truth about the soul is to be found there. It is not even a significant part of their being.

If psychology is to untangle the human mind, it has to start by getting rid of all generalizations and strict categories. It is particularly urgent to dismiss assumptions about the human nature, which are based on social conditioning. That was what led to the prejudice about women, and so much else, to begin with. It can't be annulled by other prejudice.

A grave flaw in both Freudian and Jungian psychology is that they are largely based on phenomena that have their origin in social conditioning, but mistake them for being fixed properties of the human mind. Anthropological accounts from other cultures have shown that they are not. It is also confirmed by the variations within a certain society.

Most of what the gender roles contain are examples of this. Masculinity and femininity are in the eyes of the beholder, also when the beholder is the one beheld. We are compelled to play our roles, but that does not mean we identify with them. This is a very important distinction.

Carl G. Jung talked about it as the *persona*, the behavioral mask we wear to direct how others will perceive us. We know that we are playing a role. We may take delight in playing that role or we might despise it, in any case we are very much aware of it. And each of us plays it differently.

Hillman's Dionysus lives alongside Apollo in us all, but so does the whole pantheon of Greek deities in a collective so big and disorderly that there is no meaning in using those archetypes to find a distinct structure. Well, not in an empirically scientific sense. If there is a claim of scientific evidence, failure is certain. But that is not the only way to do research.

What Hillman and other Jungians have used for the pursuit of understanding the human mind is a symbolic perspective, which can bring its own rewards. Their mistake was the claim that what they found were objective facts. They should have given that claim up. Their speculations just show one perspective, one way of looking at it. But as such, it can still further our understanding — indirectly.

The fact that our minds find it so easy to relate to symbols and apply them in our thinking tells us something about our cognition. They display our age-old need for simple patterns by which to make life comprehensible. The binary division into opposites is a clear example of this. In reality, though, it is rarely that simple.

Day and night do not instantly switch. Their borders are blurred by periods of dawn and dusk, and clouds influence the brightness of the day and darkness of the night. Man and woman are no absolute opposites, considering how very much they have in common, as well as how much their bodies shift from childhood all the way to old age. By symbols, the complexities are turned into simplified patterns, and life appears a little less overwhelming.

Analysts have made the mistake of regarding the symbols as factual components in us, forming our behavior, instead of analyzing our tendency to create those symbols in the first place. The significance lies not in the symbols, but in our need to invent and utilize them. In other words, they are not our masters, but our tools.

The Soul's Archetypes

The idea of symbols as imaginary inventions to grasp the complexities of reality, discussed earlier, was also in a way promoted by James Hillman. There are several indications of it in his writing, even in the books previously examined. He did so again in *Re-Visioning Psychology* from 1975, where he explains how his archetypal psychology differs from and also to some extent agrees with Jungian analytical psychology.

It is when he presents his ideas of the soul that he ventures into its capacity to create an imaginary version of its experiences. He starts with this definition:

> *By soul I mean, first of all, a perspective rather than a substance, a viewpoint toward things rather than a thing itself. This perspective is reflective; it mediates events and makes differences between ourselves and everything that happens.*[582]

The soul, then, is a reflective entity, adding meaning to experience. He adds three qualities, whereof the third in particular approaches the concept of symbols invented in the mind to make sense of it all:

> *First, "soul" refers to the deepening of events into experiences; second, the significance soul makes possible, whether in love or in religious concern, derives from its special relation with death. And third, by "soul" I mean the imaginative possibility in our natures, the experiencing through reflective speculation, dream, image, and fantasy — that mode which recognizes all realities as primarily symbolic or metaphorical.*

[582] James Hillman, *Re-Visioning Psychology*, New York 1975, p. x.

So, the symbolizing stems from imagination, the mind's
fantasy at work, and it is a continuous process, involving all
experience: "Every single feeling or observation occurs as a
psychic event by first forming a fantasy-image."[583]

That would be the archetypes, except for the fact that in
Jungian psychology they are not created by the imagination
but stored in the unconscious and inherited from generation to
generation, without change. So, Hillman must have a perception of them, or he speaks about different phenomena. It is unclear.

He regards the archetypes as metaphors rather than
things, easier to describe in images than literally. That would
fit them as fantasy objects. So might his idea that they are the
"deepest patterns of psychic functioning, the roots of the soul
governing the perspectives we have of ourselves and the
world."[584] But less so what he says next:

*They are the axiomatic, self-evident images to which psy-
chic life and our theories about it ever return.*

Now, we are back at the Jungian archetypes, not invented
by individual minds but planted in them long ago. Hillman
calls them axiomatic first principles, models, or paradigms,
again taking them far away from the process of imagination.
On the contrary, by his definitions they are fixed objects locked
in our minds, impossible for us to erase or even alter. He even
compares the archetypes to gods, which certainly confirms
their unchangeable nature:

*By setting up a universe which tends to hold everything
we do, see, and say in the sway of its cosmos, an archetype
is best comparable with a God.*

[583] Ibid., p. xi.

[584] Ibid., p. xiii.

It seems, therefore, that the forming of fantasy-images he speaks of is limited to our inherent catalogue of archetypes, as if they are all the cards our imagination is dealt, and the only thing we can do is shuffle them. That leaves little room for the tremendous cornucopia of human fantasy.

Anthony Stevens

Anthony Stevens (born 1933) is a British psychiatrist who studied both psychology and medicine at Oxford in the 1950s. During his years as a student, he went through analysis with the Jungian therapist Irene Champernowne, which he found very rewarding although he was at that time doubtful about the scientific basis of the method.[585]

In 1966 he went to Greece to study attachment bonds in infancy at an institution for unwanted children. He found that psychological theories of the time failed to explain his findings, but they fit what the English psychiatrist John Bowlby had stated about the instinctual bonds between mothers and children, contrary to a learned behavior —just like with other animals. He found the explanation in *ethology*, the study of animal behavior in the wild, which had been pioneered by Konrad Lorenz. The pattern was visible also at the Greek institution, though the children made bonds with women who were not their mothers.[586]

He wrote about this in his most renowned book, *Archetypes: A Natural History of the Self* from 1982, basing his take on psychology as a combination of Jungian theory about archetypes and ethology, akin to what Joseph Campbell concluded about their connection in his 1959 book *Primeval Mythology*, as discussed earlier.

He had a firm stance on the importance of psychology learning and including the findings of biology, without which it was but a doctrine of faith:

Possessing no solid basis in biology, psychology could only lend itself the semblance of coherence by adopting the

[585] Anthony Stevens, *Archetypes: A Natural History of the Self*, New York 1982, p. 15.

[586] Ibid., pp. 1ff.

quasi-theological subterfuge of establishing dogmas that it became heresy for the faithful to deny.[587]

Stevens was also a practicing analyst, before retirement. He has not written extensively about mythology or religion, but his focus on the Jungian archetypes and his effort to shed new light on them in accordance with biological science serves an example of how this Jungian concept has been adapted to later discoveries about the human mind.

In Defense of the Archetypes

In his 1982 book about the archetypes, Anthony Stevens claims credibility for having initially been a doubting Thomas regarding analytical psychology as a whole, including the unconscious and the archetypes.

He had also come to question behavioral psychology, which was the paradigm of that time. The latter was easier to dismiss, since it just did not correspond to what he had discovered in his research in Greece. Jung's theories would, but he was hesitant about them:

> *Jung's theory of 'archetypes' operating through a 'collective unconscious' was exactly what I was after. The only problem was that I could not be sure if I believed in it, because I had never quite grasped what he meant.*[588]

He got over the hesitation after raising the issue with his former analyst Irene Champernowne, who told him that there was a biological explanation:

> *Archetypes, she declared, are biological entities. They are present, in related forms, throughout the animal kingdom. Like all biological entities they have a natural history: they*

[587] Ibid., p. 6.

[588] Ibid., p.14.

are subject to the laws of evolution. In other words, arche-
types evolved through natural selection.[589]

That made them comparable to Konrad Lorenz's innate releasing mechanisms and species-specific patterns of behavior, as well as John Bowlby's goal-corrected behavioral systems. Animals in the wild have shown similar patterns, and humans are animals, too. Stevens studied Jung's ideas about the archetypes and concluded: "Jung's assertion that the archetype does not 'denote an inherited idea, but rather an inherited mode of functioning' was biologically unimpeachable."[590]

That makes some sense, but Stevens may have read Jung with the hope of finding just that, since Jung's theory contains a lot more than a mode of functioning. As mentioned in the chapter about Joseph Campbell's similar idea, Jung's archetypes are entities with their own definite powers and not just some instinctual patterns, not to mention the vast number of details they are supposed to contain. There is a limit to what instincts can carry through the genes. Furthermore, there is still the need for evidence of the archetypes Jung claimed to exist.

It is, by the way, surprising that Stevens makes no mention of Joseph Campbell regarding this, although familiar with his writing. The only Campbell text he refers to is *The Hero With a Thousand Faces*, which does not treat this specific subject. But Campbell did so in *Primitive Mythology*, published more than twenty years before Stevens' book. He even claims that, "until now," no one has attempted to link together ethology and analytical psychology.[591] But that was exactly what Campbell did already in 1959.

What is clear all through Stevens' book is the high regard he has for Jung and his continued, even increased relevance to

[589] Ibid., p. 17.

[590] Ibid., p. 18.

[591] Ibid., p. 29.

psychology as well as other related sciences — contrary to Freud, whose ideas have largely been dismissed:

> *Whereas many of the original concepts of Freud have been superseded, those of Jung are just beginning to receive the attention they deserve: in many respects it is true to say that it has taken science until now to catch up with him.*[592]

Stevens refers constantly to Jung's writing, as if it were a gospel of the nature of humankind. Still, some of his interpretations tend to stray away from Jung's ideas in an effort to prove them currently valid.

Mother and Child

Stevens has one objection to the perspective of ethology. It neglects the experience of the individuals. There are emotions involved, not just a biologically programmed pattern of behavior.

As in the case of the child and the mother, "the child does not experience his mother as a mere behavioural sequence with punishing or rewarding attributes but as a person, an indispensable 'other', with recognizable features and personality characteristics which are uniquely precious to him."[593]

The lack of this perspective in ethology made him search for a theory including "what it is like":

> *What I needed was a generally comprehensive theory capable of embracing both the behavioural manifestations of attachment and the inner psychic manifestations occurring in consciousness in the form of symbols, images, intuitions, feelings, words, etc.*[594]

[592] Ibid., p. 142.

[593] Ibid., p. 12.

[594] Ibid., pp. 13f.

He found it in Jung's archetypes: "In contrast to Jung, the ethologists are concerned with the outer manifestations of living organisms rather than with their subjective experiences."[595] Stevens searched a theory combining the two.

But that raises several questions, the first being if he is correct to merge two phenomena into one, i.e., an instinctual behavior and an emotional experience. If instinct triggers the behavior, then the emotion is a response to it, and if the emotion is the trigger, then the behavior is not really instinctual.

What Stevens suggests is that the instinct is in the form of an archetype, which is the one triggering the behavior, but that is a weirdly roundabout way for instincts to work. It might make some kind of sense for some archetypes, such as the mother and the child, but those relations and their responses are sufficiently explained by basic animalistic instincts. The mother and child archetypes may be convenient ways of describing them, but that is symbolical and not factual. It is merely a fancy terminology, implying that the instincts of our species can't be as simple as those of other animals.

Then there are all those archetypes that do not automatically lead to certain instinctual behaviors, such as the trickster, the scapegoat, the artist, mana and mandala, the tree, and water. Stevens would need to exclude them if claiming that archetypes are inherited modes of functioning, since the responses to them differ substantially between people and in many cases trigger no response at all.

A more rewarding perspective to explore would be the emotions as reactions to instincts. The child's connection to the mother is instinctual, and the emotions differ according to how that connection plays out. For example, the child reacts with sadness when the mother is absent and with relief when she returns, disappointment when she neglects the child and delight when she does not, frustration when their communication errs and merriment when it does not, et cetera.

[595] Ibid., p. 27.

The emotions can also be in direct opposition to the instincts, when either the mother or the child dislikes the other, momentarily or constantly, which is not that rare. The instincts make a bond between them that can be called mutual love, but it doesn't guarantee that they like each other. It can even lead to them hating the bond between them, revolting against their instinctual connection.

The concept of the archetypes suggests that they are constants, just like the instincts, but life is more complicated than that. Constants are rare in the human psyche. Still, it is possible to describe variations like those mentioned above with archetypes. The mother archetype can turn into that of the evil stepmother, when the relation to the child goes sour. But it did not start with a change of archetypes. They give a symbolic description of the change, but they don't explain it.

Like Jung, Stevens hangs on to the archetypes as causes, although they are mere depictions at best. As such, though, they have their merits in making life and fate relatable to us — not necessarily relevant, but relatable. We turn reality into fiction and symbols, not to explain it as much as to deal with it, for solace as well as entertainment. We rarely insist that our fantasies are real, but if we do then mayhem ensues. That has been known to happen, surely also in analytic therapy.

Male and Female
There is a consistently narrow view among Freudians and Jungians about the genders, with ingredients of both misogyny and homophobia. For Freud and Jung it may be at least partially excused by the culture they lived in, but for later analysts it gets increasingly disturbing. Anthony Stevens with his 1982 book is no exception.

Discussing the male initiation rites of many cultures, he claims that there are those who do not pass this test, and are therefore not accepted as men. He gives an example of what that leads to:

In some cultures, for example, failed initiates become 'berdaches' - shamans who must dress as females and if they are permitted to mate the union has to be a homosexual one.[596]

This example was also used by James Hillman in his 1967 book *Insearch*, discussed earlier. It is a grossly uninformed statement. Homosexuality is not a punishment for insufficient maleness, but a known and in many cultures through time accepted variation of sexuality. There are numerous examples of that in numerous cultures. As for masculinity, both Hillman and Stevens should have taken a look at the sexual attitudes of the Spartans, who were not exactly famous for lacking traditional masculine traits. Greek mythology shows the same.

What is expressed by Hillman and Stevens, as well as by most of their colleagues, is a prejudice from their own heritage, the doctrine of the Christian church and its morals. Stevens praises it as "the traditional patriarchal values enshrined in Judeo-Christian civilization for millennia."[597] It is disappointing that they were unable to rise above that in their theories about the human psyche, but easy to see how this prejudice got so widespread and persistent among Freudians and Jungians.

Freudians are fixed on the Oedipus complex, which is a purely heterosexual theory not even allowing a female counterpart, and it regards any homosexual tendency as a malfunction. Jungians adhere to the archetypes of anima and animus, the female in men and the male in women, which may sound like a liberated standpoint but again just confirms the binary conception of gender and sexuality, where deviations are psychic maladies in need of analytical therapy. Both theories are formed on the principle of heterosexuality as the healthy state, and those who are different can and should be cured. Stevens confirms this attitude when he states:

[596] Ibid., p. 157.
[597] Ibid., p. 121.

*In our own society, the vast and, I believe, growing popu-
lation of homosexual males may be seen as the result of
failed initiation - not through any innate deficiencies of
masculinity, but because, it seems, the masculine principle
requires culturally sanctioned trials and ordeals if it is to
be actualized in maturity.*[598]

In other words, he states that homosexuality is a cultural
thing, created and multiplied by how people (and he means
males) are raised. So, he assumes that "societies which provide
no puberty rites will produce a large population of males in
whom the masculine principle is only partially actualized. Certainly, this would seem to be the case in contemporary Western
Society."[599]

That narrowminded view is Western in the cowboy movie
sense. Boys should be raised so that they toughen and become
real men, or they will be cowardly sissies prone to homosexuality. It is not psychology, but pure fiction.

Stevens does find one advantage with an increase of homosexuality — it counters overpopulation.[600] Well, that is one
way of looking at it. He continues by assuring the reader that
it doesn't stand in the way of individuation, the Jungian concept of self-realization: "From the purely psychological standpoint, the homosexual relationship, like its heterosexual counterpart, is a perfectly valid way of working out the individuation process." And he has an archetypal explanation for both
those types of sexuality:

*For both sexes, and especially in adolescence (the period of
the 'crush'), a beloved person of the same sex is experienced
as a living embodiment of the Self, in much the same way*

[598] Ibid., p. 157.

[599] Ibid., p. 158.

[600] Ibid., p. 198.

as a beloved person of the opposite sex is experienced as an embodiment of the Animus/Anima.

So, homosexuals love themselves, whereas heterosexuals love their inner entity of the opposite sex. Would that mean the former reject their anima or even lack one, and the latter can't love themselves? What Stevens suggests is an overly complicated way to explain that some people love members of their own sex and others love those of the opposite sex. He applies a psychological terminology to it, but that in itself is no explanation as to either why or how, nor can it be empirically tested outside of Jungian analysis. To begin with, that would need evidence of the existence of anima and animus, which is yet to be presented.

Stevens spends several pages of his book comparing his binarity of male and female to the Chinese concept of *yin* and *yang*.[601] He calls it Taoist, but it predates that philosophy with hundreds of years. Yang represents the light and yin the dark, as with a tree or a hill where one side is exposed to sunlight and the other is in the shade. This duality is applied to a lot of other phenomena, such as the two sexes, warm and cold, and heaven and earth. Taoism and other Chinese traditions describe the dynamic between yin and yang as a process in the world creation. Chapter 42 of *Tao Te Ching*, the primary Taoist text, states:

> *All things carry yin and embrace yang.*
> *They reach harmony by blending with the vital breath.*[602]

The yin and yang concept is not primarily about the sexes, and Stevens takes it far beyond what the Chinese philosophy contains in his interpretation of it, but it has one aspect that

[601] Ibid., pp. 175-180.

[602] Stenudd 2015, p. 182. The vital breath is *qi*, the Chinese life energy concept.

does seem to connect to the Jungian idea about the sexes.

Its famous symbol, the circle consisting of two identically shaped fields, where one is dark representing yin and one light representing yang, also has a light dot in the dark field and a dark one in the light field. They represent the idea that there is always some yang in yin and vice versa, which is not far-fetched to link to the Jungian idea of a female anime in man and a male animus in women.

Not that it was what the ancient Chinese considered, but still there is a similarity.

It must be pointed out, though, that *Tao Te Ching* does not make the connection between the sexes and yin and yang. There, the female is compared to water, which humbly floats to the lowest places, and this is a Taoist ideal. In fact, Tao itself, the supreme cosmic principle ruling existence, is called the mother of the whole world.[603] In that way, Taoism promotes the idea of the ultimate matriarchate.

Religion

In his book, Anthony Stevens does not investigate the phenomenon of mythology, unlike several other Jungians presented above. What he does, in line with just about every Jungian, is to apply mythological concepts to psychology. Mainly he uses deities, particularly Greek ones, as symbols of archetypes. Also, he compares some mythical events and components to psychological dynamics. They are merely tools in his psychology.

Religion, on the other hand, he treats somewhat differently, although not with that many more words. He explains its structure and functions in society a well as in the individual mind, leaning mainly but not exclusively on his interpretations of Jung on those issues.

Stevens connects it to biology, stating that "religions are like other biological phenomena: they evolve in directions

603 Ibid., chapter 25, p. 123.

which enhance the welfare of those who have them."[604] That would make religion an evolutionary ingredient promoting the survival of the species and its societies. He stresses the crucial importance of it and the dire consequences of its absence:

> *History teaches that civilizations which lose faith in their gods normally crumble into barbarism and a protracted dark age, which endures until such time as a new culture arises or is imposed.*[605]

On the other hand, religious conviction has also been known to lead to barbarism and dark ages.

He claims that the image of a primordial god is imprinted in our minds, however science may reject it, and it is quite clear that he refers to a monotheistic deity very much like the one in the Bible:

> *Science may continue to dismantle the ancient myths of our culture, but it can never entirely exorcise God from the story of creation. God as Will and First Cause, the Original Detonator of the Big Bang, He who set the whole universe in motion and is immanent in all its parts, the God of 'process theology', the God who as* imago Dei *is built into the Self.*[606]

That statement fails on the simple fact that there have been so many different conceptions of creation and deities in our world through time, and still are. There are even creation myths where no deity was responsible for the world to appear.

Another objection to Stevens' claim comes from none other than Laplace, the French scholar, in the famous anecdote about his conversation with Napoleon, who wondered why

[604] Stevens 1982, p. 218.

[605] Ibid., p. 220.

[606] Ibid., p. 223.

there was no mention of God in Laplace's science. He replied, "I had no need of that hypothesis."

As for the functions of religions, Stevens states that they have been "broadly the same" in all of them. His list of those functions is similar to other theories on the subject:[607]

1. *Mythological-explanatory*, mainly about creation and our role in it;
2. *Sanctification of the social and ethical code*, which he regards as "the most crucial function";
3. *Ritual*, "the method by which sanctification is prescribed and maintained";
4. *Spiritual*, "the perception of a transcendent meaning, the sense of participating in a higher purpose," which in "the most advanced cultures" has been regarded as the most exalted function.

None of those functions, though, are exclusive to religion. The first one is scientific by nature and has increasingly by time been replaced by science. The second, about social ethics, stands on its own, without any divine sanctification needed, which is shown by the many modern societies basing their ethics and laws on reason instead of religion. The rituals of the third function, too, obviously manage fine without a religious setting, since there are plenty of rituals and celebrations confirming a social order where deities and the like are absent or utterly peripheral. The last function, the spiritual, has often through history been fulfilled by political ideologies — for better or worse.

There is nothing in the above that makes religious beliefs crucial. Stevens and many others with similar claims insist that these functions are religious by nature, and so is any other phenomenon applying them. But it is the other way around. Religion is just one of the social entities serving these purposes.

[607] Ibid., pp. 218-220.

Stevens suggests the same when he states that "religion evolved as a means of establishing absolute values in the interests of the stable continuity of the group."[608] It is the social function that is essential, and not the religious method of achieving it. Still, he insists:

> *We shall never entirely escape from our need for mythology and religion: it is too fundamental a part of our nature, deeply irrational though it may seem.*

That is not a correct conclusion to draw from its use. If the need is social, anything that replaces and improves this function would make religion and mythology redundant. Of course, there may be other values of mythology and religion that preserve them. There surely are. But religion as such is not a necessity in itself, only to the extent it is relevant to some needs of ours, whether social or individual. Those needs may be biologically inherent in us, but religion is not.

To Stevens, though, it is the other way around. He claims that religious beliefs are inherent in us, and therefore the neglect of them is crucially detrimental:

> *Religious belief is 'planned for' in the genome. People can no longer believe in God, yet they are programmed to believe in something. If God dies, they will find other vessels, however cracked, in which to pour their faith. Both Self and society need religion; without it both suffer and both ultimately perish.*[609]

But there is no religion in the genome. We are not inherently programmed to believe in something. That programming takes place after birth. Religions are learned and not inherited. Otherwise, they would not be so elaborate and different.

---

[608] Ibid., p. 284.
[609] Ibid., p. 285.

They certainly make use of needs that are inherent in us, or they would fail to captivate. But that does not make religion one of those needs, much like we are inherently programmed with the urge to reproduce but not to wed before doing so — and we do not perish if we resist that urge.

Updated Edition

Twenty years after *Archetypes* was published, in 2003, Anthony Stevens released a revised version, where he included various findings and developments relevant to the subjects he treated in the first edition. Mainly he kept the original text, but added updates after each chapter.

According to Stevens, the most important development is the influence of neo-Darwinian evolutionary thinking on psychology and psychiatry, "which has revolutionized how we look at human nature." But he finds none of it contradicting Jung:

> *The findings of the two new disciplines, evolutionary psychology and evolutionary psychiatry, in no way contradict or supersede Jung's original insights into the nature and influence of the archetypes which make up the human collective unconscious: on the contrary, they corroborate and amplify them.*[610]

Consequently, Stevens sees no reason to revise his text or change its theme. Instead, he makes additions to it, "to trace what has happened to the archetype in the past 20 years in terms of our understanding of it and our responses to it."[611]

Recurring ingredients in those added comments are the defense of his claims in the first edition and the dismissal of critique he has received. He is not very prone to reconsider his

---

[610] Anthony Stevens, *Archetype Revisited: An Updated Natural History of the Self*, Toronto 2003, pp. xi f.

[611] Ibid., p. xiii.

position on any of the issues. Jung's texts remain revered and his theories, as Stevens interprets them, are seen as precursors to later scientific discoveries about the human nature.

Mythological Symbols

In his 1999 book on the subject of symbols, *Ariadne's Clue: A Guide to the Symbols of Humankind*, Anthony Stevens uses mythology both to find examples and to explain them. His approach is psychological and also historical, in order to track their emergence. He aims to explain "the meaning of symbols in terms of their psychodynamic importance, as well as their evolutionary or prehistoric origins."[612]

That is quite an ambition, especially regarding the prehistoric origins. About those we can do little more than speculate, which does not mean we should refrain from it. On the contrary, thorough speculation is rewarding even if the results are dubious. It is by daring to be wrong we may eventually be right.

In his pursuit, though, Stevens neglects the oldest remnants we have, such as graves, rock paintings, and sculptures from the Upper Paleolithic Period (c. 50,000-10.000 years ago). His main material is Greek, Egyptian, biblical, and later. Also, in spite of treating symbols, which are images also in the Jungian understanding — Stevens defines a symbol as "an image or a thing which acquires its symbolic value through the meanings and emotions it evokes in us"[613] — his book has few illustrations. There is none from Paleolithic times, not even a Lascaux cave painting or the Venus of Willendorf figurine. That excludes anything before the introduction of written language.

So, the prehistoric origins are really all but ignored.

No doubt, the archeological material from as far back as the Paleolithic Period is hard to interpret with any certainty.

---

[612] Anthony Stevens, *Ariadne's Clue: A Guide to the Symbols of Humankind*, Princeton 1999, p. x.

[613] Ibid., p. 12.

The graves do not necessarily indicate a belief in some afterlife, they might just have been what we would call sanitary arrangements. Even when they were decorated, it could simply be an expression of grief.

The rock paintings are often explained as ritualistic or religious, but they can just be decorations and artistic expressions. Venus of Willendorf is usually seen as some kind of deity or a celebration of woman, like the Mother Earth that Stevens and other Jungians repeatedly mention. But it could again just be an artistic expression — of female beauty or, for that matter, Paleolithic pornography.

Still, that in itself is interesting. Our distant ancestors showed no unquestionable sign of being what we call religious. So, maybe they were not. It is at least as likely as that they were. Like modern atheists, they could have been in awe of nature and its splendor, as well as of their own abilities to express that awe, without any worship of invisible entities or archetypes emerging from their unconscious.

Like his fellow Jungians, Stevens insists on forming a web of symbols with causes and meanings that only they have the theory to explain. Then the Paleolithic Period is best to leave aside.

Dreaming

In his intent to understand the symbols as archetypal and find their origin in the unconscious, Stevens emphasizes the importance of dreams since they are not products of the conscious mind. Like other Jungians as well as Freudians, he sees dreaming as major evidence of an unconscious containing more than the conscious can perceive or even fathom, but still exercising a huge influence on it. But there are flaws in his understanding of this phenomenon.

As an example of the power of dreams, he uses the 19th century German chemist August Kekulé, who had a dream of a snake biting its tail, which is the ancient *ouroboros* symbol, and thereby he realized the shape of the benzene molecule.[614] Both Carl G. Jung and Erich Fromm had previously referred to this as evidence of what dreams can bring.[615] But questions can be raised about its significance. Here is Kekulé's own account:

> *I was sitting, writing at my text-book; but the work did not progress; my thoughts were elsewhere. I turned my chair to the fire and dozed. Again the atoms were gamboling before my eyes. This time the smaller groups kept modestly in the background. My mental eye, rendered more acute by repeated visions of the kind, could now distinguish larger structures of manifold conformation: long rows, sometimes more closely fitted together; all twining and twisting in snake-like motion. But look! What was that? One of the snakes had seized hold of its own tail, and the form whirled mockingly before my eyes. As if by a flash of lightning I awoke; and this time also I spent the rest of the night in working out the consequences of the hypothesis.[616]*

Strictly speaking, that is a daydream. Kekulé claimed to have had another dream revelation about chemistry a few years earlier, which doesn't increase his credibility. He encouraged his students to dream, but wisely added, "let us beware of publishing our dreams before they have been put to the proof by the waking understanding."[617] So, he showed less confidence in his dreaming than Jung, Fromm, and Stevens did.

[614] Ibid., p. 13.

[615] Carl G. Jung, *The Psychology of the Transference* (originally published in German 1946), New York 1998, p. 4, and Erich Fromm, *The Forgotten Language: An Introduction to the Understanding of Dreams, Fairy Tales and Myths*, New York 1951, p. 45.

[616] John Read, *From Alchemy to Chemistry*, New York 1995 (first edition 1957), pp. 179f.

[617] Ibid., pp. 174 and 180.

Science has found strong indicators that all mammals and some other animals also dream, though nothing can be stated for certain about what those dreams contain. Do they have their own sets of archetypes, sending messages that push the dreaming animals towards individuation? At some point, those concepts lose their meaning.

If dreaming is not exclusive to humans, then neither its origin nor its function can be specifically human. Other explanations, which are applicable to all dreaming species, must be sought. There is still no scientific consensus on what those explanations might be.

What is easier to scientifically confirm than dreaming is that all animals sleep or, to be precise, they "exhibit a restorative cycle of rest following activity."[618] Again, though, there is no consensus as to why, but two reasons seem likely. One is simply rest, and the recuperation it brings. The other is to conserve energy at times when activity is neither practical nor needed, such as nighttime for daylight creatures and winter for hibernating species.

What has confused evolutionary biologists is the risk sleep entails, since it is a state when awareness of the surroundings is reduced. The sleeper becomes an easy prey. This is indicated by the fact that predators (and humans) tend to sleep for longer periods than prey.[619] On the other hand, in sleep we are the least noticeable, being both still and silent. That would be difficult when awake.

Sleep is of vital importance. Being deprived of it for too long is even lethal to animals. Dreaming, on the other hand, seems not to be equally crucial. People can be deprived of REM sleep, which is when the main and sophisticated dreaming occurs, for weeks without damaging effects on their behavior.[620]

---

[618] Dale Purves et al. (ed.), *Neuroscience*, 5th edition, Sunderland 2012, p. 645.

[619] Ibid., p. 627.

[620] Ibid., p. 637.

So, sleeping is far more essential to us than dreaming. This opens for the possibility that Sigmund Freud was right when stating that dreams help to keep us asleep:

In a certain sense all dreams are dreams of convenience; they serve the purpose of continuing sleep instead of awakening. The dream is the guardian of sleep, not the disturber of it.[621]

Even when we are asleep, our brain needs something to do, a game to play, or it will get bored and awaken. However, that reveals nothing about the content of dreams. They may just be distractions, haphazard mixes from bits and pieces in the brain's memory storage, loosely linked together into what appears to be stories, or fractions of stories. Sort of like vaudeville.

Considering the vital priority of sleep over dreams, especially if the latter are what Freud called guardians of sleep, the Jungian theory of a number of archetypal symbols in a collective unconscious (or the *phylogenetic psyche*, as Stevens also calls it)[622] contributing to our self-realization is very far-fetched, indeed. Also, since it seems likely that all mammals dream, one must wonder what self-realization they have going for them.

That does not mean dreams can't contain symbols, i.e., symbolic representations of phenomena known from wakefulness. They would be sort of shorthand for significant ingredients in life, and could as such be components in the dreams of humans as well as other mammals.

Not only in dreams do we simplify by the use of symbols. Also the perception of the awake mind simplifies and categorizes, so as to handle impressions swiftly and accurately. That

[621] Sigmund Freud, *The Interpretation of Dreams*, transl. A. A. Brill, New York 1913 (originally published in German 1899), p. 197.

[622] Stevens 1999, p. 93.

is similar to the typical pattern of animals immediately noticing and reacting to movement, but not so much to static objects. It is a priority beneficial to survival.

We tend overall to react to changes in our surroundings, but be almost blind to the already familiar and constant. That function in our minds is likely to generalize and simplify, thereby turning complex phenomena into what can be labeled symbols. But to the extent that these symbols are innate and shared by the whole species, they are tools for survival and not for some complicated process by which to know oneself. That's the least of worries to animals in the wild. They don't care about who or what they are, but about threats to their very existence.

These symbolic representations appearing in dreams as well as in wakefulness, are for the most part composed from our personal experiences when awake. They do not consist of innate building blocks in a hidden unconscious. This is evident from the fact that our dreams mainly, if not completely, contain familiar persons, objects, and settings.

Also strangers as such are familiar to us, since we meet them all the time in most modern societies. Even objects we never came across and places we never visited can be familiar if we have some impression or fragmentary knowledge of them. Those ingredients in dreams may be characterized as archetypal, in the meaning of a generic symbol of something, but it must be remembered that they are made up of our own impressions of them when awake.

Accordingly, the fears or delights that the events in our dreams evoke are well-known to us and relate directly to our daily life. Those events may be highly unlikely, for better or worse, but what makes us react is the prospect of experiencing them when awake. Otherwise we would be indifferent to them.

Dreams are staged by waking experiences, and not the other way around.

The same can be said for symbols. They are formed and

upheld by our waking experiences, or we would not be able to relate to them. This is shown by the simple fact that they symbolize phenomena belonging to waking and not to sleeping. Well, not to the subjective state of being asleep, anyway. Symbols of sleep concern its relation to being awake, but symbols of waking life need no reference to sleep.

Not that it is always easy to tell those things apart. A famous example of the enigma was told by the Chinese Taoist Chuang Tzu in the 4th century BC. When he woke up from dreaming that he was a butterfly, he was not sure if it was instead a butterfly now dreaming of being him.[623] Yet, he was sure that there must be a difference, which he called the Transformation of Things.

Indeed, there is a difference. We may not know that we are dreaming when we are, but we do know that we are awake when we are — if sound and sober, at least. There are surely exceptions, but not to the extent that we should base our understanding of reality on them.

Instinct

Somewhat in accordance with what can be said about the content of dreams, it is reasonably safe to state that our symbols are products of our conscious minds, relating to our waking life. The characteristics of the symbols are evidence of this, since they are products of conscious observation and interpretation and collectively adopted.

The symbols Stevens includes in his books show this, too. Such classical symbols as the *caduceus* and the *ouroboros* stem from observations of nature, modified by conscious imagination. The same can be said for the planets, the discovery of which demanded persistent study of the night sky over long periods, and the elaborate mythologies connected to them — without which they would have been completely meaningless

---

[623] James Legge, *The Sacred Books of China: The Texts of Taoism*, part 1, Oxford 1891, p. 197.

— were culturally developed. The fact that those white dots way up there in the nocturnal darkness were at all considered, although having no apparent effect on human life whatsoever, can only be explained as expressions of the conscious mind at work.

All the socially shared symbols are conscious products. We learn or invent them, or a combination thereof. They are not genetically transmitted between generations.

There is one exception, though, and Anthony Stevens has repeatedly pointed it out. Animals have instinctual reactions to some phenomena of grave importance to their well-being. Even symbolical representations of these phenomena trigger reactions, as discussed above regarding Stevens' book about the archetypes and also regarding Joseph Campbell's book *Primitive Mythology*. Konrad Lorenz, who made pioneer research on this behavior in animals, referred to it as *innate releasing mechanisms* (IRM).

To Stevens, this is evidence of the innate Jungian archetypes. In his book on symbols discussed here, his definition of archetypes points directly at the IRM behavior:

> *Essentially, archetypes are genome-bound units of information which programme the individual member of a species to perceive, respond, and behave in ways which are adapted to the circumstances prevailing in the environment at any given time.*[624]

He compares it to birds building their nests:

> *The bird may not have a clear 'idea', in the human sense, of precisely what it is doing, but it must have some kind of 'image' of what the nest — the (arche)typical nest of the species — should be like when completed.*

[624] Stevens 1999, p. 22.

Well, that is instinctual, which is a heavily researched and confirmed fact about animal behavior. Instincts exist also in humans, although it seems that our complicated brains and social structures tend to alter or repress some of them — as Freud in particular had stated, but also Jung.

Actually, it is not that easy to find verifiable examples of IRM in humans.

A commonly used example of instinctual reactions is how we behave when confronted with spiders or snakes, even if they are just images and not the living creatures. But it remains to be proven how instinctual these reactions really are. The results of studies vary. It might be a learned or conditioned behavior, i.e., having been told that spiders and snakes are scary, or having been scared by them earlier in life.

One strong indicator of the fear of spiders and snakes not being innately instinctual is the fact that we do not all share it. As mentioned above in the chapter about Carl G. Jung, a 2020-2021 survey found the fear of reptiles in only 25% of the respondents, and that of spiders and other insects in only 23%. If it was genetically engraved in the instincts, these number should have been significantly higher. How can an instinct just exist in a quarter of the population? Natural selection would erase it in a few generations, by outnumbering alone. It is not that these fears significantly increase the chance of survival.

Instincts in general are rather elusive in humans, and scientific consensus is rare. Jungians and Freudians may have weakened their arguments when trying to base so much of their psychological theories on what they regarded as instinctual urges.

For example, self-preservation is seen as a basic instinct, but that would make both suicide and personal sacrifice for one or other reason impossible. Another instinct is to procreate, or at least to copulate, but this urge is resistible even for long periods, and some have no yearning at all to do it with the opposite sex. Feeding might be the most crucial instinct for survival, yet there are many who voluntarily fast for long periods or even choose to starve to the point of it being fatal. There may be no instincts that we are unable to control or even suppress by conscious effort.

Not even very rudimentary reflexes are immune to conscious effort. We can create designed reflexes by persistent training, even when they are quite different from our innate behavior. When such fundamental natural programming can be altered, it is far-fetched to assume that there would be anything in our minds inaccessible to us.

A psychology founded on anything else than the conscious mind is bound to lead to an inadequate perception of our nature.

Memes

There is an interesting alternative explanation to the emergence and spread of symbolic concepts. It comes from the famous evolutionary biologist Richard Dawkins. With his profound understanding of the role of the genes in evolution, he doesn't even bother to refute the Jungian idea of the archetypes being genetically inherited. But in the last chapter of his bestselling book *The Selfish Gene* from 1976, he presents the concept of *memes* as transmitters of cultural content, compared to genes and their biological content.

The memes are ideas that spread culturally, where some are successful and others just fade away. It is similar to the success or failure of mutated genes, or for that matter viruses, which are more or less contagious and have varying levels of influence on those infected. This is how he came up with the term:

> *We need a name for the new replicator, a noun that conveys the idea of a unit of cultural transmission, or a unit of im-*
> *itation. 'Mimeme'*[625] *comes from a suitable Greek root, but*

---

[625] From the Greek word *mímēma*, something imitated, which in turn stems from *mimos*, imitator or actor.

*I want a monosyllable that sounds a bit like 'gene'. I hope
my classicist friends will forgive me if I abbreviate mimeme
to* meme. *If it is any consolation, it could alternatively be
thought of as being related to 'memory', or to the French
word* même. *It should be pronounced to rhyme with
'cream'.*[626]

He ends his book with a hopeful message, where he actually argues for the human capacity to overcome the biological inheritance of the genes as well as the cultural inheritance of the memes. Our species has that capacity:

*We have the power to defy the selfish genes of our birth and,
if necessary, the selfish memes of our indoctrination. We
can even discuss ways of deliberately cultivating and nur-
turing pure, disinterested altruism — something that has
no place in nature, something that has never existed before
in the whole history of the world. We are built as gene machines and cultured as meme machines, but we have the
power to turn against our creators. We, alone on earth, can
rebel against the tyranny of the selfish replicators.*[627]

Anthony Stevens is not completely satisfied with the meme concept, which is hardly surprising. What Dawkins proposes has nothing to do with symbols innate in a collective unconscious. His memes are socially upheld and transmitted. That is far from the Jungian archetype theory.

Stevens bases his critique of Dawkins on the French cognitive anthropologist Dan Sperber, who pointed out that memes are less stable than genes, since they tend to undergo some degree of change every time they are transmitted.[628]

[626] Richard Dawkins, *The Selfish Gene*, New York 1978 (first edition 1976), p. 206.

[627] Ibid., p. 215.

[628] Stevens 1999, p. 162.

Of course they are, and Dawkins has certainly not claimed the opposite. Ideas that spread across society not only change in the process, but add content along the way. It is not even sure that they are recognizable at the end of it, evolving into very different ideas. Then again, some ideas can stay remarkably the same across time and separate cultures.

Since memes move through thought and not through the complicated process of genetic mutations, their evolution can be very swift and often is. But of course genes change, too, though it takes much longer for the effect to be significant and noticeable. So, the comparison is not between something mutable and something immutable, but between two mutable phenomena of different speed and modus operandi. Everything in the universe changes, in its own fashion and tempo.

But Sperber claims that some concepts do not. Stevens quotes him about supernatural ideas, "throughout the world's cultures, the same kinds of gods, dragons, devils and ghosts recur again and again," which is due to "commonalities of the human mind."

These "same kinds," though, deteriorate upon closer inspection, since they stem from the prejudice of the observers. The myths and beliefs around the world have been documented and interpreted mainly by researchers from a Christian tradition, and this influenced their perception substantially. It still does. But gods are very different indeed, to the point where it is meaningless in some cases to speak about gods at all. That also goes for dragons, devils, and ghosts. Actually, it is equally true for mythology and the whole concept of religion.

The simple truth is that the similarities are mostly in the eyes of the beholder. Searching for similarities you are sure to find them, just as you are sure to find differences if searching for those. Furthermore, even to striking similarities there can be a lot of explanations other than archetypes in a collective unconscious.

After all, there are indeed commonalities of the human

mind, which means that similarities are to be expected also in what is believed about what is not known.

Richard Dawkins' clear distinction between the gene and the meme remains far more convincing. They are separate processes. Their connection is that genes led to a brain able to create memes. But memes, ideas, symbols, and beliefs are not genetically transmitted.

Religion
Regarding religion, Anthony Stevens follows in the footsteps of Jung, claiming that "religious beliefs and practices, which are universally characteristic of human communities, are archetypally determined." He insists that a religious inclination is innate in human beings, like an instinct of sorts. Not a specific religion, of course, but the urge to be devoted to one or other. He compares it to language, "the propensity for religious beliefs and behaviour is innately 'prepared for', like the propensity for speech."[629] He explains:

> *The particular set of religious beliefs and rites practised in a given society has to be learned by each generation in the same way as its language. But the idea that there will be a religious system and a language which will have to be learned appears to exist in all growing individuals as* an a priori *assumption.*

It is an odd comparison, since language is a prerequisite for religion. Some kind of religious belief might have been possible in the isolated non-communicative mind of the primeval human. There is probably no way of knowing. But all of what is meant by religion needs to be expressed and shared, in order to develop and continue.

Claiming that the existence of religion is evidence of its innate nature, like the ability to form language is necessary to

[629] Ibid., pp. 170f.

learn it, is misleading. The human mind is able to grasp all kinds of concepts and perspectives, which does not mean they were all inherently present. It would be more adequate to state that the human mind is able to understand and use abstract concepts — or, really, that the mind can think of all kinds of things.

With his argument, Stevens approaches Plato's idea of all knowledge being innate or it would not be possible to express. Accordingly, there is no learning, only recollection. He had Socrates prove it in an experiment where an uneducated slave was able to solve a geometrical problem, only by Socrates' encouragements.[630] Those encouragements, though, contained a number of hints and clues. It would not pass as a proper empirical experiment.

Yet, Plato is clear about all knowledge, and not just some of it, being innate. Therefore it cannot be used to emphasize the significance of one certain knowledge. Also, of course, neurology has proven Plato wrong. Recollection is not enough to acquire knowledge. It has to be learned.

Whatever we think, it is with language we convey it to each other, and it is by the exchange of ideas that they take fixed forms. Abstract ideas, in particular, can hardly travel from one mind to another without a language to express them. To state the obvious: There would be no religion to speak of, without language.

Stevens insists with his Jungian perspective on religion and all its aspects. Discussing rites, he makes this distinction between the sacred and the profane:

At the psychic level, the realm of the sacred corresponds to the archetypal realm of the collective unconscious, while the profane corresponds to that of the personal psyche.[631]

[630] Plato, "Meno," 82-85, *The Dialogues of Plato*, vol. II (of 5), transl. Benjamin Jowett, Oxford 1892 (first edition 1871), pp. 41-47.

[631] Stevens 1999, p. 216.

But how to experience the sacred without conscious awareness? Promoting something to sacred is a social process, shared with those who are likeminded and expressed in rituals. Without the conscious social connection it is meaningless. That is also true for rites practiced in solitude. They are established and upheld socially, and we relate to them conscious of their social meaning.

We may have personal experiences of higher meaning, but it takes social confirmation for something to be sacred.

As for the profane, there is nothing about it that excludes it from the collective. We share the profane at least to the extent that we share the sacred. Actually, the polarity as such is false. The sacred and the profane are not opposites. We relate to reality and our perception of it as a whole. Some of it we may agree to regard as sacred, and the rest not. We still relate to it all with the same mental apparatus.

Gods

Discussing gods, Anthony Stevens starts with a theory of their origins, which has been around for centuries:

> *The earliest religions probably arose through the attribution of deity to natural forces and phenomena, such as the sun, moon, sky, earth, earthquakes, thunder, the rain, and the wind.*[632]

It is far from the only theory about the emergence of the belief in deities, but it is a reasonable one. Primeval humans would have been likely to think that any activity they observed on earth as well as in the sky must be caused by something or someone, just like they themselves made things happen by willful action. How else could the sun and moon be moved across the sky, the earth shake, the rain fall, and so on?

[632] Ibid., p. 173.

There must have been what Aristotle called a mover. Without any knowledge of the physics behind those things, it was a reasonable conclusion. And since there was no visible explanation to those movements, the ones causing them must be invisible.

If our distant ancestors were able to think rationally, and remnants of their tools and customs show that they were, then the idea of unseen powerful beings responsible for the events that lacked visible causes made sense — until more plausible explanations were revealed much later in our history.

But Stevens goes on, shifting the perspective from the rational to the symbolical, though that is not really called for: "Essentially, gods and goddesses are personifications of archetypal potential."[633] He remarks that it takes people of psychological sophistication to understand this, and people without it "actually *believe* in their gods and goddesses as existing and real." But it is not simply so that by understanding this, everything is fine. There is a risk with the insight:

> *This sophistication is achieved at a price, however, for a culture that no longer believes in its gods is spiritually adrift and in danger of disintegration.*

As usual, his source to this rather extreme conclusion is Jung. But the danger of disintegration has been known to plague cultures with those beliefs, too. Religion is no vaccine against social unrest. Frequently it has instead been the instigator of it.

As for "spiritually adrift," one must wonder what it means apart from a loss of religious belief, which is just saying that losing the belief is losing the belief. If being spiritual means more than that, then there are so many other ways to experience and express it than by worshipping a specific set of deities.

[633] Ibid., p. 174.

Even when it comes to changing gods instead of deserting them altogether, societies may have gone through some tumultuous times for a while, but hardly disintegration. If anything is to be concluded from such developments, it is that cultures adapt to new religions rather smoothly, perhaps because their function in society is not dependent on the names by which the gods are known.

Certainly, deities often have the dignity and significance that can be called archetypal, and they play symbolic roles in the myths. Their appearances and behaviors can almost be seen as caricatures of what they represent, both larger and more extreme than humanly possible.

But that does not mean their origin and nature is archetypal in the Jungian sense. Their function is better explained as symbols of natural forces, which is what also Stevens suggests. In mythology, the deities are anthropomorph embodiments of powers that lack other explanations. For example, in creation myths they are mainly components in the story, pieces of the puzzle of how the world might have come to be.

Creation Myths

Stevens also discusses creation myths, and there is good reason for it. Cosmogonies are at the core of many mythologies, probably most of them, and they are usually given huge importance in worship as well as rituals. Originally, those myths were efforts to answer the question of how the world in all its vastness began, and this was done in what Stevens calls "the pre-scientific terminology of myths and symbols."[634] He continues:

> *When all these mythic and scientific explanations are compared, a profoundly interesting fact emerges; they often overlap in such a way as to suggest that the primordial mind and the modern mind have been working along similar lines.*

[634] Ibid., p. 195.

It is true that there are some similarities between how creation myths and modern science conceive the origin of the world, but they are in the reasoning and not in the details. Since the question is the same, so must some of the speculative answers be.

The basic idea that the world would have had a beginning, instead of eternally being the same, was deducted from observations of the cyclic phenomena — from the movements of the sun and the moon up in the sky, to the birth, growth, and decay of living things down on earth. Especially the latter. Since all creatures are born and eventually die, even plants, the idea rose that this might be true for everything in the world.

Thus, darkness before the sun, the moon, and the stars lit up the sky, and a barren land before the first plants grew and the first animals and humans were born, ancestors to all the following generations. Creation myths were formed on speculations about what the primordial state would have been and how the world and everything in it emerged. This was done with a combination of reason and imagination, which is also how scientific discoveries are made.

Stevens mentions the big bang theory as an example of how myth and science overlap, pointing to Buddhist mythology as an example. But there is one more nearby, in Genesis 1 where God begins creation by ordering light to appear in the darkness, indeed similar to the moment when stars ignited in the universe, although that was hardly done in a day.

He gives another example: "The notion that all life originally emerged from the sea is common to a great many mythic cosmologies."[635] It is true that many creation myths start with a primordial sea, but not that all life emerged from it. Much more typical is that the earth rose from the sea and then plants, animals, and people appeared there, on land. Few myths mention fish or submarine vegetation.

[635] Ibid., p. 196.

It is no mystery that so many myths begin with a sea. Those people who lived close to one, or a lake so big that the land on its other side was not visible, would be in awe of its vastness and permanence. Also, anyone standing by the shore could see that the land rose out of it, so it made sense that the whole earth had done the same.

Stevens makes another claim, which is as bold as it is questionable:

> *A large number of peoples hold the belief that the moon and the earth were originally of the same substance.*

Most if not all creation myths describe the earth and the moon as completely separate entities of different substances. The moon is instead linked to the sun and the stars, usually appearing in the same phase of creation. What is very clear in mythology, as Stevens also repeatedly points out, is the strict division between heaven and earth. Things up high are nothing like things on earth. Stevens should have given at least one example of what he claims. I cannot think of any.

Those similarities, real or imagined, between the myths and scientific facts lead Stevens to this conclusion:

> *These fascinating parallels are hints that archetypal processes are links between physical and psychic realities — that the laws on which the universe proceeds may also help shape our mental attitudes to them and the hypotheses we formulate to comprehend them.*

Certainly, creation myths consist of elements that can be seen as archetypal, such as the deities and the grand events in primordial times. It is less evident that scientific cosmogony can be said to contain archetypes. Most of it is just very advanced mathematics based on astronomical observations. An archetypal perspective on it is of limited use.

Also, the parallels between myth and science are neither

as obvious as Stevens portrays them, nor explained the most convincingly by archetypal theory. As for creation myths, their components can be unraveled by examining the plausible thought process leading to them.

There were some great enigmas our ancestors had to wrestle with, when trying to figure out how the world may have begun. Stevens mentions some of them, first of all what he calls the ultimate *koan*, borrowing the Zen term, which is how something can come out of nothing. Still today, that is a paradox lacking a solid explanation.

In most creation myths this problem was escaped by the primordial state not being nothing, but something, such as a sea or a gap. Genesis 1 is an example of this, although that creation myth is usually categorized as *creatio ex nihilo*, creation out of nothing. Before starting his week of work, God's spirit hovers in darkness over the water. That means at least three things were preexistent — the water, a space above it, and God's spirit. And, whether in this void or outside it, God existed, too.

It was, of course, very hard for our ancestors to imagine a complete nothing to begin with. At the very least, there would be a space, a void, in which creation took place, but often more than that. It is the same with a primordial deity. Most myths mention one deity, sometimes two or more, already before creation began, and the rest have a deity appear early on.

It is noteworthy that an original state without any deity is found in several creation myths, but not one without some kind of space or substance in which that deity can appear. In other words, even a primordial deity starting the creation of the world was believed to exist inside of it.

In the case of a single primordial deity, it is almost always male. That may be counterintuitive to us, but it is not necessarily only an expression of patriarchy. In ancient times the male seed was known but the female egg not, so it seemed that new life was the product of male essence and women were mere vessels of it.

Strangely, Stevens presents the opposite view, when later in his text discussing the virgin birth:

> *The story of the virgin birth predates the Christian myth by a very long time: it probably owes its origins to that epoch of human emergence when the significance of male semen was unappreciated. The woman was thought to be entirely responsible for the child's creation, its conception being attributed to the numinosum[636] — the divine wind or the spirit of the ancestors. If the phallus played a part, it was merely as a means to 'open the way' for the generative spirit to enter the womb and cause the accumulation of blood to be miraculously transformed into a child.[637]*

That is unlikely bordering on the absurd. Of course our ancestors were aware that to reproduce, both man and woman are necessary. It is evident in many mythologies, too, where also deities procreate in the conventional way. In mythological reasoning, children who are born by a divine wind or some other superhuman agent will be divine, too. There are stories about children of human mothers and divine fathers, and they are always exceptional, if not superhuman.

Stevens also mentions the cosmic egg, which is found in a number of creation myths. To him it is a symbol of the primordial deity, but there is another explanation of it nearer at hand. When the very simple and pure form of the egg cracks, a living being exits and grows. That makes it a tempting object by which to explain the emergence of the world.

Every ingredient and event in creation myths is possible to explain without the use of archetypes or other psychological references. It is usually enough to apply reason, and often some very imaginative solutions adding flair to the story. Cre-

[636] From *numinous*, the religious sense of awe and wonder, a concept introduced by Rudolf Otto.

[637] Ibid., p. 209.

ation myths are stories, which means that they need to make sense within their own premises, and to entertain their intended audiences.

Stevens summarizes the function of those myths differently:

> *Creator gods give rise to other gods and these give rise to heroes, whose ordeals, trials, battles, adventures, loves, and exploits define the archetypal modes of human existence.*[638]

That is one way of putting it, but he excludes one thing, which is the main characteristic of creation myths — their effort to explain how the world was created. When that perspective is excluded, they don't make much sense anymore, and alternative explanations get overly complicated, which makes it very difficult to argue for them convincingly.

Stevens makes a similar mistake explaining the fall of man, when Adam and Eve are expelled from Eden for eating the forbidden fruit:

> *This 'loss of Eden' can be understood on at least five symbolic levels: the migration of our early ancestors from forest to savannah; the transition from the hunter-gatherer existence to pastoral and farming life, and the emergence of civilization; the expulsion of the baby from the womb; the differentiation of the ego from the Self; and the development of human consciousness.*[639]

The first levels make some contextual sense, already by the fact that this the second creation story of the Bible relates to earthly life and agriculture, whereas the first one has more of a cosmic perspective. But the last three are far-fetched, indeed. What the story tells, instead, is how humans became

---

[638] Ibid., p. 200.

[639] Ibid., p. 202.

mortal and their life filled with hardship and suffering. Those are themes recognizable from many other creation myths.

The creation myths around the world and through human history are far from homogenous. The common patterns to be found in them are not in their setting or pantheon, but maybe in how certain settings and certain pantheons lead to similar chains of events.

For example, where there is only one divine creator of it all, such as in the Avesta of Zarathustra, the Bible, and the Quran, human beings are soon at center stage, whereas in polytheisms they tend to appear late in the story and not really become main characters. The deities stay in the spotlight.

Also, regarding deities, no matter how many they are, there seems to be one in charge, distinctly more powerful and important than the others. In the history of religion this deity is called a high god. It is not necessarily so that this supreme deity created the world, although that is often the case, but he — yes, it is always a he — is the ruler of the other deities and just about everything else. Except for their elevated position, though, these high gods can be quite different in character, abilities, and activities.

A strict monotheism is actually hard to find. In the Bible and the Quran there are other superhuman beings, the devil and the angels, who are refused the title of god but are quite comparable to deities in polytheism. They are not bound to earth and they seem not to be mortal. Also, they have powers beyond what is humanly possible. So, they are deities in every sense, whatever they are called.

Avesta has the supreme god Ahura Mazda, but also originally the benevolent spirit Spenta Mainyu and the destructive spirit Angra Mainyu. In later Zoroastrianism, the three became two, Ohrmazd (Ahura Mazda) and Ahriman (Angra Mainyu), but never just one.

To Stevens, the devil represents the shadow archetype,

who is "the stranger/predator/evil intruder."[640] That is one way of putting it. Similar figures exist in many mythologies, and the term used for them is *trickster*. They are often involved in creation or the continued formation of the world, tricking deities to act against their own intentions, often to the benefit of humans. Although always deceitful, they are not necessarily evil.

The serpent in Genesis is a clear example of a trickster, making Adam and Eve eat of the forbidden fruit — but that was what gave them knowledge of good and evil, by which they became a threat to God and had to be expelled from Eden.

Satan in the Old Testament is the accuser, acting like a kind of prosecutor in God's service by questioning and testing people's faith. So, he is not so much evil as strict. It is in the Christian tradition he has turned into the personification of evil.

The trickster is one of Jung's archetypes, but it is not his invention. Nor was he the one to introduce it in the study of mythology. He just applied his own theories on that figure, as he did on many other mythical characters and phenomena, and Stevens repeats his approach without question.

[640] Ibid., p. 176.

David Adams Leeming

David Adams Leeming (born 1937) is not a psychologist, but an American professor of English and comparative literature, who has spent most of his professional life at the University of Connecticut, presently as professor emeritus. The bulk of his writing is on mythology, especially creation myths, where he has applied Jungian perspectives.

His first book on mythology was published in 1973. Several books on the subject followed. In 1994 he released a dictionary of creation myths, written together with his daughter Margaret Adams Leeming. An expanded second edition of it came in 2010, with him as the sole author.

Voyage of the Hero

The Jungian influence on Leeming's treatment of myth is evident already from the title of his first book on the subject, from 1973: *Mythology: The Voyage of the Hero*. The hero was the favorite archetype of Carl G. Jung, since he meant it to represent the human quest for individuation, the self-realization of becoming conscious of one's unconscious and its content. It is also the perspective and theme of Joseph Campbell's famous book *The Hero With a Thousand Faces* from 1949, previously discussed, which has evidently also influenced Leeming considerably.

He refers generously to both Jung and Campbell as sources to his perspective on myths, and stresses their importance in the study of mythology. As for Jung, he praises him in particular for not shunning the mystical:

> *Most of all, Jung broke the path into regions scientists had feared to explore — regions which had been labeled "mystical" and therefore unworthy of attention.*[641]

---

[641] David Adams Leeming, *Mythology: The Voyage of the Hero*, second edition, New York 1981 (first edition 1973), p. 2.

In an appendix, Leeming goes much further in his praise of Jung, calling him "an individual endowed with keen extra-sensory perception" and comparing him to the mythical hero: "Like the hero of the monomyth, Jung was a pathfinder in search of the elixir of life."[642] He describes Jung's development from childhood to old age in terms that portray him as something of a mage or an enlightened being:

> *Jung at Bollingen succeeded in creating a mythical consciousness — in establishing meaningful contact with the life force which is everywhere and in everything.*[643]

Leeming's respect for Joseph Campbell is also way up there. He regards Campbell as the one who has "perhaps done more than anyone else to revive the study of myth"[644] and continues:

> *Campbell is particularly important because he makes the next step in our approach to mythology much simpler by demonstrating that mythology is the property of no single theorist or theory.*

That is a strange statement, since Campbell leaned heavily on Jung's theories, and his own main contribution — the universal hero myth, which he called the *monomyth* — argues for a rather narrow way of understanding the content and meaning of mythology. He just added another theory to the many competing ones around.

But it happens to be the one Leeming admittedly applies: "This book of myths is built upon a simplified form of the

[642] Ibid., p. 329.

[643] Ibid., p. 332.

[644] Ibid., p. 3.

monomyth."[645] And his definition of it is, as is that of Campbell, decidedly Jungian:

> *The monomyth itself is an expression of the journey of the hero figure, of our own journey through physical and psychic life, and of the evolutionary path of humanity to full consciousness.*

Leeming also insists that there are inherited themes in myths as well as dreams, "buried in the very depths of the human psyche."[646] They are universal in humankind and have an effect on us that we are unable to explain:

> *These are themes — archetypes — which, when we come across them, in literature, for instance, "strike a chord" for no apparent reason.*

But of course there are apparent reasons. When those ingredients labeled archetypes — whether characters, things, or events — strike a chord, it is quite easy to grasp why. Simply put, they relate to our own fears and wishes.

The hero myth is a typical example. Who doesn't want to be a hero? All those stories attract us because we long to make that journey, and they scare us because we know that so much can go wrong on the way. At the outset, it is impossible to know if the journey will end in success or failure, which is why we are hesitant about it.

Also, our own lives may be described the same way, though less spectacular. It is the human adventure from cradle to grave, with disappointments followed by delights followed by disappointments, obstacles and breakthroughs, where the staircase of all those events hopefully leads upwards, at least to an increased understanding of how we and the world work.

[645] Ibid., p. 6.
[646] Ibid., p. 4.

So, of course we can relate.

Even Leeming confirms it when on the same page he states that "myths reveal concerns which are common to all of us as a species." Such concerns cannot be unfamiliar to our conscious minds. And later in the book he expresses the same, with additional Jungian terminology:

The beginning of the path to psychic wholeness is the recognition that the hero's voyage is in reality the voyage of each and all of us.[647]

Like Campbell, Leeming divides the hero's voyage into separate phases. They differ somewhat in number and specifics, but are overall quite similar. Leeming lists eight such phases, and for each he goes through a number of examples from mythology and other myths of distinction. Those eight phases are:

1. The miraculous conception and birth and the hiding of the child;
2. Childhood, initiation, and divine signs;
3. Preparation, meditation, withdrawal, and refusal;
4. Trial and quest;
5. Death and the scapegoat;
6. The descent to the underworld
7. Resurrection and rebirth;
8. Ascension, apotheosis, and atonement.

In myths about heroic quests, and there are plenty of those, certainly some or even several of these phases can be found, but what the monomyth idea implies is that they should all be present in every hero myth. That is definitely not the case.

There is, though, one particular story fitting this structure

[647] Ibid., p. 333.

remarkably well — that of Jesus. The Gospels, when combined to form a complete story from conception to ascension, contain all eight phases quite clearly.

Jesus is conceived miraculously, born with several signs of his importance, and hidden from Herod by the escape to Egypt. Already in his childhood he shows remarkable insights, and an affinity for the temple. He gets baptized and then withdraws into the desert to meditate his calling, where he is tempted by the devil but resists. He begins his preaching, meeting dismissals and hostility but persisting. Then he is put to trial and dies as sort of a scapegoat for our sins. He doesn't descend to the underworld, but is kept in a cave and stays dead until the third day, when he is resurrected. After meeting and giving some final teachings to his disciples, he gloriously ascends and by that makes atonement with God possible for all people then and since.

This story fits Leeming's model so well that its influence on the model must be assumed, considering Leeming's cultural heritage and also the fact that his father was an Episcopal priest.[648] Leeming refers to Jesus and parts of his story frequently in the book, with examples in each of the eight phases, but he doesn't discuss what this similarity to his model might reveal about his own preconceived notions when constructing it. That should be obvious.

The problem is that his intention is to present a monomyth formula applicable to all hero myths, so he regards any story fitting it as proof, also the one that is very likely to have made him decide on the formula to begin with.

He is not alone among Jungians to exhibit that flawed reasoning.

Creation Myths

In an appendix of the above discussed book, Leeming presents seven creation myths without any comment. It is understand-

---

[648] "Leeming, David Adams 1937-," *Encyclopedia.com*.

able that he felt the need to add a few such myths to his book, since those stories are essential parts of many mythologies, even though they cannot be fit into the hero monomyth model. He was to expand considerably on this topic, in particular with an anthology of creation myths, first published in 1994 as *The Encyclopedia of Creation Myths*, and in 2010 an expanded second edition with the title *Creation Myths of the World*.

Both books show a clear change in Leeming's attitude towards Carl G. Jung. In the earlier book he is just mentioned once, and that is in the text about his student Marie-Louise von Franz. None of his books are in the bibliography, nor any by Joseph Campbell, who is not mentioned at all.

Jungian concepts are present, though. In his definition of myth, Leeming writes:

> *A myth is a projection of an aspect of a culture's soul. In its complex but revealing symbolism, a myth is to a culture what a dream is to an individual.*[649]

The comparison between myths and dreams is popular among Jungians, who link the former to the collective unconscious and the latter to the personal unconscious. That is a neat model, but what is thereby claimed is that myths are not formed by conscious minds, which is particularly doubtful when it comes to creation myths with their elaborate speculations about the emergence of the world and everything in it.

Leeming also makes use of the archetype concept, though with some reservation regarding its dominance over cultural aspects:

> *While it is true that each creation myth reveals the priorities and concerns of a given culture, it is also true that*

---

[649] David Adams Leeming & Margaret Adams Leeming, *A Dictionary of Creation Myths*, New York 1995 (first published in 1994 as *The Encyclopedia of Creation Myths*), p. vii.

when creation myths are compared, certain universal or archetypal patterns are discovered in them.[650]

Even the creation myth as such, he describes as an archetype, and a grand one at that:

In short, the archetype of the creation myth speaks to the equally universal drive for differentiation from nothingness that is expressed by everything that exists in the universe.

Another approach to creation myths, popular among Jungians as well as others studying them, is the division into categories. Those models are seldom identical, but usually similar. Here are the five categories Leeming suggests:

1) from chaos or nothingness (ex nihilo), 2) from a cosmic egg or primal maternal mound, 3) from world parents who are separated, 4) from a process of earth-diving, or 5) from several stages of emergence from other worlds.[651]

Such models are of limited use. The sorting of them into such categories doesn't lead to any further understanding of the nature and function of creation myths. It is not even used for that. The models are created and myths are placed in the categories, and that's it. Nor do they really convey the significances in each myth, but tend to blur them into types where deviations are neglected — and there are plenty of deviations.

Already the first category is problematic, since a pure creation out of nothing is hard to find in mythology. I am yet to find one. Genesis 1, for example, is certainly not it, although this has been claimed in Christian theology through its history. Another anomaly is that many creation myths contain more

[650] Ibid., p. viii.

[651] Ibid.

than one of the categories, and others are such that it is only by far-fetched reasoning they can be put in any one of them.

The problem with this kind of model is evident also in Leeming's writing, since he presents a slightly deviating set of categories in his expanded second edition of the book, from 2010: ex nihilo creation, creation from chaos, world parent creation, emergence creation, and earth-diver creation.[652]

Reduced Archetypes

This later edition of Leeming's book also deviates from the first in how Carl G. Jung is treated. There is still no book of his in the bibliography, which is odd, but he is mentioned several times and there is even a short biographical text about him.[653] Joseph Campbell is also given room this time around, even with a couple of his books in the bibliography.

There is also a difference in Leeming's treatment of archetypes. In the first edition he recognized it as an important ingredient in myths, but in the second edition it is treated more or less as just one way of looking at it. He is distancing himself from it, almost as if the concept is a deserted theory of the past. He writes in the introduction:

> *Universal patterns or common motifs in mythology have been called archetypal, that is, reflective of psychological tendencies that are common to the human species as a whole.*[654]

That is quite different from his previous elevation of its meaning. Also, he stresses the importance of understanding that the archetypes "only take on life and meaning when they are clothed in cultural particularity." That is practically the op-

---

[652] David Adams Leeming, *Creation Myths of the World: An Encyclopedia*, Santa Barbara 2010, p. vii.

[653] Ibid., p. 443.

[654] Ibid., p. xix.

posite of the Jungian use of the concept, which emphasizes that the archetypes are shared by all, regardless of time and place.

In the encyclopedic text on the archetype, where Jung's, Campbell's, and Eliade's use of it are explained, he ends with a similar reservation:

> *It must be emphasized, however, that the universal archetypal language of myth requires the elements of particular cultural experience in order to be realized, just as dreams require the local experience of individuals.*[655]

The prerequisite of a cultural experience is that it cannot be innate, nor can it be completely unconscious. So, there is just about nothing Jungian left in Leeming's view on the archetypes. Quite a change from the 1994 edition, and even more so from his 1973 book on mythology, discussed earlier. Leeming has gone from his initial adoration of Jung to distancing from him, almost dismissing him completely.

That doesn't stop him from frequently presenting Jungian perspectives on the myths, but by quoting other sources, such as Marie-Louise von Franz and Charles H. Long.

There is another problem with Leeming's encyclopedia of creation myths, but it doesn't concern its Jungian perspectives. It is how he treats the sources to the myths he recounts. He doesn't quote those sources, but re-tells most of the myths with his own words.[656] That is probably for copyright reasons. Still, it leads to doubts about the accuracy of his versions, and therefore also to what grounds he has for his interpretations.

Furthermore, as a source for many of the myths he uses *The Beginning: Creation Myths around the World* by Maria Leach, who has done the same. So, he has re-told stories already re-told by her, instead of going to her sources, although she has referenced them all commendably.

---

[655] Ibid., p. 376.

[656] Ibid., p. 31.

Religious Myth

In between the two above discussed editions of his book on creation myths, in 2002, David Adams Leeming published *Myth: A Biography of Belief*, where he discusses myth and religion more freely, in a personal way, allowing himself to speculate and make claims that are based on his opinion more than objective facts. That is certainly his prerogative as an author, and the result is a stimulating read in spite of his claims often being questionable.

On the other hand, all through the book it is often unclear if he just refers to the opinions and theories of others, or declares his own support for them. Since he often doesn't quote sources but interprets the views of others with his own words, it is hard to sort out where the line goes between their views and his.

This ambiguity is shown also in his treatment of Carl G. Jung, whose theories are referred to frequently, although without either approval or dismissal. Contrary to the above discussed books, this one's bibliography contains several texts by Jung. That has some significance but is easily explained by the many references to Jung's theories. Leeming's own opinion about those theories often remains unclear.

The book is based on a series of lectures he held in the year 2000, intended to define patterns of archetypes in the myths he presents as examples, also interpreting those archetypes and their functions. Doing so, he uses myths from religions, well aware that some people may be offended by his labeling of religious stories as myths, which would imply that they are fabrications.[657] He explains:

Myths reflect our spiritual and psychological development, our spiritual and psychological biography as a species, and

[657] David Adams Leeming, *Myth: A Biography of Belief*, New York 2002, pp. ix f.

it seems fair to hope that religions can also reflect that de-velopment.

He may be right, but there is also a possibility that he gives religion more credit than it deserves. There are many indications, and he mentions several of them in the book, that religions have primarily opposed development, and to a large extent still do. But Leeming has religion in very high regard, indeed, stating that "all cultures are joined in their many different ways in the great 'religious' and mythological process of examining the Unknown."[658] The ultimate goal of this examination is self-awareness of the whole creation:

> *Mystics of all the great religions have especially been in agreement about their own traditions being non-exclusive vessels for the eternal and continuing process of making creation conscious of itself.[659]*

It is a thought-provoking idea, which is proposed also in modern speculations about cosmology. Whether intentionally or not, the universe has given birth to creatures who are able to observe it and shed some light on its birth and development. That this is at all possible is not something given, we might just as well have been unable to explore the world beyond our own limited habitat — and up until very recently we were.

Tradition

As for the relation between myth and religion, Leeming states:

> *Traditionally, religions have been the repositories and interpreters of sacred stories — of myths — and the creators of rituals to express them.[660]*

[658] Ibid., p. 15.

[659] Ibid., p. 23.

[660] Ibid., p. 19.

It is likely that religions, in the meaning of socially shared and upheld beliefs, have developed rituals enacting those beliefs. But, as Leeming implies, the myths are likelier to have been the sources of religions than the other way around. The beliefs were developed and transmitted in the form of myth, speculations turning into imaginative stories, which by time became the building blocks of religious doctrine. Time is what makes myth sacred.

Religious belief systems consist essentially of myths that became traditional and cherished as such. The myths may have started as speculation or mere entertainment, but as time passed their value increased because of their long tradition. What made them sacred was not primarily their content, but their cultural presence through multiple generations. They were preserved as legacy from the ancestors.

This is indicated by the very common response anthropologists have received as to why a culture holds on to certain rites and the beliefs they promote — it was the way of the ancestors. What has been cherished for long tends to continue to be cherished, even through cultural and social changes. The power lies not primarily in the symbolism or the dogma, but in the long history. It is sort of what is expressed by the saying that old habits die hard.

We have numerous traditions also in this modern world, which we stick to although they have more or less lost their original meaning. We don't need to believe in the old myths and rituals. It is usually enough that they are old. For example, there is a Germanic tradition of raising a maypole, covered in leaves, when celebrating spring or midsummer. It is not known what this tradition originally meant or how it started. It is simply done because it has been done for so long.

Leeming makes the claim that "as our experience as cultures and as a species changes, so do our myths."[661] That may

661 Ibid., p. 19.

be true for some myths, but the overwhelming number of them are faithfully kept unchanged from generation to generation, even in societies having to rely solely on oral transmission. It is quite remarkable, showing our reverence for tradition.

This also explains why it is not a problem that myths are not realistic and the meaning of rituals often are clouded or even misguided. As Leeming puts it, "we celebrate events that are clearly impossible according to the laws of reason."[662] That has nothing to do with why we keep them around. Regardless of how fictional they may be, the myths and rituals are true in the sense that they truly belong to our traditions. We can, and we do, appreciate what our ancestors treasured for whatever reason.

Although myths tend to remain the same, reason is something that changes when our knowledge and culture does. Leeming writes that "the very essence of myth and ritual is anti-rational,"[663] and regards this as an essential aspect of them. But rationality and reason are in the eyes of the beholder. Many of the myths made sense to our ancestors, and the fabulous events described were regarded as possible or at least plausible.

It is even one of the attractions of the old myths that they contain ancient beliefs, which we can grasp through those myths — and appreciate. We get a chance to think like our ancestors did and understand them, as if sitting beside them when they told those tales. It is akin to time travel.

That is particularly true for creation myths, which tried to make sense of the world from very little factual knowledge about it. The cleverness and imagination by which this was pursued are fascinating to us, although we now know how wrong they were. What is wrong to us was right to them, and right for them.

Leeming hopes for a new mythology, whereby he seems

[662] Ibid., pp. 12f.
[663] Ibid., p. 12.

to dismiss the traditional value of the ones we already have. He sees all kinds of new myths and mythical concepts appearing in modern society, for example in the arts and in politics, but what he looks forward to the most is a mythology bringing together religion and science. He already sees signs of it:

> *Perhaps the best indication of the beginnings of the acceptance of a new mythology is the relatively recent recognition of the common purposes and understandings of the old enemies, religion and science, spirit and reason.*[664]

But he also sees a persistent refusal to modify religion in accordance with scientific progress, and he describes it as "a general resistance or inability of ordinary people — those not on the radical fringes of theology and those out of touch with the esoteric disciplines of astro and microphysics."[665]

That is quite a prejudiced view, as if "ordinary people" would be incapable of understanding that scientific discoveries contradict old religious cosmology. We don't need deep insights into either theology or physics to be aware of the consequences to religious dogma.

A much more plausible explanation to the slow or non-existent adaption of religion is, as discussed above, that it is not about facts but about tradition. Religions of old are conserved because of their age, and in that perspective deviations from later scientific findings are irrelevant.

Even fundamentalists who insist on a cosmology rejected by science do so because of their commitment to tradition, whether or not they use scientific counterclaims. Their incentive is that their religion should remain in accordance with tradition, since that is to them essential to its value and meaning.

It is true that religion and science have been colliding a lot for hundreds of years, but not all religions and not always. The

[664] Ibid., p. 24.

[665] Ibid., p. 48.

animosity to science has mainly been within Christianity, already in the Middle Ages when the works of the Greek philosophers were rediscovered and much of their thinking was found to contradict the dogma of the church. Many other religions were not similarly provoked by scientific theories and discoveries.

And it must be remembered that there was a time when there was no conflict between religion of whatever kind and science, because they were merged into one. Mythologies are inseparable combinations of spirit and reason.

New Myths

Leeming's book is divided into three parts, which concern three main aspects of mythology: creation, deity, and the hero. He ends each part by discussing the prospects of a new mythology, adapted to modern mentality and knowledge, which he presumes and hopes to emerge. It would consist of a new creation myth, a new perspective on divinity, and a new hero monomyth.

To Leeming, the content of these new myths must be universalistic, in the meaning that the archetypes of which they consist are revealed by comparing many mythologies and lead to a universal symbolic language.[666] Accordingly, he speaks of those who promote the new myths as universalists.

The new universalist creation myth should be "based on our new understandings of the universe, but using traditional language patterns," where humans play a much larger part than in the old myths-[667]

He sketches what that new myth would be like, starting by replacing the creator god with another concept: "In the beginning was the Great Mystery." It was energy with "the potential for everything that was, is, and will be," which burst into "the explosion that became the Universe."

[666] Ibid., p. 10f.

[667] Ibid., p. 49.

That is an image of the Big Bang, except for the significant fact that it was not an explosion, but an expansion. In an expansion the center remains, whereas in an explosion it is emptied — and that would be an odd universe, even in a mythical sense. Leeming should have held on to astrophysics on this point.

He goes on with the solar system and Mother Earth as other parts of the continuing creative process driven by the Great Mystery. We humans have an obligation to retell the story:

> *In our paintings, our thoughts, our words, and our stories we have learned to imitate creation and make creation conscious of itself. As long as we keep doing this the Mother will not discard us.*[668]

He insists that all creation stories are spiritual parables, "never meant to be taken literally,"[669] but symbolical celebrations of the creation archetype, which is the pattern of chaos to order. The re-creation of this pattern is essential to us, or even crucial:

> *If we do not re-create, if we do not make creation conscious of itself, we have no reason for being.*

Harsh words. It is kind of an ouroboros circle that the universe would appear for the sake of discovering that it did. It is also a parallel to those types of mighty gods whose main concern is to be worshipped by the people they created. For being new, this creation myth carries a lot of baggage from the old ones.

As for the new deity, Leeming describes it as one sole supreme being of which "all deity myths are partial meta-

---

[668] Ibid., p. 51.
[669] Ibid., p. 52.

phors."[670] Another distinct characteristic is that this deity has no gender, which to Leeming means that it must be nonpersonal:

> *However we perceive of deity now in the intellectual sense, it is likely to become neither masculine nor feminine and, therefore, in any human sense nonpersonal as it slowly takes form in our collective psyche.*

Why a deity without gender therefore must lack personality is doubtful. There is more to personality than gender, especially with deities, who are notoriously sexually ambiguous. In some cases, gender is not at all applicable. If there is just one single deity, it can but be genderless. Still, such deities can be very personal, indeed.

It is also very questionable that all deities are metaphors for one supreme being. Mythologies prove this wrong. In polytheism, the many deities are clearly separate characters with their own roles in the world, and in monotheism the deity can't be a metaphor for itself.

Leeming is biased by belonging to a culture impregnated by Christian ideas for two thousand years — and even that tradition he misunderstands. Christianity is not strictly monotheistic, since the deity is divided into a trinity, whereof the son is obviously separate from the father, also according to his own words as retold in the Gospels. In addition, there are angels, including the fallen one, who can rightly be compared to the deities of polytheism.

Leeming's claim of all deities really being one would meet with approval from the proponents of the trinity, but hardly from comparative religion.

Thirdly and lastly, Leeming demands of the new hero monomyth that it leaves the old patriarchal value systems, instead to promote inclusiveness and universal interrelatedness,

---

[670] Ibid., p. 105.

as the human perspective becomes increasingly global.[671] In the new hero myth, which Leeming calls ecological, we are the heroes.[672] And for us to be comfortable with the hero myth, it has to change substantially:

> *What we know is that the old mythologies represented by the old patriarchal and individualistic hero masks are no longer viable as expressions of who and what we are.*

It is no longer a question of brave men in battle with each other to save the day, but a realization that the world is in dire need of unity:

> *The crucial salvation now is communal salvation; without it our species will die and creation will lose its conscious-ness.*[673]

The path of the ecological hero who has the whole planet in mind is to discover the Self, his own as well as that of the species.[674]

It is somewhat unclear if Leeming means that these new myths are de facto taking form in society, or if it is wishful thinking on his part. Probably both.

Certainly, new myths appear frequently, some to quickly disappear and others to remain. But it is also true that many of the old myths stay with us, regardless of how they fit our present understanding of the world.

As discussed earlier, it is very much a question of tradition. The longer myths have been around, the likelier it is that they continue to be. That is particularly the case with those connected to religious mythology. They are part of our cultural

[671] Ibid., p. 151.

[672] Ibid., p. 158.

[673] Ibid., p. 160.

[674] Ibid., p. 162.

heritage, which is why their content is not that important to us. It is enough that they once were relevant to our ancestors.

New myths are easily formed, but it is extremely difficult for them to replace the old ones. They will coexist.

Another problem with Leeming's theory of new myths is its claim of homogeneity, i.e., that they would be adapted by society as a whole, even across the globe. It is very unlikely. Many things in society can be said to move towards homogeneity, such as political and economic structures, but spiritual beliefs and their myths are not similarly conforming. Quite the opposite. They tend to go their separate ways, rejecting any adaptation to other beliefs.

A culture can surely be dominated by one religion and its mythological content for as long as hundreds of years, but not forever. Although the religion remains, its monopoly does not. And if it is missionary, it might spread over the world but not convert everybody. We humans are alike in that we are reluctant to conform to others, especially if they are from other cultures than our own.

So, Leeming's vision of globally adapted new myths fitting the needs of our time is not realistic. Already the fact that he sketches myths with what he regards as utopian qualities, perfectly fulfilling optimal individual as well as social realization, should tell him that he is naïve. Perfection is nowhere in sight, only steps hopefully getting us closer to it. But always many steps remain, if there is at all a final step.

Jordan B. Peterson

Jordan Bernt Peterson (born 1962) is a Canadian clinical psychologist, who has reached significant fame way beyond his peer group through his Internet presence, especially on YouTube. His videos have reached millions, as have the few books he has written so far. The biggest bestseller is the 2018 life advice book *12 Rules for Life: An Antidote to Chaos*, but the first one was published already in 1999, *Maps of Meaning: The Architecture of Belief*, where he presents his admittedly Jungian perspective on psychology and what it says about mankind as well as the threats facing society.

Before switching to psychology he got a BA in political science in 1982. Soon after that he started to study clinical psychology, earning his PhD in 1991 with research on the predisposition to alcoholism.

His thoughts are controversial, to the extent that many praise them and many dismiss them categorically, but few who are familiar with them are in between. His refusal in 2016 to accept a legal mandate in Canada to use personally preferred gender pronouns caused calamity at the University of Toronto campus and far beyond it. In 2021 he resigned from his teaching position, becoming Professor Emeritus.

Already in 2013, he started a YouTube channel with videos of his university lectures. Later the content switched to lectures aimed directly at the YouTube audience. The channel now has close to six million subscribers and his videos have a total of over 460 million views (September 2022).[675] He has also been interviewed on several other major YouTube channels and podcasts.

With his modest literary production of only three books so far, but an overwhelming and highly noted social media presence, Peterson is the first psychologist to rise to world-

---

[675] youtube.com/c/JordanPetersonVideos.

wide fame in this manner. Furthermore, it is completely independent of his academic achievements, which seem not to be as prominent. It is an interesting path, likely to be followed by others in the field.

Meaning and Belief

In more ways than the above-mentioned Internet prominence, Jordan B. Peterson deviates from his peers. His first book, *Maps of Meaning: The Architecture of Belief* from 1999, starts with a twelve pages long preface of an autobiographical nature, and a daringly frank one at that. He tells openly of his personal anguish and torment when working his way towards the discipline of psychology and his Jungian take on it.

Peterson is quite dramatic about his experience, which is evident already in the Latin title he has given his preface: *Descensus ad Inferos.* It is usually translated as *Descent into Hell*, though the Netherworld would be more accurate. The expression is mainly connected to the Christian tradition that Jesus went there after the crucifixion to liberate souls held captive, and ascended from it at his resurrection.

Jordan's Ordeal

Jordan B. Peterson took the first significant step in his search for meaning at the age of 12. While participating in the confirmation classes of his church he realized, "I could not swallow what I was being taught."[676] Concluding that religion was "for the ignorant, weak and superstitious," he stopped attending church.

At about the same time, he developed an interest in political issues, bothered by social injustices and the Cold War. A question that stood out to him was, "how did evil — particularly group-fostered evil — come to play its role in the world?" That led him to start as a volunteer for a "mildly socialist" po-

676 Jordan B. Peterson, *Maps of Meaning: The Architecture of Belief*, New York 1999, p. xii.

litical party. "Economic injustice was at the root of all evil, as far as I was concerned."

His political engagement continued into college, but with growing doubts. He saw a flaw in the attitude of his socialist friends, which he found confirmed in George Orwell's book *Road to Wigan Pier*: "Orwell said, essentially, that socialists did not really like the poor. They merely hated the rich."[677]

That is not exactly what Orwell stated, though. According to him, the socialists were no lovers of the working class, though claiming to be. And their hatred was aimed at the class they themselves belonged to — the bourgeoisie. He wrote about the socialist:

> *Though seldom giving much evidence of affection for the exploited, he is perfectly capable of displaying hatred — a sort of queer, theoretical, in* vacuo *hatred — against the exploiters. Hence the grand old Socialist sport of denouncing the bourgeoisie. It is strange how easily almost any Socialist writer can lash himself into frenzies of rage against the class to which, by birth or by adoption, he himself invariably belongs.*[678]

Peterson wrongly interpreted Orwell to mean that socialists, because of their own failure, hated those who were successful. He came to a general conclusion about any ideology, not just that of socialism: "Anyone who was out to change the world by changing others was to be regarded with suspicion." It made him leave political science after finishing his bachelor's degree.

But he did not stop pondering the problem of the Cold War and its threat of total nuclear destruction. To find what caused it, he began to study psychology.

As a psychology student, he visited a prison where he met

677 Ibid., p. xiii.

678 George Orwell, *Road to Wigan Pier*, London 1937, p. 212.

men who had committed brutal crimes. It made him wonder if he would ever be able to do the same. He had a recurring compulsion during university lectures: "I would unfailingly feel the urge to stab the point of my pen into the neck of the person in front of me."[679]

Although resisting it, he found the urge disturbing. He had never been aggressive, which he explained by mostly having been smaller and younger than his classmates — a strange argument from a psychologist, since it would rather imply suppressed aggression. And he did indeed come to a similar conclusion: "I was not much different from the violent prisoners — not *qualitatively* different. I could do what they could do (although I hadn't)."

Also, he began to have trouble conversing, because of a sort of voice inside his head, critically commenting the opinions he expressed. It repeated, "You don't believe that. That isn't true."[680] He wondered what part of him this voice was, and decided to experiment: "I tried only to say things that my internal reviewer would pass unchallenged." It made him more confident, which led him to conclude that he was that criticizing part, and the thoughts it approved were truly his. Reading Jung about the concept of *persona*, "the feigned individuality," he found an explanation.

But his ordeal was far from over. He was getting terrible nightmares, mostly on the theme of nuclear war. He had those apocalyptic dreams two or three times a week, for a year or more. In search for their meaning, he read Sigmund Freud's book on dream interpretation. Contrary to Freud's theory, he could not regard those nightmares of his as wish-fulfillments, nor as sexual in nature. He experienced them as more religious.[681]

His point about wish-fulfillment is clever. It can hardly be

[679] Peterson 1999, p. xvi.

[680] Ibid., p. xvii.

[681] Ibid., p. xix.

applied to nightmares. His dismissal of the sexual content of his dreams, though, might have been hasty. In an apocalyptic dream described in the book, his cousin, who was "the most beautiful woman I had ever seen," had been butchered by dogs offering the meat to him and other survivors, but he discovered the truth before eating it.[682] That could be interpreted as a dream treating a forbidden wish of his, a sexual attraction to his cousin. Of course, I do not suggest this was the case, but such a Freudian interpretation is possible.

Another episode, though not a dream, was when he came home from a college drinking party, self-disgusted and angry, and started to paint: "I sketched a harsh, crude picture of a crucified Christ — glaring and demonic — with a cobra wrapped around his naked waist, like a belt."[683] It disturbed him, as he found it sacrilegious. He didn't know why he painted it or what it meant, but again a sexual interpretation is not unthinkable, considering the party he came from and the naked demonic Christ with a serpent around his waist. It can be seen as an image of desires he felt were sinful. The symbolism gets even more suggestive by the fact that he hid the painting in his closet.

Still, Peterson found it all pointing at myth and religion, which made him start to study Jung's writing, although having trouble understanding it at first. In spite of that, this study made his nightmares cease, and he reached a revelation:

> I discovered that beliefs make the world, in a very real way — that beliefs are the world, in a more than metaphysical sense.[684]

He also learned that there are "universal moral absolutes" and furthermore:

682 Ibid., p. xviii.

683 Ibid., p. xix.

684 Ibid., p. xx.

I learned why people wage war — why the desire to maintain, protect and expand the domain of belief motivates even the most incomprehensible acts of group-fostered oppression and cruelty — and what might be done to ameliorate this tendency, despite its universality.

There is brave honesty in Peterson's deeply personal account of his way towards Jungian psychology, where he exposes himself more than what has been customary among Jungian and Freudian theorists, who have tended instead to regard themselves as objective observers, detached from what and whom they observe. In their role as therapists, they even see it as instrumental. They are supposed to remain completely disengaged in their relation to their patients, their own feelings untouched in the process, like innocent bystanders.

Whether they have managed that is another matter. Prejudice spreads easily in those who think they are immune to it, and emotions roam freely in those who deny them. By being transparent about his own emotional roller-coaster ride, Peterson admits to the intricate role the psyche plays also in a psychologist.

Nevertheless, his conclusions about the power of beliefs are debatable.

Beliefs

Peterson's claim that beliefs make the world is so general, it has to be interpreted figuratively, which is also what he seems to indicate. But he gets concrete when stating that beliefs are the reasons for wars and their cruelty.

It is true that beliefs, religious or ideological, have often been used to justify wars, and such justifications might have escalated the cruelty of them. As causes of war, though, beliefs are rarely sufficient explanations. Wars are initiated by rulers, and not by the people they rule. Accordingly, the reasons for war are those of the rulers — such as the pursuit of power, fortune, and glory. Peterson must surely have learned that from political science. Rulers are rarely driven by beliefs, although they often claim to be.

The soldiers, too, are usually driven by other things than beliefs when they march to war, if they at all have a say in it. Mostly they do not. They are simply commanded, whatever they think about the reason given to them by their rulers. True, their morale is increased if they believe the war is just, and deteriorates if they do not. But very rarely, if ever, is their conviction the cause of war, though it can have a great influence on its outcome.

Basically, war consist of an attacker and a defender, and the strongest argument for waging a war is being the latter, or pretending to be. It is not always clear. Both sides want to claim to be the defender — of their land, their religion, their well-being, their way of life. The attacker claims there was an imminent threat to those values, blaming the defender and thereby trying to switch their roles. It has been known to succeed.

The sad truth is that many wars are started as precautions, a defense in advance. Sometimes it is pretense and sometimes accurate. In any case, it is a vicious spiral, hard to escape.

Peterson reported his anguish since youth about the Cold War, which was an escalation of two sides preparing for defense. The nuclear arms race was called the balance of terror, where peace between the two sides was kept by the threat of total annihilation. A risky business, but it managed to keep a third world war off, and maybe still does. Until it doesn't.

Anyway, the Cold War had very little to do with belief.

Science and Myth

Peterson's book has the subtitle *The Architecture of Belief*. It may not be the most adequate description of the book's content. He ends the preface summarizing the arguments he is to present in the book, and there is no mention of belief. Instead, he describes a polarity of *things* as opposed to *narrative*, where the former is connected to science and the latter to myth, literature, and drama. The difference is one between objects and action.[685]

It is an oversimplification that doesn't hold up to scrutiny. Science deals with things as well as action, where the latter is definitely given the most attention. It is the activity of things, their internal and external movements, that science focuses on. Newton and Einstein calculated how celestial bodies move, Darwin explained how animals and plants evolve over time by natural selection, and so on. Without action, without change, there would not be anything to examine. Nothing in the universe is static. Science is a narration of the processes of nature, i.e., how things came to be and how they proceed.

Of course Peterson is right about myth, literature, and drama describing a series of events, but that is not different from how science describes reality. It is all action.

He continues by calling science the objective world, and the other one the world of value. That makes more sense, though both *objective* and *value* need to be defined, especially the latter. Science strives to figure out the laws of objective reality, which has through history proven to be a tricky task, but the aim is clear enough. What value means to myth, literature, and drama, on the other hand, is much more of a handful.

Peterson explains it as "what is and what should be, from the perspective of emotion and action," which is not very clarifying. He probably refers to emotional attitudes towards reality and how to deal with it. Some events are wanted and others are shunned. Value is subjective, of course, and when we attach it to things as well as actions, we are definitely leaving objective reality. Still, it is very real to us. Since we are part of the world, we relate to it by how it affects us.

A scientific description of the world that succeeds to be truly objective has little relevance to us. We need the subjective perspective, whether fictional or realistic. That is very likely to be an essential ingredient in the formation of our mythologies. They are tools to turn the world we live in into our world.

[685] Ibid., p. xxi.

Science is not different. We explore and explain the world so that we understand it. Whatever we do, it is always about us.

Peterson continues by dividing the world "as a forum for action" into three parts, which "tend to manifest themselves in typical patterns of metaphoric representation," and here he enters the domain of myth, as well as Jungian interpretations of it:

> *First is unexplored territory — the Great Mother, nature, creative and destructive, source and final resting place of all determinate things. Second is explored territory — the Great Father, culture, protective and tyrannical, cumulative ancestral wisdom. Third is the process that mediates between unexplored and explored territory — the Divine Son, the archetypal individual, creative exploratory Word and vengeful adversary.*

So, it is the mother, the father, and the son. The way Peterson describes them, the first is a typical Mother Earth deity, the second an authoritarian high god, and the third a hero character with similarities to Christ.

When he speaks about unexplored and explored, he probably means exploited. Nature is largely explored, but not yet completely exploited — well, we are rapidly getting there. One could also use the concepts of nature versus civilization. That makes the third entity, the mediator, some kind of balancing factor between them. An ideal, like the image of Christ.

Personal Interest

To Peterson, the devilish threat is when group identification is made absolute, whereby civilization turns tyrannical, and the antidote is loyalty to personal interest, which he also calls subjective meaning.

That is what the hero archetype represents:

Loyalty to personal interest is equivalent to identification
with the archetypal hero — the "savior" — who upholds
his association with the creative Word in the face of death,
and despite group pressure to conform.[686]

The Jungian ideal of individuation is self-realization, but
not necessarily loyalty to personal interests. This is Peterson's
own twist to the story, and it is a significant one. He claims that
it "provides the individual with a standpoint that simultaneously transcends and maintains the group,"[687] by which he
seems to mean that an individual of integrity is capable of interacting constructively with the collective.

That is probably true, up to a point. But if the individual
is regarded as more important than the group, which is what
loyalty to personal interests indicates, then that person is more
likely to be detrimental to it — and definitely so if all members
have the same priority. The collective would cease to function
and break apart. On a larger scale, society would crumble.

Both Jungian and Freudian psychology have distinct individualistic characteristics, already in their premise that personal psychological issues mainly have internal causes and
should be treated accordingly, by individual analysis. Freud
went so far as to describe the conflict between personal needs
and social demands as something akin to war. Jung had a less
dramatic view, where his idea of the collective unconscious instead formed sort of a bridge between the individual and the
collective. But he did stress the importance of individual self-
discovery, symbolized by the archetypal hero's quest.

So, Peterson's insistence on loyalty to personal interests
may be tendentious, but it is not that far-fetched as an interpretation of depth psychology. It is provocatively expressed,
which is probably quite intentional.

His autobiographical account, with the significant title

---

[686] Ibid., pp. xxi f.

[687] Ibid., p. xxii.

Descensus ad Inferos, shows disgust at what society can be at its worst and how this brings out the worst in men. Loyalty to personal interests and resistance towards group pressure as a model for the hero implies personal responsibility. The malady of society is no excuse to submit, but a call to rise and resist. No doubt, that is one kind of hero, and Peterson seems eager to follow that path.

To apply his own definitions, his text is not aimed at being objective, but at value.

What Is and What It Means

The polarity of object and action, or science and myth, boils down to the two perspectives of *what is* and *what it means,* whereof the latter dominates in the human mind. According to Peterson, we are practically unable to relate to things without assigning some specific meaning to them, and that meaning is inseparable from the thing itself. In other words, it is what it means. This thinking is established already in early childhood:

> *Everything a child encounters has this dual nature, expe-*
> *rienced by the child as part of a unified totality. Everything*
> *is something, and means something — and the distinction*
> *between essence and significance is not necessarily*
> *drawn.*[688]

That is one way to describe the child's unavoidably subjective perception of the world it lives in. All things are seen in relation to what they are to the child. That includes priorities. Things are more or less meaningful to the child, based on their influence.

This is probably true for all animals, as an effective way to deal with the complexity of reality, such as the division of things into edible or not, other species into predator or prey, and members of its own species into friend or foe. It is a sur-

[688] Ibid., p. 2.

vival instinct, so we keep it into adulthood, and by time it gets increasingly intricate. Yet, as a behavioral process it is quite transparent.

Peterson uses other words for this: "The 'natural,' pre-experimental, or mythical mind is in fact *primarily* concerned with meaning."[689] Calling it natural is so uncontroversial that the quotes are redundant, and mythical depends on its definition. If he suggests that this basic behavior is a kind of personal myth-making, he is going too far. It would be enough to describe it as symbolic representation — or better yet, classification. We sort things into categories according to how we need to relate to them.

But it is the concept pre-experimental that is the most questionable. Experimenting is not something exclusive to modern science, nor is the mental process involved in it. It is safe to say that people have experimented for ages, also applying the trial-and-error procedure.

Animals do it, too. The cat lightly touching an unfamiliar object with its paw, and jumping away if it moves, is experimenting. It is the curiosity that famously killed the cat. A toddler puts strange things in its mouth to check if they are edible, children test how long they can hold their breath or who runs the fastest, and so on. The experiments of our distant ancestors led to the use of fire, flint tools, and clothing. There never was a pre-experimental mind.

Peterson limits the experimental mind to what goes on in modern science, which he calls objective, but that is a question of method and not of mental capacity and inclination. People have always made research, with the quality of the results depending on previous knowledge and technical resources.

Also the scientific demand of being evidence-based is just as old. What has changed is what our increased knowledge allows as evidence, and the sophistication with which it is applied. The underlying thought process is the same.

[689] Ibid., p. 3.

Peterson's narrow definition of scientific thinking leads him to dismiss the possibility that it exists in mythology. He states, "Myth is *not* primitive proto-science."[690] Instead, he defines it as "description of the world as it *signifies* (for *action*)." In other words, myth describes the world as what it means to us and how we should act in it. But that doesn't exclude it from also being scientific.

Nor do the rather elaborate definitions he gives science:

Science might be considered "description of the world with regards to those aspects that are consensually apprehensible" or "specification of the most effective mode of reaching an end (given a defined end)."

It is strange that he makes the reservation "might be." Just about anything might be. The question is if he claims it or not — and he must, since he uses it in his further reasoning. Peterson often makes reservations of this kind, while still continuing to apply those proposals as if they were established facts. Something that might be cannot be used as evidence for something else, it just makes the latter another might be.

Nevertheless, his definitions of science can be applied to myth as well. Their description of the world is consensually apprehensible, and was so even more when they were formed. That doesn't mean they are correct, which is anyway not demanded by Peterson's definition. When the myths were formed, they were at least plausible, or they would have been quickly dismissed — unless they had a significant entertainment value, which is the main reason for their persistence to this day.

His second definition is so vague that it can be applied to much more than science. The most effective mode of reaching an end can be running in a straight line from start to finish, the fall of the curtain in the theater, or for that matter a swift sui-

690 Ibid., p. 9.

cide. Peterson might refer to the scientific principle of Occam's razor, which is to find the solution reached by the fewest steps. If that is what he suggests, then mythology has an abundance of examples of it.

For example, an almighty deity creating the world is at least as direct as the Big Bang theory, also considering the question of what preceded it. Among creation myths in particular, there are many instances of evident rational thinking showing that they were composed from deep pondering of what the beginning of the world might have been like. The results were often quite ingenious, considering the few facts known at the time.

Peterson gives the account of a Sumerian creation myth, which leads him to the above statement about myth not being protoscience, i.e., ancient science with insufficiently developed methods. He makes an odd choice, since his source is a modern reconstruction of the myth, because of the lack of primary sources.[691] A better choice would be the Babylonian creation story *Enuma Elish*, which is preserved on clay tablets from that distant era, and it carries a lot of Sumerian influence.

When examining any myth, it is crucial to get a trustworthy source, the older the better. In the book Peterson uses, Mircea Eliade's *A History of Religious Ideas*, volume 1, *Enuma Elish* appears just a few pages after the Sumerian example, unfortunately also retold by Eliade, albeit with several quotes from translations of the original text.

Peterson actually treats *Enuma Elish* extensively later in his book, and there he quotes big chunks from a translation of the Babylonian text.[692] It is an unfortunate choice of translation, though, namely that of Alexander Heidel, originally published in 1942 and revised in 1951. His interpretation of the text is ad-

---

[691] Ibid., p. 8. Quoted from Mircea Eliade, *A History of Religious Ideas*, vol. 1, transl. Willard R. Trask, Chicago 1978 (first published in French 1976), pp. 57f.

[692] Ibid., pp. 108-136.

mittedly focused on comparisons with Genesis of the Bible, and for Christian scholars and priests: "This little study is intended primarily not for the professional Assyriologist but rather for the Old Testament scholar and the Christian minister."[693] Such sources should be used with caution.

That being said, the reconstruction of the Sumerian myth still shows evident signs of rational thinking when describing the forces at work in the creation of the world.

In the beginning is the goddess Nammu, who represents the primordial sea. This is a very common starting point in creation myths, which can be explained by the vastness of the sea to the beholder. It seems to have no end and be eternally the same through time. Nammu gives birth to the first couple, An and Ki, representing the sky and the earth, who in turn produce Enlil, god of the atmosphere, separating the sky from the earth.

This is as far as the quote in Peterson's book goes, and it is enough to conclude that rational thinking was involved in putting the myth together.

It all makes sense. Out of the primordial sea come the sky and the earth, and the atmosphere holding them apart. It is a cosmology that was very plausible to people who had no knowledge of the universe, which is why this pattern can be found in many ancient creation myths.

But Peterson objects strongly to the idea that this is a sign of any kind of scientific thinking:

We appear to have made the presumption that stories such as these — myths — were equivalent in function and intent (but were inferior methodologically) to empirical or post-experimental description.[694]

[693] Alexander Heidel, *The Babylonian Genesis: The Story of Creation*, Chicago 1963 (first edition 1942), p. v.

[694] Peterson 1999, p. 8.

He calls such understanding of myths fundamentally absurd, and explains that "the Sumerians could not describe (or conceive of) many of those things the processes of science have revealed to us."[695] Of course they could not, and surely the future development of science will reach conclusions we are not yet able to fathom. Still, we claim to be capable of scientific thinking — such as it is today — and the Sumerians could make the same claim in their time. They possessed the ability to reason and applied it to their creation myth, as did so many other ancient cultures.

Peterson states, "The mythic universe is *a place to act*, not *a place to perceive*." But of course it can be both. It has to be, or action would be blind.

Science is to Peterson about *what is*, as opposed to myth, which is about *what should be*, or *value*, as he also calls it. This value is to him nothing but moral. With such a polarity, he needs to claim that myth is not about what is, and science not about what should be. It is doubtful that any of those claims are valid.

Firstly, all values are not moral, nor can it be said that moral values are the most important ones. We also cherish survival, pleasure, humor, intellectual stimulation, and so on. If he wants to claim that moral is the only significant value, he should simply call it that, i.e., replace value with moral. Otherwise, he is mistaken. He states that "no functioning society or individual can avoid rendering moral judgment,"[696] but whether true or not, it doesn't exclude other values.

As for *what is* as opposed to *what should be*, creation myths have many components of what there is that cannot be changed, such as the sea, the sky, and the earth. Also, the many deities of mythology, with their different powers, indicate vast areas out of human control. That is even a functioning definition of deity — an invisible power to explain what is beyond

[695] Ibid., p. 9.

[696] Ibid., p. 10.

human control and comprehension. It would in most religions be absurd, even blasphemous, to state what the deities and their actions should be.

In science, *what should be* has very often been part of the equations and still frequently is. Some examples are monstrous, like the theories of racial biology and eugenics, which flourished at the universities quite recently in our history. Others strive to be globally benevolent, like ecology, climate change research, and gender studies. Science is rarely as objective as many of its proponents claim. Behind a lot of research lies an idea of what should be.

The whole discipline of medicine is an obvious example. The research is all about how things can be improved. Viruses are not studied solely to understand what they are, but also to find how they can be fought. Still, that can hardly be regarded as unscientific.

So, Peterson's model doesn't hold, at least not as he defines it, which is partly quite fuzzy. In spite of that, he uses this model to explain the major function of mythology as an aid for us when making choices in life, also when we lack sufficient information to do it comfortably:

> *It is, traditionally speaking, our knowledge of good and evil, our moral sensibility, that allows us this ability. It is our mythological conventions, operating implicitly or explicitly, that guide our choices.*[697]

That may be applicable to some mythologies, but far from all. Certainly, there are religions with myths firmly based on moral teaching, and Christianity is a prominent example of this. It can be said about all three Abrahamic religions, as well as Zoroastrianism, which had an influence on them. Beyond that, it is less clear or even all but absent.

For example, the immoral behavior of the deities in Greek

697 Ibid.

mythology was a gripe already among the philosophers of that time. Still they were worshipped. Also the deities in Norse mythology were known to use deception to get what they wanted, not to mention brute force. The pantheon of Indian mythology is so complicated, as are the ancient texts about them, that it is difficult to come to any general conclusion about their messages. Mythology is about so much more and so much else than good and evil.

Nevertheless, Peterson is convinced that the study of "mythological commonalities might comprise the first developmental stage in the conscious evolution of a truly universal system of morality."[698]

It may seem like a good thing, but is actually scary. Very scary. A universal system of morality means one single moral code to be applied to all. It has been tried again and again in history, and the result has never been a thing of benevolence. Instead, it has been an instrument of oppression and cruelty — just the things that terrified Peterson in his youth. When based on religious beliefs it has allowed for even more oppression and cruelty.

We would all like to see the world become a better place, but moral is the wrong word for what we need. Moral is the forceful application of rules, where the force is not concerned with the suffering it brings, nor does it invite criticism or even discussion. The words that indicate a positive and genuinely healing direction are compassion and empathy, which are in essence opposites to moral. Where moral is constraining, compassion and empathy are liberating. Where moral is vindictive, compassion and empathy are forgiving. The former leads to blame and persecution, but the latter to tolerance and mutual understanding.

It cannot be stressed enough — a universal system of morality should be avoided. It has proven to lead to immense suffering and injustice.

[698] Ibid., p. 12.

Jordan B. Peterson, who is evidently familiar with and sympathetic to Christian values, should contemplate how Jesus treated the woman brought before him, who had been caught in adultery. Those who brought her said that the law of Moses demands that she should be stoned. He replied that the one without sin could cast the first stone. When they had left, he told the woman that nor would he condemn her.[699]

That surpasses moral.

The morally based quest that Peterson proposes involves three subqueries:

1) What is? What is the nature (meaning, the signifi-cance) of the current state of experience?
2) What should be? To what (desirable, valuable) end should that state be moving?
3) How should we therefore act? What is the nature of the specific processes by which the present state might be transformed into that which is desired?[700]

Had he not previously specified that what should be and what is valuable are of a moral nature, this list seems to point to the desirable, whatever that is, whether moral or not. But he has, and it is emphasized by the use of the word *should*. This is a moral path, which makes it more of a trap.

Apart from that, it is a straightforward three-step procedure for just about any situation: observe it, evaluate it, and improve it. Easier said than done, especially the second and third phase.

Scanning mythology for optimal moral solutions is hardly going to do better than it has done in the past. If our predecessors did not succeed, although they put faith in their myths, we are not likely to do any better. New definitions of what should be improved and new ideas on how to do it are needed,

[699] John 8:3-11.

[700] Peterson 1999, p. 13.

but they are surely hard to find. If they were not, it would have been fixed long ago.

Peterson's vague recipe contains nothing new and gives no workable instruction. It just says that we should solve the problem. We already knew that. He points to "proper analysis of mythology" leading to the solution by showing what should be and what should be done, but he doesn't specify what that is.

We are just to trust that the solution is there, and go search for it. He should at least tell us what he has found.

Metamythology

Peterson lists four classes of myths, which he clams to provide a more complete answer to the three questions mentioned above. These four classes are:

> (1) *myths describing a current or pre-existent stable state (sometimes a paradise, sometimes a tyranny);*
> (2) *myths describing the emergence of something anomalous, unexpected, threatening and promising into this initial state;*
> (3) *myths describing the dissolution of the pre-existent stable state into chaos, as a consequence of the anomalous or unexpected occurrence;*
> (4) *myths describing the regeneration of stability [paradise regained (or, tyranny regenerated)], from the chaotic mixture of dissolute previous experience and anomalous information.*[701]

This seems more like four stages of one myth than different classes of myths. Together, the four parts form a story from beginning to end. Peterson doesn't explain in what way they are to be seen as separate myths. None of them on its own forms anything even similar to a complete story.

[701] Ibid., p. 16.

Then he speaks of *metamythology* and *metamyth*, which he doesn't define, but the term *meta* indicates that he means myth about myth, i.e., a myth that comments on itself. Also, his metamyth concept is similar to Joseph Campbell's *monomyth*, discussed in the chapter about him, which he applied to hero myths. Campbell used the concept for the general pattern he claimed to exist in all hero myths. Peterson seems to suggest that his four classes, or stages, form a pattern that is also universal.

That may well be, since what he describes is very close to the structure in any plot, according to dramaturgy, which is based on Aristotle's *Poetics*. First, there is an initial situation, then something unexpected happens that needs to be dealt with, the drama intensifies into a crisis, and finally there is the resolution. This structure is found in just about every drama and myth, for the simple reason that it is how, as Aristotle put it, a story gets a beginning, a middle, and an end.

The dramaturgical perspective is extremely useful, even necessary, when analyzing myths. They are stories and must be understood as such.

Peterson uses his four classes of myth to describe what he calls the *Metamythological Cycle of the Way*, which starts and ends at the same point, with the "establishment of conditional, but determinate moral knowledge (belief)."[702]

Some things about this are unclear. Does he mean that belief is synonymous to moral knowledge? But belief can consist of so much more than moral. Also, what part of it is conditional and what is determinate? He probably means that any condition has its determinate moral, but that would lead to a vast number of different morals, which makes a universal system of morality so complicated that it must be close to impossible to utilize. If he means that this moral is a formula of sorts that can be applied to any situation, then he should present that formula.

[702] Ibid., p. 17.

He is yet to present his conception of the universal system of morality. What are its principles and rules?

The *way* of which he speaks, he connects to the Chinese concept *Tao*, and gives it a definition: "The 'way' is the path of life and its purpose."[703] That is a clear definition, which also fits the Chinese concept quite well, provided that the perspective is not individual.

The *Tao Te Ching*, which is what Peterson refers to regarding Tao, does put demands on the individual, but the purpose is for the world as a whole. Humankind should adapt to what is natural, and not interfere with it.

Peterson mentions chaos in the third of his four classes. It is what happens when a system of belief, which he calls its "stories," is shook by something unexpected to which the proper response is not known. That induces fear:

> *When we are in the domain of the known, so to speak, there is no reason for fear. Outside that domain, panic reigns.*[704]

The "so to speak" seems redundant, but is probably Peterson's way of stating that the known doesn't have to be factually correct as long as it is believed to be. The fear of the unknown results in all kinds of overreactions, whereof some can be very detrimental. When new circumstances demand modifications of the stories of a belief, the fear of the unknown tends to keep those modifications at a minimum. Too much of it brings chaos, but too little causes stagnation, which turns to chaos as it leaves us unprepared for future change.

This fear of the consequences of change is where Peterson sees a significant cause of social unrest:

> *It is for this reason that individuals are highly motivated to avoid sudden manifestations of the unknown. And this*

[703] Ibid., p. 16.
[704] Ibid., p. 18.

There are many indications in all levels of society that this
is correct. The fear of the unknown leads to resistance towards
change. It is the comfort of knowing what you have, as opposed to the uncertainty of what you might get. Accordingly,
change is often rejected with the argument that it will not lead
to perfection, although it should be enough that the change is
an improvement of the present situation.

Also, loud calls for change are often propagating the return to a real or imagined previous state, which is referred to
as the good old days. The past is regarded as known, but the
future is not.

As Hamlet in his famous monologue concludes, the unknown is why people fear death, which "makes us rather bear
those ills we have, than fly to others that we know not of."[705]

Another example is xenophobia, the fear of strangers,
which has caused a lot of animosity, even hatred and horrific
brutality.

Indeed, Peterson is right about the fear of the unknown as
a strong and often destructive force in humankind. What is less
convincing is his roundabout way of reaching this conclusion.
The fear has little to do with mythology and beliefs. It is more
about instinctual behavior, relating to the threats we know as
opposed to the ones we don't. The latter makes our imagination go wild. That is the trigger in just about every horror story.

It is about what we can expect. When we don't know what
that is, we tend to expect the worst. That is why we avoid being
exposed to the unknown, individually as well as socially. It is
not about holding on to what Peterson calls our protective cultural stories, though they may be used as excuses for our actions. It is about fear.

---

[705] Act III, Scene I. William Shakespeare, *Hamlet*, edited by John Livingstone Lowes, New York 1914, p. 68.

Peterson's concept of the cultural story is still interesting. There is definitely such a thing as cultural identity — and it is fiercely protected in any culture. Its power lies in its tradition, which is a value continuously increasing over time. The older a culture gets, the more firmly its components are cherished and protected. Any change will be opposed by most members of that culture. In this identity, mythology plays a role, as does just about every other aspect of the culture, such as language, customs, and history.

Protection of the cultural identity, its heritage, is not mainly based on fear, but on habit. We humans are habitual creatures. As a cultural component is repeated it becomes habitual, a tradition by which the culture identifies itself. A drastic change of it risks damaging that identity and thereby the bonds of commonality the members of the culture share.

A culture consists of countless components, on the individual as well as the social level, which have been established by time. It is traceable through its history. Therefore, it can be seen as a story — the history of the formation of a cultural identity. Of course, the mythology and religion of that culture are important parts of its story.

Enuma Elish
Examining mythology in greater detail, Peterson applies the three "constituent elements of experience" he calls the unknown, the knower, and the known. Those three basic components can be creative as well as destructive. There is also a primal source, "the precosmogonic chaos," for which he uses the ouroboros symbol, the serpent biting its own tail.[706]

It is a neat set, in which the knower is the process of exploration, which sort of mediates between the unknown and the known. The chaos existing prior to creation is the primal source without which there would be nothing out of which anything could emerge.

706 Peterson 1999, pp. 89f.

But it gets complicated when he continues by applying it to the Babylonian creation myth *Enuma Elish*, where he sees four main characters: Tiamat, who is both the ouroboros and the Great Mother, which contradicts his model and yet he says that combination is frequently the case; Apsu (also spelled Abzu), who is her mate; the elder gods he calls their children, which is true for the first four of them; and Marduk, who is the hero deity:

> *Tiamat symbolizes the great unknown, the matrix of the world; Apsu the known, the pattern that makes regulated existence possible. The elder gods symbolize the common psychological attributes of humanity (the fragments or constituent elements of consciousness), and constitute a more thorough representation of the constituent elements of the patriarchal known; Marduk, greatest of the secondary deities, represents the process that eternally mediates between matrix and regulated existence.*

That is one way of interpreting the symbolism of the myth, but it is hardly how the Babylonians saw it. Nor is it in any way evident how Peterson came to these conclusions. They are quite far-fetched as explanations of the content in a myth dating thousands of years back.

Tiamat, a name that means ocean, is the primordial sea so common in creation myths, and Apsu is a lake. One water is salt, the other fresh. When these waters met, deities were born, marking the beginning of creation. Those deities also represent main entities in the world. About the first two mentioned in the myth, Lahmu and Lahamu, nothing is known for sure. They may have to do with light, since some translations say that they shone, or they may be connected to mud. Both are possible and make sense — light would appear at some point, and mud is found where water is.

The next deities, Anshar and Kishar, represent what is above and below the horizon, i.e., heaven and earth. They gave birth to Anu, a sky deity, who in turn gave birth to Nudimmud, a deity of fresh water, also called Ea, or Enki in Sumerian.

After that, the story of the battle between those primeval beings begins, which is something often seen in polytheistic mythologies. A number of such powerful creatures is bound to trigger rivalry. The primordial deities, Tiamat and Apsu, clash with the younger ones. Apsu is swiftly killed by Ea, but it takes his son Marduk to defeat and kill Tiamat, on the condition that this will grant him supreme power. Out of her corpse, he builds the world. Finally, he lets Ea create humans to serve the deities.

Humans entering the story late is also typical for polytheistic mythologies. All those deities are busy interacting with each other, before even thinking of creating humans. Another characteristic of those myths is that humans have a lesser role in them, since they can't measure up to the magnificent deities.

It should be noted that Marduk is a deity of Babylonian origin and worship, whereas the previous ones are connected to Sumerian mythology. So, the story is also one of how a Babylonian deity became the ruler of the Sumerian deities. His sovereignty is emphasized at the end of *Enuma Elish*, when the other deities praise Marduk and give him fifty names describing aspects of his might.

One character is missing in Peterson's short summary, also in his longer treatment of the myth. It is Mummu, Apsu's vizier, who is present at these primeval events, maybe already when the waters of Tiamat and Apsu are mixed. He may have been a mist connecting them, like rain from a cloud. He is both eager and instrumental in Apsu's efforts to kill the other deities, but while Ea kills Apsu, he just imprisons Mummu and holds him with a nose-rope. It is unclear what his fate is.

These are traits of the mythological character called the trickster, active in many creation myths, sometimes benign and sometimes causing misery — to the deities as well as to humans. The trickster has his own intentions, often unknown to others, and his own clever methods. It is definitely a figure to examine when analyzing myths, and an archetype frequently discussed in Jungian discourse. Considering this, it is odd that Mummu is completely absent from Peterson's treatment of *Enuma Elish*.

Jordan B. Peterson insists on a symbolic interpretation of the myth that is closer to his psychology than to the minds of the Babylonians. He rejects emphatically the possibility of creation myths being in any way scientific:

> *Creation myths are generally considered primitive or superstitious attempts to perform the magic of modern science. We assume that our ancestors were trying to do the same thing we do when we construct our cosmological theories and describe the generation of the objective world. This presumption is wrong.*[707]

I beg to differ. His wording is one of exaggeration. Of course our ancestors were not trying to perform modern science, of which they knew nothing, nor were they at all able to do the same as we when constructing our cosmology — which, by the way, most of us today are also unable to comprehend, as complicated as it has gotten. But they were thinking rationally and they were trying to explain, at least speculate in a plausible way about the creation of the world. Plausible to people at their time, that is. *Enuma Elish*, too, shows several examples of this reasoning.

One would expect Peterson to argue for his view by pointing out the limited intellectual abilities of our ancestors, but he goes in the opposite direction. He claims that they were wiser than that: "Our ancestors were not as simple-minded as we think they were, and their theories of the generation of the cosmos were not merely primitive science." He has a point when he continues:

[707] Ibid., p. 108.

Archaic theories of creation attempted to account for the existence of the world, as experienced in totality (which means, including meaning), and not for the isolated fact of the material world.

Just about all ancient creation myths show a belief in a world that is not only material. Already the presence of deities proves that. Rational thinking alone would lead to it, since there was so much in the world that could not be explained by what was seen. There had to be invisible powers at work. And actually, our distant ancestors were right. How else to explain gravity, the warmth of sunshine, the movement of the celestial bodies, and so on? Invisible powers shape and act on our world.

As for meaning, it is a word with several possible definitions. Our ancestors would assume that what happened in the world was intentional, like their own actions, or nothing would happen. Invisible powers had intentions with their actions, and it would be advantageous for humans to understand those intentions, so as to predict and adapt to them. Again, that was rational, if not to say scientific, in the time of our ancestors.

Myths are stories, which means there is a narrative with characters interacting, and the Aristotelian beginning, middle, and end. That is true for creation myths as well, but their beginning takes us all the way back to the birth of the world. Those speculations about that utterly unknown time usually have a cosmological perspective, telling how the earth, the sky, and the heavenly bodies appeared. They are quite logical, in the sense that they were at least plausible to their original audiences.

Once the fundamental components of the world are at place, the creation myth leaves its beginning and enters the middle, where distinct characters engage in all kinds of drama. Deities get personalities and conflicting aims, whereby calamity ensues. Additional creatures may appear on the way, but they are incorporated in the character driven drama, which is the main thing. The plot thickens. The end of the story comes when the world reaches the state it had at the time of the original audience.

This pattern can be seen in a vast majority of creation myths, including *Enuma Elish*. They start with cosmological events, continue with an anthropomorph drama, and end in the world familiar to the original audience.

Accordingly, the beginning of Enuma Elish is the birth of the first few deities. When they start to interact, we have entered the middle part of the story, and when they have settled their differences to unite under Marduk's reign, the end is reached. The drama is over and the story completed.

This structure of myths is age-old and still very familiar to us. Otherwise, we would not be able to connect to them.

Ouroboros

A central figure in Peterson's perspective on creation myths is *ouroboros*, for which he uses the alternative spelling *uroboros*, the serpent forming a circle by biting its own tail. He applies it to *Enuma Elish*, as discussed above.

In another chapter he expands the meaning of the concept considerably:

> *The uroboros symbolizes the union of* known *(associated with spirit) and* unknown *(associated with matter), explored and unexplored; symbolizes the juxtaposition of the "masculine" principles of security, tyranny and order with the "feminine" principles of darkness, dissolution, creativity and chaos.*[708]

That's not all. It also stands for "the *knower*, who can transform chaos into order, and order into chaos." It exists "everywhere, and at all times," and furthermore:

[708] Ibid., p. 141.

*It unites the beginning and the end, being and becoming,
in the endless circle of its existence. It serves as symbol for
the ground of reality itself.*

He goes on about it in equally majestic terms, too many to quote here. Peterson describes it as the original force of creation and recreation, without which nothing would have emerged. That is as close to an omnipotent ever-present high god as one can come: "It has served mankind as the most ubiquitous and potent of primordial gods."[709]

Other Jungians have also stressed the importance of this symbol, as discussed earlier in this book, and it can be found in several mythologies — but far from as many as should be expected if it had the grand significance Peterson ascribes to it. The image of the serpent forming a circle is not far-fetched in human fantasies. The mere fact that this animal is devoid of any limbs makes the image near at hand. That has certainly been used as a symbol for mythological and cosmological concepts — but again, far from globally, and even less so with the meaning Peterson gives it.

The risk with this attitude is that any circle or serpent in myths, dreams, and ancient symbolism is explained as representing ouroboros, which is what Peterson tends to do in his book and several other Jungians in their writing. But a circle can be just a ring, and a serpent just a snake. That's most often the case.

Even in mythology, the appearance of a serpent biting its tail is not necessarily of central importance and significance. For example, the Norse myth about the Midgard Serpent growing so big that it encircled the whole world and bit its own tail, does in no way point to its primordial sovereignty. It is the child of a deity and a giantess, so it could not have been present from the beginning. Its role is more important at the end, since when it releases its tail, the final battle of Ragnarök begins.

[709] Ibid., p. 142.

Making generalizations about myths and their components leads to misconceptions and negligence towards their differences. Although similarities are easy to find, so are differences, and it is a mistake to allow the former to overshadow or even discard the latter.

Still, it has been a favorite pastime among Jungians, as well as many mythologists.

Inconsistencies

In his wordy and partially inconsistent text, Peterson makes some strange statements, which give the impression that he jumps to conclusions in the eagerness to present arguments for his theories. In some cases it gets rather amusing.

For example, he says about creation myths: "Primordial myths of creation tend to portray the origin of things as the consequence of at least one of two related events."[710] Well, how else would processes of creation, or any process, advance if not as consequences of events? Regarding theories about myths in general, he states:

A good theory about the structure of myth should let you see how a story you couldn't even understand previously might shed new and useful light on the meaning of your life.[711]

There is no reason to assume that a myth should shed light on the meaning of an individual life, or for that matter the life of humankind. We may feel that some myths do, in one way or other, but it cannot be assumed that it is a prerequisite. A theory containing this condition is most likely to have started with such a demand, and molded itself around it. That might be scientific in some way, but it is not what is expected of objective science.

[710] Ibid., p. 110.

[711] Ibid., p. 98.

Occasionally, Peterson also contradicts himself, which easily happens in a text as long and complex as the well over 500 pages of his book. To give one example, he says about our attitudes towards similarities and differences, "We seem peculiarly aware of our differences, however, and not of our similarities."[712] Just a few pages later, he makes what is in essence the opposite statement: "We cannot see the unknown, because we are protected from it by everything familiar and unquestioned."[713]

Are we blind to the familiar, or does it blind us from seeing what is not familiar? It can't be both, or we would be completely blind.

As a matter of fact, we would be unable to see our differences if we could not see our similarities, and vice versa. The one is dependent on the other. As for the unknown and the familiar, or simply the unknown and the known, it is like saying that we can't know what we don't know. That may be true in some sense, but it is also meaningless. The words are conditional. What is definitely accurate, though, is that we can get to know what we don't know, or we would never have been able to expand our knowledge.

Yin and Yang and Tao

Peterson is, like several other Jungians, prejudiced towards the material he uses, so that he sees what he wants to see in it, even when that is doubtful or just wrong. Comparing mythological cosmologies, he states:

> *In the Far East, similarly, the cosmos is imagined as composed of the interplay between* yang *and* yin, *chaos and order — that is to say, unknown or unexplored territory and known or explored territory.*[714]

[712] Ibid., p. 94.

[713] Ibid., p. 99.

[714] Ibid., p. 100.

No. Yang and yin do not represent chaos and order, nor unexplored and explored territory. They are linked opposites in the sense of heaven and earth, male and female, light and dark, warm and cold, and so on. The basic meaning of the concepts is the sunny side and the shadow side, such as with a hill, where the sunshine only reaches one side and the other is in constant shade. That is why the two are connected and together form a whole. It is not one or the other, but one and the other.

Then there is an illustration with an extended description of yin and yang.[715] Here he has added characteristics that are even farther from the meaning of those two concepts. He correctly gives yang the characteristics of masculinity and day, but wrongly adds order, the known, authoritarianism, and fascism. Yin represents femininity and night, but not his additional suggestions chaos, the unknown, decadence, and nihilism.

Apart from his misunderstanding of yin and yang, how could Western concepts of the 19th and 20th centuries at all be contained in this thousands of years old cosmology from China? When comparing ancient phenomena to modern ones, it is first of all necessary to assure a proper understanding of them, and not just twist them into what fits a favored model.

One source Peterson uses for his understanding of yin and yang is Richard Wilhelm's explanation in his famous translation of the Chinese ancient classic the *I Ching*, where yin and yang are fundamental. But Wilhelm doesn't use any of the descriptions criticized above.

He states instead that "speculations of a gnostic-dualistic character are foreign to the original thought of the *I Ching*; what it posits is simply the ridgepole, the line."[716] The line in

<hr>

[715] Ibid., p. 338.

[716] Richard Wilhelm, *The I Ching or Book of Changes*, transl. Cary F. Baynes, Princeton 1971 (originally published in German 1924), p. lv.

question is the basic component of the *I Ching* trigrams and hexagrams.

As for chaos, the *Tao Te Ching* describes it as a primordial state out of which Tao, the Way, rose and caused order. Chapter 25 states that Tao, born before heaven and earth, finished chaos. Therefore, "it can be called the mother of the whole world."[717] The chapter ends:

> *Man is ruled by Earth.*
> *Earth is ruled by Heaven.*
> *Heaven is ruled by the Way.*
> *The Way is ruled by itself.*

Yin and yang are only mentioned once, in chapter 42, where it says:

> *All things carry yin and embrace yang.*
> *They reach harmony by blending with the vital breath.*[718]

The vital breath is *qi*, comparable to the Indian concept of *prana*, or to Western ideas of a life energy. More relevant here, though, is the description that all things carry yin and embrace yang, which means that both are present in everything, sort of like a chemistry consisting of just two particles, or physics with just two energies, one positive and one negative.

Idealism

Jordan B. Peterson's attitude towards mythology can be categorized as idealistic. He is a knight in shiny armor fighting the dragon of the evil in the world, which is the suppression of individualism. That is the trap of group identification, and it has to be overcome for society to be rejuvenated:

[717] Stenudd 2015, p. 123.
[718] Ibid., p. 182.

This means that pursuit of individual interest — development of true individuality — is equivalent to identification with the hero. Such identification renders the world bearable, despite its tragedies, and reduces neurotic suffering, which destroys faith, to an absolute minimum.[719]

He states that this is the message everyone wants to hear, and continues:

Risk your security. Face the unknown. Quit lying to yourself, and do what your heart truly tells you to do. You will be better for it, and so will the world.

It is with this goal in mind that he interprets mythology to contain the same message. His language becomes religious when he insists on the necessity of liberating the individual. On the last page of his text, between two quotes from the non-canonical *Gospel of Thomas*, he declares:

A society predicated upon belief in the paramount divinity of the individual allows personal interest to flourish and to serve as the power that opposes the tyranny of culture and the terror of nature.[720]

That is Jordan B. Peterson's gospel.

It is highly doubtful that glorified individualism will save the world. Some of the misery seems instead to be caused by just that, when personal interest rules over the collective. Tyranny, for instance. In any case, this credo is not a suitable formula for understanding mythology, which relates to a collective and not an individual.

[719] Peterson 1999, p. 447.

[720] Ibid., p. 469.

Rules for Life

After the above discussed book, *Maps of Meaning* from 1999, it took almost 20 years before Jordan B. Peterson published the next one — but it became a big international bestseller, selling millions of copies, mainly due to his Internet fame and the media debacle caused by his refusal to use personally preferred gender pronouns.

In *12 Rules for Life* from 2018, he gives his advice on how to improve one's life quality and be successful.

Contrary to what was the case with his previous book, which is quite a demanding read, this one is aimed at the general audience. Still, it contains a lot of the same claims regarding mythology and religion, as well as Peterson's stand on the individual and social functions of morality.

In the introductory chapter, which is titled "Overture," he presents the central theories of his first book, insisting on the dubious claims discussed above, such as that of the original intent of myth:

> *I proposed in* Maps of Meaning *that the great myths and religious stories of the past, particularly those derived from an earlier, oral tradition, were* moral *in their intent, rather than descriptive.*[721]

He also persists with his division and definition of chaos and order, the former feminine and the latter masculine, and their wrongly proposed link to yin and yang in Taoism. Considering his view on chaos, the subtitle of his book, *An Antidote to Chaos*, is surprising. He doesn't propose a transition from chaos to order, but a balance between them. That is how he interprets yin and yang:

> *For the Taoists, meaning is to be found on the border be-*

---

[721] Jordan B. Peterson, *12 Rules for Life: An Antidote to Chaos*, Canada 2018, p. xxvii.

*tween the ever-entwined pair. To walk that border is to stay
on the path of life, the divine Way.*[722]

Except for his comparison of yin and yang to chaos and
order, he is correct about the traditional Chinese ideal — also
before and outside of Taoism — that there should be balance
between the two opposites. Chaos has nothing to do with it,
though, but the Chinese philosophers of old definitely regarded that balance as orderly. Order was the ideal, just as Tao
emerged out of the primordial chaos to bring the world to a
natural order, according to the *Tao Te Ching*.

Also Peterson, in his twelve rules, mainly propagates
some kind of order — as his subtitle suggests. He admits to it
in his explanation of the subtitle, "It indicates clearly that people need ordering principles, and that chaos otherwise beck-
ons."[723] The same is shown by his sixth rule: "Set your house
in perfect order before you criticize the world."[724]

He seems close to obsessed with order, or more accurately
discipline. You should stand up straight with your shoulders
back, akin to a soldier on guard; not let your children do anything that makes you dislike them, which is an odd perspective
on parental attention; be precise in your speech, as if everything to talk about is, and so on. He even prefers that people
share a belief system in order to understand one another, and
live by the same code so that they are mutually predictable,
and thereby they can act together to "tame the world."[725] That
is so orderly, the ancient Chinese philosophers would applaud.

To Peterson, it is the "heroic path" and he insists that we
should all follow it to save the world:

[722] Ibid., p. xxviii.

[723] Ibid., p. xxxiv.

[724] Ibid., p. 147.

[725] Ibid., p. xxx.

We must each adopt as much responsibility as possible for individual life, society and the world. We must each tell the truth and repair what is in disrepair and break down and recreate what is old and outdated. It is in this manner that we can and must reduce the suffering that poisons the world.[726]

Easier said than done, especially since most of it is unspecified. What his words boil down to is simply: fix it! Yes, but how? Peterson, too, admits to not having the perfect answer:

Being is far more complicated than one person can know, and I don't have the whole story. I'm simply offering the best I can manage.[727]

That goes for all of us.

The Lobster

In the chapter of Peterson's first rule for life, "Stand up straight with your shoulders back," his use of the lobster as an argument has caused some buzz in the media, including some amusement.

In a fight between lobsters, the winner gets an increased ratio of serotonin over octopamine, which makes it able to extend its body to look bigger and thereby boost its potential to win additional challenges, kind of like a natural internal doping. The loser suffers the opposite effect. Thereby, the winner is prone to keep on winning, and the loser to keep on losing.

Peterson sees the same phenomenon in human interaction: "It's winner-take-all in the lobster world, just as it is in human societies."[728] And not just in fights. In most things in life — for lobsters as well as humans — the winners continue

[726] Ibid., p. xxxiii.

[727] Ibid.

[728] Ibid., p. 8.

to triumph and the losers to fail. He refers to it as a dominance hierarchy. So, we should follow the lobster's lead, by standing up straight to look bigger and prouder.

Why the life of lobsters should at all be relevant to us humans, Peterson explains by pointing out that they have been around for at least 350 million years. He concludes:

This means that dominance hierarchies have been an essentially permanent feature of the environment to which all complex life has adapted.[729]

That demonstrates a poor understanding of evolution. Humans and lobsters have evolved on different branches of the evolutionary tree, since at least 500 million years ago. That means no lobster traits could have been inherited by our kind. Furthermore, the dominance hierarchy he describes is far from the only social order in the animal kingdom, and never was. Nor is it the ruling norm among humans.

While lobsters are solitary, humans are social. That fact alone should have warned Peterson not to compare the two, especially since he confirms it clearly in another chapter of his book:

Our brains are deeply social. Other creatures (particularly, other humans) were crucially important to us as we lived, mated and evolved. Those creatures were literally our natural habitat—our environment.[730]

Societies can certainly have prominent leaders, but they still rank as part of the group and need its continued approval. At least they must avoid disapproval. Their status is given by the others, and can be retracted. Strength may cause others to yield, but it is popularity that makes them do it willingly.

[729] Ibid., p. 11.
[730] Ibid., p. 39.

The societal form that has been with humankind for the very longest is that of hunter-gatherers. It lasted from way back in prehistory to the introduction of agriculture a mere 10,000 years or so ago. That means we are still genetically programmed mainly for the former, since evolution takes a lot of time. As far as we can deduct from archeological findings and from present day hunter-gatherers, their society was egalitarian, and very much so. No dominance hierarchy, but a sharing of power as well as of resources. This is what comes naturally to us — well, to most of us.

Agriculture changed a lot of that, mainly by the establishment of property of cultivated land and the emergence of organized force above the level of the local community. But that has not yet had the time to reprogram our genes. We remain willing social creatures, more prone to share than to hoard, and to cooperate rather than compete. It is those deviating by doing the opposite who preach that we are all like them, and they still need some kind of added force to get their way. They are the problem, not those they aim to subdue.

Jordan B. Peterson suggests instead that we should grow to intimidate others into submission, to avoid them doing it to us. That can only become a vicious spiral, where the strongest and most aggressive person has a moment of triumph before an even stronger and more aggressive person comes along, and so on, like an eternal game of king of the hill, but with devastating consequences. Whether accomplished alone or in alliances, such victories can never last, since the vast majority of our species denounce and oppose them.

We don't want to be lobsters.

Shame

The second of Jordan B. Peterson's twelve rules for life is "Treat yourself like someone you are responsible for helping," which has a sympathetic ring to it. Help yourself as you would help others. It is the age-old Golden Rule, albeit reversed. The most famous expression of it is that of Jesus in his Sermon of the

Mount, commonly worded "Do unto others as you would have them do unto you." The same principle is expressed in a multitude of religious and philosophical ethics. It is the ideal of reciprocity, which was practiced already among hunter-gatherers in Paleolithic times.

Peterson's take on it is individual instead of social. Help yourself like you would someone in your care. It presumes that you have the compassion to care for others, at least those you deem to be responsible for, but the focus here is you. Don't neglect yourself in the process. In other words, take good care of yourself. That is important, too, no doubt, as expressed in the Christian decree to love your neighbor as yourself. You need to love yourself, as well.

This is what Peterson finds lacking — we don't love ourselves as we should. He gives the example of how we treat our pets with more concern, which he finds evident by the common negligence to take prescribed drugs for our own sake, but not so when it is for our pets: "People are better at filling and properly administering prescription medication to their pets than to themselves."[731]

To Peterson this shows that people love their pets more than themselves, and he concludes that it is because of shame:

> *How much shame must exist, for something like that to be true? What could it be about people that makes them prefer their pets to themselves?*

He is jumping to conclusions. It is not necessarily about shame, but more likely about compassion and affection. We do have a willingness to treat those we are closely connected to with more care than ourselves. We would definitely do it to our loved ones, and that may include our pets.

But do we really put our pets before ourselves? Some might, but Peterson's argument about prescriptions is not def-

[731] Ibid., p. 33.

inite proof of it. Any animal shelter can give numerous examples of neglected and mistreated pets. Also, the mere fact that a pet owner visits the vet shows the care that surely includes following the prescription. Some pet owners do not. So, the statistics may have a huge flaw right there. The general attitude is that humans are more important than animals,

A better test would be to inquire what pet owners do if their pet causes them serious health problems, for example an escalating allergy or being repeatedly bitten by an aggressive pet. Would they suffer for the sake of the pet? Some probably would, up to a point, but I doubt that it is a majority.

To explain the self-sacrificing priority of pets that Peterson claims to exist, he turns to the second creation story of Genesis, with Adam and Eve in the Garden of Eden. When they eat of the forbidden fruit, they realize that they are naked and feel ashamed, hurrying to cover themselves. Their nakedness reveals their weaknesses and flaws. Peterson finds this shame to be the key:

> *Why should anyone take care of anything as naked, ugly, ashamed, frightened, worthless, cowardly, resentful, defensive and accusatory as a descendant of Adam? Even if that thing, that being, is himself? And I do not mean at all to exclude women with this phrasing.*[732]

Peterson points out a major reason for shame, which is the human proclivity for malevolent actions, not found in other animals: "Only man will inflict suffering for the sake of suffering. That is the best definition of evil I have been able to formulate."[733] As far as we know, he is right about the first statement. Animals may cause suffering, but it is instinctual instead of intentional. They kill for food and fight for mating — not from any evil will. Or we just don't know them well enough.

[732] Ibid., p. 53.
[733] Ibid., p. 54.

He has also found a conceivable definition of evil, but it is not without gaps. What it describes is sadism. Evil deeds can also be for personal gain, indifferent to, but not necessarily wanting, others suffering. That would be cynicism. Then there are the concepts of vengeance and punishment, where suffering is brought on someone who is believed to deserve it. Those who execute such acts probably regard them as good, and others may agree on it. They would call it justice.

Evil is a difficult concept. There are many cases where the word can be applied without controversy, but also lots of cases where the jury is still out.

One important distinction to make is evil as a character trait as opposed to an action — evil persons or evil acts. In the former case, it is a judgment made by others, and it is a very difficult one to make. It has been debated just about forever if there are evil persons or just evil deeds. The Christian credo is rather the latter, since there is always a chance of forgiveness. An evil deed can be forgiven, but hardly a truly malevolent mentality. If there is such a thing as a genuinely evil personality, it can probably only be defined by its intent to be just that. Then, evil are those who commit acts that they themselves regard as evil. Anything else is open to debate.

Peterson seems convinced that there are such persons, even that we all have that streak in us. It makes him consider if we should exist at all:

Perhaps Man is something that should never have been. Perhaps the world should even be cleansed of all human presence, so that Being and consciousness could return to the innocent brutality of the animal.[734]

Yet, he admits that there are people who behave with admirable compassion, even in hardship, and they are not the exception but the norm: "This sort of everyday heroism is the

[734] Ibid., p. 55.

rule, I believe, rather than the exception."[735] That is definitely the case, or our species would have eradicated itself long ago.

So the question is why he still persists with that dark image of the human psyche, tormented by shame and prone to evil. It seems that he is far from convinced of it. He confesses that in his own periods of darkness he sees admirable traits in fellow humans:

> *I find myself frequently overcome and amazed by the ability of people to befriend each other, to love their intimate partners and parents and children, and to do what they must do to keep the machinery of the world running.*[736]

One would hope he sees even more of it in his light periods.

Do what You Can

In his text about the fourth rule, "Compare yourself to who you were yesterday, not to who someone else is today," Jordan B. Peterson expresses a concise view on the content of religion, emphasizing with italics that it is about proper behavior.[737] In other words ethics, but "older and deeper." It is a dogmatic value system promoting stability and order, demanding of people to be obedient, or "properly disciplined."

To Peterson, that is what we need, whether we are religious or not. In fact, he claims that we are all religious, even atheists: "You might object, 'But I'm an atheist.' No, you're *not*." He means that your deepest beliefs are not what you think they are, but what you show in your actions:

> *You can only find out what you actually believe (rather than what you think you believe) by watching how you act.*

[735] Ibid., p. 60.

[736] Ibid.

[737] Ibid., p. 102.

*You simply don't know what you believe, before that. You
are too complex to understand yourself.*[738]

Peterson continues by comparing the god of the Old Testament to the god of New Testament. Considering the harsh terms of life and the deep flaws in human behavior, he finds the former more realistic and believable because of his stern and uncompromising rule, adding a strange comparison: "He was a Force of Nature. Is a hungry lion reasonable, fair or just? What kind of nonsensical question is that?"[739]

But Peterson neglects that contrary to the lion, the god of the Old Testament is a thinking and reasoning god, who speaks and acts in terms of justice, defending his actions and sometimes even allowing human arguments to influence him. The comparison of him to a lion is what's nonsensical.

As for the belief of atheists and belief in general, it depends on how it is defined. Here Peterson seems to speak about conviction rather than belief, i.e., ethics without the need of a divine source. Of course it is possible to have ethical principles and still be an atheist. Environmentalism is one example of this, as is altruism and so much more. Even in religious doctrines it is easy to extract god from the equation and still find convincing reasons for most of their rules on proper behavior.

Peterson suggests treating the Old and New Testament gods, the stern and the loving god, as if they could be one and the same, which leads him to conclude:

*In other words, you decide to act as if existence might be
justified by its goodness — if only you behaved properly.*[740]

So, the goodness of existence depends on you. That's a Herculean task, to say the least. But Peterson does not expect

[738] Ibid., p. 103.
[739] Ibid., p. 105.
[740] Ibid., p. 107.

you to complete it all. Instead, he proposes that you focus on things near at hand: "Notice something that bothers you, that concerns you, that will not let you be, which you *could* fix, that you *would* fix."[741] This is a variation of the popular aphorism originating in the *Serenity Prayer* by the American theologian Reinhold Niebuhr, from the 1930s:

> *Father, give us courage to change what must be altered,*
> *serenity to accept what cannot be helped, and the insight*
> *to know the one from the other.*[742]

That is sound advice, whether or not a deity is involved.

Theodicy

The sixth chapter in Jordan B. Peterson's book, "Set your house in perfect order before you criticize the world," is basically a repetition of the previously discussed chapter four, which in turn is a variation on Reinhold Niebuhr's Serenity Prayer. It can be summed up into the advice do what you can.

In this chapter, though, Peterson gets there by involving one of the most discussed problems in Christian discourse, which is that of *theodicy*. The term was invented by the German philosopher Gottfried Leibniz in his 1710 book *Essais de Théodicée sur la bonté de Dieu, la liberté de l'homme et l'origine du mal* (*Theodicy: Essays on the Goodness of God, the Freedom of Man and the Origin of Evil*). The question it raises is how an omnipotent and benevolent god can allow evil and suffering in the world, and that was discussed long before Leibniz, even in the Old Testament of the Bible.

Carl G. Jung wrote extensively about it in his 1952 essay on the Book of Job, discussed above in the chapter about Jung. He found the story of Job to reveal flaws in the psyche of God.

[741] Ibid., p. 108.

[742] Fred Shapiro, "You can quote them," *Yale Alumni Magazine* 2010 (yalealumnimagazine.org/articles/2709-you-can-quote-them).

Peterson pursues another line of reasoning, which must be regarded as more religiously pious. He presents the problem quite precisely:

> *A religious man might shake his fist in desperation at the apparent injustice and blindness of God. Even Christ Himself felt abandoned before the cross, or so the story goes.*[743]

An agnostic or atheist, he continues, would blame fate or the brutality of chance. The burning question is, "Why is there so much suffering and cruelty?" For those who believe in an almighty deity, that would be the one to blame. Still, Peterson states, "Whole peoples have adamantly refused to judge reality, to criticize Being, to blame God."[744]

He claims that this is particularly true for Judaism, but that is questionable. The Old Testament has more examples than Job of a frustrated relation to God and his rule, sometimes even bordering on condemning him. And in Christianity the question has been frequently discussed ever since Jesus on the cross exclaimed, "My God, my God, why have you forsaken me?"[745] Still, the conclusion within Christian theology has always been one or other argument for God either being innocent or having a masterplan justifying all the human suffering. Of course a religion would not dismiss their highest deity for any reason. That would be the end of it.

Peterson is on the same track. He means that the fault is ours, since we have become complacent and neglect to pay attention, which causes our misery. For example, when the hurricane hit New Orleans, the damage was utterly severe because the city had failed to complete precautions already decided in 1965. He concludes:

[743] Peterson 2018, p. 151.

[744] Ibid., p. 156.

[745] Mark 15:34 and Matthew 27:46. It is a quote from the beginning of Psalm 22 in the Old Testament.

That is harsh. Also, it is unfairly simplistic. Some misfortune might be avoidable, and neglecting to do so deserves blame. But so much else is beyond our capacity, as the Serenity Prayer points out.

There are plenty of dreadful diseases for which we have yet to find a cure, but it is hardly a sin of ours that we haven't. We are trying. There are natural disasters that we cannot protect ourselves against. What is significant is that our society has become so resourceful and advanced, the misfortunes we are helpless against have diminished tremendously from the time of the Bible — and they continue to do so. No thanks to any deity.

This is because we don't settle for what Peterson says, "If you are suffering—well, that's the norm. People are limited and life is tragic." That is defeatism, and hopefully not what Peterson proposes. We get nowhere by accepting suffering, either individually or socially, and life doesn't need to be tragic in any other sense than that it has an expiration date — which, by the way, we have managed to extend by medical research and social reform, just about all over the world.

In regard to the theodicy problem, natural disasters have been an argument against the idea of a benevolent god, since he would be their cause or at least have the power to stop them. For individual hardship, it could be argued that the suffering was deserved or was for some ultimate good. But when a catastrophe struck thousands of people indiscriminately, it could not make any such sense. It proved that God was either indifferent or incapable.

The earthquake of 1755 in Lisbon became a symbol of just that among the Enlightenment philosophers of the time, Vol-

---

[746] Peterson 2018, p. 157.

taire being the most noted of them. It had a death toll of tens of thousands of people. Also, it struck on All Saints' Day and destroyed a number of Lisbon churches, which gave additional cause to question God.

Of course, humankind is not only able to diminish suffering in the world. We are also known to introduce new threats and disasters of our own making, whereof some are humongous. We can't blame any deity for those, nor can we expect one to save us from them. On the other hand, it would also be wrong to share the blame between us all, since few of us have the capability to do anything about it.

Suffering for Future Gain

In spite of Jordan B. Peterson's education and profession, his book deals less with psychology than with theology. Arguing for his twelve rules, he repeatedly uses his own theological interpretations of the Bible and its meaning, especially the second creation story of Genesis and the story of Jesus in the Gospels.

It is a brave venture. How to understand the biblical texts has been a major subject as long as those texts have been around, involving thousands of minds and producing thousands of texts. Within Christianity, the discussion about its message and meaning is at least as old as the letters of Paul, which were written before the Gospels. Through the centuries, the Bible has been interpreted in minute detail by numerous clerical writers, such as Clement of Alexandria, Origen, Eusebius, Augustine, Thomas Aquinas, and Martin Luther. There is little about it that has not already been proposed.

What Peterson finds in the Bible is a message about human suffering, due to our flawed character and unwillingness to accept that message. It is a dark view, where pain is unavoidable and pleasure all but completely absent. Good is merely the struggle to restrain evil, "The good is whatever stops such things from happening,"[747] and the meaning of life is discipline. Where is the joy?

In the chapter "Pursue what is meaningful (not what is expedient)," Peterson begins with this grim statement:

> *Life is suffering. That's clear. There is no more basic, irrefutable truth. It's basically what God tells Adam and Eve, immediately before he kicks them out of Paradise.*[748]

A few pages down, he repeats it, in just as firm words: "Pain and suffering define the world. Of that, there can be no doubt."[749] He is nothing if not persistent, but that doesn't make him right. There is also pleasure, without which suicide rates would have swelled to consume our species long ago. We have that option. The fact that we remain shows that there is more to life than pain.

Peterson continues by suggesting what he regards as the only way to lessen the suffering:

> *Sacrifice can hold pain and suffering in abeyance, to a greater or lesser degree — and greater sacrifices can do that more effectively than lesser. Of that, there can be no doubt. Everyone holds this knowledge in their soul.*

So, the antidote to suffering is sacrifice. Isn't that just more of the same thing?

As examples of great sacrifices he mentions the crucifixion of Jesus and Abraham willing to sacrifice his son Isaac. But for us regular folks, he recommends learning to sacrifice in the meaning of postponing — refusing ourselves something good now, to get something even better in the future, since "the future can be made better if the proper sacrifices take place in the

---

[747] Ibid., p. 198.

[748] Ibid., p. 161.

[749] Ibid., p. 172.

present."[750] He calls it the delay of gratification, and makes a bold claim about it:

> *The discovery that gratification could be delayed was sim-ultaneously the discovery of time and, with it, causality (at least the causal force of voluntary human action).*[751]

That may or may not be true, but it is an interesting idea. How was time discovered? It must have been evident long ago, even to other animals. Its cyclic nature with day and night is easily perceived in a matter of days, and the seasonal changes in a matter of years. Its linear nature of irrevocable changes is evident with children born, growing up, getting old, and finally dying.

The added complexity of gratification suggests that it was not what first made us aware of time. But it was a way to make use of that awareness.

As for causality, it is also something familiar to all animals. Predators know that if they bite their prey, it will soon cease to resist, and the prey knows that if it succeeds to flee from the predator, it will not be food that day. Humans and animals alike are aware that there are consequences to their actions. Otherwise they would not flee when threats appear or even jump out of the way when a boulder rolls towards them.

What may be particularly human, though, is the ability to plan for a causality far ahead in time. We do something now to gain something else much later — after days or even years. Agriculture is evidence of it, and so were the flint tools long before that.

It seems that other animals live more in the moment, like Zen masters. When they do some elaborate preparation, like building a nest, it is regarded as instinct, which might mean that they don't really know why.

[750] Ibid., p. 195.

[751] Ibid., p. 164.

Or they do. We should not take for granted what goes on in the heads of other animals, and what does not. Peterson is certain, though, that the animals don't know that sacrifice in the present can lead to a better future: "No other animal has ever figured this out."[752] I wonder how he can be so sure about it.

Glimpse of Light

The world described by Jordan B. Peterson is a dark place, where we must accept that we will suffer and make sacrifices. He repeats it over and over. His description of our species is equally depressing. He sees serious flaws and few redeeming qualities, except in the small number of outstanding individuals of our history, geniuses, whom he praises just about as often as he dismisses the rest of us.

He states, "Each human being has an immense capacity for evil,"[753] but he has little to say about our capacity for good. That doesn't bring much hope or consolation. Still, he insists that we should not be bitter:

> *Hating life, despising life — even for the genuine pain that life inflicts — merely serves to make life itself worse, unbearably worse.*[754]

It seems that he is not following his own advice on this point. There is hardship, and then even more hardship, which we must accept and discipline ourselves to bear. The only reward for our efforts is that we don't make it even worse for ourselves. And then we die. Not very inspirational.

Even when Peterson has a positive tone, it tends to backfire. In the eleventh chapter, "Do not bother children when they are skateboarding," he tells about his delight watching

---

[752] Ibid., p. 195.

[753] Ibid., p. 197.

[754] Ibid., pp. 346f.

skateboarders outside his university building enthusiastically struggling to improve their skills, which involves a good deal of courage and significant risks of injury. Obviously, the boys on their skateboards are enjoying themselves.

Peterson thinks that they should be allowed to continue, though not because of their joy, but for the important lesson the boys learn by it. They get daring and tough, so that they have a better chance of persevering what torments life inevitably has in store for them. Boys should be allowed to be boys, in order to become men — the kind of rugged men portrayed by John Wayne and Clint Eastwood. He quotes another movie he-man, "Don't, in the immortal words of Arnold Schwarzenegger, be a girlie man."[755] This is obviously Peterson's ideal. He thinks it is also what women want:

> *If they're healthy, women don't want boys. They want men. They want someone to contend with; someone to grapple with. If they're tough, they want someone tougher. If they're smart, they want someone smarter.*[756]

That has the prospect of turning the home into a battle zone. Competition instead of cooperation. Such an ideal is sure to create more problems than it solves. Also, it can definitely be debated if this is in line with human nature.

Certainly, the capacity for aggression is within us, but so is that of compassion. Boys occasionally fight, but most of the time they do not and have no urge to do so. There have been countless wars through history, but between them are exceeding periods of peace. We all prefer the latter. We don't seek conflict, but agreement. It comes much easier for us to love than to hate.

Peterson's world is a dark fantasy, a nightmare. The real world is much lighter, fortunately, and humanity kinder and

[755] Ibid., p. 328.
[756] Ibid., pp. 331f.

more benevolent. Otherwise our species would since long have been extinct.

As for Jordan B. Peterson's gloomy perspective, one cannot help but wonder what causes it. Not that *ad hominem* is ever a valid argument, but he invites it by openly using his own life experiences as examples in his arguments. As a clinical psychologist, he must be aware of what can be assumed about him from those generous personal glimpses. His life has not been easy.

He grew up in the small-town Fairview of Alberta, Canada, four hundred miles from the nearest city, where the freezing cold winters lasted for five months, during which daylight hours descended to their minimum.[757] That's not the ideal setting for developing a positive mentality. Also, he had skipped a grade in school and was small for his age, while the boys around him were quite rough.[758] He doesn't say so explicitly, but that would have made him vulnerable, maybe even bullied.

In his adult years, with a wife and two children, his daughter developed a severe and painful illness already as an infant, which kept its grip on her as she grew up. The whole family struggled with it as her suffering varied in intensity and she went through different treatments.[759]

It is a heartbreaking story that he tells over several pages in the chapter on the last of his twelve rules for life, "Pet a cat when you encounter one on the street." The header is paradoxical, considering its main content, but also perfectly reasonable. Sometimes life strikes as hard as Mjolnir, the hammer of Thor, so it is of crucial importance to grasp the pleasant moments appearing, no matter how insignificant they may seem. We cannot handle pain at all if we are not open to pleasure.

Contrary to dogs, cats are particular about their prefer-

[757] Ibid., pp. 67f.

[758] Ibid., p. 290.

[759] Ibid., pp. 339ff.

ences. They don't want to be petted by just anybody, and choose the moments even with those they accept. They can't be tamed, but keep their integrity. As Peterson says, "They are friendly on their own terms."[760] He explains:

> *They appear willing to interact with people, for some strange reasons of their own. To me, cats are a manifestation of nature, of Being, in an almost pure form. Furthermore, they are a form of Being that looks at human beings and approves.*

So, if they allow us to pet them, the honor is exclusively ours. And here, at the last page of his twelve rules, is the glimpse of light all but completely missing from the previous pages:

> *And maybe when you are going for a walk and your head is spinning a cat will show up and if you pay attention to it then you will get a reminder for just fifteen seconds that the wonder of Being might make up for the ineradicable suffering that accompanies it.*[761]

A mere moment of solace in the gloom of life, but solace nonetheless. And his daughter's health improved. He ends the chapter, "Things are good. For now."

Soon after the publishing of his book, his wife was diagnosed with cancer, which she survived through surgery. He, too, had serious health issues already at the time of writing his book, with several complications in the following years.

He recovered to write a sequel, published in 2021, with twelve more rules for life.[762]

[760] Ibid., p. 352.

[761] Ibid., p. 353.

[762] Jordan B. Peterson, *Beyond Order: 12 More Rules for Life*, New York 2021.

Literature

Addison, Joseph et al.:

The Medleys for the Year 1711, no 39, London 1712.

Aeschylus:

"Eumenides," *Oresteia*, transl. Richmond Lattimore, Chicago 1953.

Aristotle:

Metaphysics, transl. Hugh Lawson-Tancred, London 1998.

Poetics, transl. Stephen Halliwell, Loeb 199, London 1999.

Augustine:

Eighty-three Different Questions, transl. David L. Mosher, Washington D.C. 1982.

Bandelier, Adolf F.:

The Delight Makers, New York 1916 (first edition 1890).

Bodkin, Maud:

Archetypal Patterns in Poetry: Psychological Studies of Imagination, London 1934.

"Archetypal Patterns in Tragic Poetry," *British Journal of Psychology*, volume 21:2, 1930.

Brinton, Daniel G.:

"The Chief God of the Algonkins, in His Character as a Cheat and Liar," *The American Antiquarian*, May 1885.

The Myths of the New World: A Treatise on the Symbolism and Mythology of the Red Race of America, New York 1868.

Budge, E. A. Wallis:

The Book of the Dead: The Papyrus of Ani, New York 1967.

The Gods of the Egyptians: Studies in Egyptian Mythology, vol. 1 and 2, London 1904.

Byrom, Michael:

Punch and Judy: Its Origin and Evolution, London 1978.

Campbell, Joseph:

An Open Life: Joseph Campbell in Conversation with Michael Toms, New York 1988.

The Masks of God: Primitive Mythology, New York 1959.

The Masks of God: Oriental Mythology, London 1962.

The Masks of God: Occidental Mythology, New York 1991 (first published in 1964).

The Masks of God: Creative Mythology, New York 1976 (first published in 1968).

The Hero With a Thousand Faces, Princeton 1972 (first edition 1949).

Campbell, Joseph & Robinson, Henry Morton:

A Skeleton Key to Finnegans Wake, New York 1944.

Dawkins, Richard:

The Selfish Gene, New York 1978 (first edition 1976).

Descartes, René:

Meditations on First Philosophy, transl. George Heffernan, Notre Dame, Indiana 1990 (originally published in Latin 1641).

Deussen, Paul:

Die Geheimlehre des Veda, 2nd ed., Leipzig 1907.

Doniger, Wendy:

The Rig Veda: An Anthology, London 1981.

Duckworth, George E.:

The Nature of Roman Comedy: A Study in Popular Entertainment, Princeton 1952.

Eeden, Frederik van:

"A Study of Dreams," *Proceedings of the Society for Psychical Research*, vol. 26, Glasgow 1913.

Eliade, Mircea:

A History of Religious Ideas, vol. 1, transl. Willard R. Trask, Chicago 1978 (originally published in French 1976).

From Primitives to Zen: A Thematic Sourcebook of the History of Religions, New York 1967.

The Myth of the Eternal Return, transl. Willard R. Trask, New

York 1954 (originally published in French 1949). The 1959 edition was renamed *Cosmos and History: The Myth of the Eternal Return*, and the 1965 edition *The Myth of the Eternal Return or, Cosmos and History*.

The Quest: History and Meaning in Religion, Chicago 1969.

The Sacred and the Profane: The Nature of Religion, transl. Willard R. Trask, New York 1959 (originally published in French 1957).

Eliade, Mircea (ed.):

The Encyclopedia of Religion, vol. 4, New York 1987.

Encyclopædia Britannica:

11th edition, volume XI, New York 1910.

Evans-Pritchard, Edward Evan:

The Zande Trickster, Indiana 1967.

Flournoy, Théodore:

From India to the Planet Mars: A Study of a Case of Somnambulism with Glossolalia, transl. Daniel B. Vermilye, New York 1900.

Franz, Marie-Louise von:

An Introduction to the Interpretation of Fairy Tales, New York 1970.

C. G. Jung: His Myth in Our Time, transl. William H. Kennedy, New York 1975 (originally published in German 1972).

Creation Myths, Boston 1995 (first edition 1972: *Patterns of Creativity Mirrored in Creation Myths*).

Frazer, James G.:

The Fear of the Dead in Primitive Religion, London 1933.

The Golden Bough: A Study in Comparative Religion, vol. 1 and 2, London 1890.

The Golden Bough: A Study of Magic and Religion, abridged edition, New York 1922.

Freud, Sigmund:

Inhibitions, Symptoms and Anxiety, transl. Alix Strachey, London 1936.

Leonardo da Vinci: A Psychosexual Study of an Infantile Reminiscence, transl. A. A. Brill, New York 1916.

"L'Hérédité et l'étiologie des névroses," *Revue neurologique*, volume 4 (6), Paris, 1896.

Moses and Monotheism, transl. Katherine Jones, Letchworth 1939.

Sexuality and the Psychology of Love, New York 1963.

The Future of an Illusion, transl. James Strachey, New York 1961.

The Interpretation of Dreams, transl. A. A. Brill, New York 1913 (originally published in German 1899).

The Letters of Sigmund Freud and Otto Rank: Inside Psychoanalysis, edited by E. James Lieberman and Robert Kramer, Baltimore 2012.

Three Contributions to the Sexual Theory, transl. A. A. Brill, New York 1910 (originally published in German 1905).

Totem and Taboo, transl. A. A. Brill, New York 1918.

Fromm, Erich:

Escape from Freedom, New York 1976.

Greatness and Limitations of Freud's Thought, 1980.

Psychoanalysis and Religion, New Haven 1967.

The dogma of Christ, and other essays on religion, psychology, and culture, Greenwich Connecticut 1963.

The Forgotten Language: An Introduction to the Understanding of Dreams, Fairy Tales and Myths, New York 1951.

You Shall Be as Gods: A Radical Interpretation of the Old Testament and Its Tradition, Greenwich 1966.

Frye, Northrop:

Anatomy of Criticism: Four Essays, Princeton 1957.

Grimm, Jacob:

Teutonic Mythology, vol. 3, transl. James Steven Stallybrass, London 1883.

Grimm, Jacob & Wilhelm:

Kinder und Hausmärchen, vol. I, Göttingen 1857.

Hartmann, Eduard von:

Philosophy of the Unconscious, transl. William Chatterton Coupland, vol. 1-3, London 1884.

Hastings, James, ed.:

Encyclopædia of Religion and Ethics, 13 vols., Edinburgh 1908-1927.

Heidel, Alexander:

The Babylonian Genesis: The Story of Creation, Chicago 1963 (first edition 1942).

Henderson, Joseph L.:

Cultural Attitudes in Psychological Perspective, Toronto 1984.

Thresholds of Initiation, Middletown 1979 (first edition 1967).

Henderson, Joseph L. & Oakes, Maud:

The Wisdom of the Serpent: The Myths of Death, Rebirth, and Resurrection, Princeton 1990 (first edition 1963).

Hillman, James:

Insearch: Psychology and Religion, Dallas 1984 (first published in 1967).

Re-Visioning Psychology, New York 1975.

The Myth of Analysis: Three Essays in Archetypal Psychology, Evanston 1972.

The Soul's Code: In Search of Character and Calling, New York 1996.

"Why 'Archetypal Psychology'?" *Spring: An Annual of Archetypal Psychology and Jungian Thought*, New York 1970, pp. 212-219.

Holberg, Ludvig:

Jeppe on the Hill, transl. Waldemar C. Westergaard & Martin B. Ruud, Grand Forks 1906 (originally written in Danish 1722).

Huizinga, Johan:

Homo Ludens: A Study of the Play-Element in Culture, Boston 1955 (originally published in Dutch 1948).

Irenaeus:

Five Books of S. Irenaeus, transl. John Kemble, Oxford 1872.

Jones, Ernest:

Essays in Applied Psycho-Analysis, London 1923.

Joyce, James:

Finnegans Wake, London 1939, p. 581.

Jung, Carl G.:

Collected Papers on Analytical Psychology, transl. M. D. Eder, ed. Constance E. Long, London 1916, and 2nd edition, New York 1917.

Contributions to Analytical Psychology, transl. H. G and C. F. Baynes, London 1928.

"Instinct and the Unconscious," transl. C. F. and H. G. Baynes, *British Journal of Psychology*, X, London 1919.

Jung Speaking: Interviews and Encounters, edited by William McGuire and R. F. C. Hull, Princeton 1977.

"La Structure de l'inconscient," transl. M. Marsen, *Archives de Psychologie*, XVI, Geneva 1916.

Modern Man in Search of a Soul, transl. W. S. Dell and Cary F. Baines, London 1933.

Psychological Types or The Psychology of Individuation, transl. H. Godwin Baynes, London 1923 (originally published in German 1921).

Psychology and Religion, New Haven 1977.

Psychology of the Unconscious, transl. Beatrice M. Hinkle, New York 1916 (originally published in German as *Wandlungen und Symbole der Libido*, 1912).

The Collected Works of C. G. Jung, vol. 1, Princeton 1975.

The Collected Works of C. G. Jung, vol. 4, Princeton 1985.

The Collected Works of C. G. Jung, vol. 5, Princeton 1976.

The Collected Works of C. G. Jung, vol. 7, Princeton 1966, 1972.

The Collected Works of C. G. Jung, vol. 9.1, Princeton 1969.

The Collected Works of C. G. Jung, vol. 11, New York 1958.

The Collected Works of C. G. Jung, vol. 12, Princeton 1968.

The Collected Works of C. G. Jung, vol. 13, Princeton 1983.

The Collected Works of C. G. Jung, vol. 17, Princeton 1970.

"The Difference between Eastern and Western Thinking," *The Tibetan Book of the Great Liberation*, edited by W. Y. Evans-Wentz, London 1954.

The Integration of the Personality, transl. Stanley Dell, London 1940.

The Portable Jung, edited by Joseph Campbell, New York 1971.

The Psychology of the Transference (originally published in German 1946), New York 1998.

The Theory of Psychoanalysis, New York 1915.

The Undiscovered Self: with Symbols and the Interpretation of Dreams, transl. R.F.C. Hull, Princeton 2010.

"Traumsymbole des Individuationsprozesses," *Eranos-Jahrbuch 1935*, Zürich 1936.

Two Essays on Analytical Psychology, transl. H. G. and C. F. Baynes, London 1928.

Jung, Carl G. & von Franz, Marie-Louise (ed.):

Man and his Symbols, New York 1964.

Jung, Carl G. & Jaffé, Aniela:

Memories, Dreams, Reflections, transl. Richard & Clara Winston, New York 1965 (originally published in German 1962).

Jung, Carl G. & Kerényi, Károly:

On a Science of Mythology: The Myth of the Divine Child and the Mysteries of Eleusis, transl. R. F. C. Hull, New York 1949 (originally published in German 1941 as *Einführung in das Wesen der Mythologie*).

Kant, Immanuel:

Kritik of Judgment, transl. by J. H. Bernard, London 1892.

Kerényi, Károly:

Asklepios: Archetypal Image of the Physician's Existence, transl. Ralph Manheim, New York 1959 (originally published in German 1947 and revised in 1956).

Eleusis: Archetypal Image of Mother and Daughter, transl. Ralph Manheim, New York 1967 (originally published in German 1960).

Zeus and Hera: Archetypal Image of Father, Husband, and Wife, transl. Christopher Holme, Princeton 1975 (originally published in German 1972).

Kirsch, Thomas B.:

The Jungians: A Comparative and Historical Perspective, London 2000.

Lang, Andrew:

Myth, Ritual & Religion, vol. 1 and 2, London 1887.

Leach, Maria:

The Beginning: Creation Myths around the World, New York 1956.

Lee, Richard B. & Daly, Richard, ed.:

The Cambridge Encyclopedia of Hunters and Gatherers, Cambridge 1999.

Leeming, David Adams:

Creation Myths of the World: An Encyclopedia, Santa Barbara 2010.

Myth: A Biography of Belief, New York 2002.

Mythology: The Voyage of the Hero, second edition, New York 1981 (first edition 1973).

Leeming, David Adams & Leeming, Margaret Adams:

A Dictionary of Creation Myths, New York 1995 (first published in 1994 as The Encyclopedia of Creation Myths).

Legge, James:

The Sacred Books of China: The Texts of Taoism, part 1, Oxford 1891.

Long, Charles H.:

Alpha: The Myths of Creation, New York 1963.

"Cosmogony," *The Encyclopedia of Religion*, ed. Mircea Eliade et al., volume 4, New York 1987.

"Creation, Myths and Doctrines of," *The New Encyclopædia Britannica, Macropædia* vol. 5, Chicago 1976.

Significations: Signs, Symbols, and Images in the Interpretation of Religion, Philadelphia 1986.

Longfellow, Henry Wadsworth:

The Song of Hiawatha, London 1855.

Maury, Alfred:

"Des hallucinations hypnagogiques ou erreur des sens dans l'état intermédiaire entre la veille et le sommeil," *Annales médico-psychologiques*, vol. XI, Paris 1848.

Miller, Miss Frank:

"Some Instances of Subconscious Creative Imagination," *Journal of the American Society for Psychical Research*, vol. 1 no. 6,

New York 1907.

Mooney, James:

Myths of the Cherokee, Washington 1902.

Müller, Max:

Lectures on the Science of Language, London 1861.

Murray, Gilbert:

The Classical Tradition in Poetry, London 1927.

Myers, Frederic W. H.:

Human Personality and Its Survival of Bodily Death, vol. 1, New York 1903.

Neumann, Erich:

Depth Psychology and a New Ethic, transl. Eugene Rolfe, London 1969 (originally published in German 1949).

Johann Arnold Kanne: Ein Beitrag zur Geschichte der mystischen Sprachphilosophie, University of Erlangen 1927.

The Great Mother: An Analysis of the Archetype, transl. Ralph Manheim, Princeton 1972 (first edition 1955).

The Origins and History of Consciousness, transl. R. F. C. Hull, New York 1970 (originally published in German 1949).

Noll, Richard:

The Jung Cult: Origins of a Charismatic Movement, Princeton 1994.

Orwell, George:

Road to Wigan Pier, London 1937.

Otto, Rudolf:

The Idea of the Holy: An Inquiry into the non-rational factor in the idea of the divine and its relation to the rational, transl. John W. Harvey, 1943 (originally published in German 1917).

Owens, Lance S.:

C. G. Jung and Erich Neumann: The Zaddik, Sophia and the Shekinah, PDF 2017.

Parsons, Elsie Clews & Beals, Ralph L.:

"The Sacred Clowns of the Pueblo and Mayo-Yaqui Indians," *American Anthropologist*, vol. 36:4, 1934.

Pertegato & Pertegato, ed.:

From Psychoanalysis to Group Analysis: The Pioneering Work of Trigant Burrow, London 2013.

Peterson, Jordan B.:

12 Rules for Life: An Antidote to Chaos, Canada 2018.

Beyond Order: 12 More Rules for Life, New York 2021.

Maps of Meaning: The Architecture of Belief, New York 1999.

Philo:

Philo I, transl. F. H. Colson and G. H. Whitaker, Loeb 226, London 1929.

Plato:

The Dialogues of Plato, vol. I and II (of 5), transl. Benjamin Jowett, Oxford 1892 (first edition 1871).

The Republic, transl. Paul Shorey, vol. 2, London 1942.

Plotinus:

The Enneads, transl. Stephen MacKenna, revised by B. S. Page, London 1956.

Plutarch:

Essays and Miscellanies, vol. 3, transl. William W. Goodwin, Boston 1909.

Purves, Dale et al. (ed.):

Neuroscience, 5th edition, Sunderland 2012.

Radin, Paul:

The Trickster: A Study in American Indian Mythology, New York 1956.

Winnebago Hero Cycles: A Study in Aboriginal Literature, Baltimore 1948.

Radin, Paul et al.,

Der göttliche Schelm: Ein indianischer Mythen-Zyklus, Zürich 1954.

Rank, Otto:

The Double: A Psychoanalytic Study, transl. Harry Tucker jr, New York 1979.

The Myth of the Birth of the Hero: A Psychological Interpretation of Mythology, transl. F. Robbins and Smith Ely Jelliffe, New York 1914.

The Trauma of Birth, London 1929.

Rasmussen, Knud:

Festens gave: Eskimoiske Alaska-Æventyr, Copenhagen 1929.

Read, John:

From Alchemy to Chemistry, New York 1995 (first edition 1957).

Riklin, Franz:

Wishfulfillment and Symbolism in Fairy Tales, transl. Wm. A. White, New York 1915.

Rohde, Douglas L. T. et al.:

"Modelling the recent common ancestry of all living humans," *Nature*, vol. 431, London 2004.

Schelling, Friedrich von:

System of Transcendental Idealism, transl. Peter Heath, Charlottesville 1978.

Segal, Robert A.:

Jung on Mythology, Princeton 1998.

Shakespeare, William:

Hamlet, edited by John Livingstone Lowes, New York 1914.

The Complete Works of William Shakespeare, London 1973.

Shamdasani, Sonu:

"A woman called Frank," *Spring: Journal of Archetype and Culture*, volume 50 (1990), New York 1991.

Smith, Winifred:

The Commedia Dell'Arte: A Study in Italian Popular Comedy, New York 1912.

Sproul, Barbara C.:

Primal myths: Creation Myths around the World, San Francisco 1991 (first edition 1979).

Stenudd, Stefan:

Psychoanalysis of Mythology: Freudian Theories on Myth and Religion Examined, Malmö 2022.

Tao Te Ching: The Taoism of Lao Tzu Explained, Malmö 2015.

Stevens, Anthony:

Archetypes: A Natural History of the Self, New York 1982.

Archetype Revisited: An Updated Natural History of the Self, Toronto 2003.

Ariadne's Clue: A Guide to the Symbols of Humankind, Princeton 1999.

Sundstedt, Kjell:

Att skriva för film, Stockholm 2000.

Suzuki, D. T.:

An Introduction to Zen Buddhism, New York 1964.

Taylor, Eugene:

The Mystery of Personality: A History of Psychodynamic Theories, New York 2009.

Theophrastus:

The Characters of Theophrastus, transl. J. M. Edmonds, Loeb 225N, London 1929.

Thomas, Edward J.:

Early Buddhist Scriptures, London 1935.

Tylor, Edward B.:

Primitive Culture: Researches into the Development of Mythology, Philosophy, Religion, Art, and Custom, vol. 1 and 2, London 1871.

Researches Into the Early History of Mankind and the Development of Civilization, London 1865.

Vogler, Christopher:

The Writer's Journey: Mythic Structure for Writers, Saline Michigan 2007.

Werblowsky, Raphael Jehudah Zwi:

Lucifer and Prometheus: A Study of Milton's Satan, London 1952.

Wilhelm, Richard:

The I Ching or Book of Changes, transl. Cary F. Baynes, Princeton 1971 (originally published in German 1924).

Williams, Griffith Wynne:

"Highway Hypnosis: An Hypothesis," *International Journal of Clinical and Experimental Hypnosis*, vol. 11:3, Philadelphia 1963.

Williams, Griffith Wynne & Shor, Ronald E.:

"An Historical Note on Highway Hypnosis," *Accident Analysis and Prevention*, vol. 2:3, New York 1970.

Wittgenstein, Ludwig:

Philosophical Investigations, transl. G. E. M. Anscombe, New York 1953.

Zweig, Stefan:

Mental Healers: Franz Mesmer, Mary Baker Eddy, Sigmund Freud, transl. Eden and Cedar Paul, New York 1932.

Web Sources

Acton, Lord:

Acton-Creighton Correspondence, 1887 (libertyfund.org).

Amirazizi, Roxy:

"The Chapman University Survey of American Fears" 2021 (chapman.edu).

Centre-dp.org

Research and Training Centre for Depth Psychology according to C. G. Jung and Marie-Louise von Franz (centre-dp.org).

Encyclopedia.com:

"Leeming, David Adams 1937-" (Encyclopedia.com).

Eranos:

"Welcome to Eranos," a yearbooks PDF list (daimon.ch/Eranos.pdf), Daimon Verlag, p. 28.

Jabr, Ferris:

"Study of Fetal Perception Takes Off," 2015 (scientificamerican.com).

Ledbetter, Sheri:

The Chapman University Survey of American Fears 2015 (chapman.edu).

New York Times:

"Comet's Poisonous Tail," *The New York Times*, 1910 (nytimes.com).

Peterson, Jordan B.:

YouTube Channel (youtube.com/c/JordanPetersonVideos).

Quote Investigator:

"There But For the Grace of God, Go I" 2014 (quoteinvestigator.com/2014/07/06/grace/).

Saint-Lambert, Jean-François de (ascribed):

"Genius," *The Encyclopedia of Diderot & d'Alembert Collaborative Translation Project*, transl. John S. D. Glaus, Ann Arbor 2007 (umich.edu).

Shapiro, Fred:

"You can quote them," *Yale Alumni Magazine* 2010 (yalealumnimagazine.org/articles/2709-you-can-quote-them).

University of Chicago:

Charles H. Long (1926-2020), 2020 (divinity.uchicago.edu/news/charles-h-long-1926-2020).